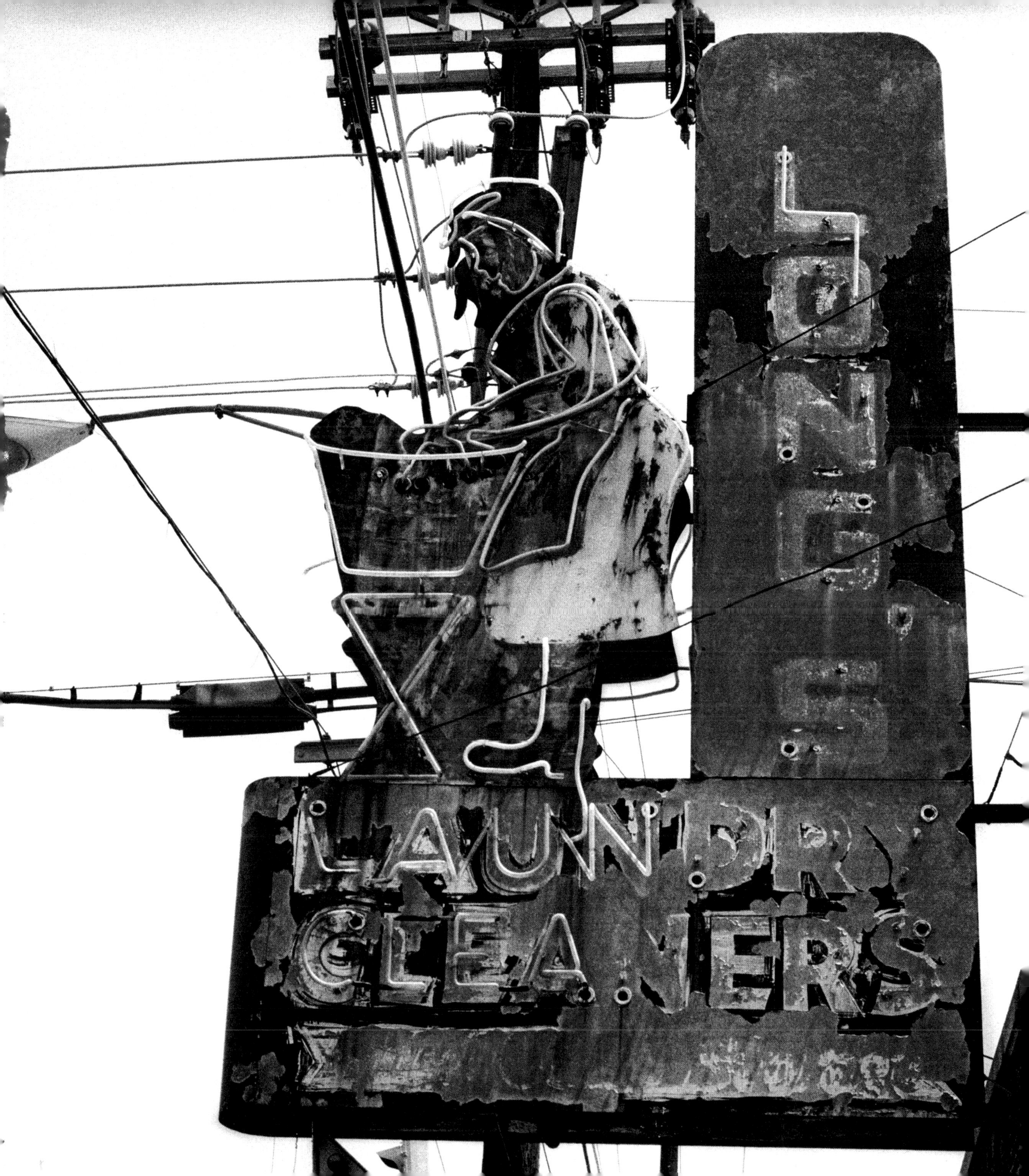
LAUNDRY
CLEANERS

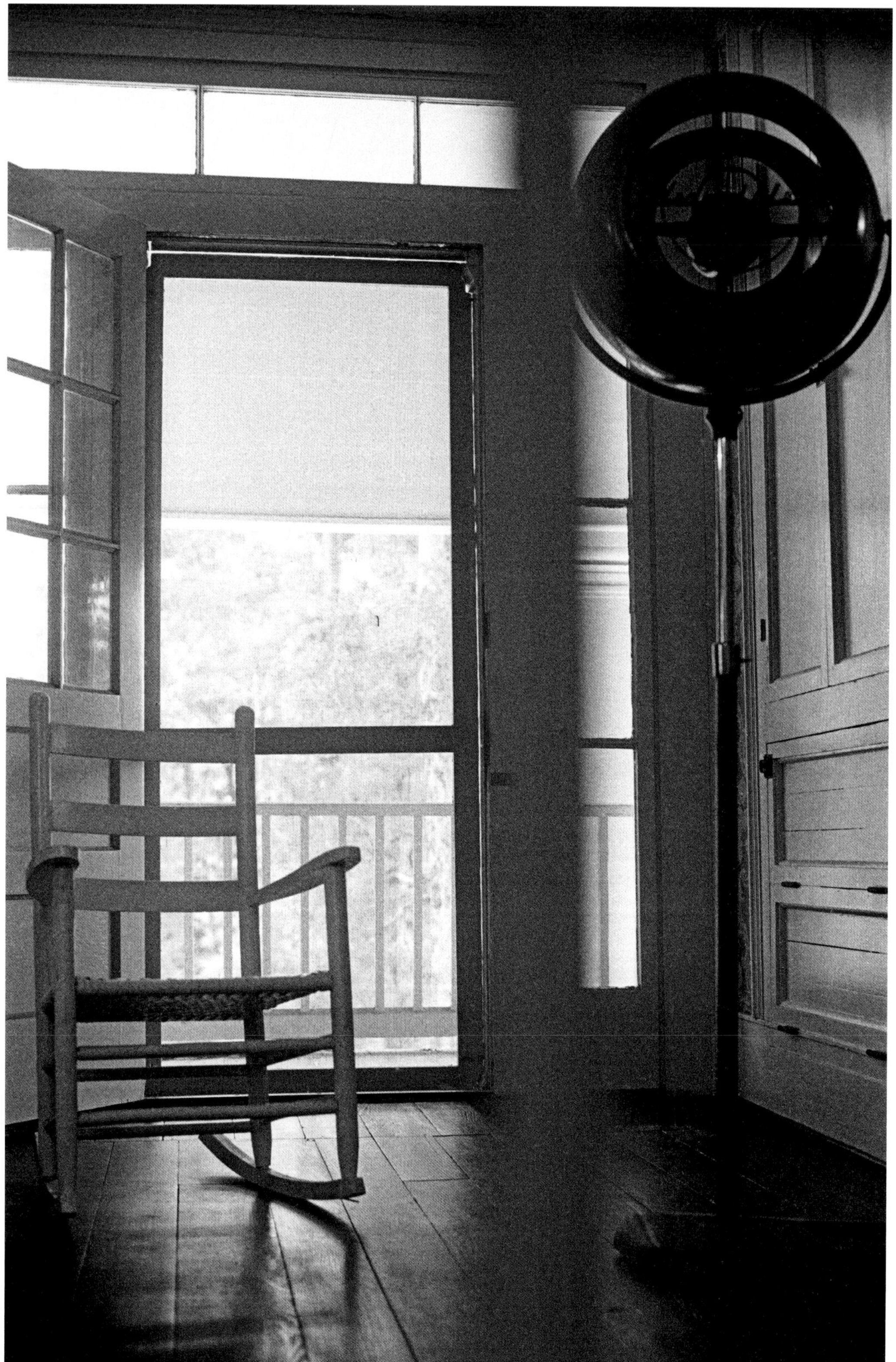

GILLES MORA

# ANTEBELLUM

UNIVERSITY OF TEXAS PRESS AUSTIN

*Walker Evans, Ben and Bernarda Shahn, Eudora Welty, Françoise, my wife:*
*They echo through these photographs. . . . Their South was mine.*

Gilles Mora

# ANTEBELLUM

*Antebellum South*: words designating the Deep South in the United States whose accepted meaning is associated with a rejection of modernity.

Following my move there in 1972, and in subsequent years, I crisscrossed it end to end by myself and with my wife. The aspiration of the Old South to erase the present always fascinated me. It was there that I sowed all my fantasies—sensual, musical, literary, and photographic—with both joy and persistence.

Beyond the hardening corruption of words, frequently hurtful, have I become a "Southerner," or better said, a "devotee of the past"? I have always run after time, grasping each opportunity to erase it, allowing myself to forget into which abyss it may lead me. Antebellum, as in many haunted realms . . .

*Françoise, Jena, Louisiana, 1973*

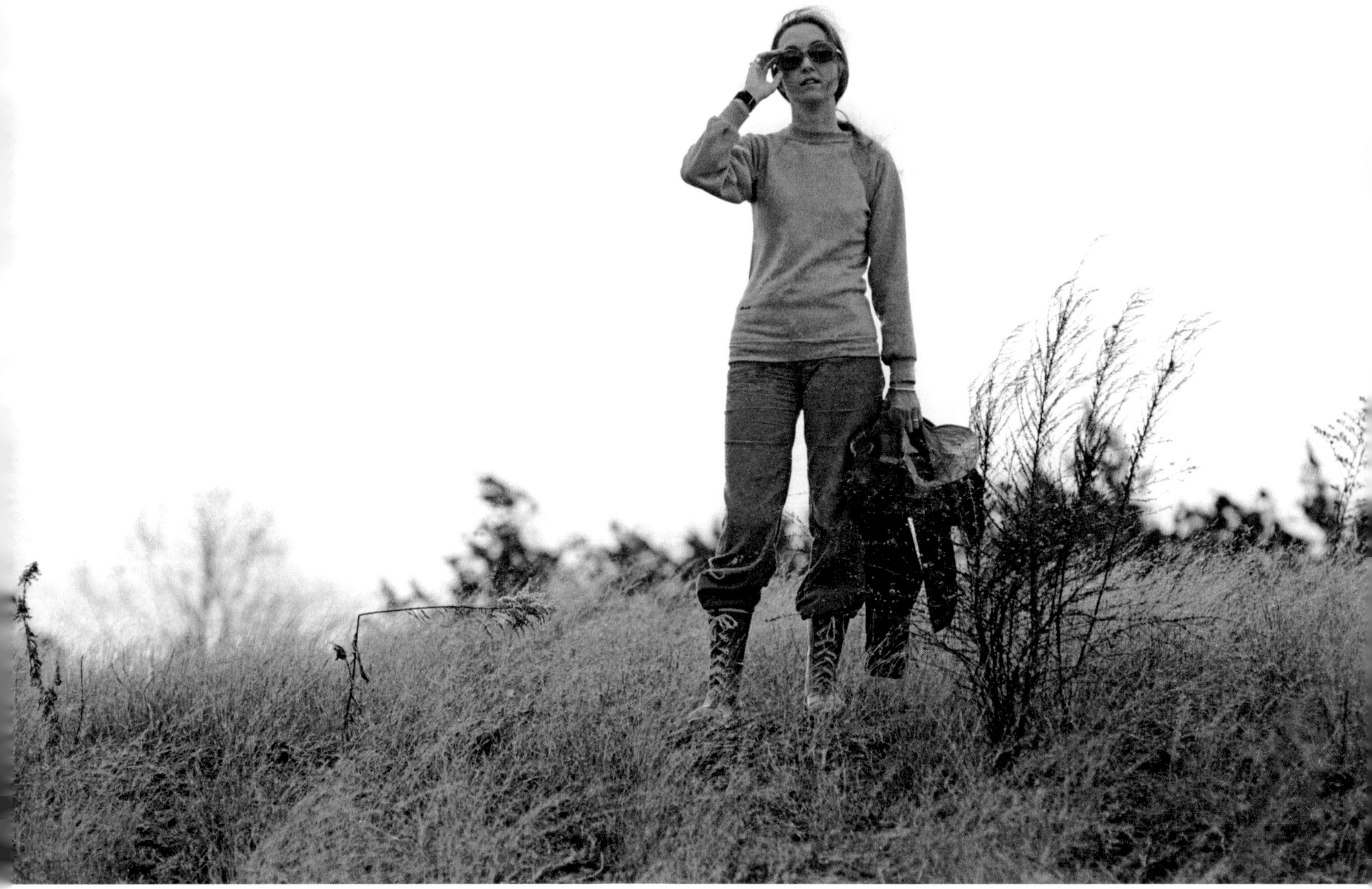

# HAUNTED REALMS BY GILLES MORA

We had barely settled in Louisiana at the beginning of the 1970s, and already I was deploring what was referred to as the "New South." This recently created term contradicted so much what I had hoped to find there—a surviving Antebellum, that ancient world—that it was for me treason incarnate. This triumphant "New South," which was supposed to replace the pre-Civil War order with readily adopted Yankee values, luckily was not limited to the promise of racial equality. That promise had barely been won at the end of the 1960s after a brave struggle, but four years later, we had the hardest time seeing progress, aside from rhapsodic but ineffective legislation. The black passengers on the Greyhound linking Memphis to New Orleans were still not allowed to get off the bus when it stopped in the small town in eastern Louisiana where Françoise and I now lived. Jena—eleven churches, two banks, and a supermarket—was a "dry" parish where the sale of alcohol was forbidden. Furthermore, in the school where we taught, we still roll-called our students by gender and race. As for our pharmacist, he was offered leadership of the local Klu Klux Klan, admittedly now reduced to a few outdated, albeit well-represented, rites. . . .

Thanks to an economy revitalized by the meteoric rise of oil prices, the "New South" aimed to promote a modernized image of the paternalistic agrarian structures of an old cultural system, whose stubborn stereotypes the rest of the world had devoured with delight ever since *Gone With The Wind*. In Louisiana, Mississippi, Arkansas, or Alabama, everywhere below the Mason-Dixon Line, the white middle class still clung to the illusion of this obsolete world's survival. Every time this movie was shown locally, more than forty years after its release, the audience was on its feet, applauding what it still hoped to salvage from the foretold disaster: the sanitized and sleek "New South" attempting to vie with the still persisting "Deep South" for a supremacy that, when we lived there, was still alive and kicking. This resilience fascinated me.

It has long been believed that to photograph is to unabashedly match reality, or the present. Whoever accepts this premise extinguishes forever the power of the photographic shot, of the delayed flaring of time and its subsequent waves. From the very first moments spent aiming my camera at the Deep South, the land that would be mine for so many years and trips, I knew that I was mostly interested in a vanished past whose presence could still be felt. This mental characteristic of mine is a life-long constant and, depending on how you see it, perhaps a failing. It colors the way I look at the world, people, landscapes, and objects. Instead of accepting them as they are, I have a tendency to take them backward. Of which past are they—or will they be—the relic, the sign, the remembrance? Ensnared by the rural America I was witnessing, I refused to believe that its transitional state differed from that which I had imagined it to be, thanks to an old issue of the *Saturday Evening Post*, purchased by my brother at a Bordeaux train station newsstand in 1955 or 1956. Its advertising imagery —Norman Rockwell illustrations of a timeless America—would blend with the Walker Evans photos that I would soon discover in Louisiana, in aficionado magazines such as *Popular Photography* or *Modern Photography*, which I then thoroughly enjoyed. These magazines formed the foundation of my budding photographic interest in its early "technological fetishism" phase. They stoked my infatuation with the cameras they widely advertised every month, which in the end often determined my photographic activities.

I still have a pronounced taste for cameras of that era. The month after I settled in Louisiana, I bought my first Canon F-1. That same rainy evening, in the grip of excitement, I drove our Chevy into a ditch, which required the Jena sheriff to come and get us out of that quagmire. The next day a rumor had spread throughout the whole county that the newly arrived French couple were alcoholics. . . .

Sensuality is not something I will omit from my relationship with the Deep South; from my very first contact with this land, I had unreservedly felt its attractive power. The enveloping and almost liquid quality of the climate, the black population's immediate physical effusiveness, often offered unreservedly, and the violent contrast it presented to white middle-class prudishness, all accentuated the Southeast's sensuality. With each occurrence, the South offered as many examples as well as exceptions, through personal contacts, landscapes, and the overall breadth of things. The author Eudora Welty immediately comes to mind. The work of this woman from the Jackson (Mississippi) white upper-middle class is resolutely open to that sensuality, whether through the subjects of her so delicate and so complex short stories or through her photographs. Because of her, I became truly aware of the mysterious filters that delineate Southern character. One should perhaps mention the almost gothic influence of the writer Ambrose Bierce I identified with delight in Ralph Eugene Meatyard's work. This Kentucky optician/photographer dried his prints on a dissection table that he purchased from the Lexington (Kentucky) morgue—the sight of which, at his place, had frightened me. . . .

When I think of Eudora Welty, I recall her aristocratic elderly lady's kind and unprepossessing face, winning me over during a delightful afternoon spent at her Jackson house in November 1989, where I sampled her refined

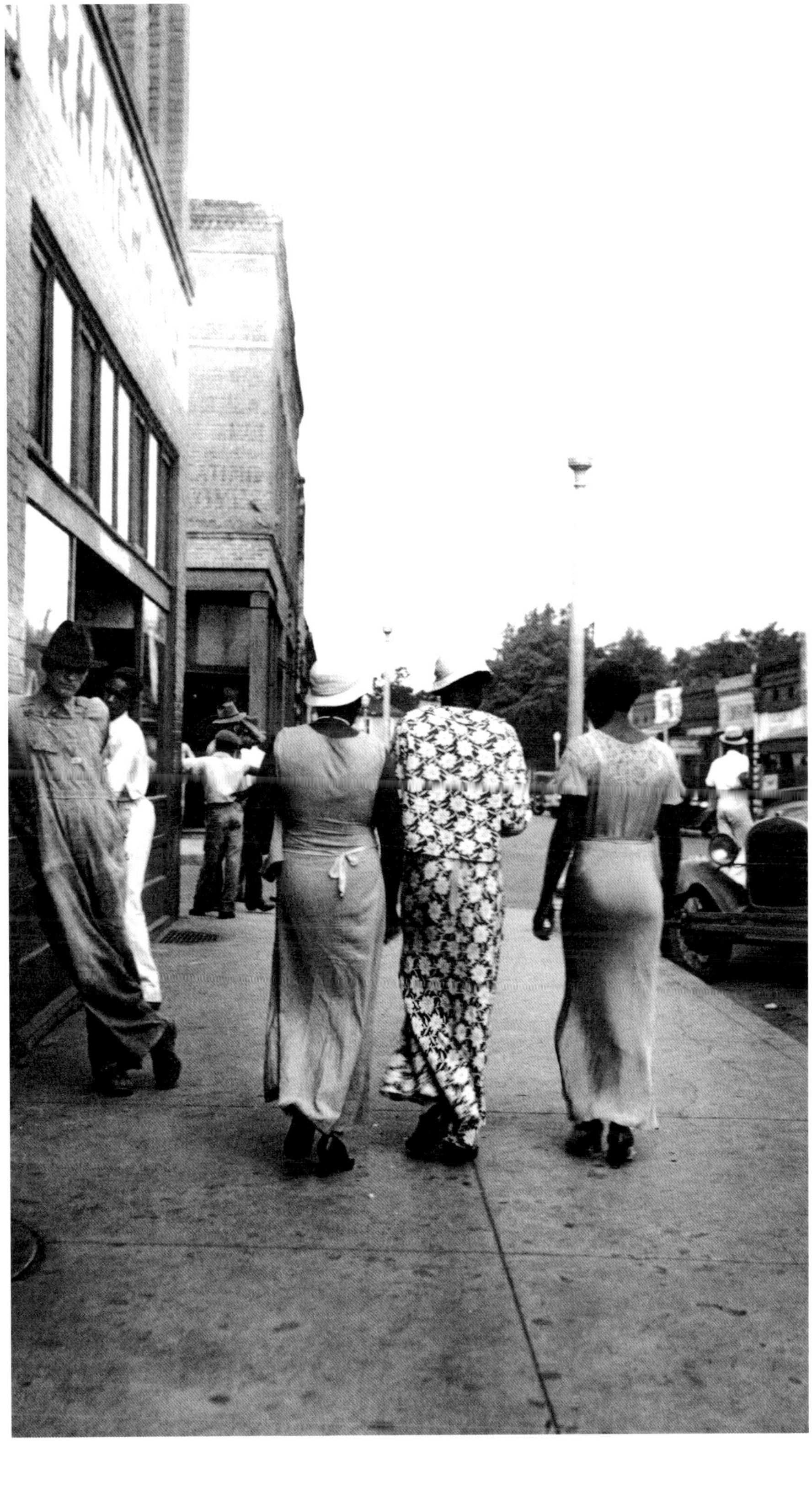

*Saturday strollers, Granada*

pastries while discussing Southern women. That same summer in France, I had just shown her relatively unknown photographs. In my eyes, she was the most astute and most profound famous writer among her Southern peers, from William Faulkner to Walker Percy, without forgetting Flannery O'Connor and many others. She did not take very seriously the photography she had done—briefly but intensely—at the end of the 1930s in Mississippi, in the midst of the Great Depression.

In her photographic work, I found the same mysterious, indescribable sympathy for the dispossessed and the same physical attraction to white or black women's bodies that characterized her literary work. A few of her images are at the heart of ones that I created also, probably the result of a kinship I told her about the day we met, which made her smile with a kindness I still cherish. I did not photograph her; I intuited the painful distance she had created between herself and her face's unprepossessing image, she whose strange beauty so nourished her writing.

The first photographer to whom I showed my images was John Clarence Laughlin from Louisiana. I had visited him several times in his New Orleans house on Marignan Street. He lived there with his wife semi-reclusively, always pained by the condescending contempt American museum institutions showed him. His dazzling knowledge of European literature, which was barely contained within the limits of an overflowing and untidy library where he spent his days, was coupled with his constant belief in a gothic surrealism, of which his entire body of work bore the trace. It maintained him in a kind of generalized state of confoundment. I could only be attracted to the decay, the destruction, and the dread of a morbid past that infused his photographic work even as New Orleans was beginning to wipe out its architectural heritage in favor of standardized urban development. I recall a New Year's Eve (1980, I believe) spent at his place where, under the shade of a table lamp from another era, I had listened to him evoking, one by one, the memories of bygone days, those of an agony-filled Louisiana where he had planted his fantastical theater of spectral shadows, ghosts, and mysterious veiled women erect on the New Orleans cemetery tombstones. His sagging face, plowed by wrinkles, displayed the same painful unattractiveness as Eudora Welty's. They had never met but held each other in great regard. I find a reflection of their faces in several images I took back then, portraits of older people that, inexplicably, imposed themselves on my lens. My fascination for buildings in ruins, for the lush exuberances flowing out of their gaping sockets, torn-out doors or windows, owes a lot to the morbid visions held dear by Laughlin, and which intersected my own. I realized that in 1935, the year Laughlin embarked on his photographer's journey, Walker Evans was on the same ground, in identical places, unaware of Laughlin; however, sustained by the same interest, Evans also was archiving a decomposing past as visible in decaying plantations as in the Louisiana capital's dilapidated facades. This coincidence of intentions in all probability reinforced my own. My South would be theirs, or so I believed. . . .

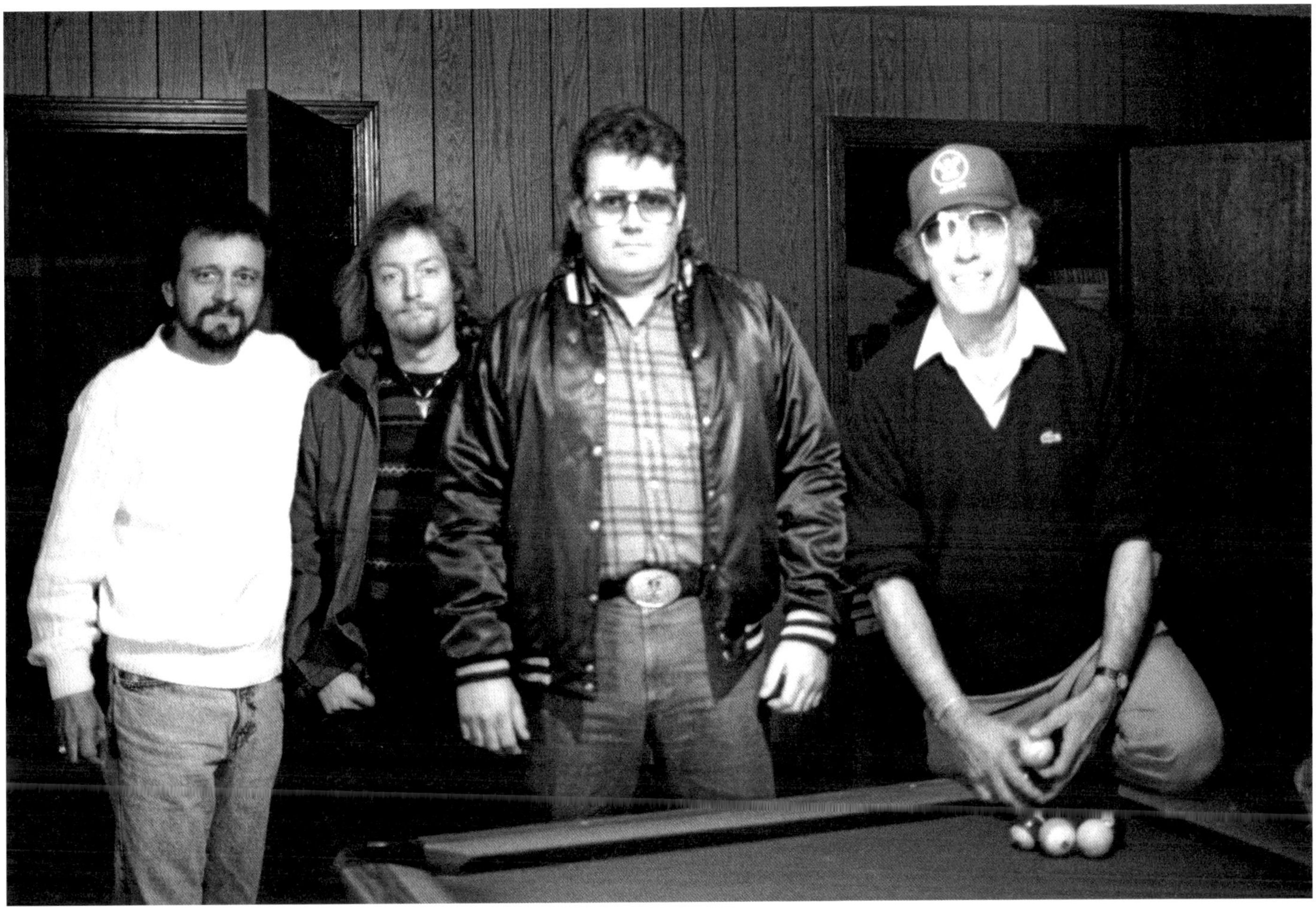

Carl Perkins, at home, with his musicians, Jackson, Tennessee, 1989

This obsession pushed me toward Alabama in the summer of 1982, more precisely Hale County, where the aforementioned Evans and his friend, the author James Agee, had in 1936, during an unforgettable July, carried out their literary and photographic project chronicling the experiences of an impoverished sharecropper family. It was published under the title *Let Us Now Praise Famous Men*. Being equipped with various documents, including Evans's contacts, my mind filled with their images and texts, and I explored the places to which their works bore witness as if in a hallucination, outside of time. In Greensboro, I managed to find the ruins of the hotel where Evans had stayed while Agee settled in the dingy shack of the sharecroppers whose existence he wanted to share for a few days. A few years later, in 1991, in the company of William Christenberry, a photographer from Selma (Alabama), who was as obsessed as I was by the mythical book of these two men, I revisited Hale County. I liked in him that unfailing affection for his birth county, his unshakeable claim of the Southern spirit, his very personal way—a little like Elvis Presley in his first

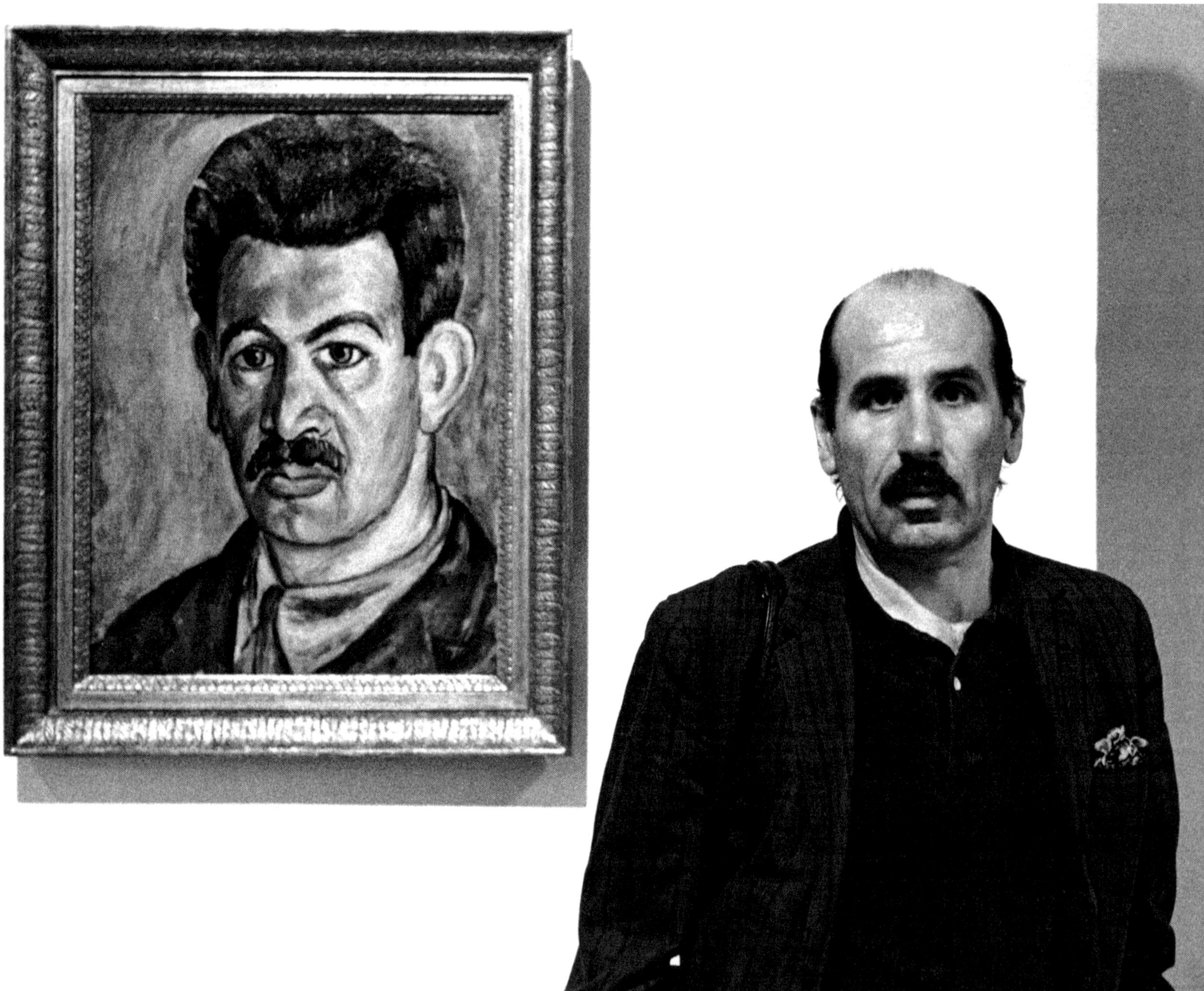

movies—of taking out his comb to smooth down his slicked-back hair, at every moment, as if a teenager from the rock 'n' roll era whose inconsolable nostalgia Christenberry shared with me. . . .

That same year in Memphis I visited his photographer colleague William Eggleston. He received me in his great colonial mansion near Sun Studio where Presley, Jerry Lee Lewis, and Carl Perkins had engraved their rockabilly monuments. I still doggedly celebrate their masterpieces with my band, formed during adolescence but consisting today of a gang of immature sixty-year-olds incapable of retiring their musical love to the lockers of old age. Under the initiative of the academic William Ferris (born in Vicksburg, Mississippi), a great sociologist of the Deep South, and of the singer Carl Perkins (from Tiptonville, Tennessee), who had become my friend and had let me extend my teenage dreams by playing several times at his side in France and Memphis, our band had come in 1996 to Memphis for two weeks of performances, sharing the stage with Elvis's first musicians during a symposium dedicated to him. From this luminous evening spent with Eggleston, who was fascinated by my friendship with Henri Cartier-Bresson whose work he profoundly admired, I remember an immense, empty living room where a monumental upright piano sat imposingly as well as the high-fidelity speakers for which he was known (more than for his photos). As for the rest, his images left me quite cold, as they owed much to the superficial effects of their colors, their subjects having been drained of all sensuality in favor of a banality devoid of any depth. I told him this quite openly; he did not take offense, his aristocratic tact prevailing absolutely. But we never saw each other after that.

My travels throughout the South never constituted a purely photographic experience. When I was accompanied by my wife, Françoise, a kind of amorous excess took over everything, conferring to my Southern stage a new dimension, born from the intimacy where our common sensual excitement was insatiable. I was struck by a kind of unconscious projection about which I was never clear, regarding the real or imagined parallels between our relationship and that of the painter/photographer Ben Shahn and his wife, Bernarda. Both couples had, at different times, traveled through the Deep South with the same amorous complicity. Shahn had been enrolled from 1935 with Walker Evans in the Farm Security Administration team. He was then a complete beginner in photography. His only plan was to instinctively heed the visual callings born of his contacts with a wild, rural world, oftentimes characterized by an ignorant brutality amplified by economic crisis and particular Southern traits. This universe had frustrated any expectation of Americanization, which Shahn and his wife resisted politically as fierce activists affiliated with the omnipresent American Communist Party. As they were freely roaming an unknown territory which fascinated them, the couple would experience what I imagined would be a sort of double adventure, which was aesthetic as well as amorous.

*Self-portrait in front of Ben Shahn's portrait, Houston, 1986*

My identification with Ben Shahn long constituted the driving force behind my relationship to the South. On a day in September 1987 in New York, we had just returned from a long trip though Georgia and South Carolina. I decided with Françoise to go visit his widow, Bernarda, still alive in her New Jersey home in Roosevelt City, a house she had shared with Shahn since the beginning of the 1940s. I called her, she accepted immediately to receive us despite her advanced age. The meeting, in particular between her and Françoise, was an unexpected and inexplicable moment of mutual understanding. As I was explaining that our photographic journeys represented for us the trips undertaken by her and Ben, Bernarda suddenly took Françoise in her arms to kiss her with surprising tenderness. It was done with a spontaneity that seemed to tacitly give us her blessing. I took several shots of them in that complicit moment, telling myself that one day, the wrinkled yet still delicate face of Bernarda, then deceased, would be substituted in my mind by Françoise's, aged but with its beauty intact.

I kept those Southern photos to myself for a long time, mixed with the memories of my encounters, which I engraved in my mind and on my rolls. I told myself I had no real legitimacy to aspire to their publication, even if I unconsciously knew that one day it would happen. One does not visit, as I did, the literally thousands of images taken by others, some of them among the greatest, without deciding the value of one's own. Some of the images would constitute a credible counterpoint to the others in the lot . . . by others, which focus on many of the same themes. I clearly remember taking some of the shots. Others only survive in the form of the final image, as if their production circumstances mysteriously evaporated; they rendered me unfamiliar with their origins, making me doubt their reality. However, in those countless smiles, in the straight gazes directed at me by the women and men I photographed, which were rarely stolen without their knowledge (I would need their tacit agreement to secure the fleeting complicity I imposed on them), and in all those proliferations of signs, what I now find after all these years seems hardly possible since any impromptu shot today is suspicious. It is perceived as an unacceptable violation or transgression: the harmony obtained through photography between a very real and trivial universe and the strangely dreamy or lost gaze of a traveler determined to find only what he wanted to see there, defying all objectivity.

For more than twenty years, I was that wandering, subconscious-laden euphoria that, from Alabama to Mississippi, established the cartography of a universe that existed only in my mind, improbable mirror of my own haunted realms.

February 2016

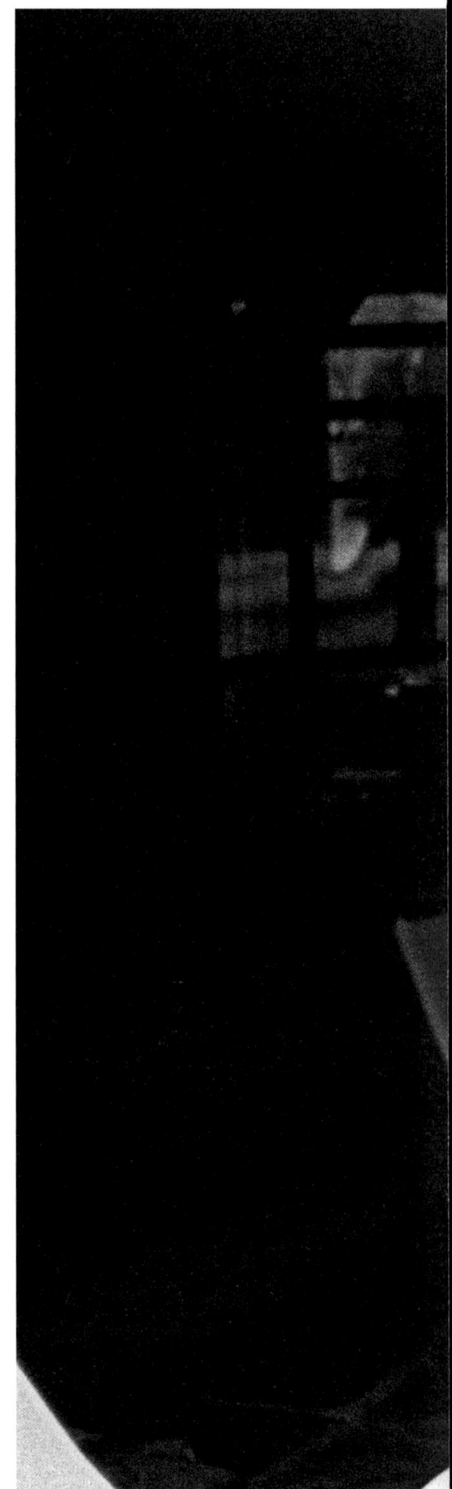

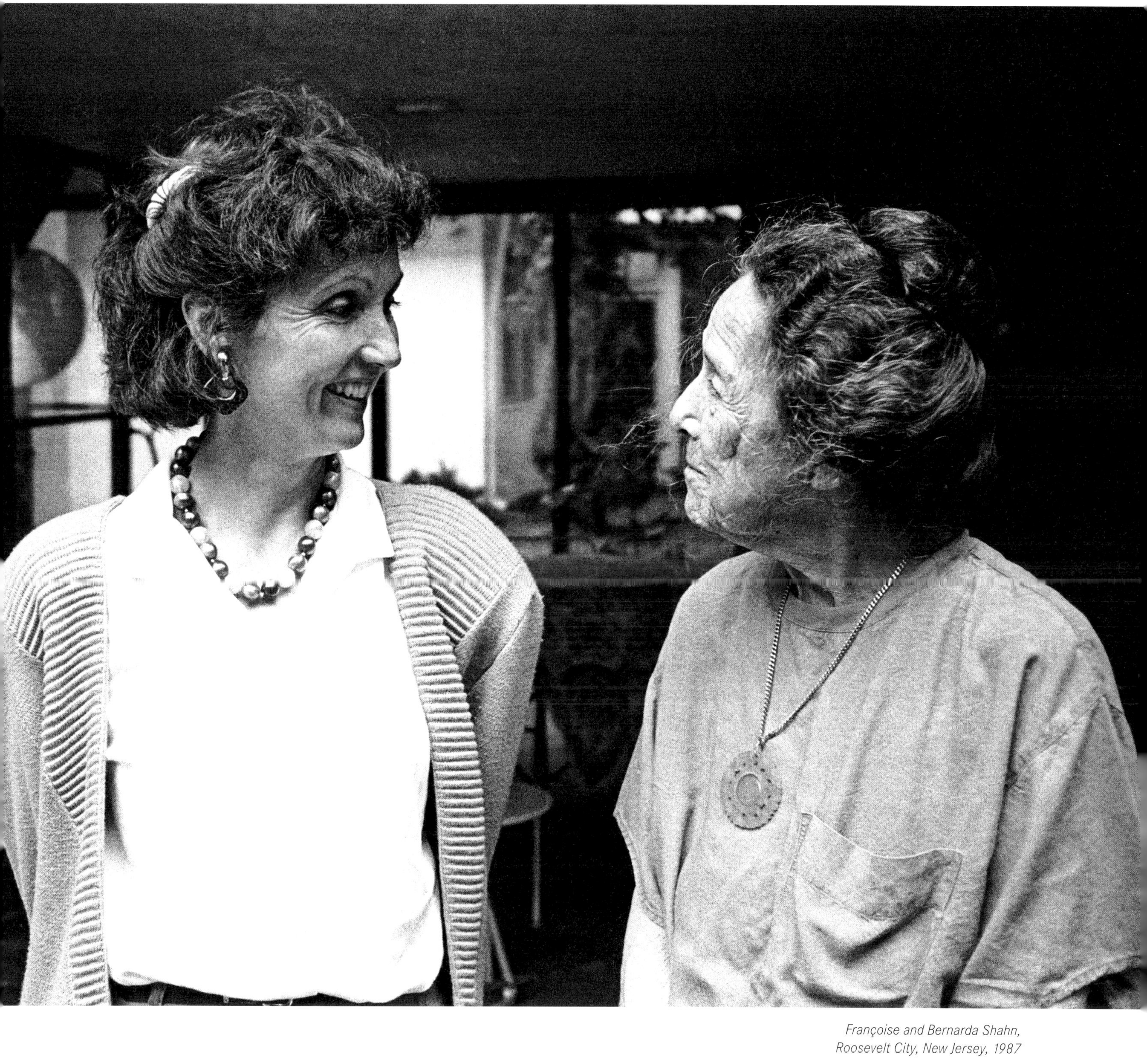

*Françoise and Bernarda Shahn,*
*Roosevelt City, New Jersey, 1987*

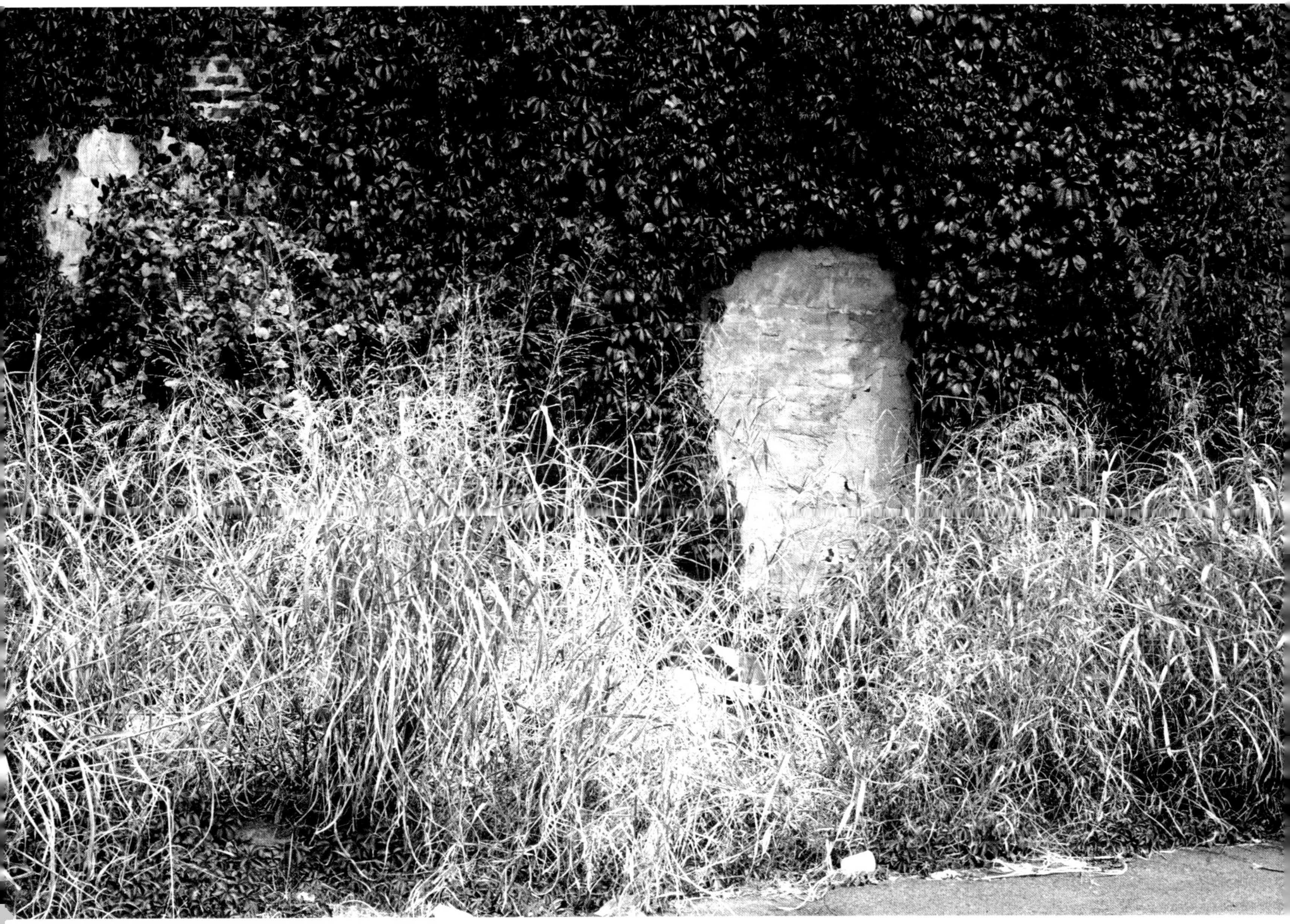

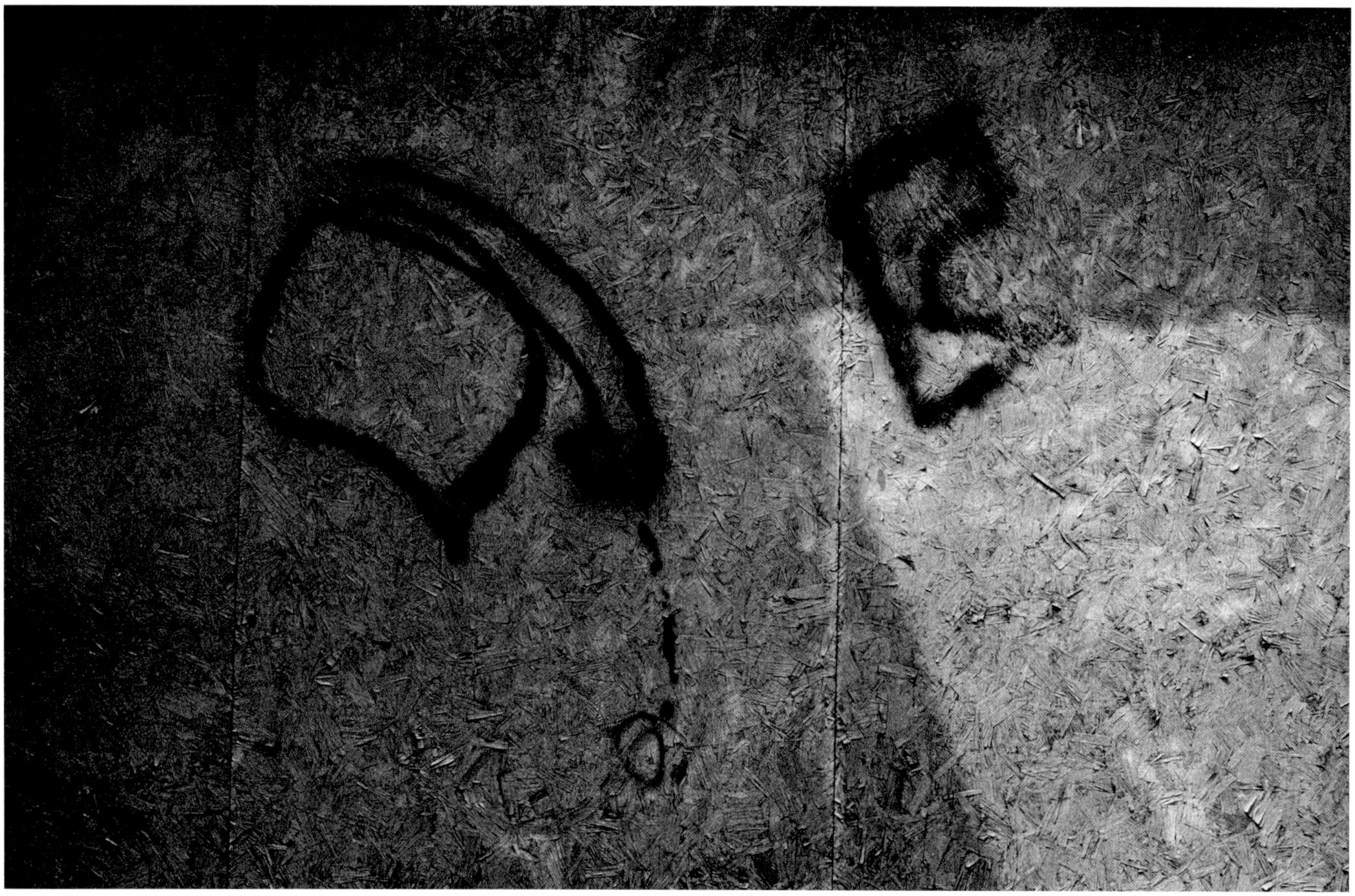

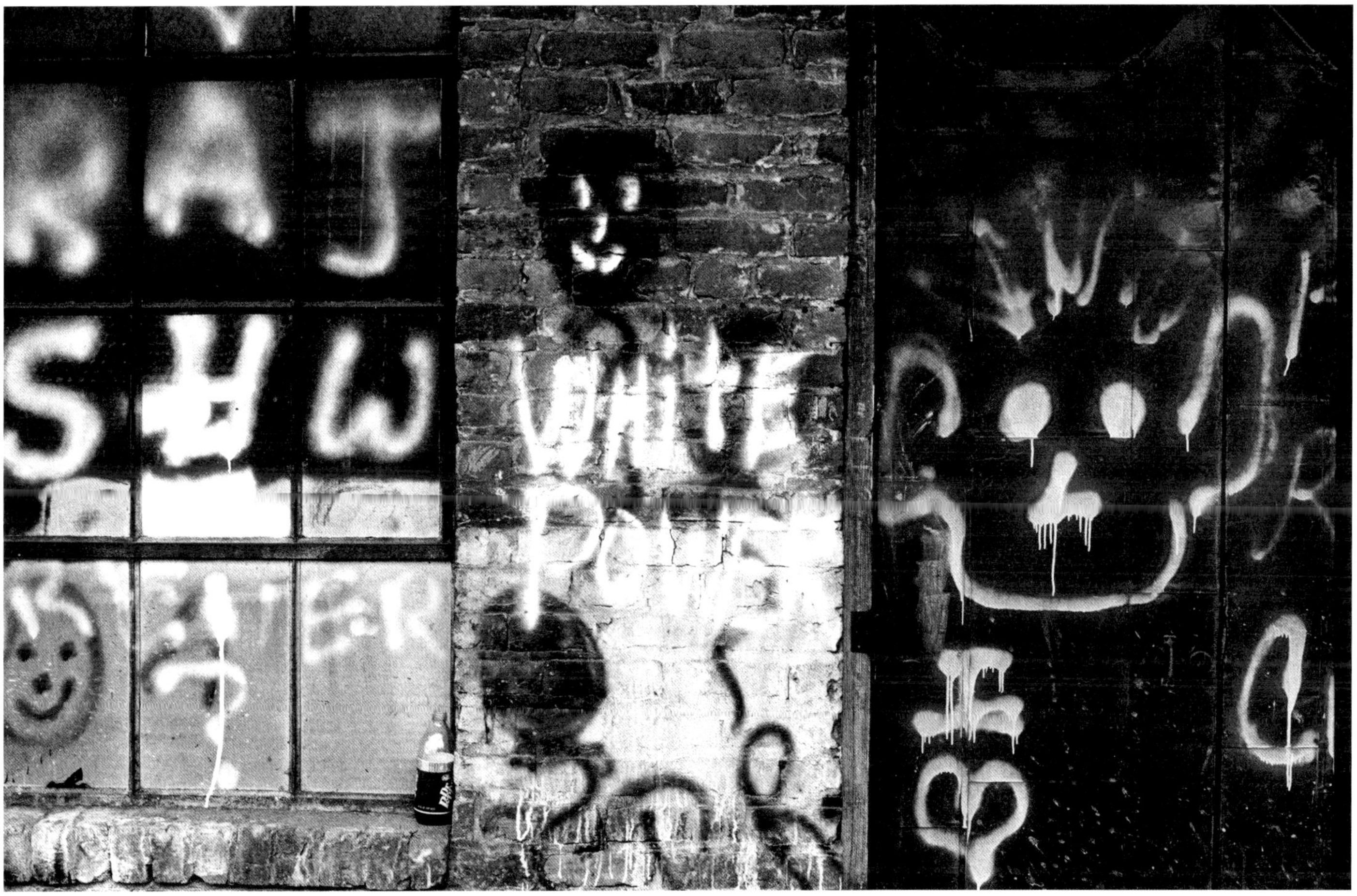
WHITE

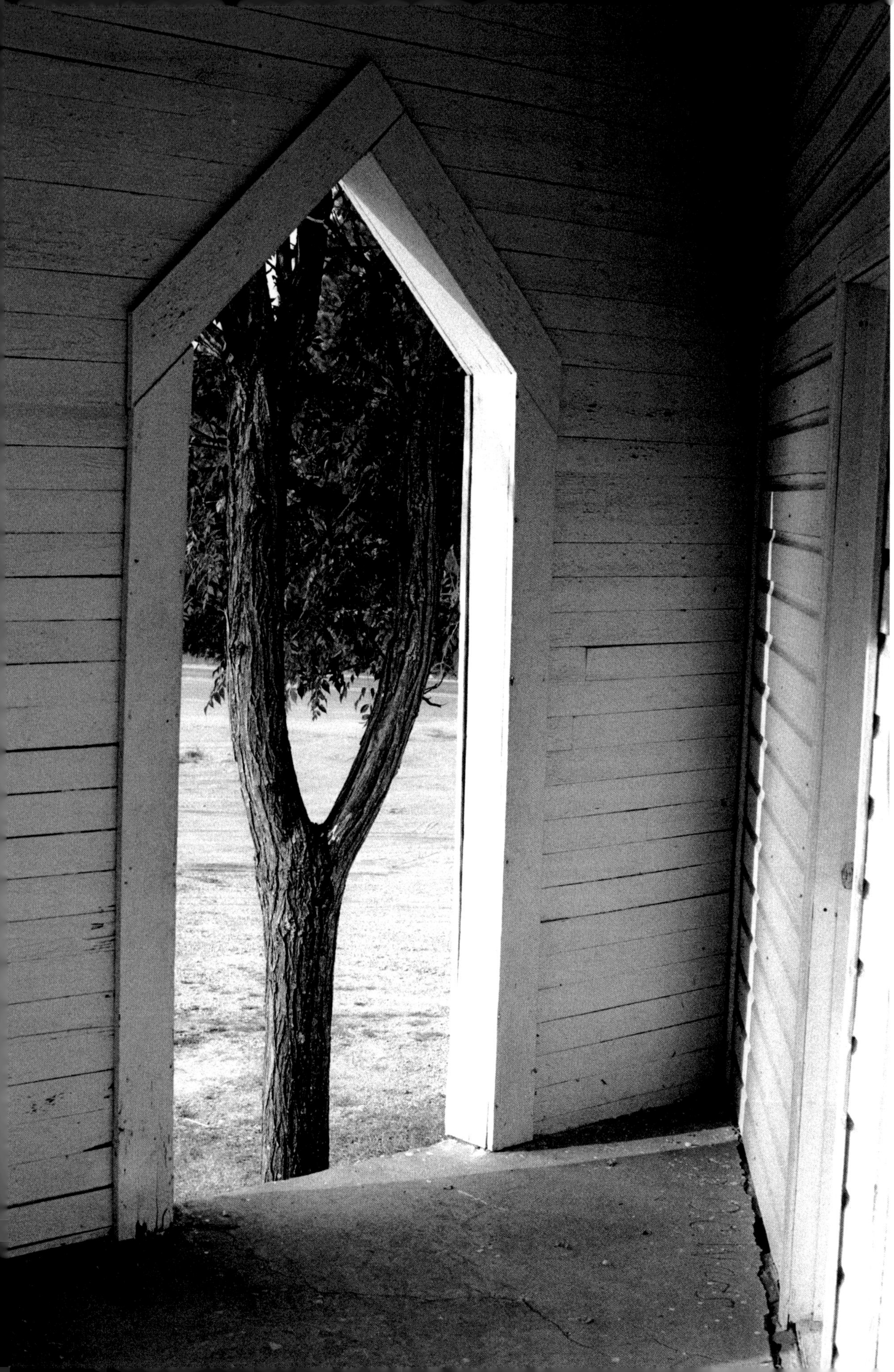

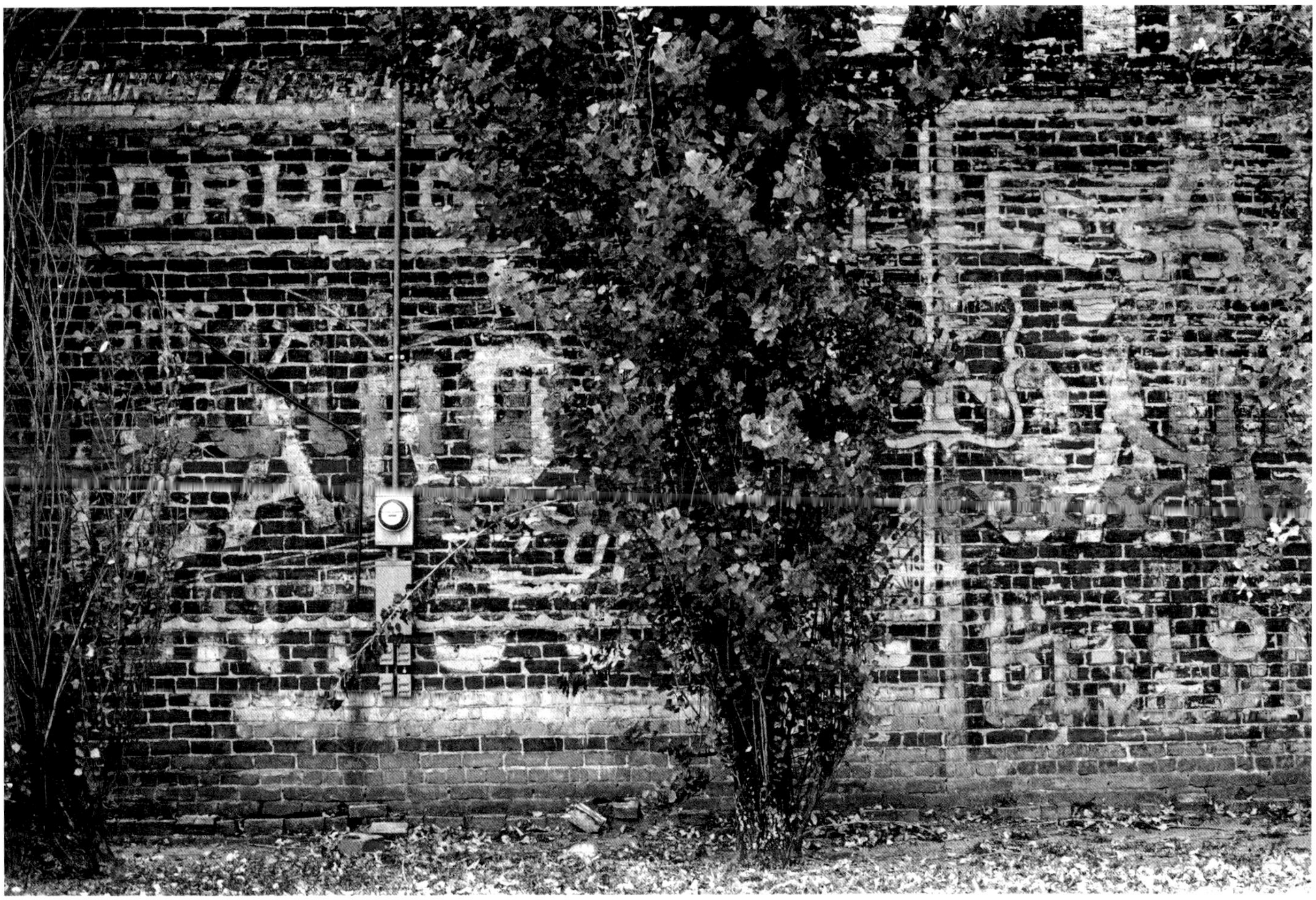
DRUG

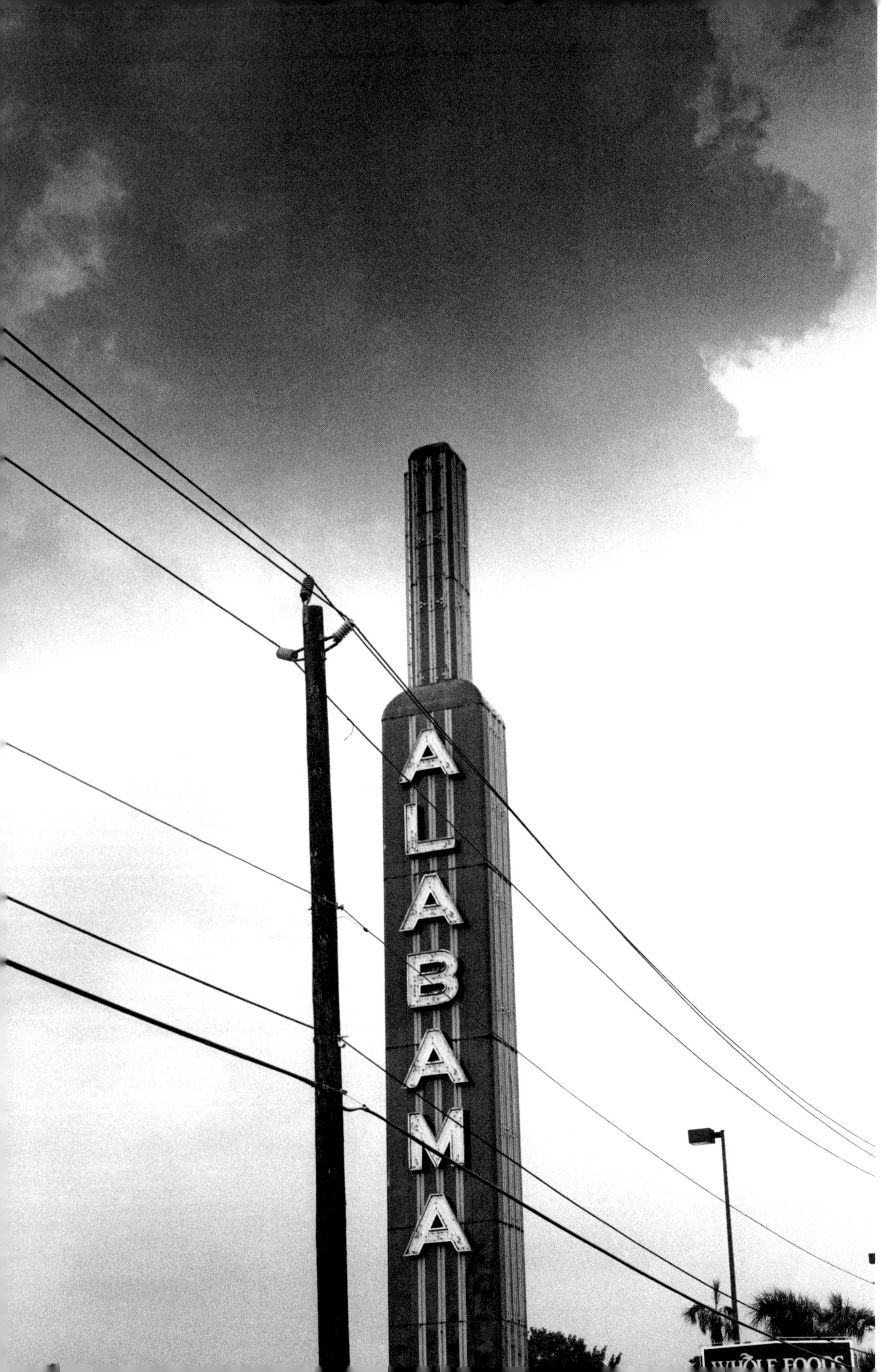
ALABAMA

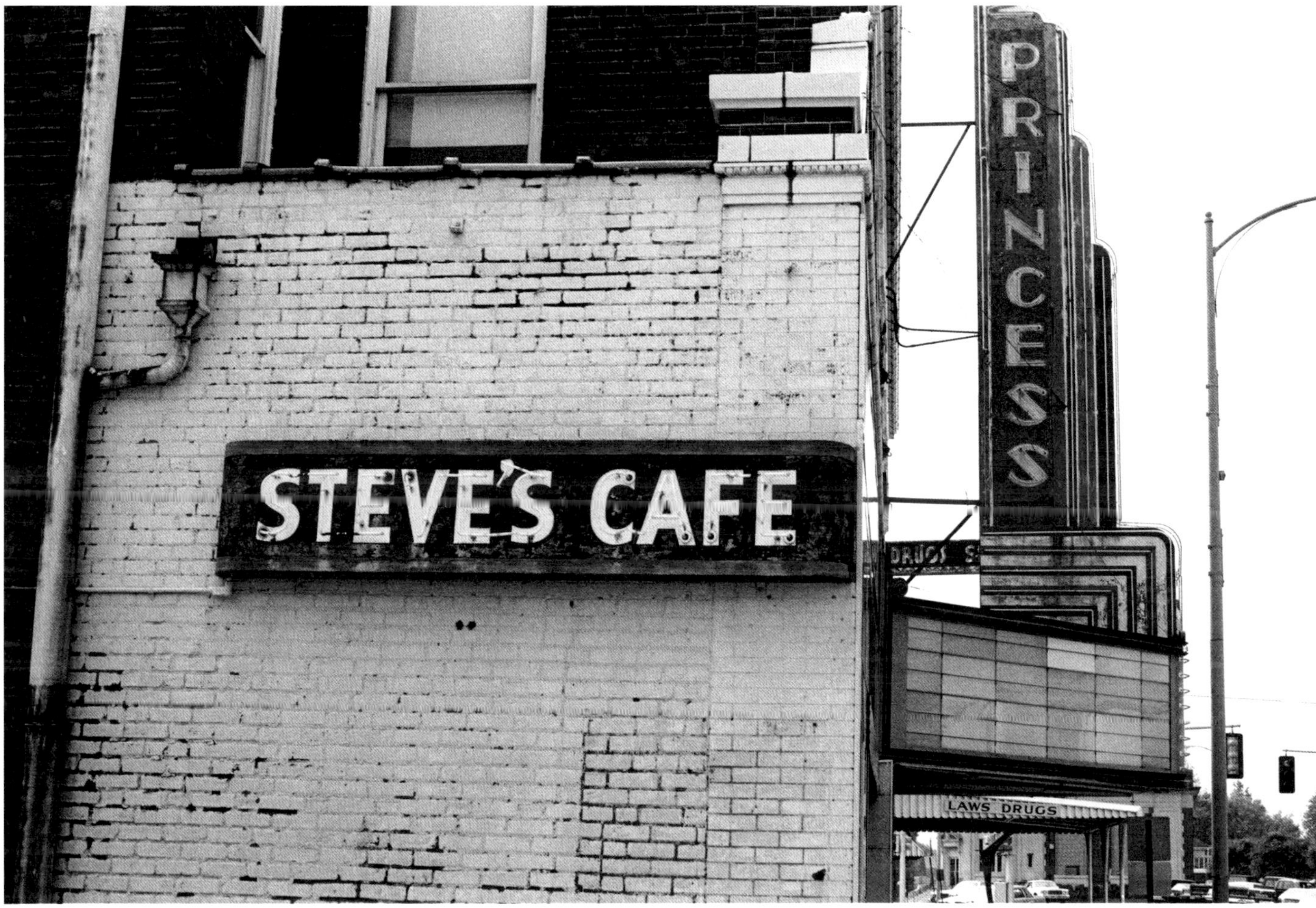
STEVE'S CAFE
PRINCESS
LAWS DRUGS

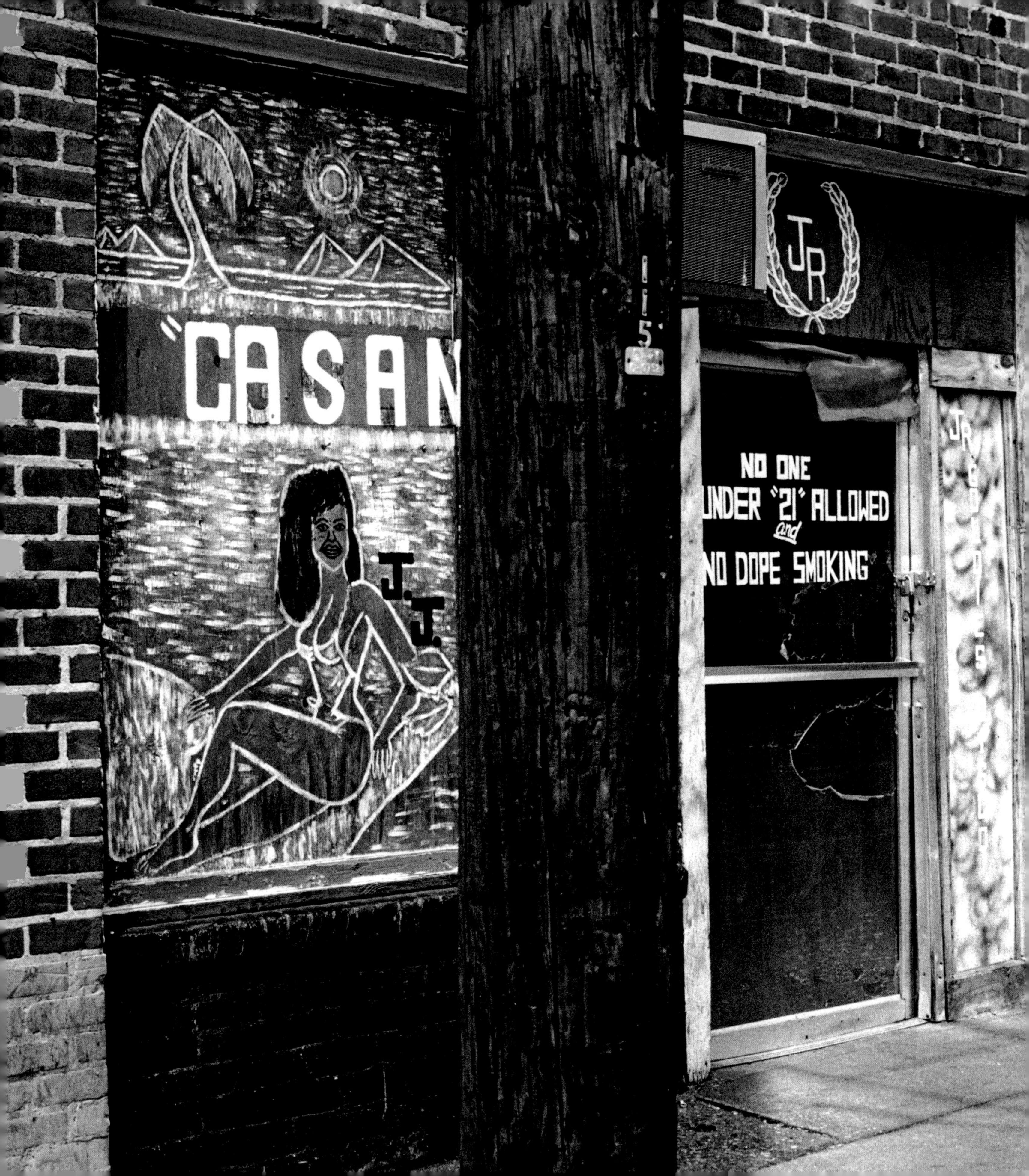
"CASAN
J.J.
115
JR.
NO ONE
UNDER "21" ALLOWED
and
NO DOPE SMOKING"

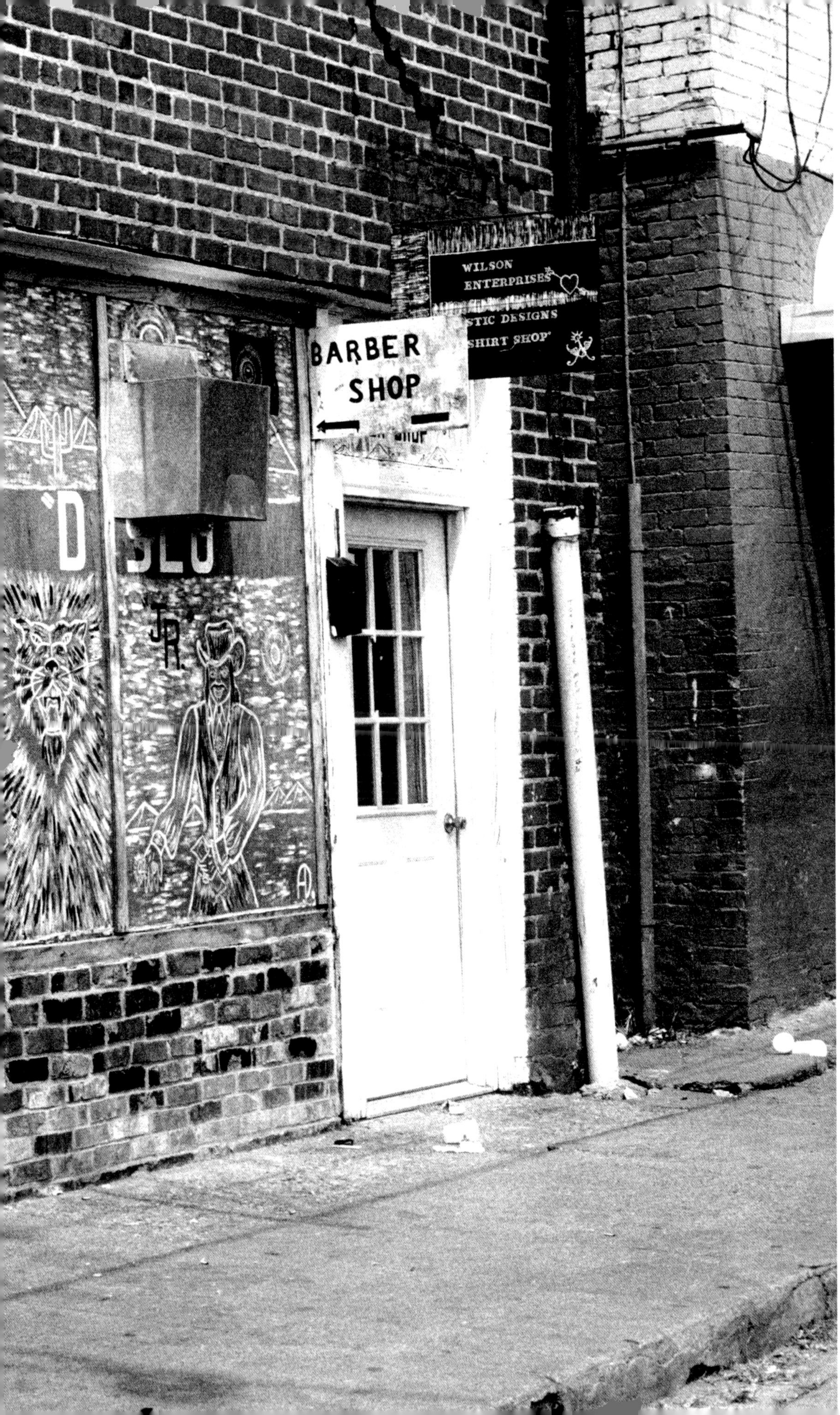
BARBER
SHOP
WILSON
ENTERPRISES

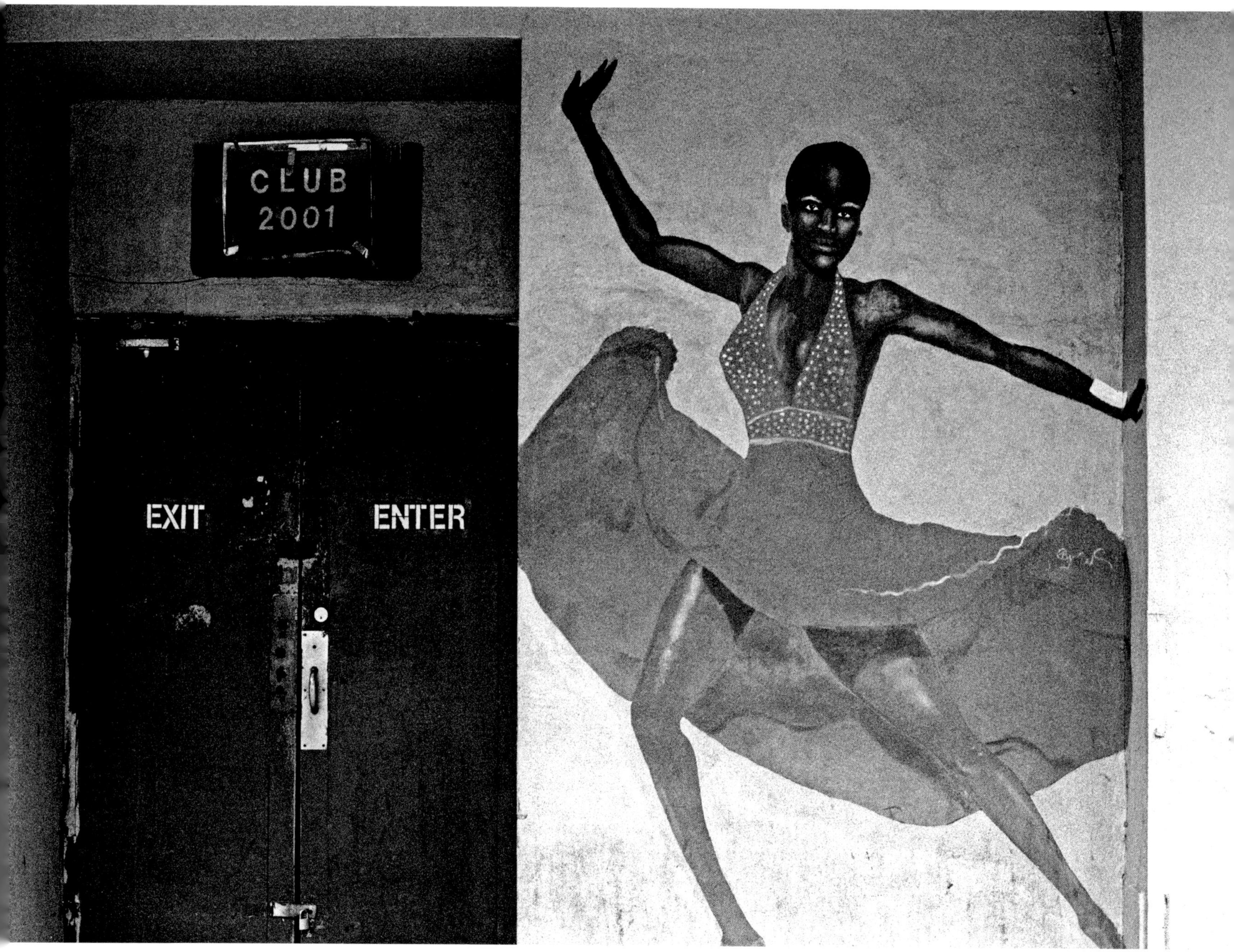
CLUB
2001
EXIT
ENTER

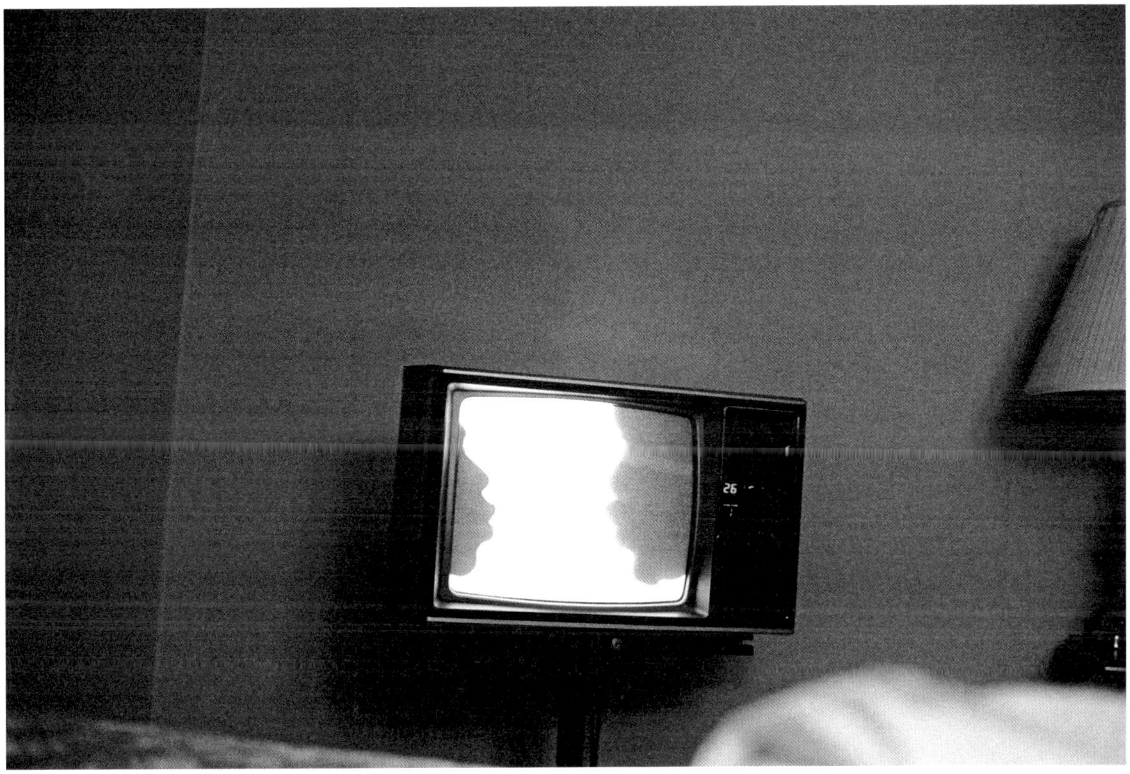

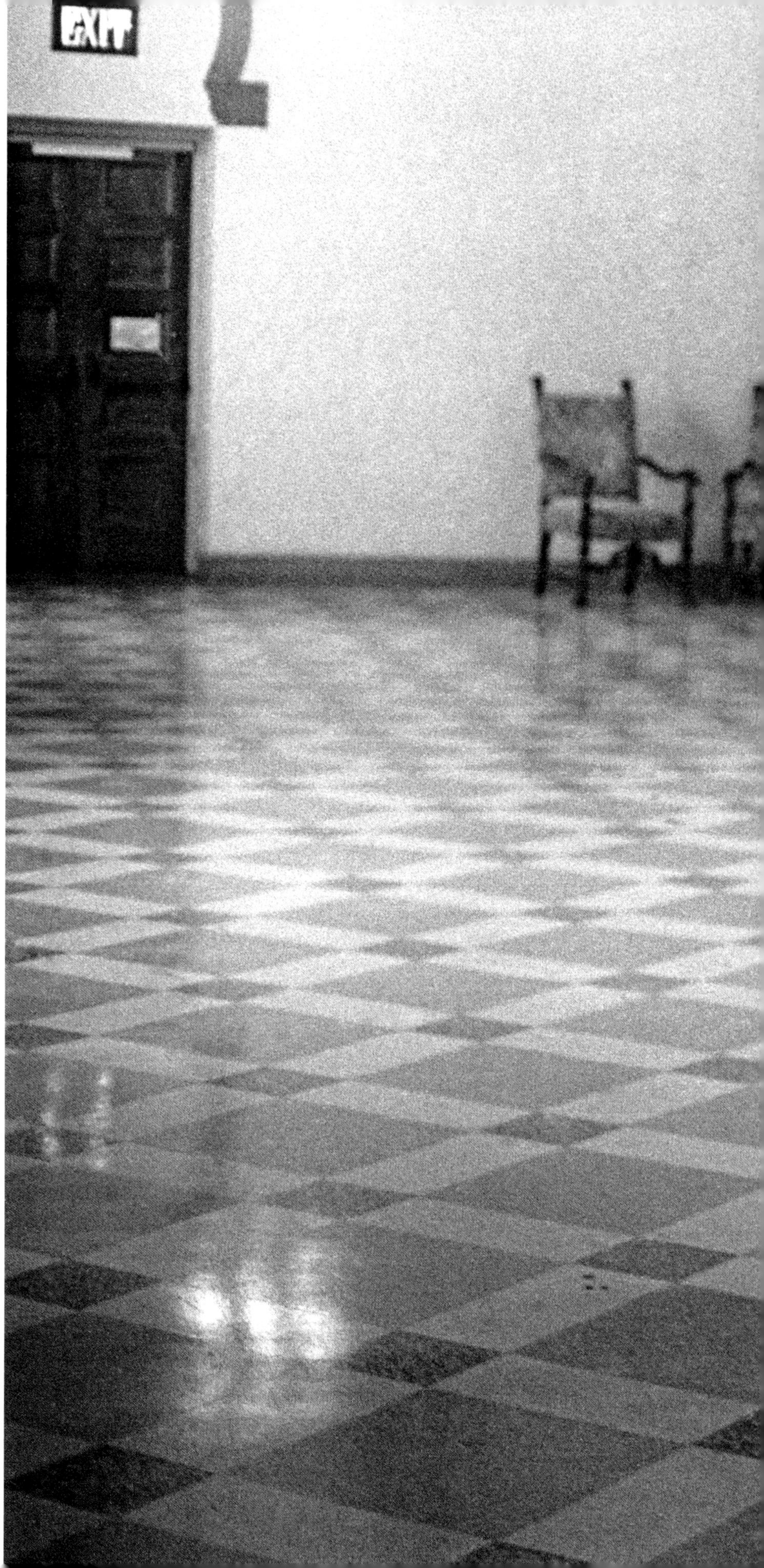
EXIT

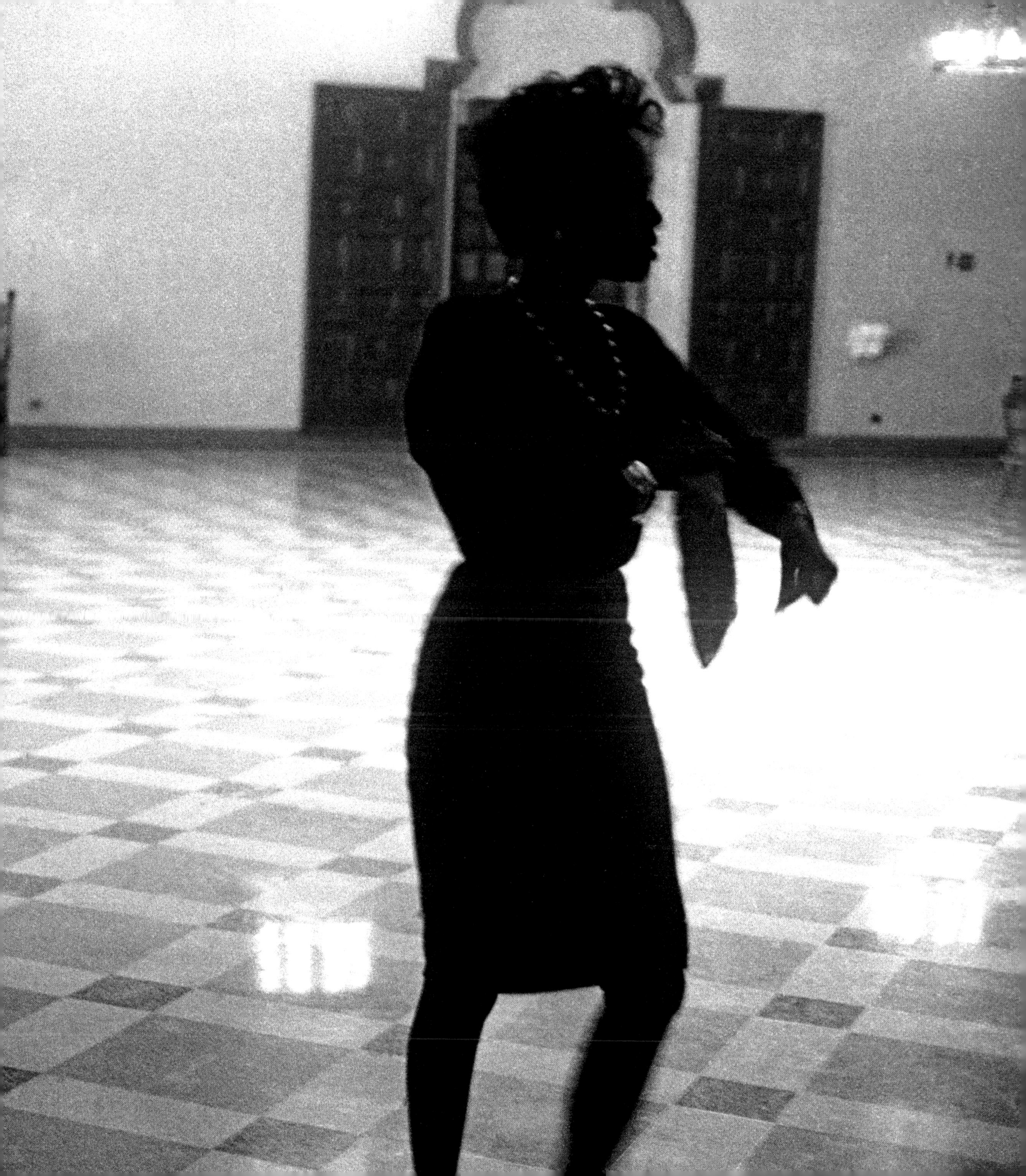

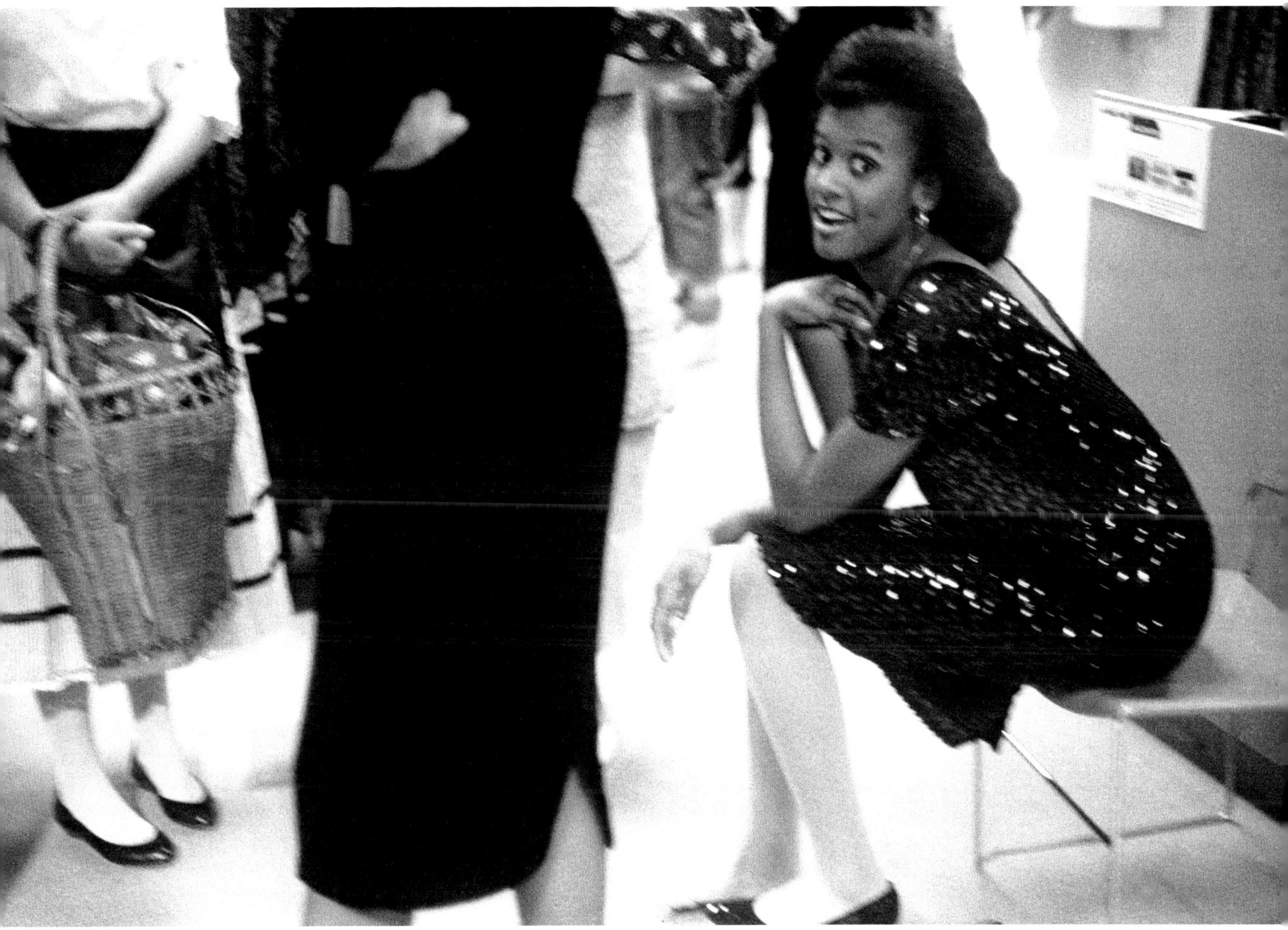

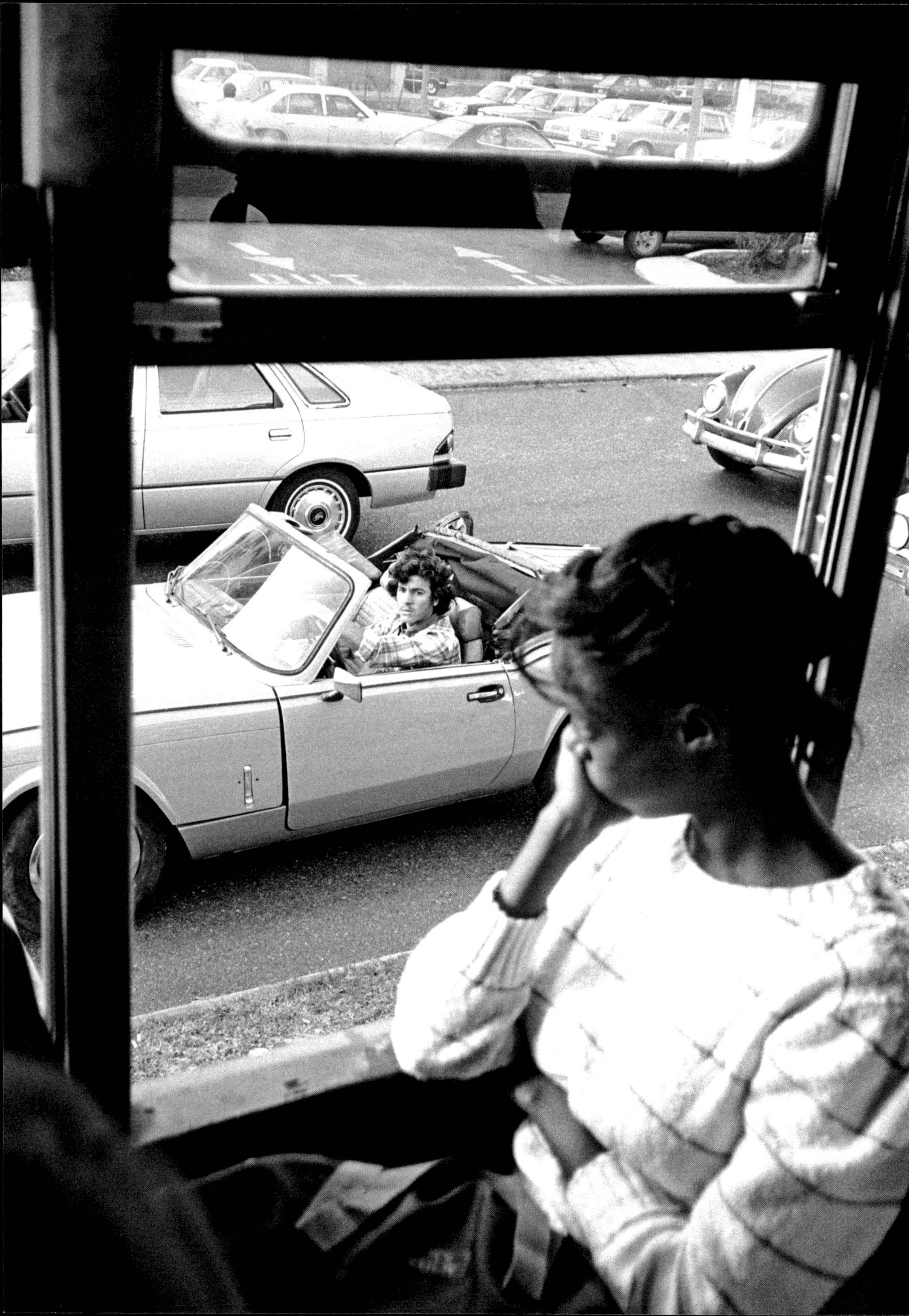

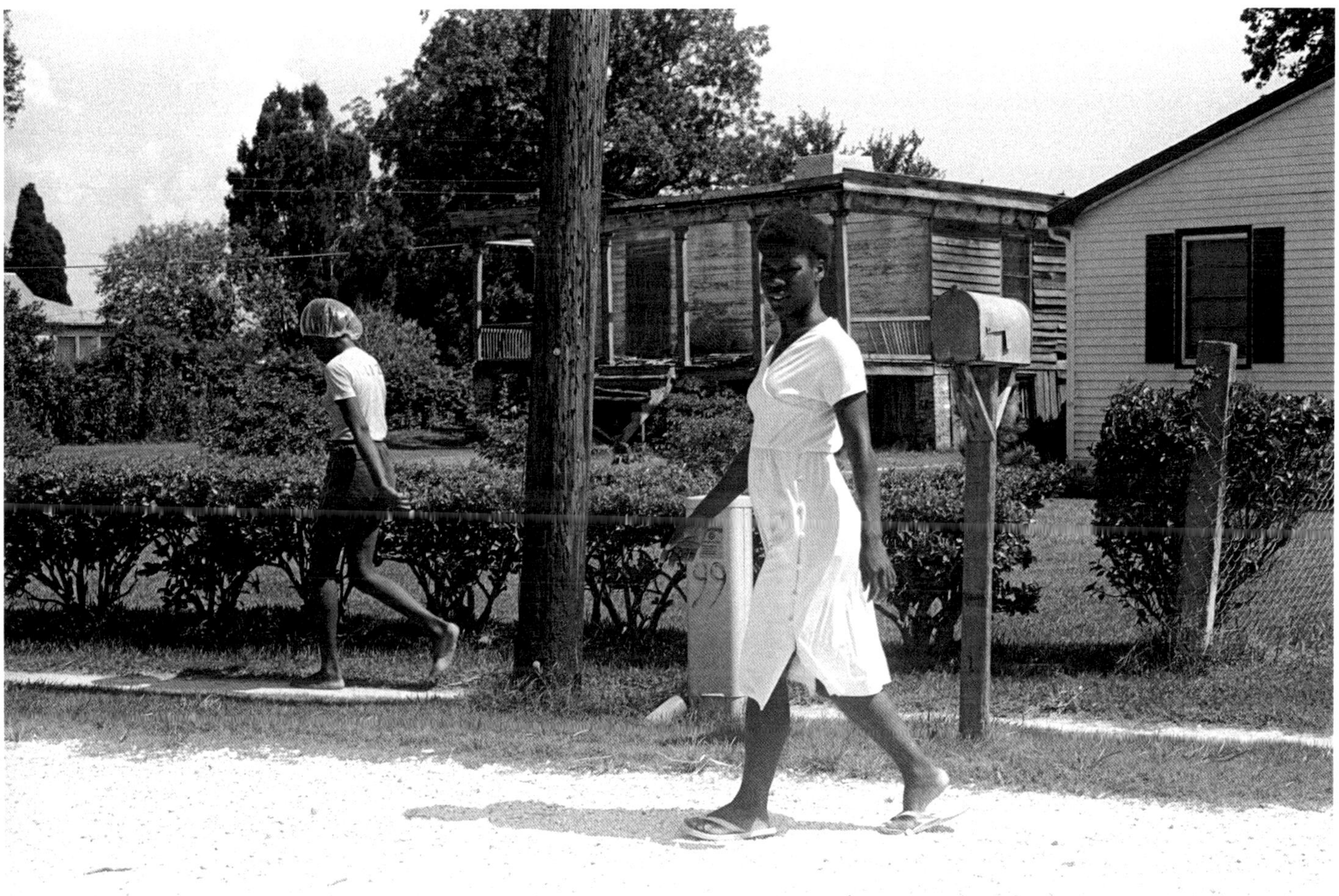

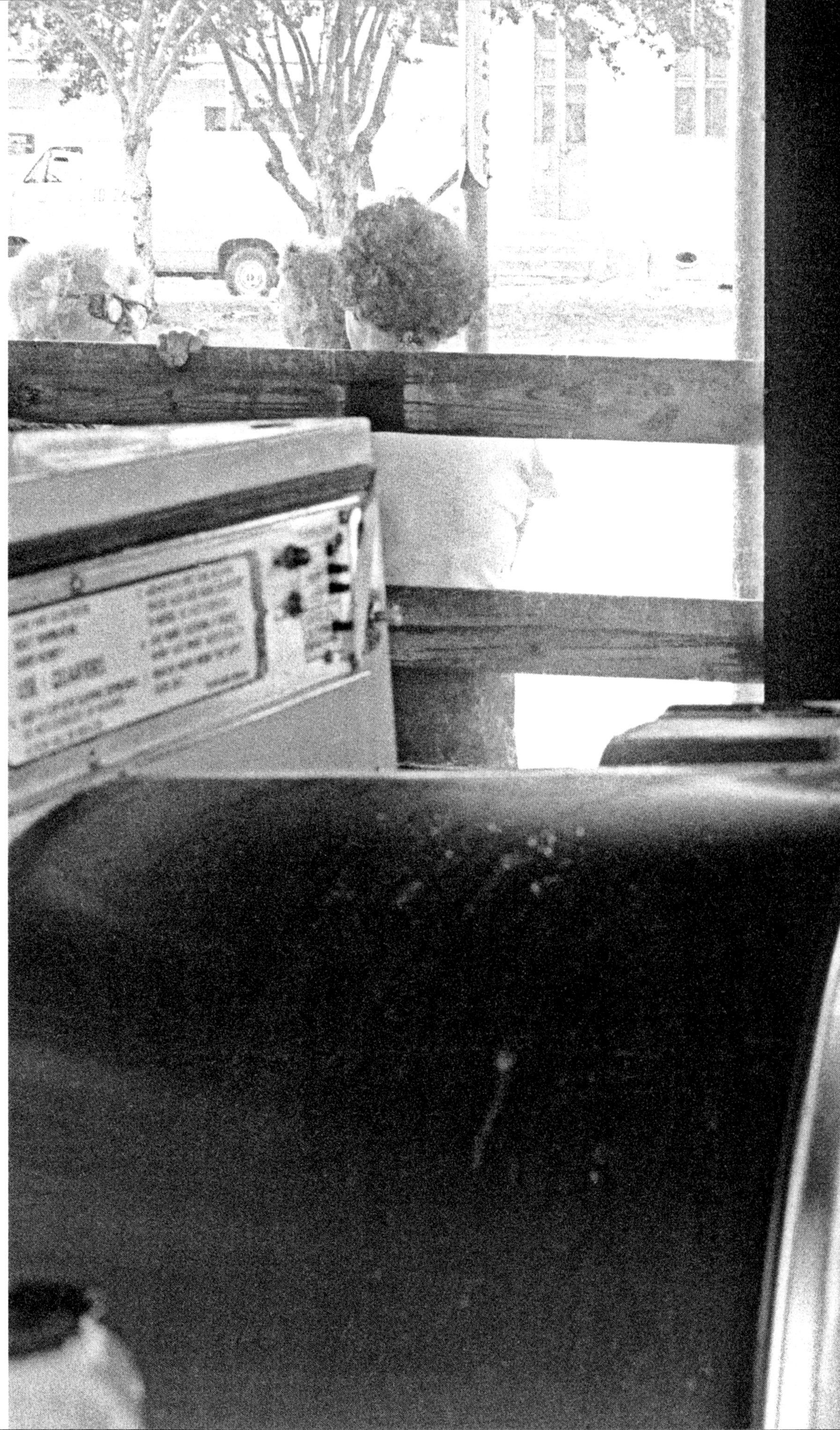

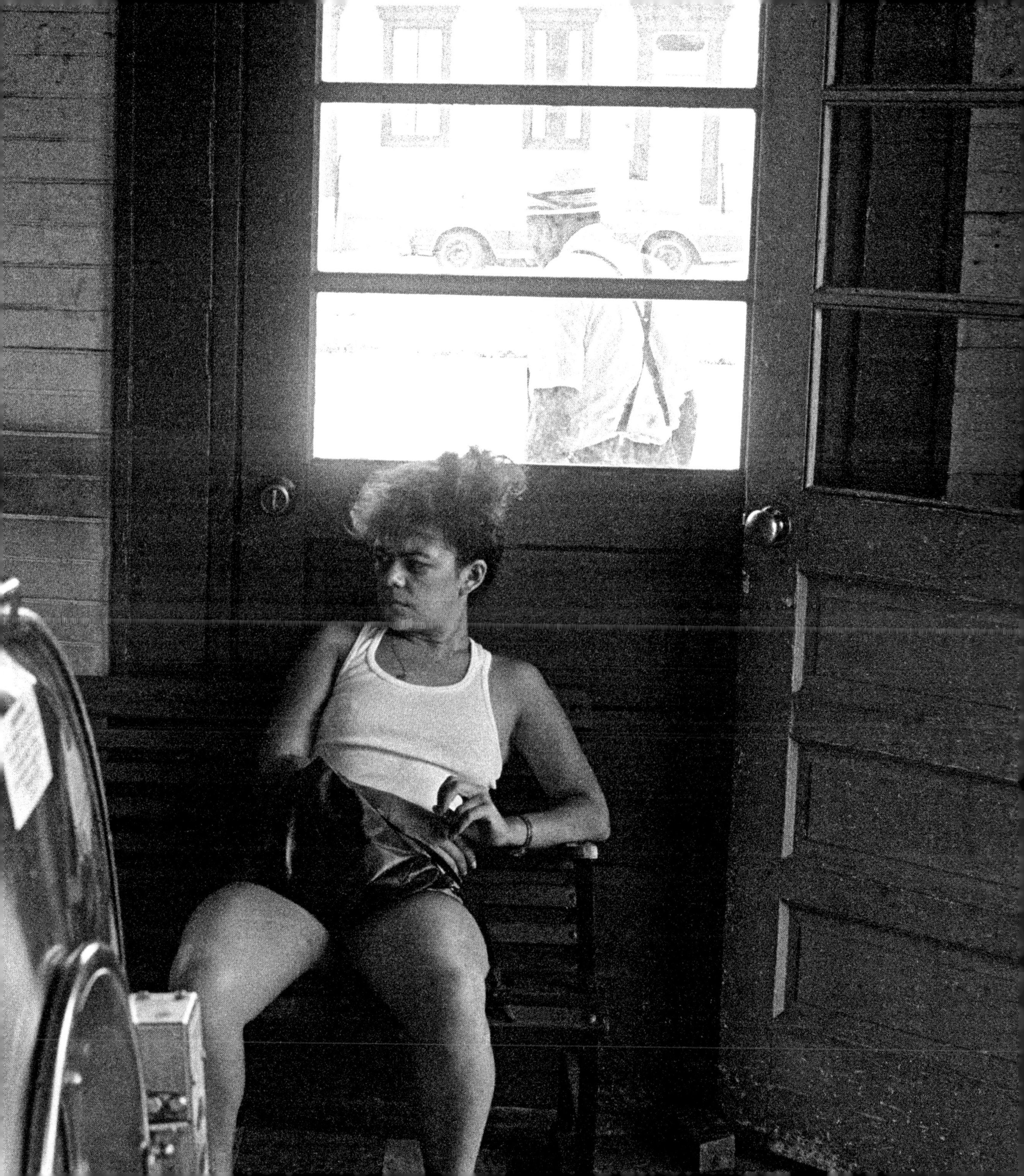

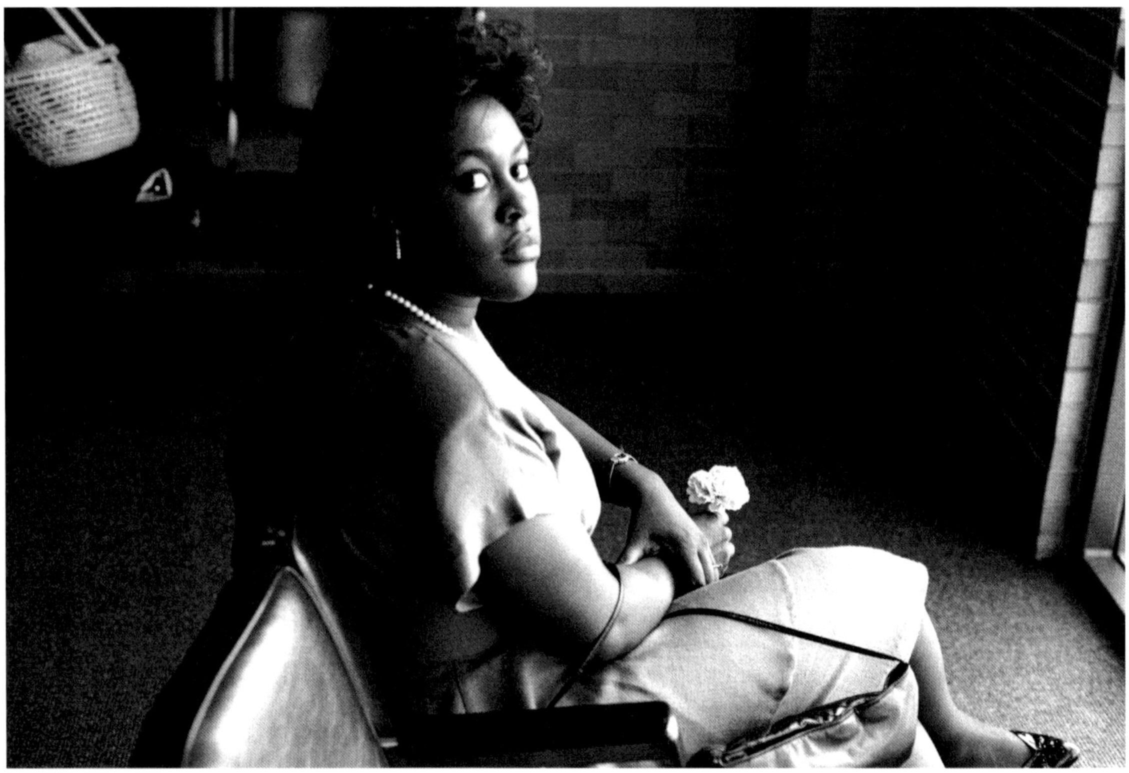

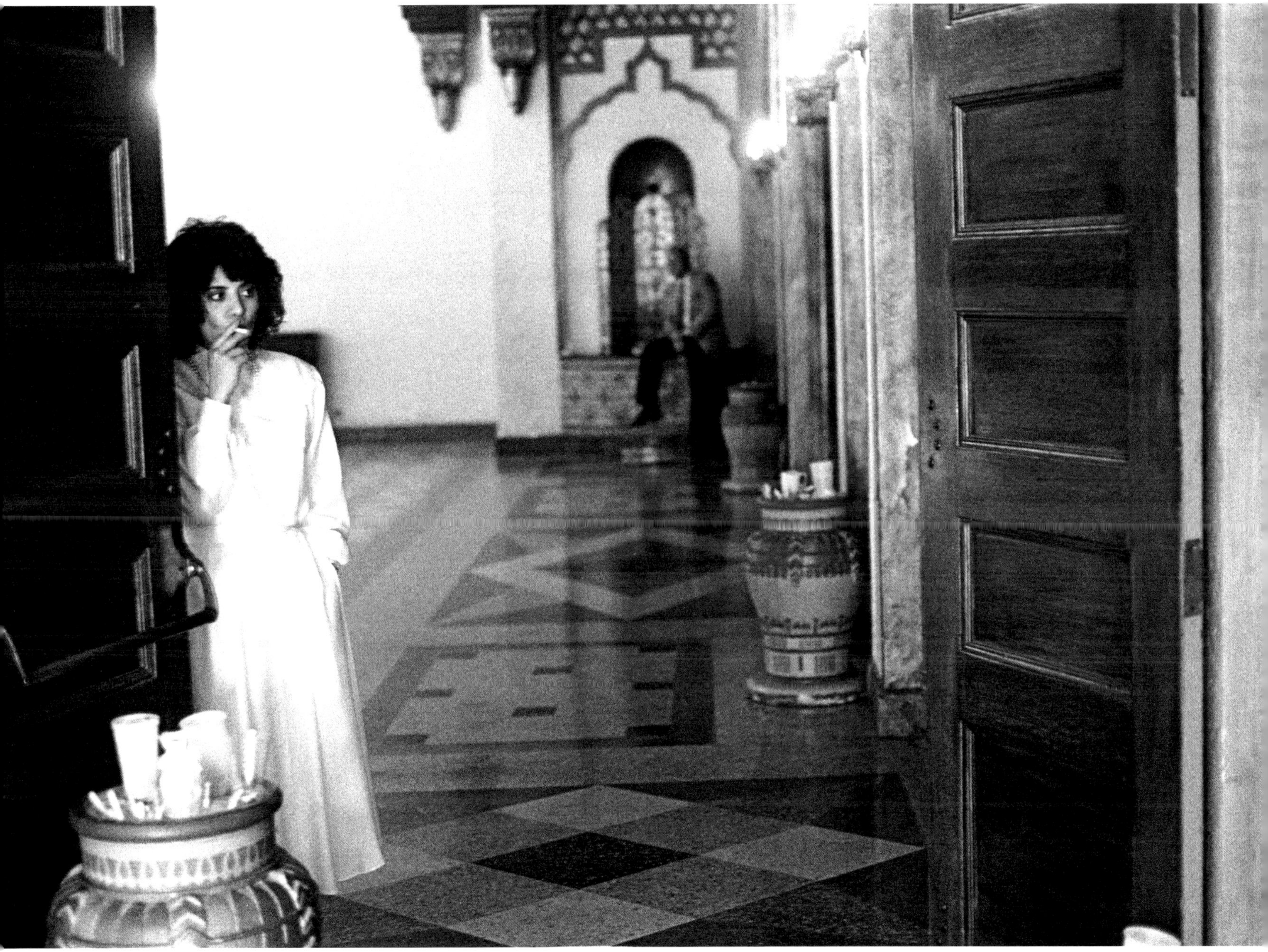

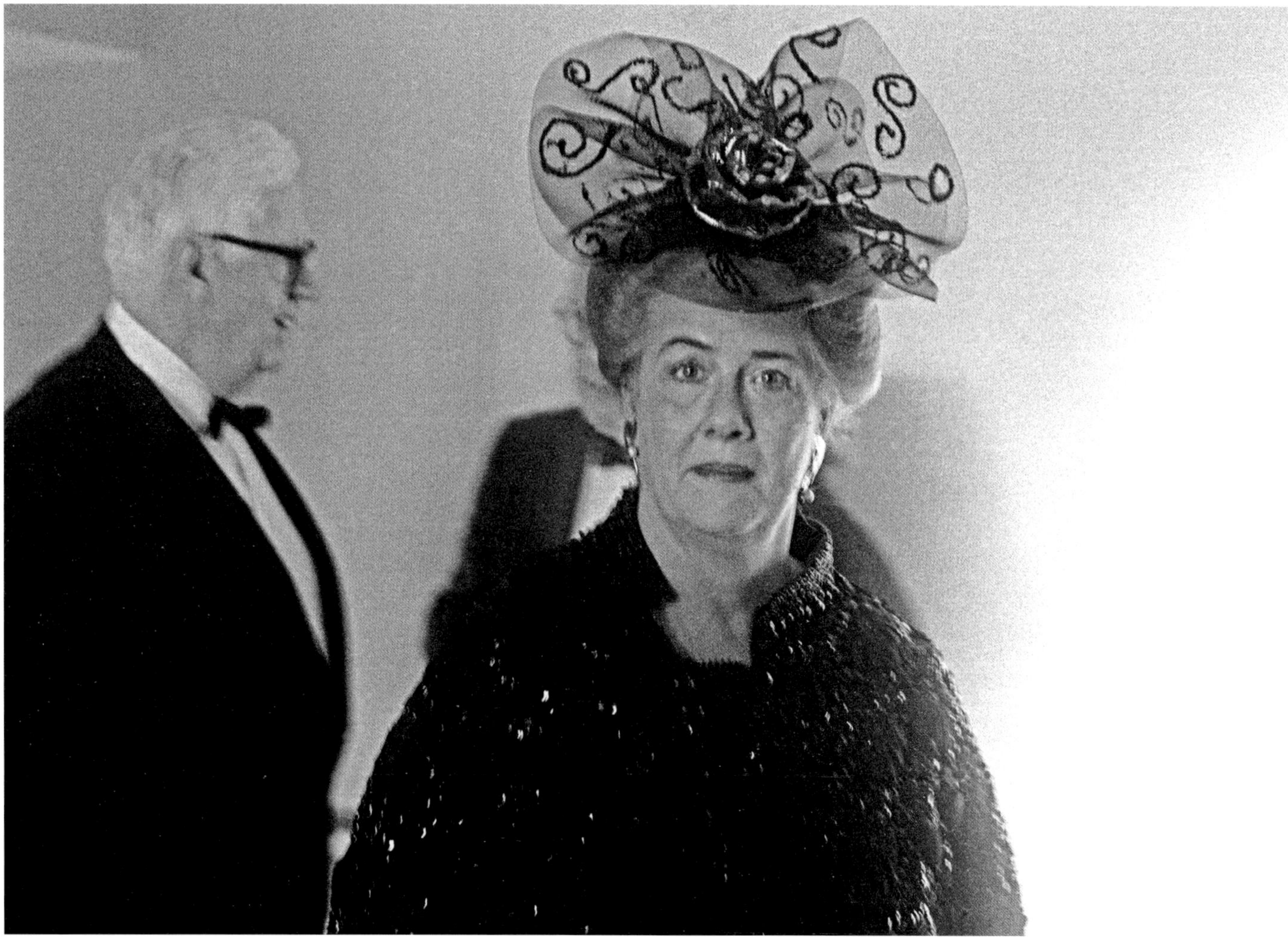

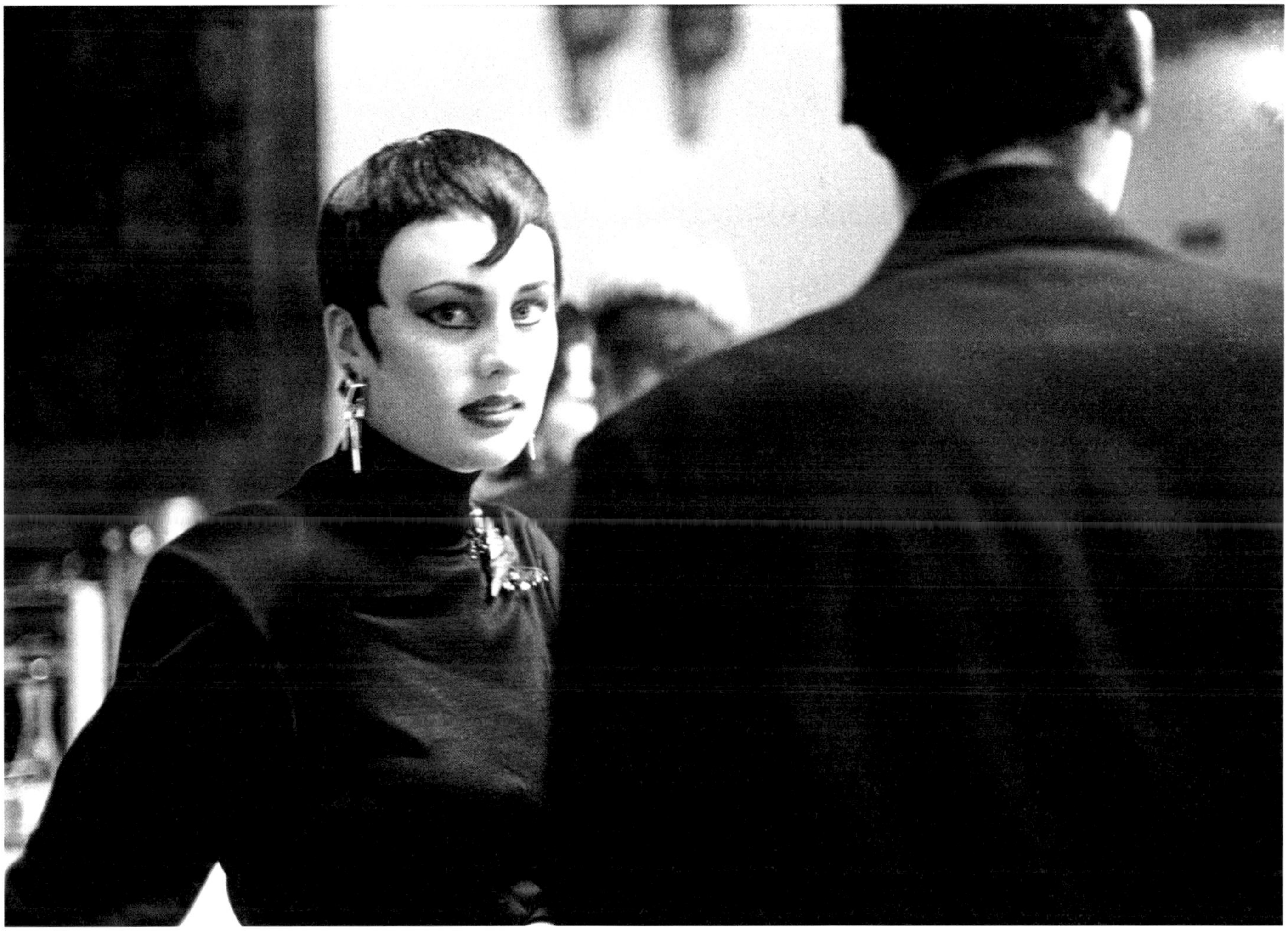

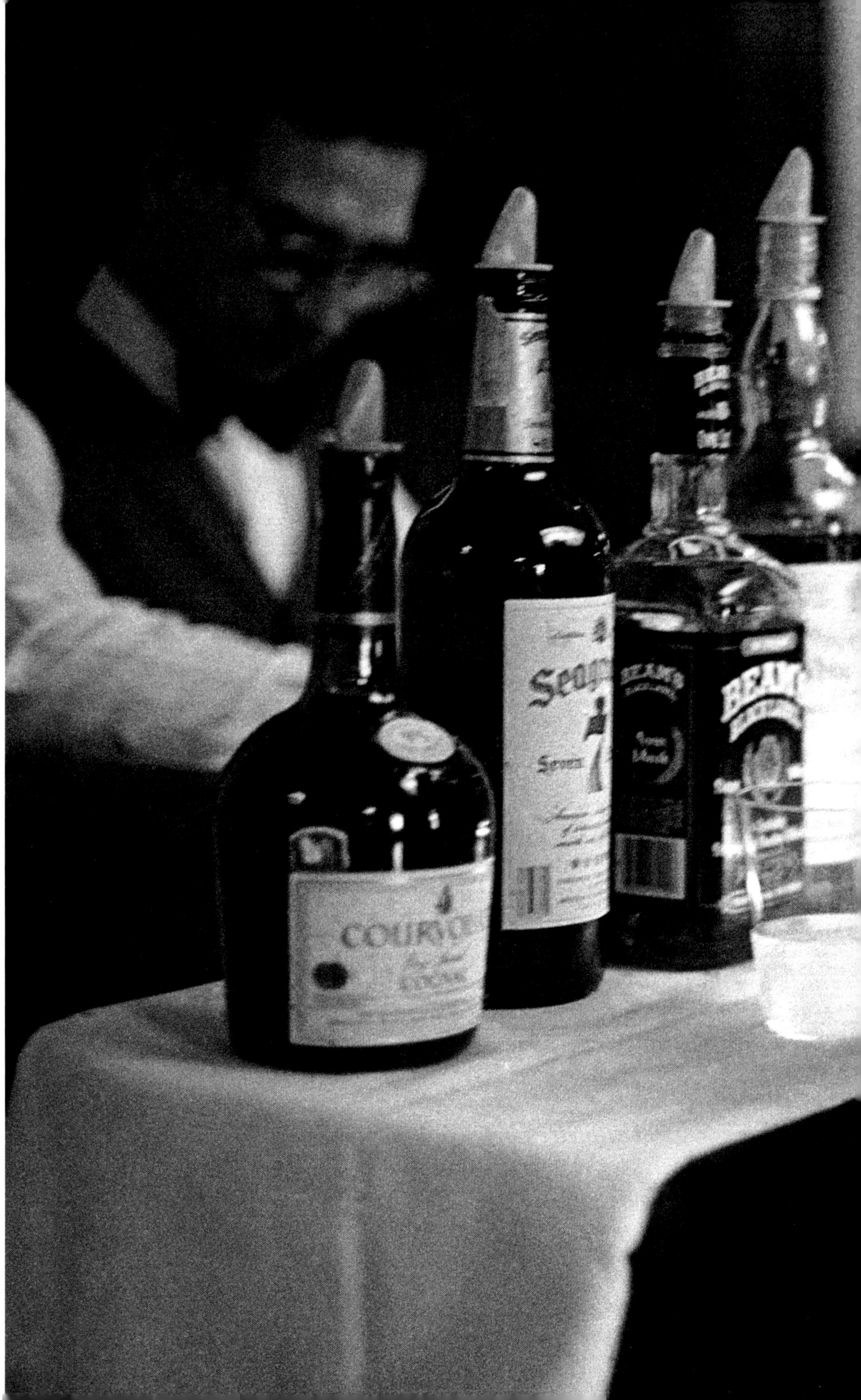

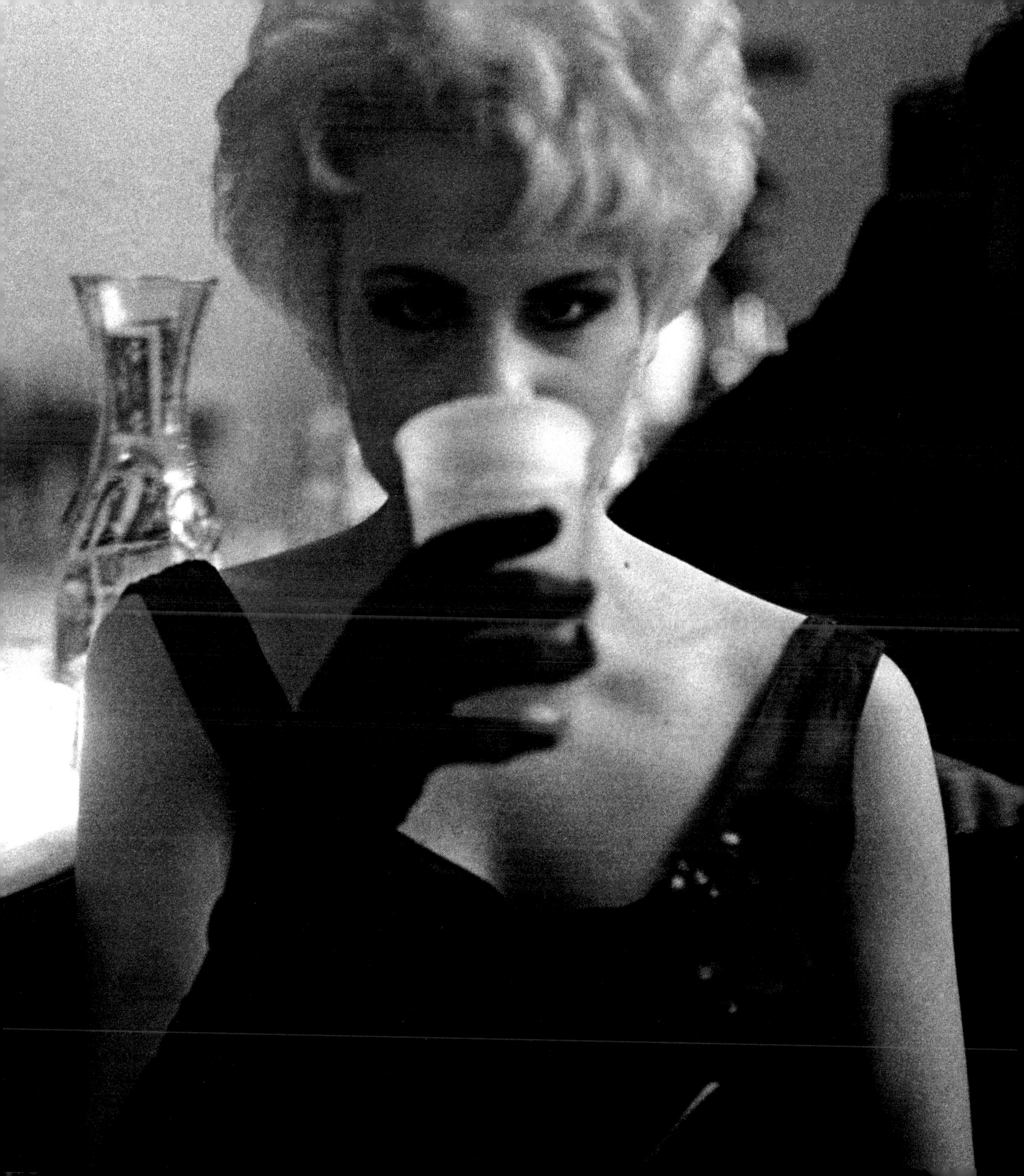

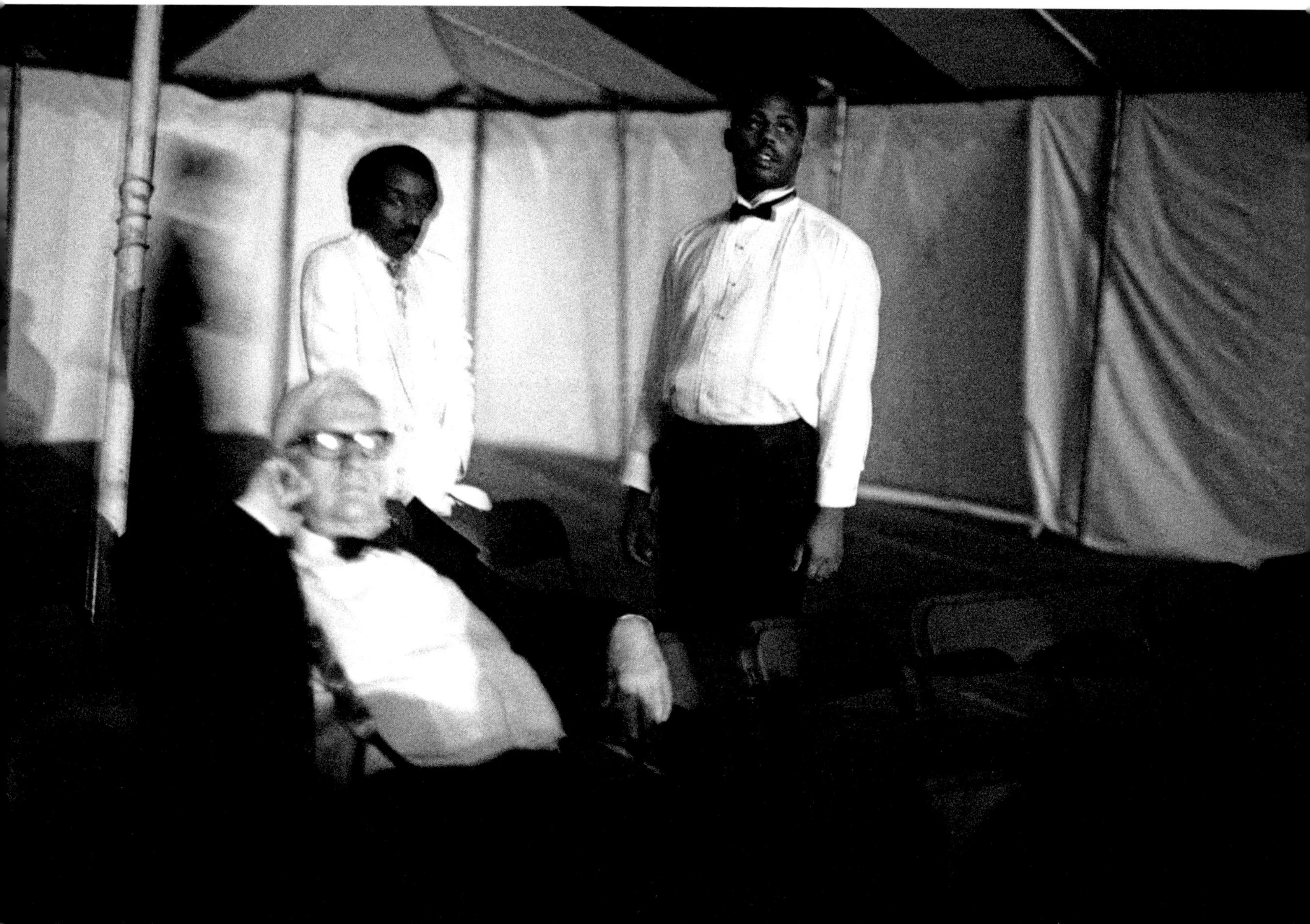

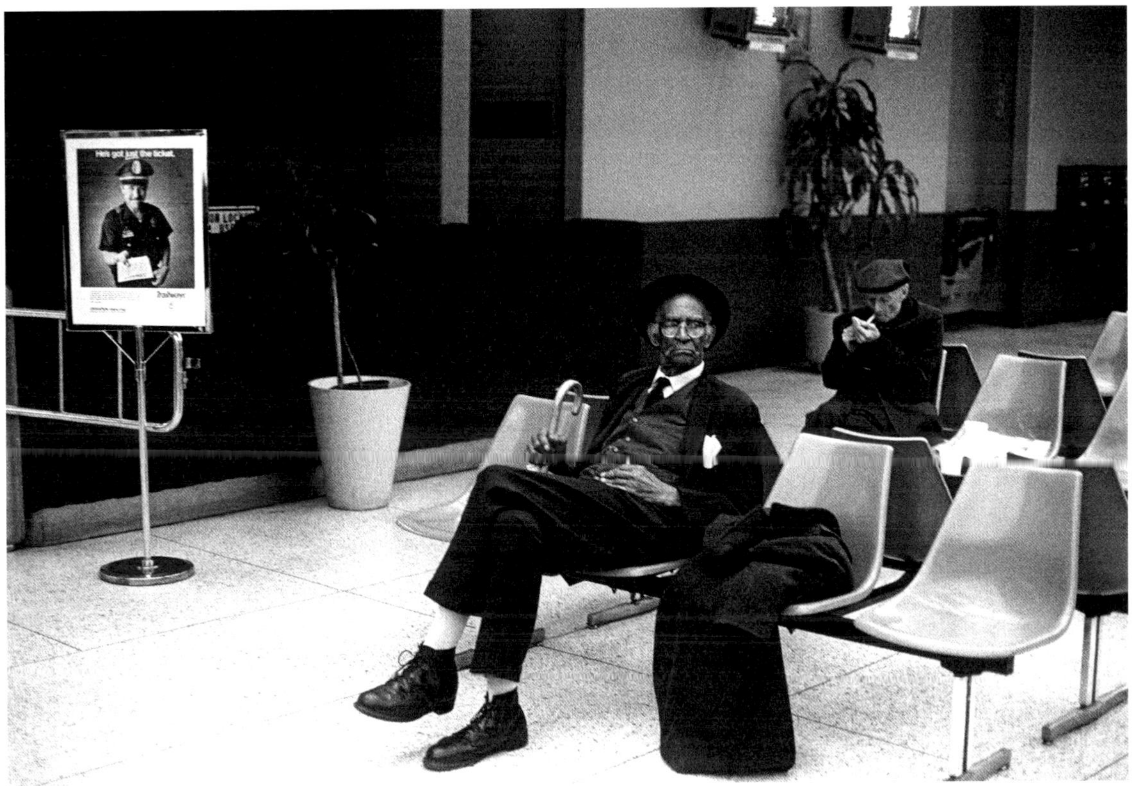
He's got just the ticket.

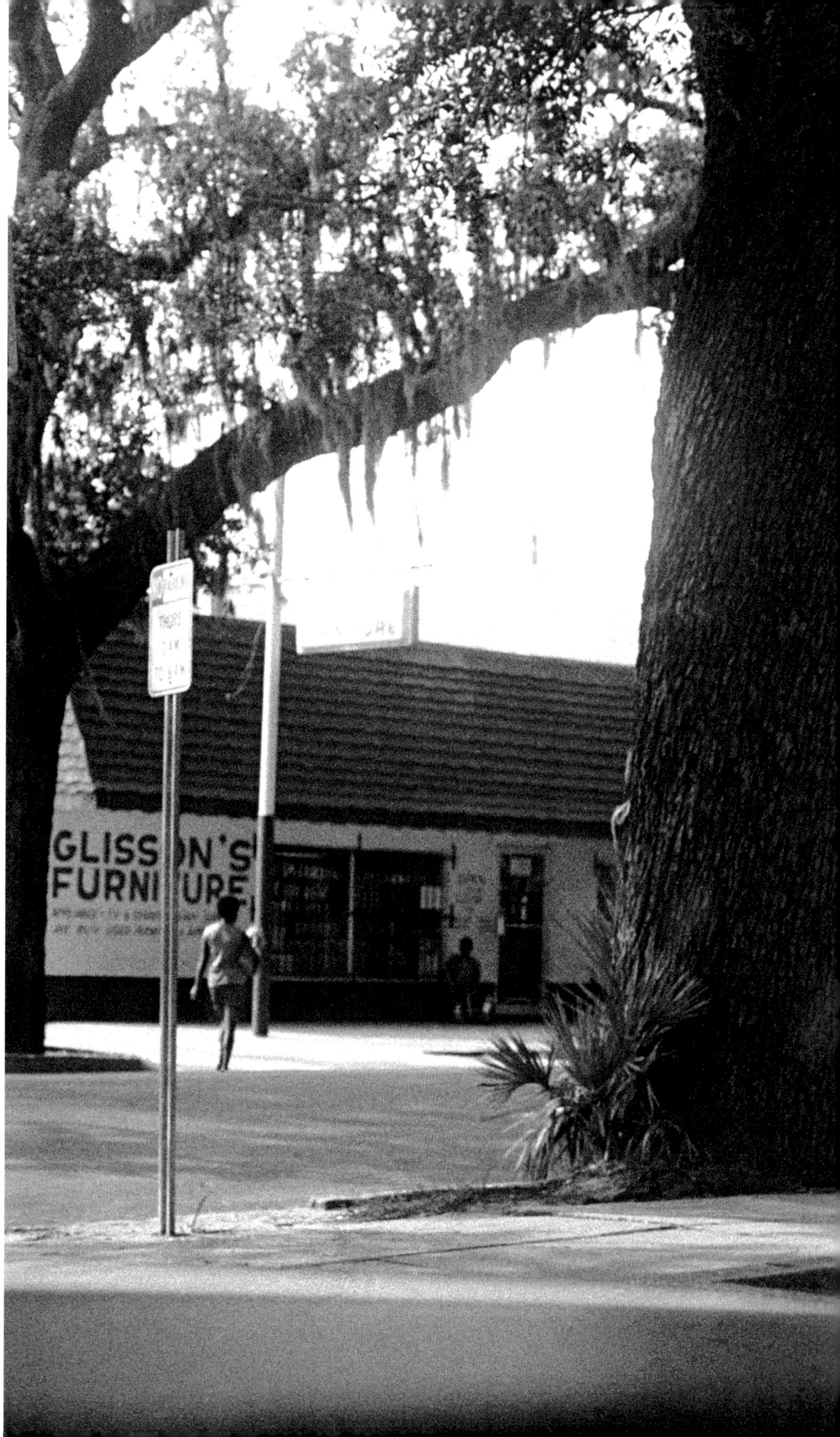
GLISSON'S
FURNI URE

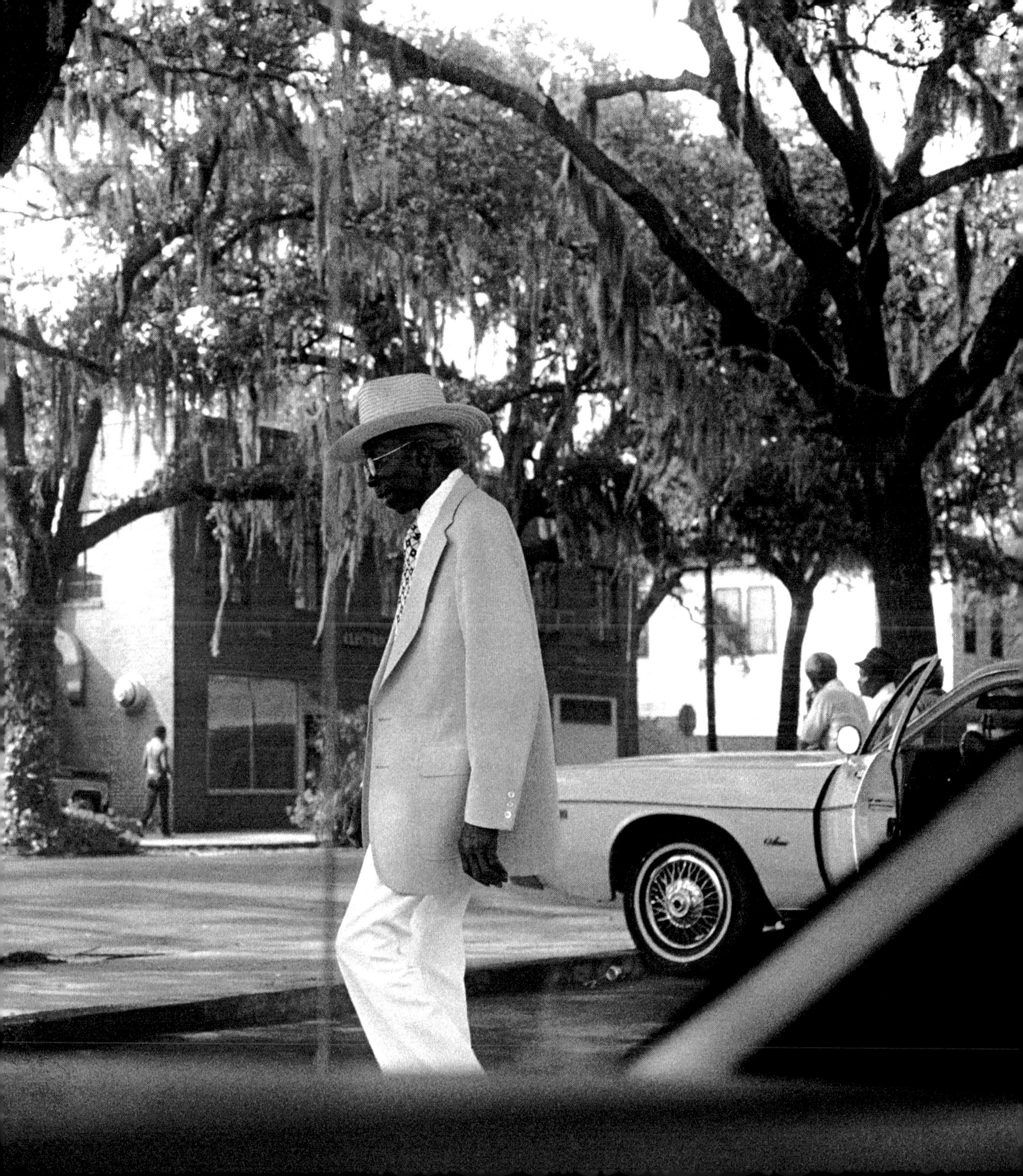

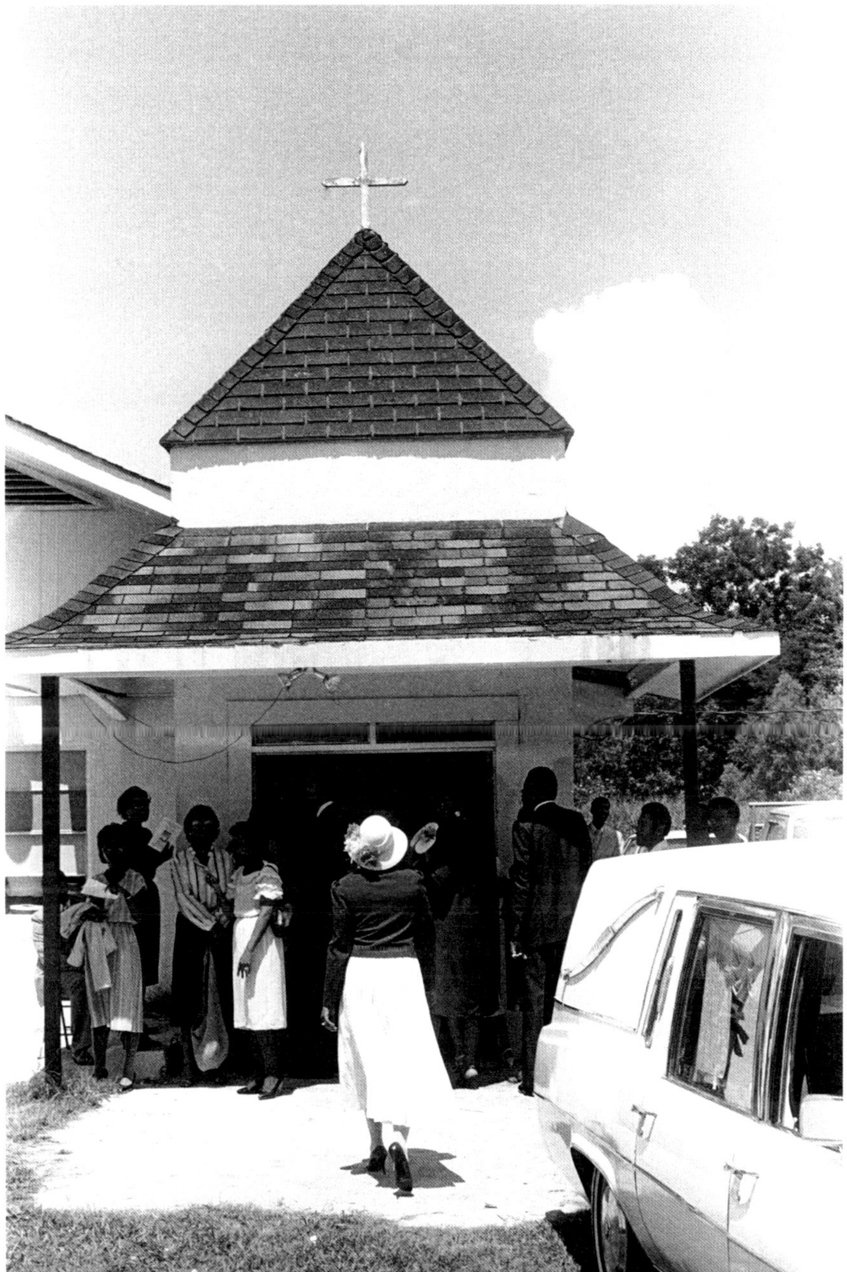

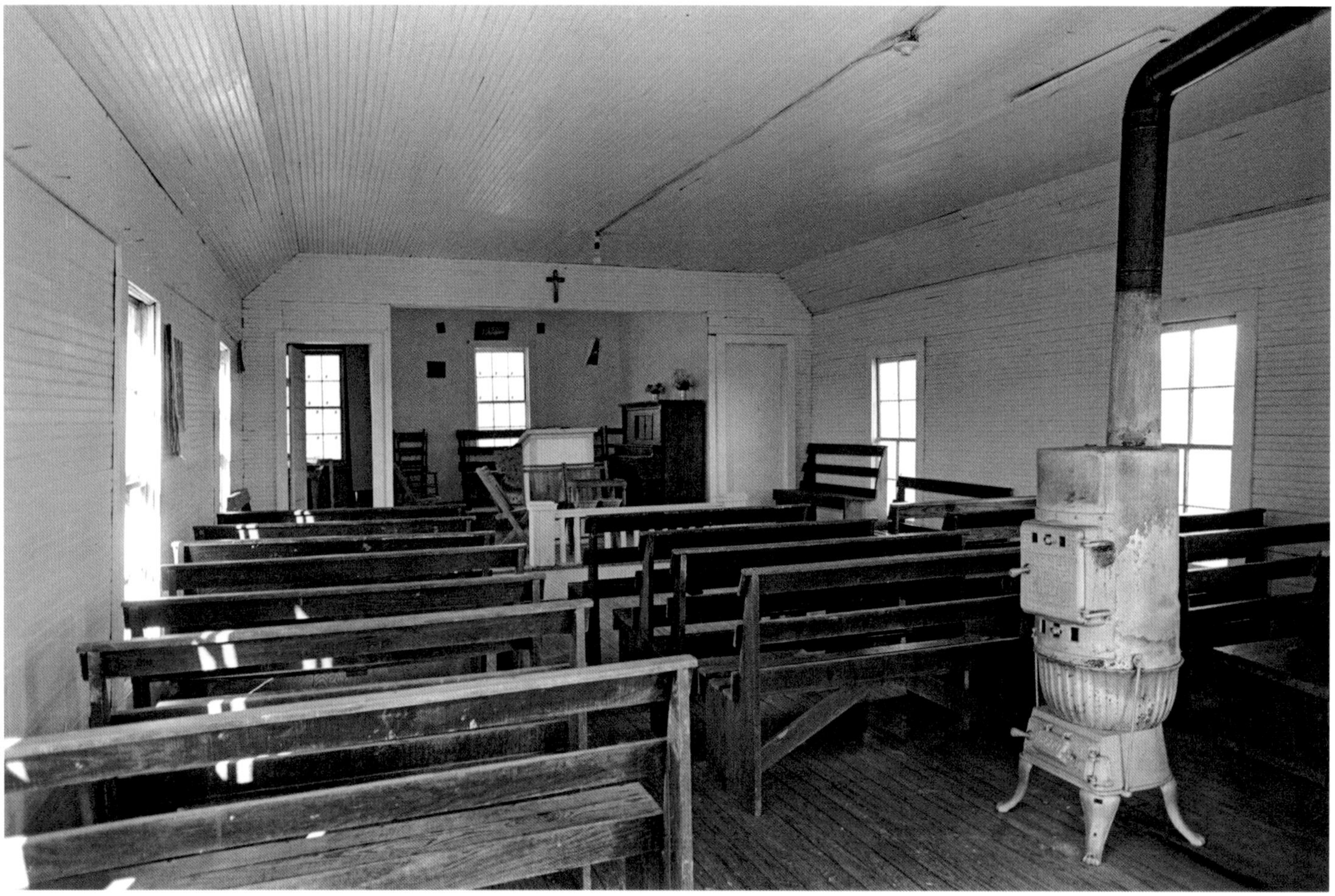

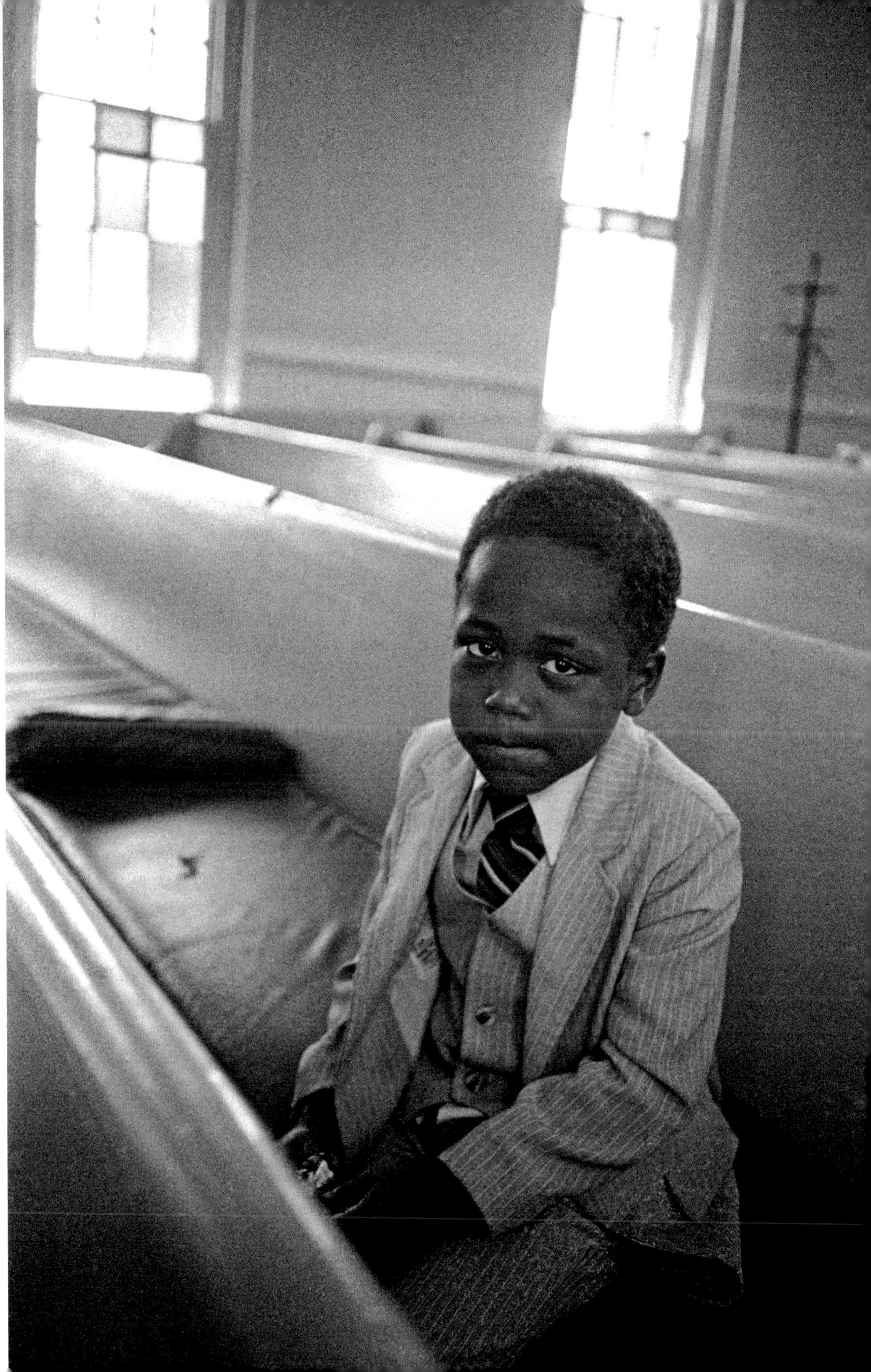

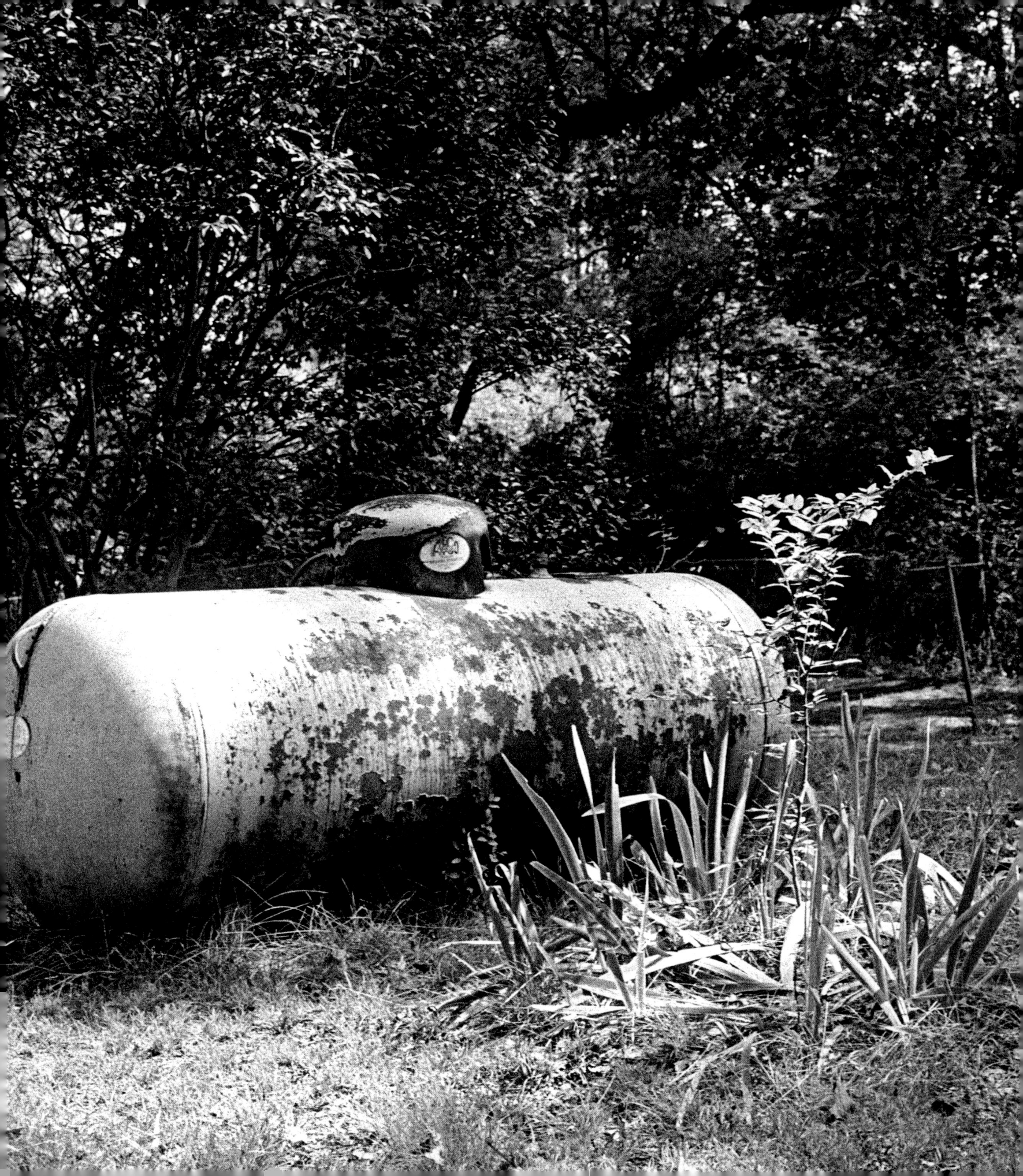

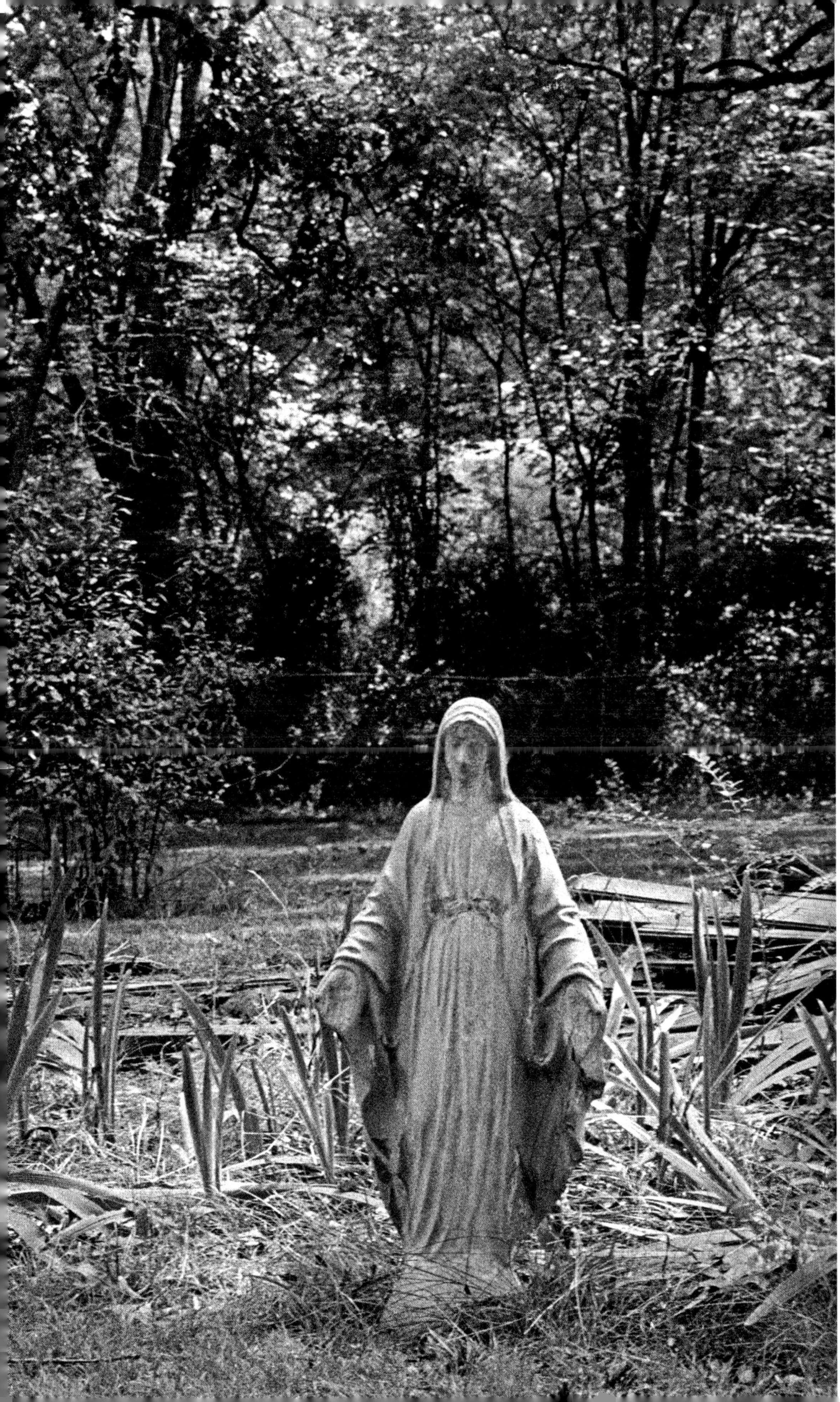

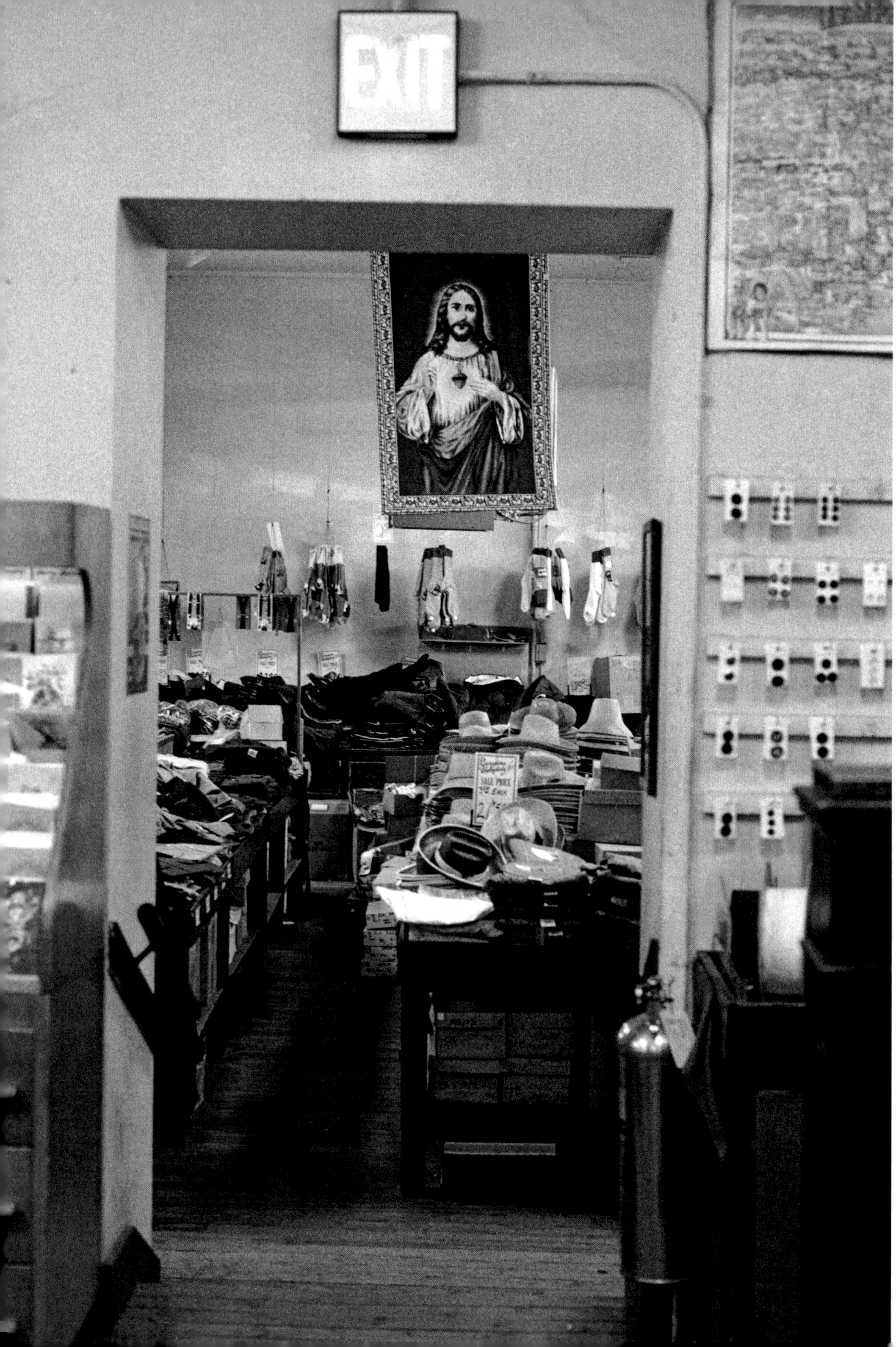
EXIT
SALE PRICE

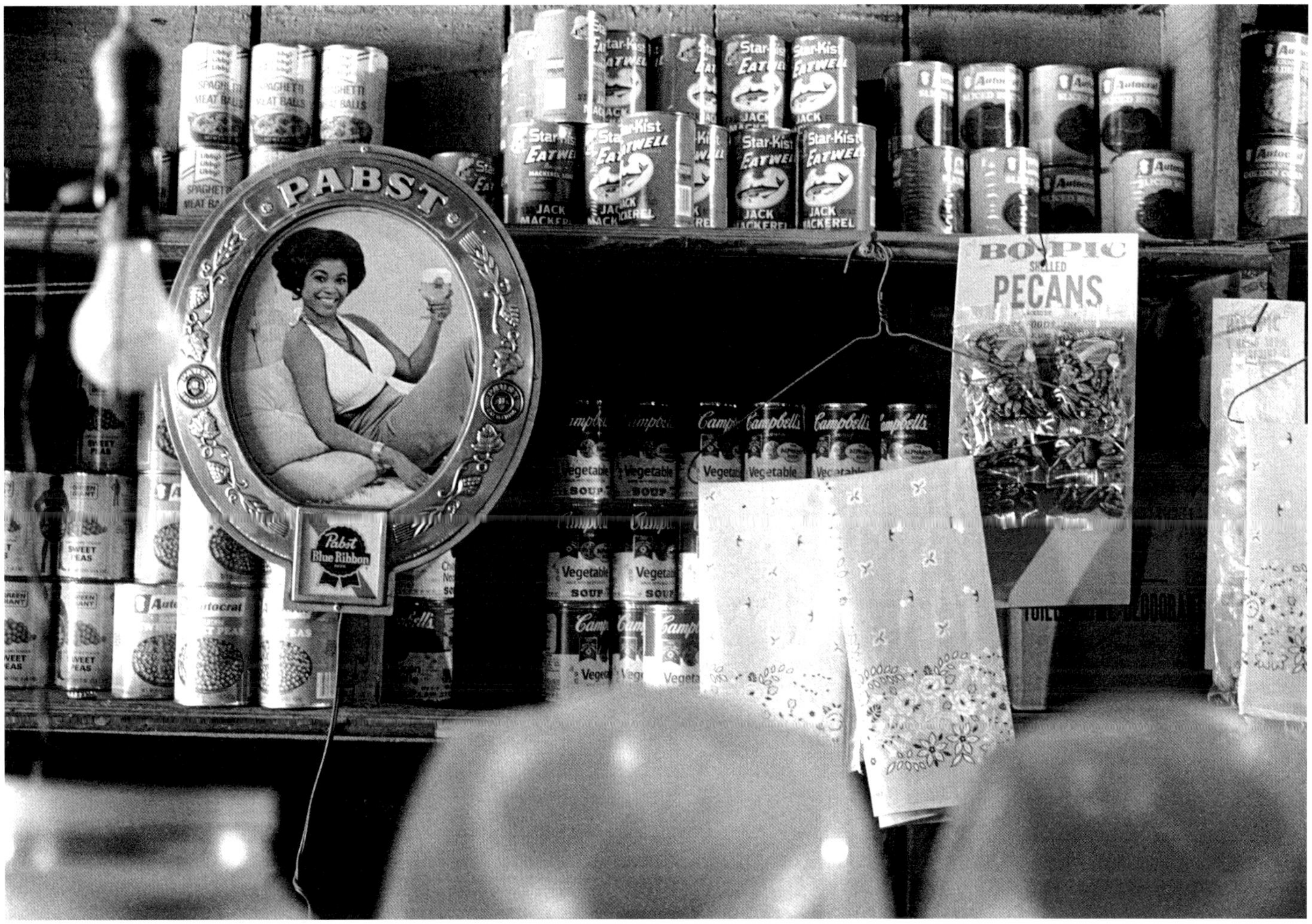
PABST
Pabst Blue Ribbon
Star-Kist
EATWELL
JACK MACKEREL
SPAGHETTI MEAT BALLS
Autocrat
SWEET PEAS
Campbell's
Vegetable SOUP
BO-PIC
SHELLED
PECANS

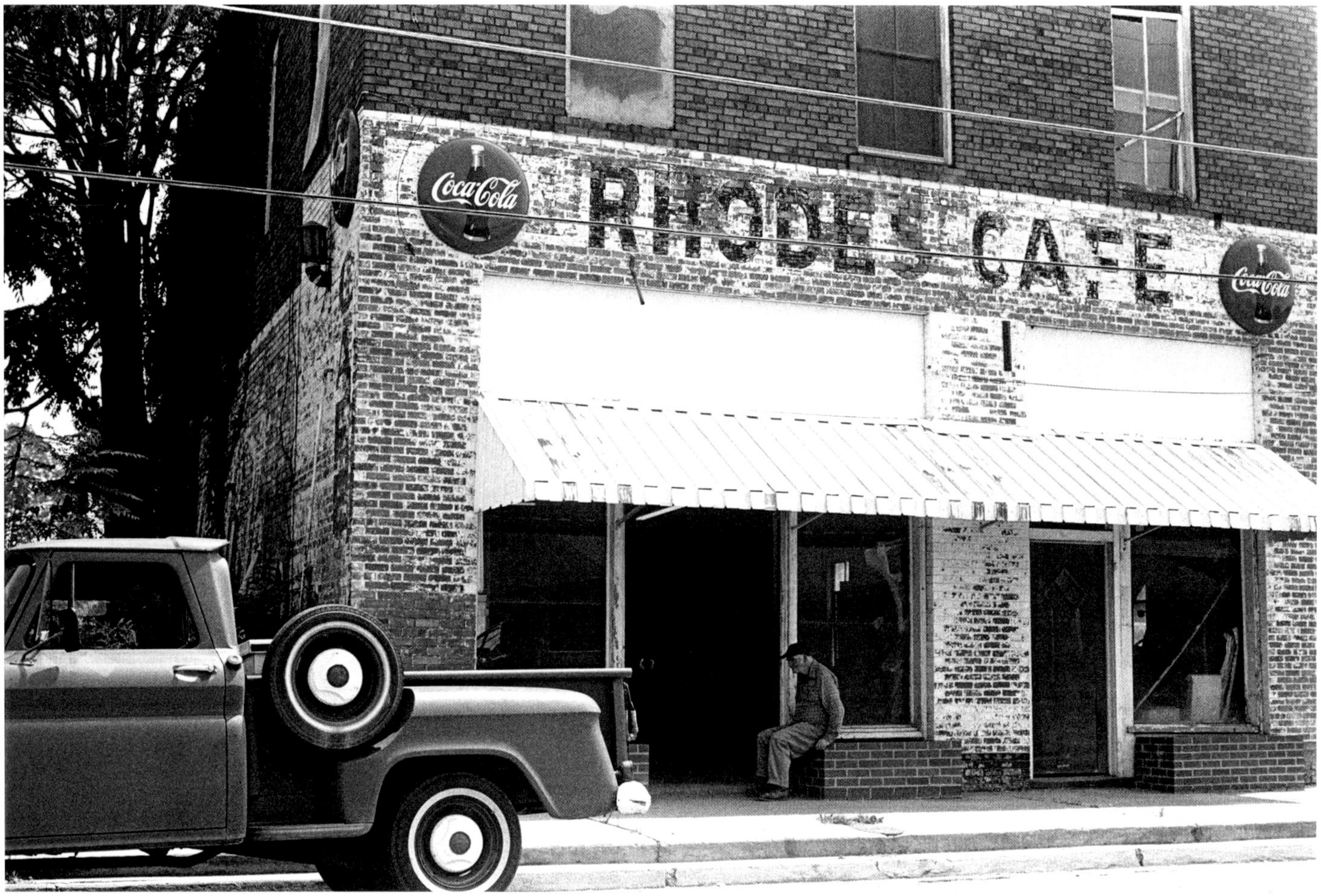
Coca-Cola
RHODES CAFE
Coca-Cola

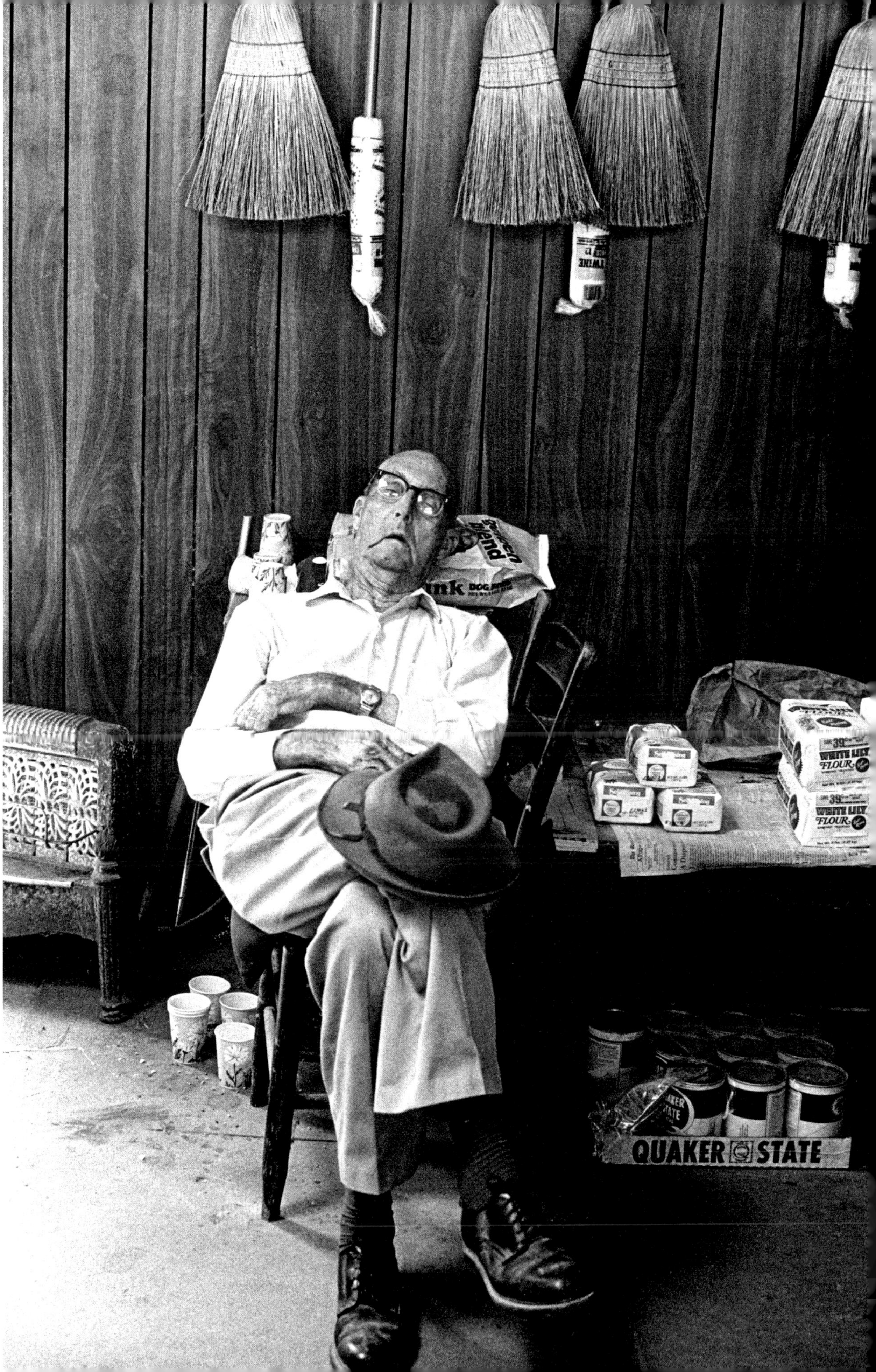
WHITE LILY FLOUR
WHITE LILY FLOUR
QUAKER STATE

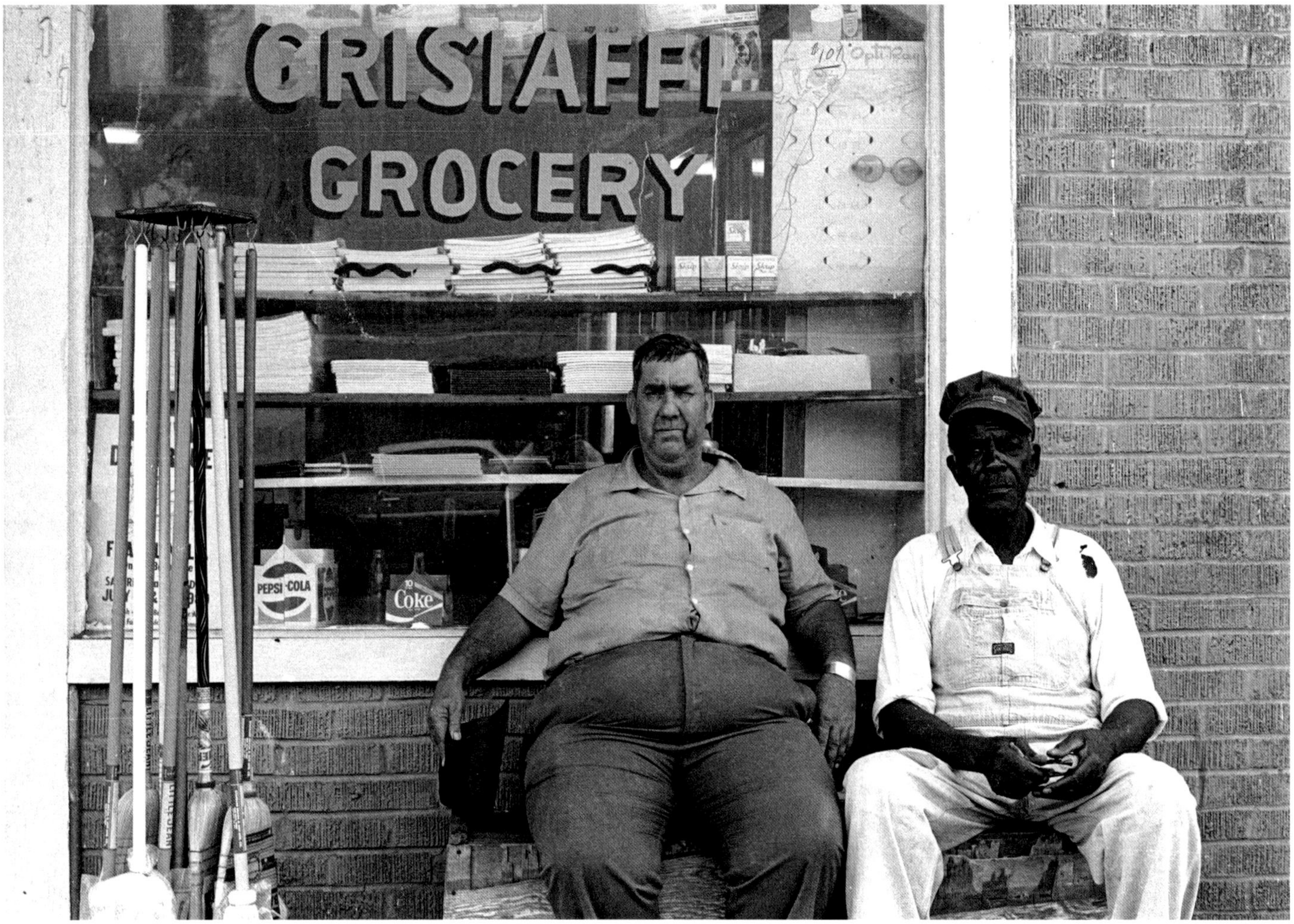
CRISIAFFI
GROCERY
PEPSI-COLA
Coke

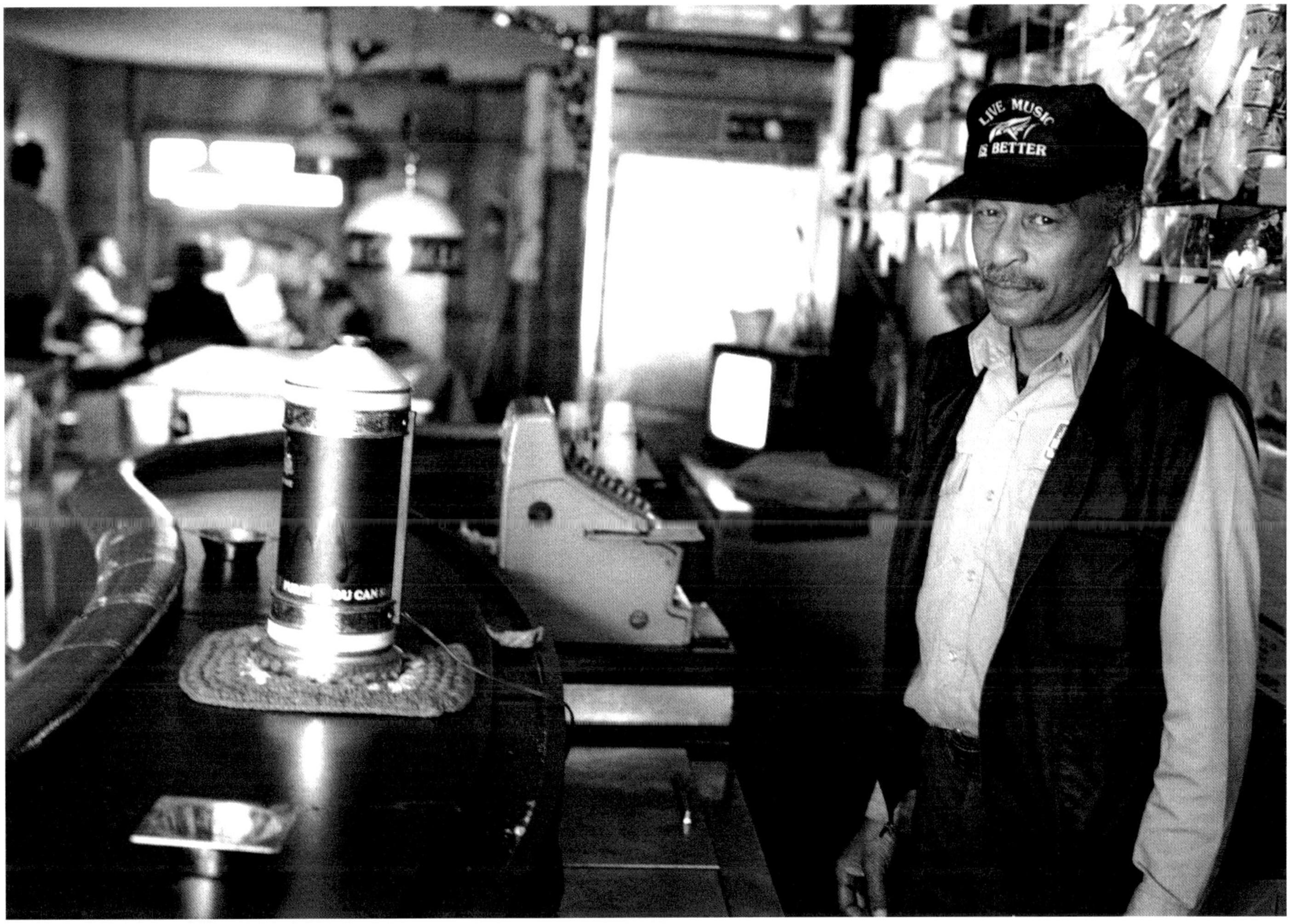
LIVE MUSIC
BETTER

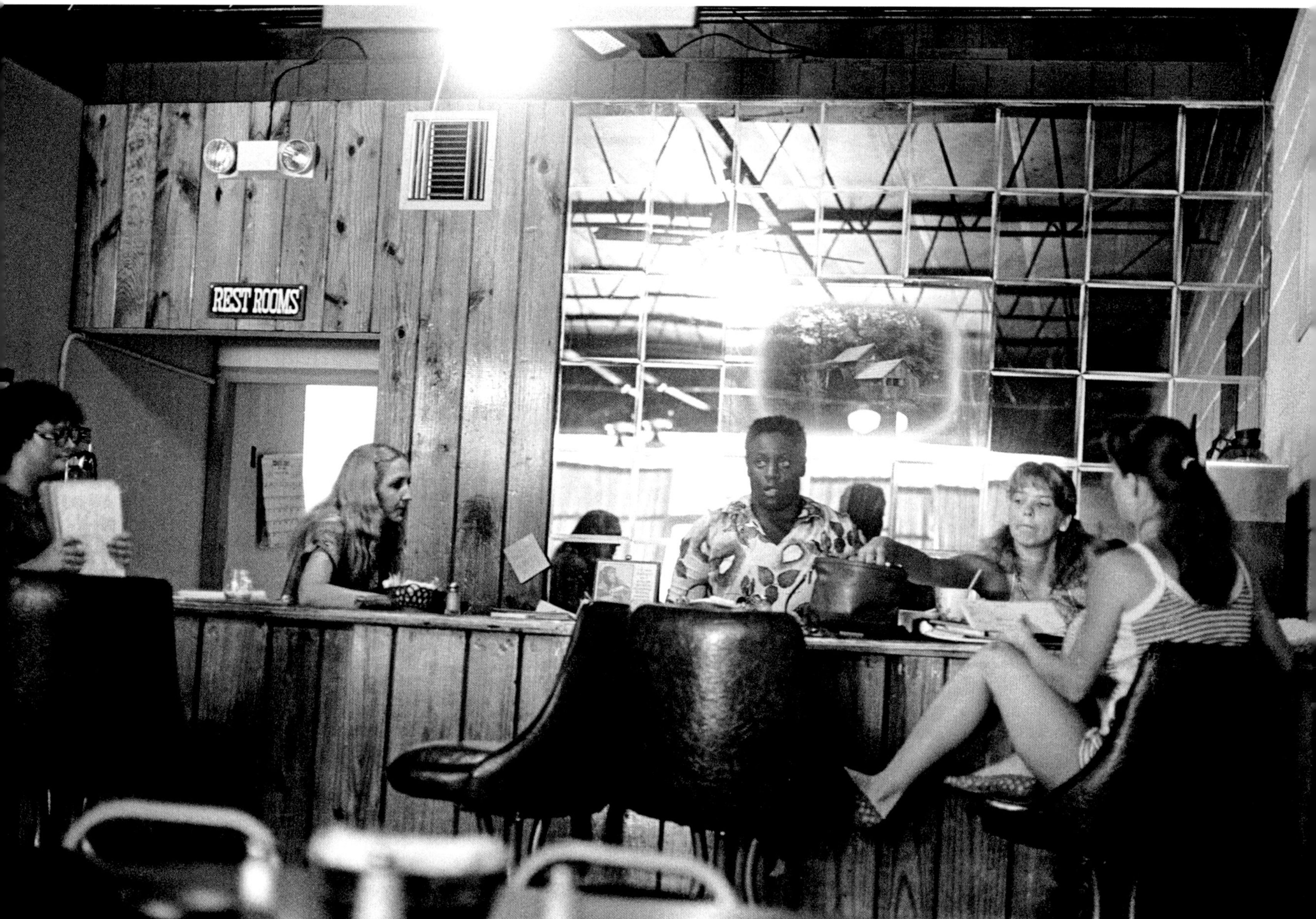
REST ROOMS

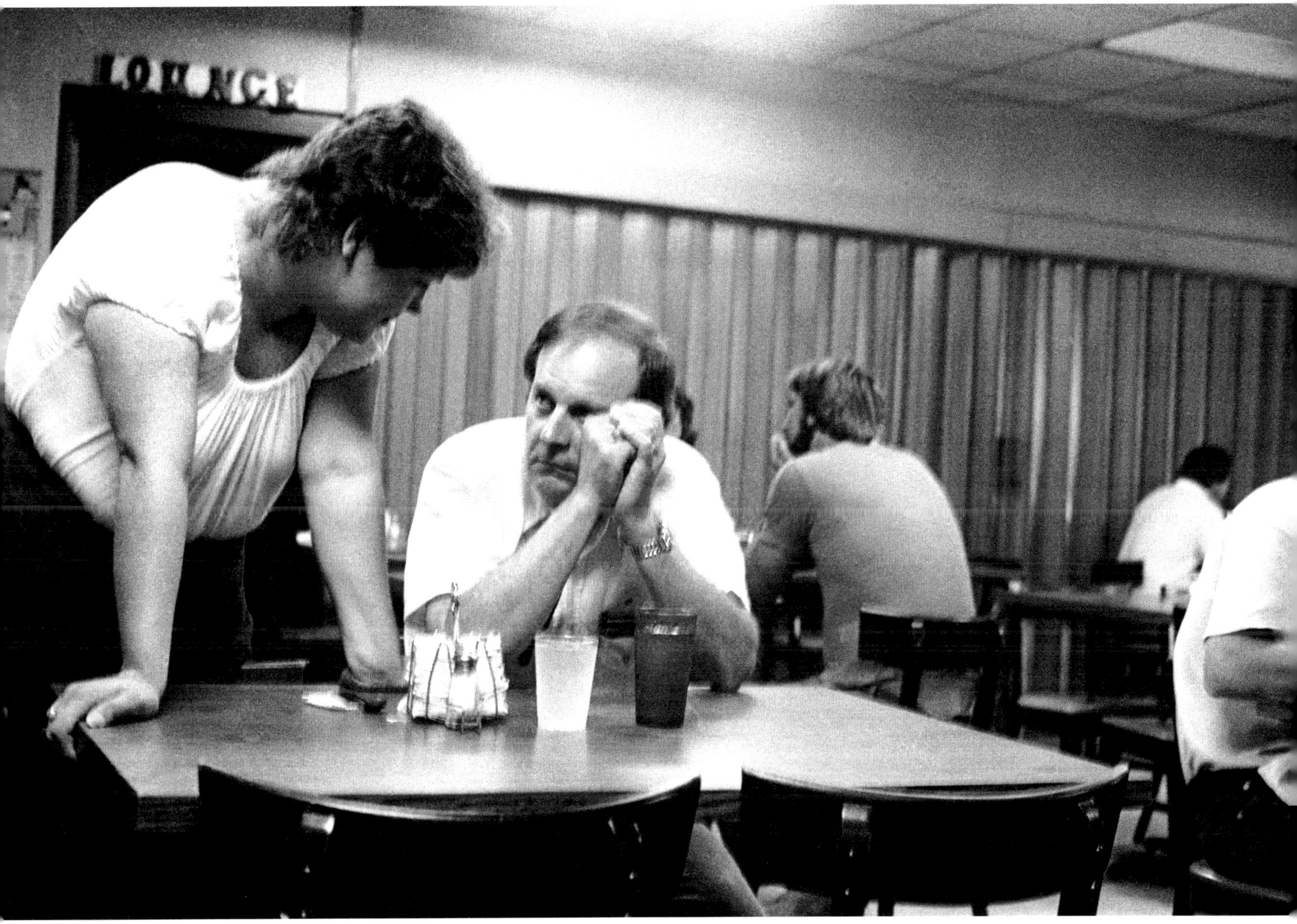
LOUNGE

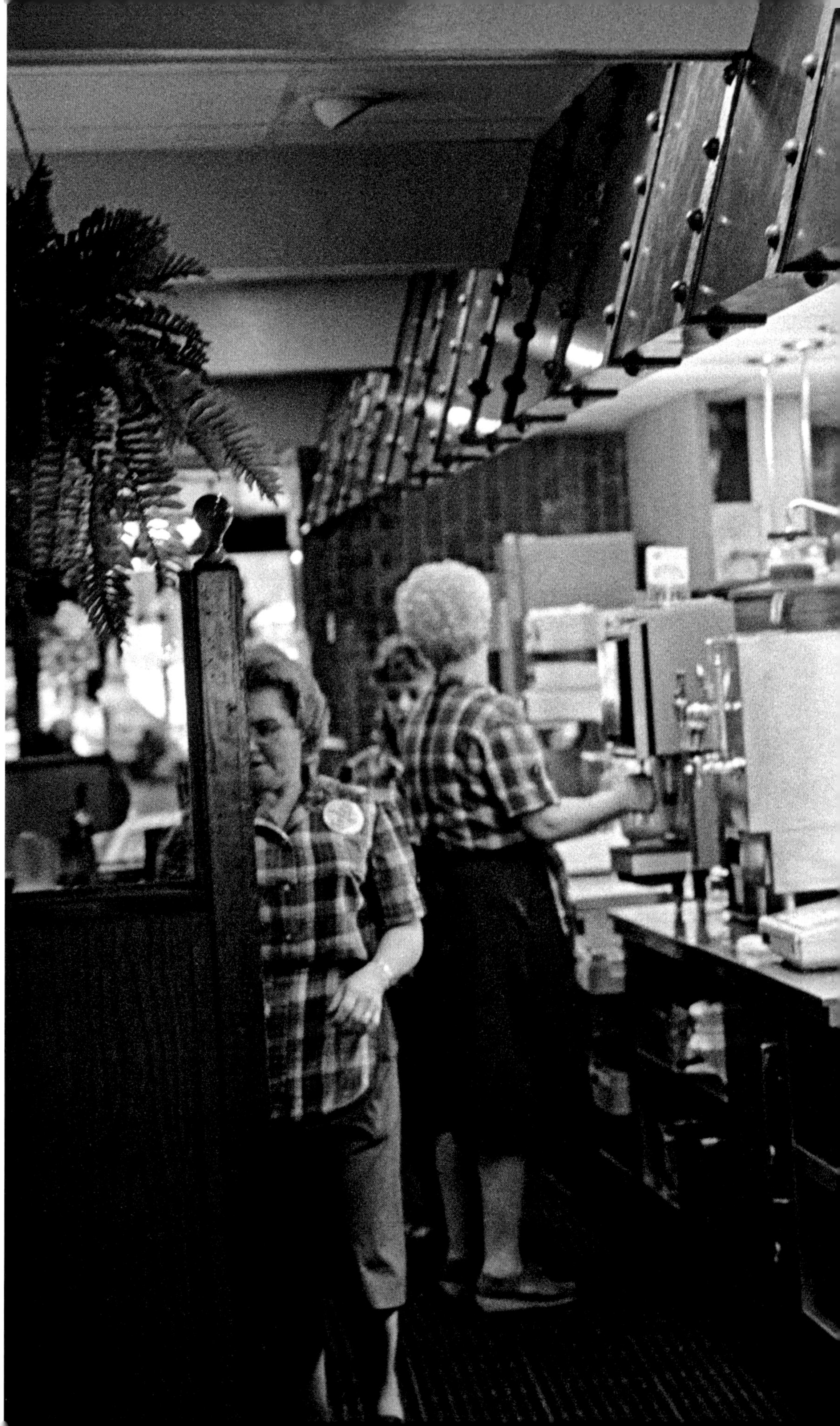

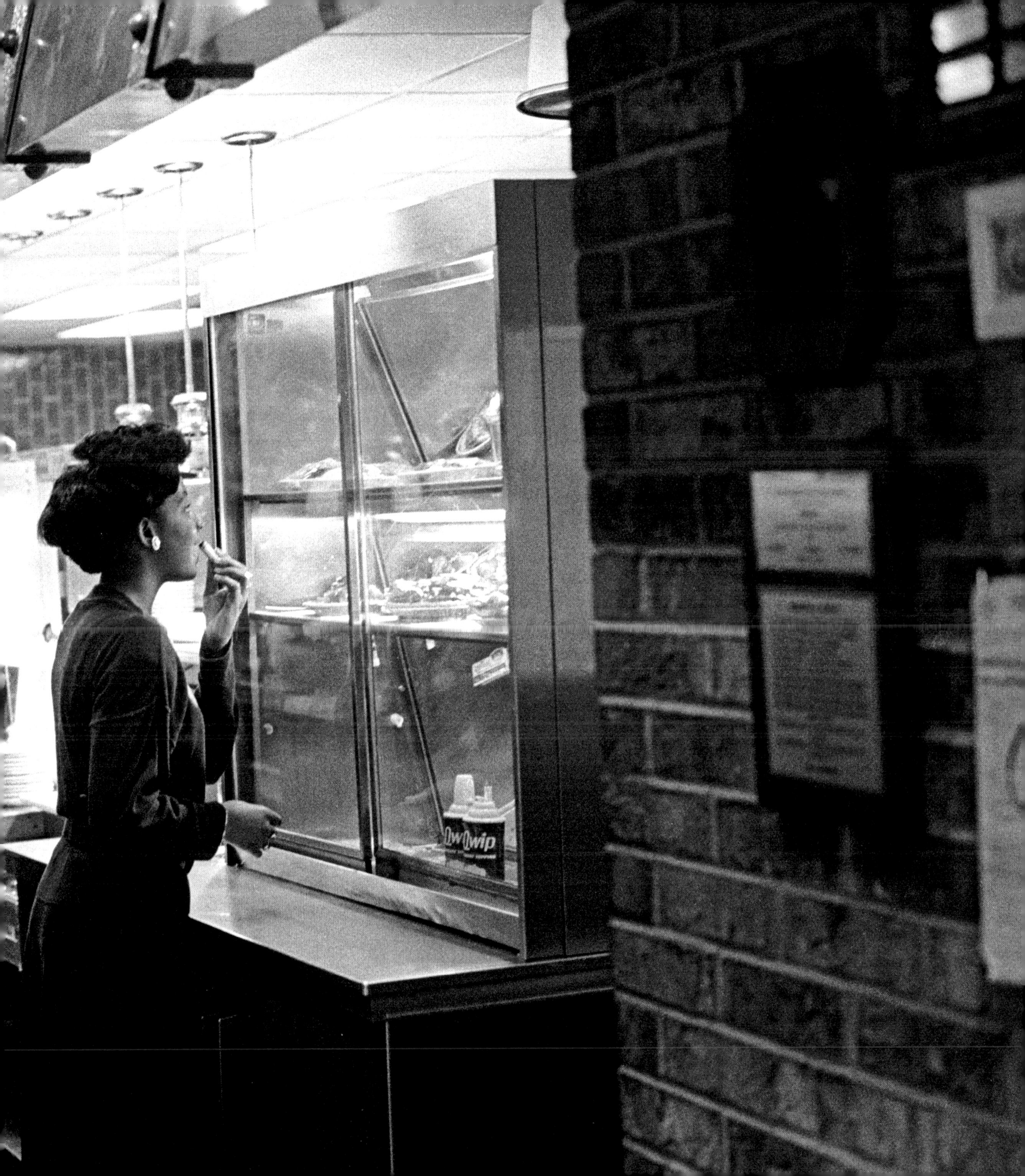

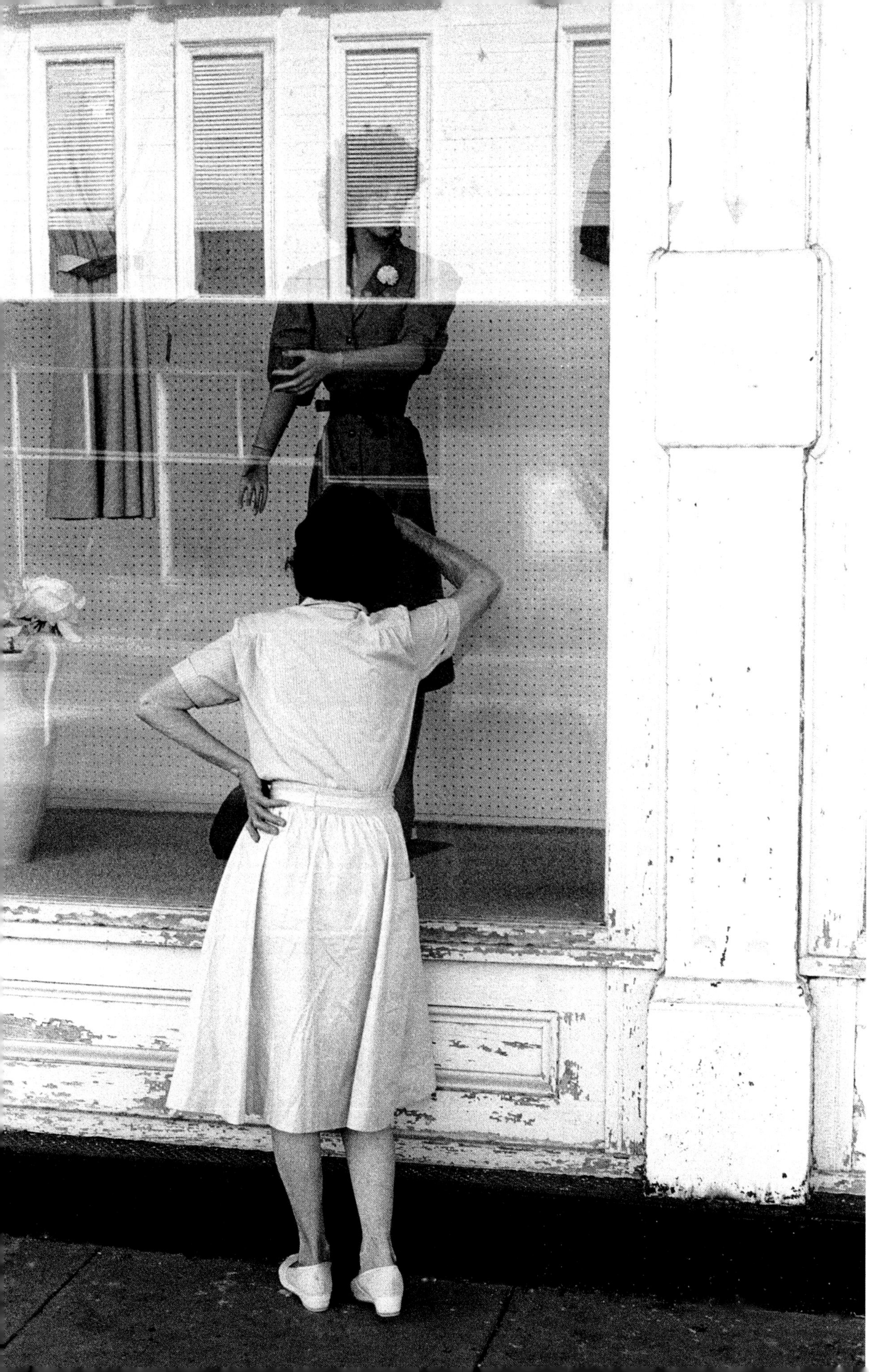

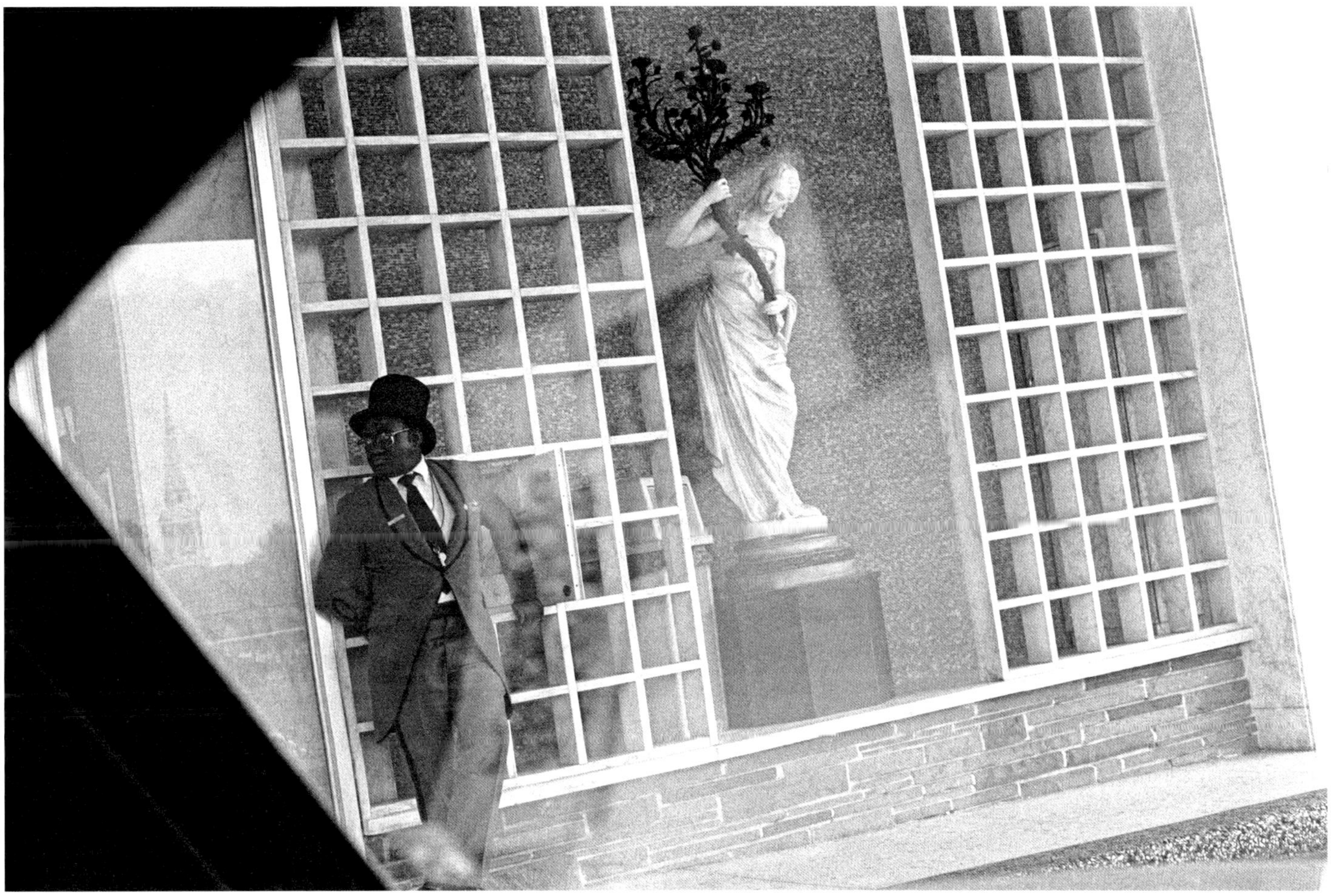

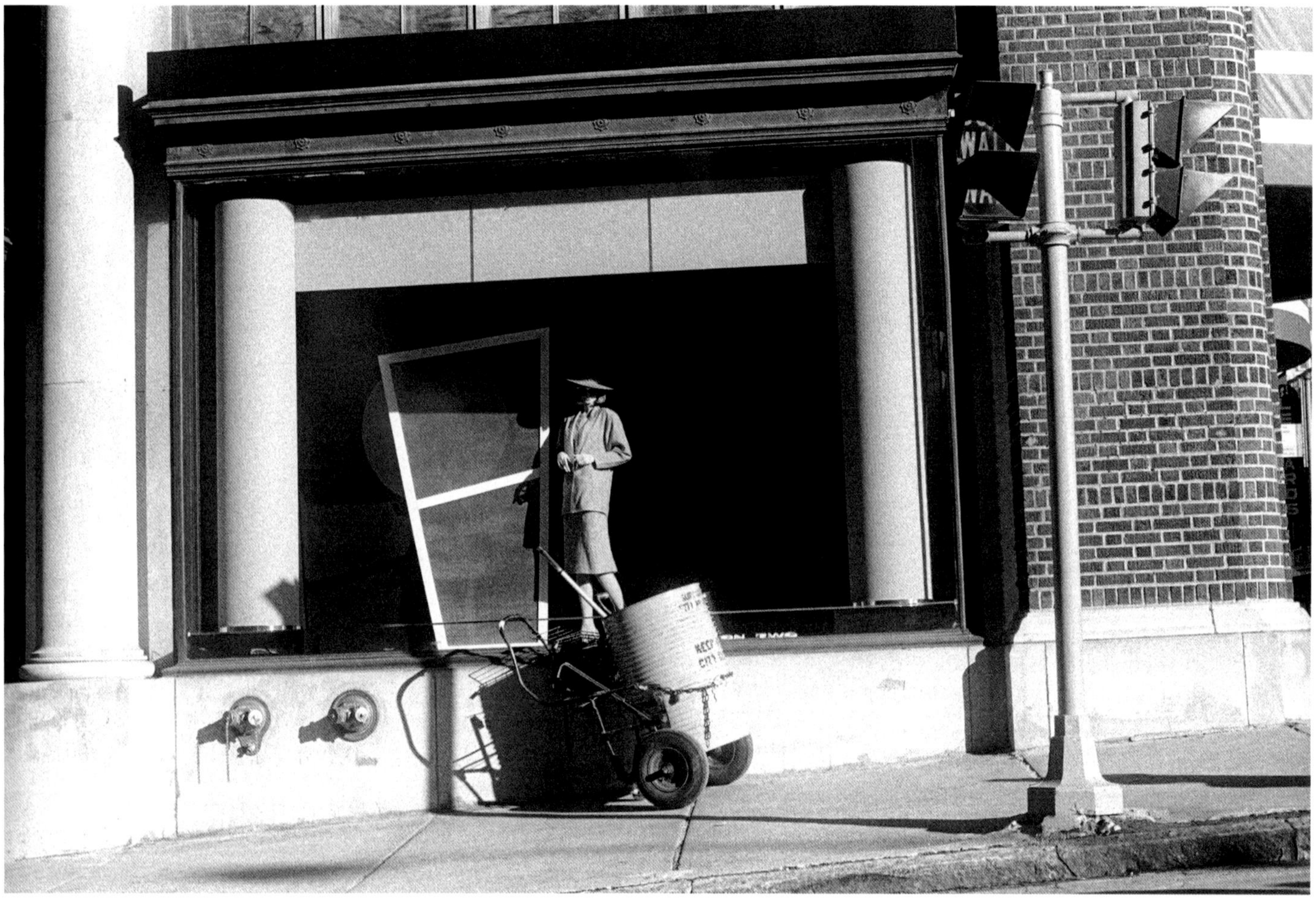

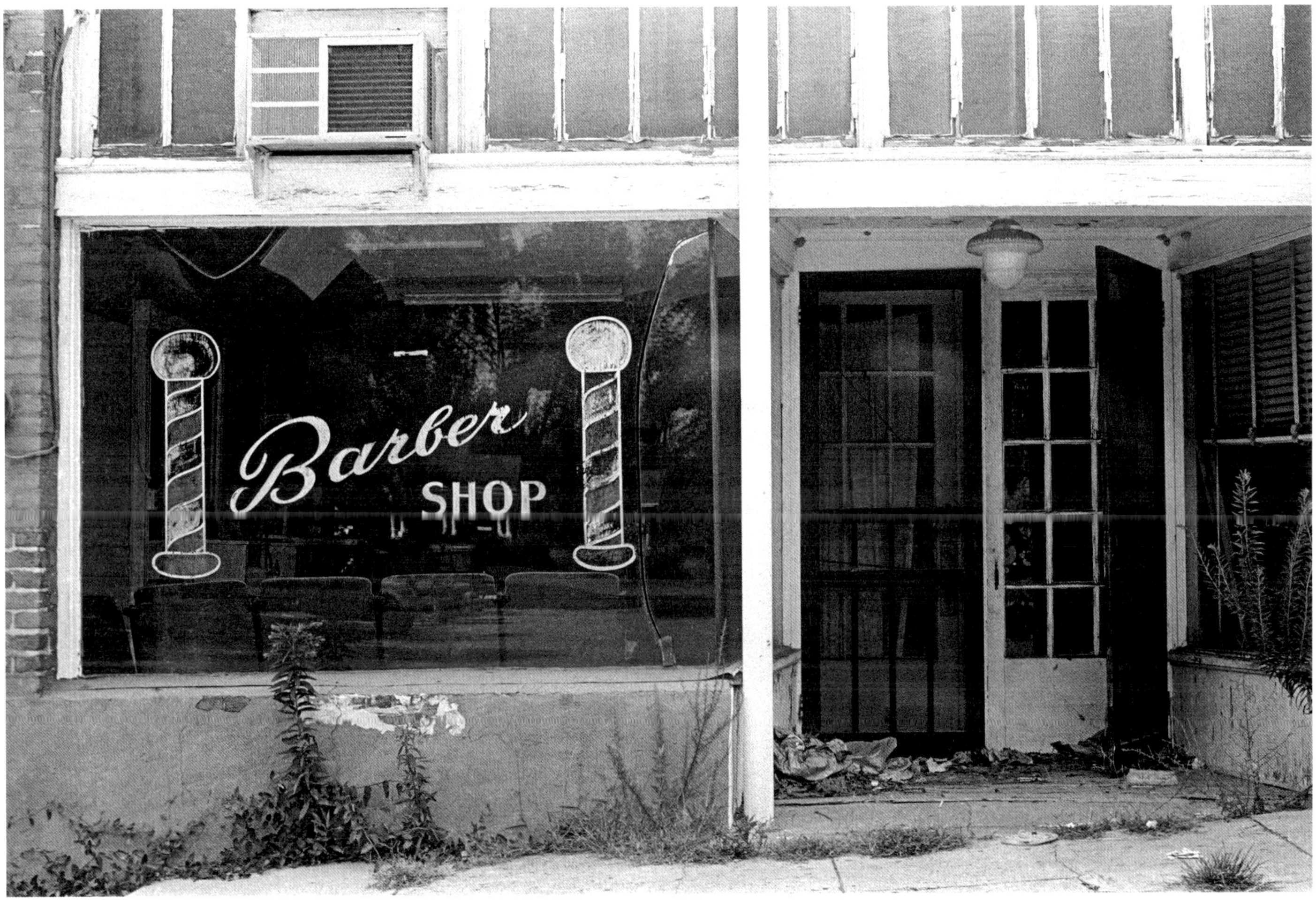
Barber
SHOP

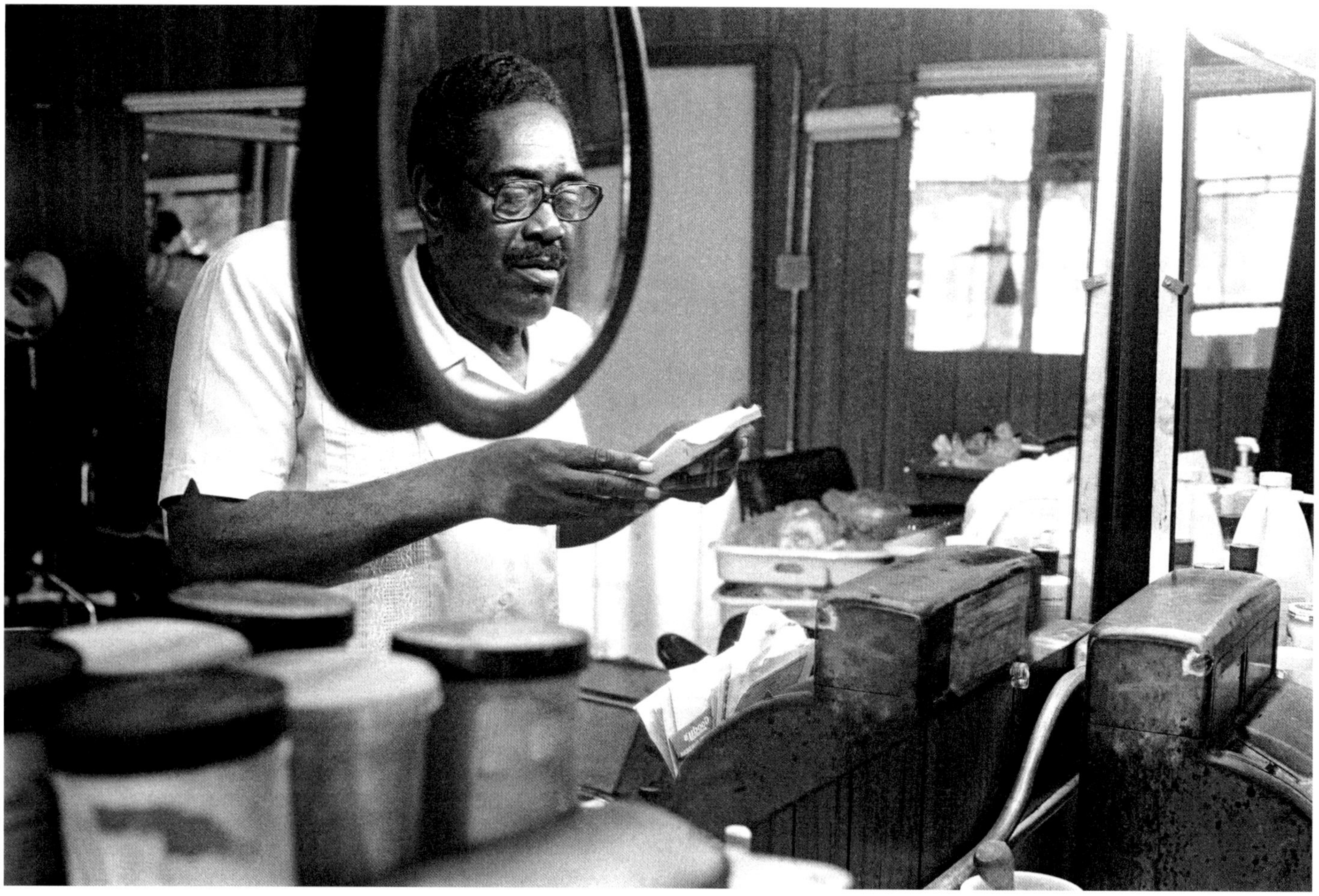

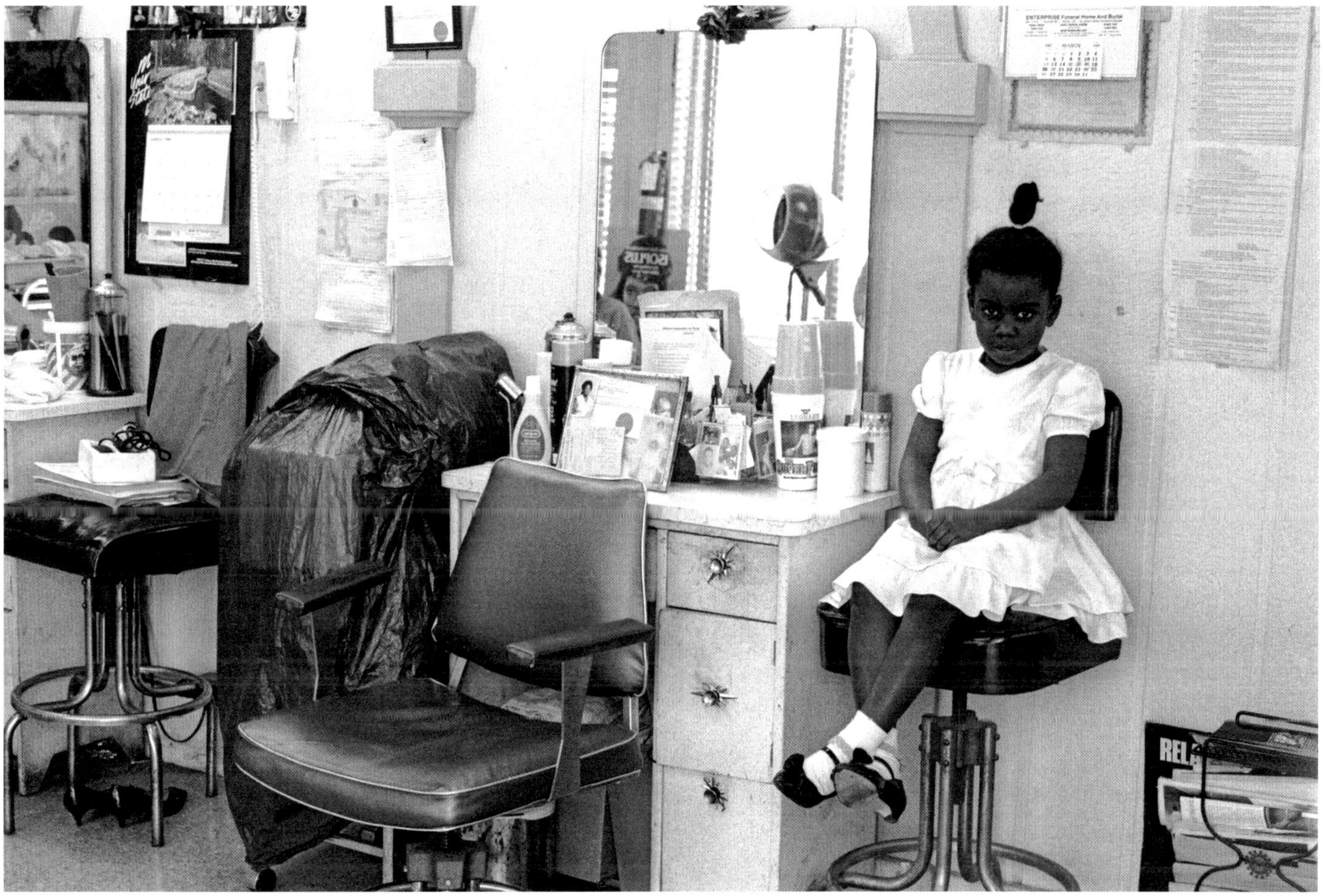
ENTERPRISE Funeral Home And Burial
MARCH

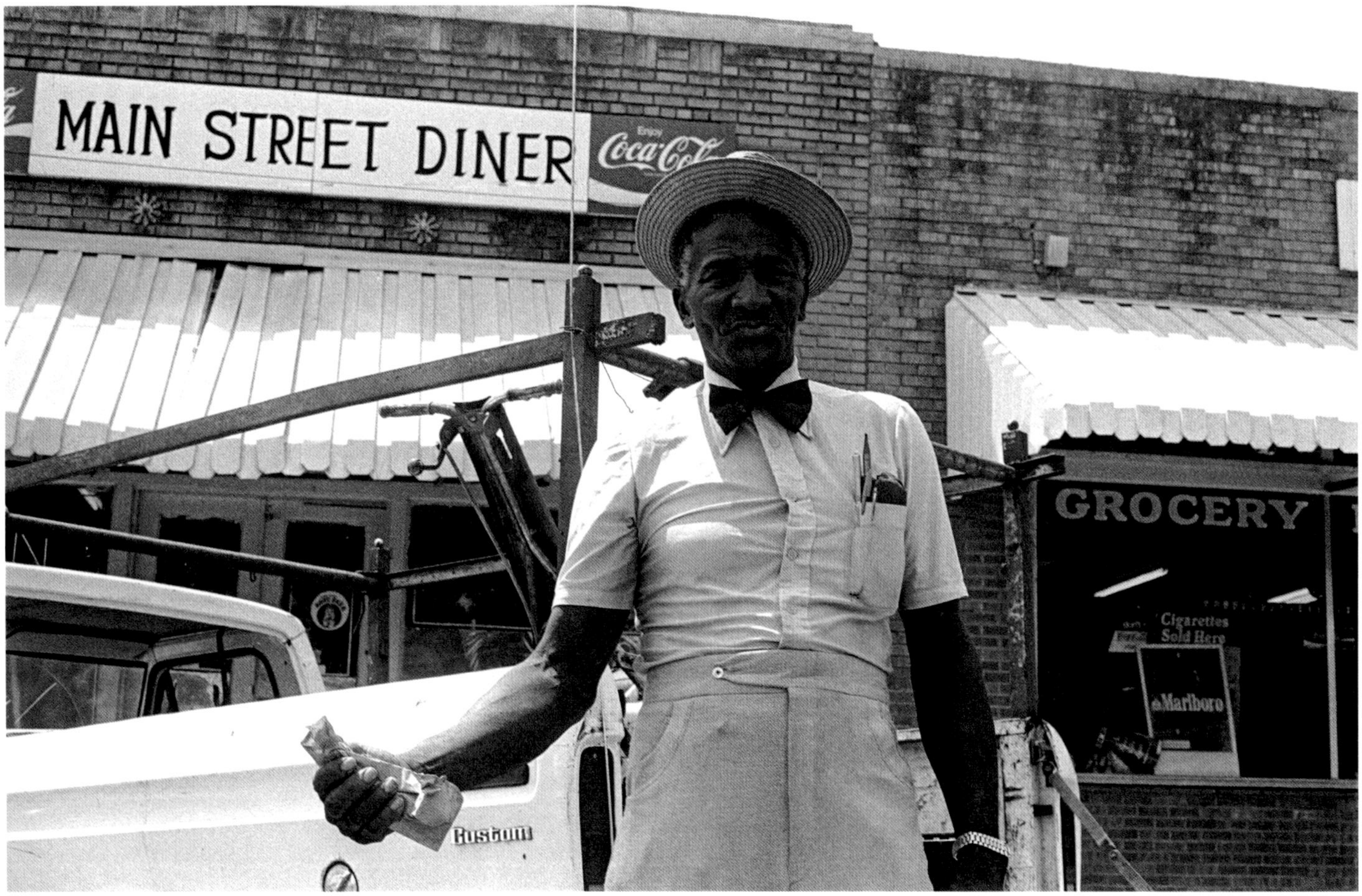
MAIN STREET DINER
GROCERY
Cigarettes
Sold Here
Marlboro
Custom

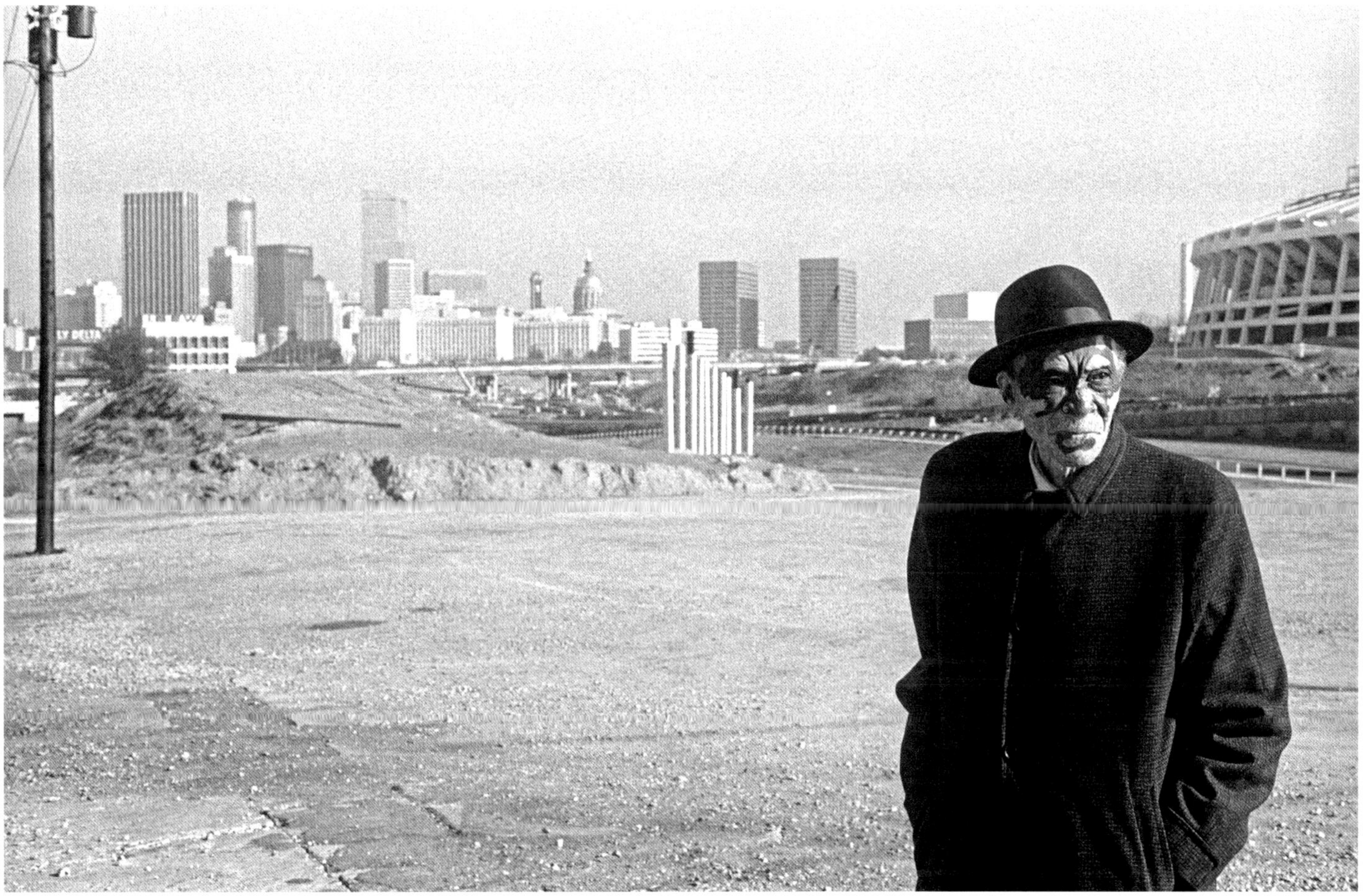

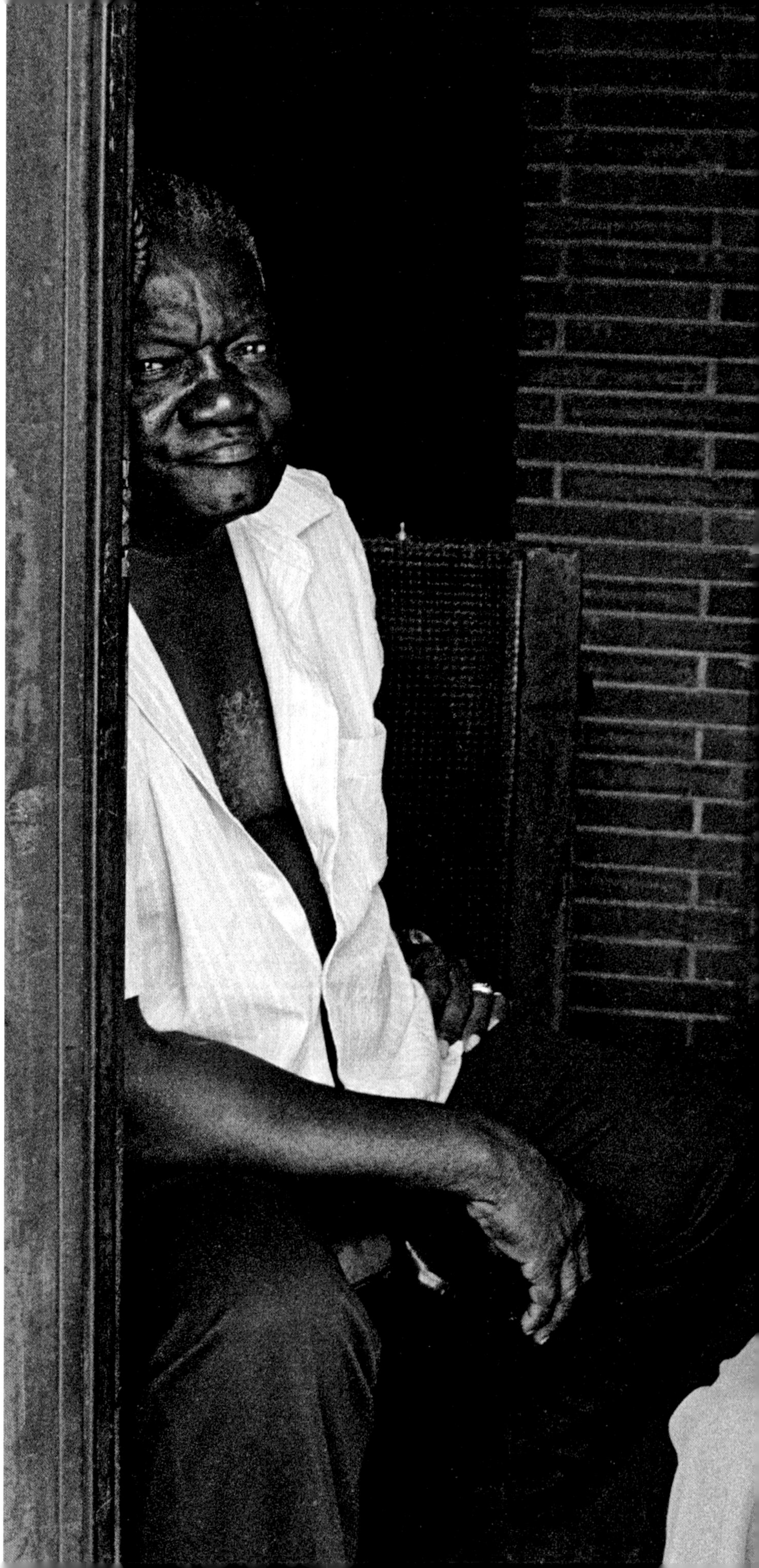

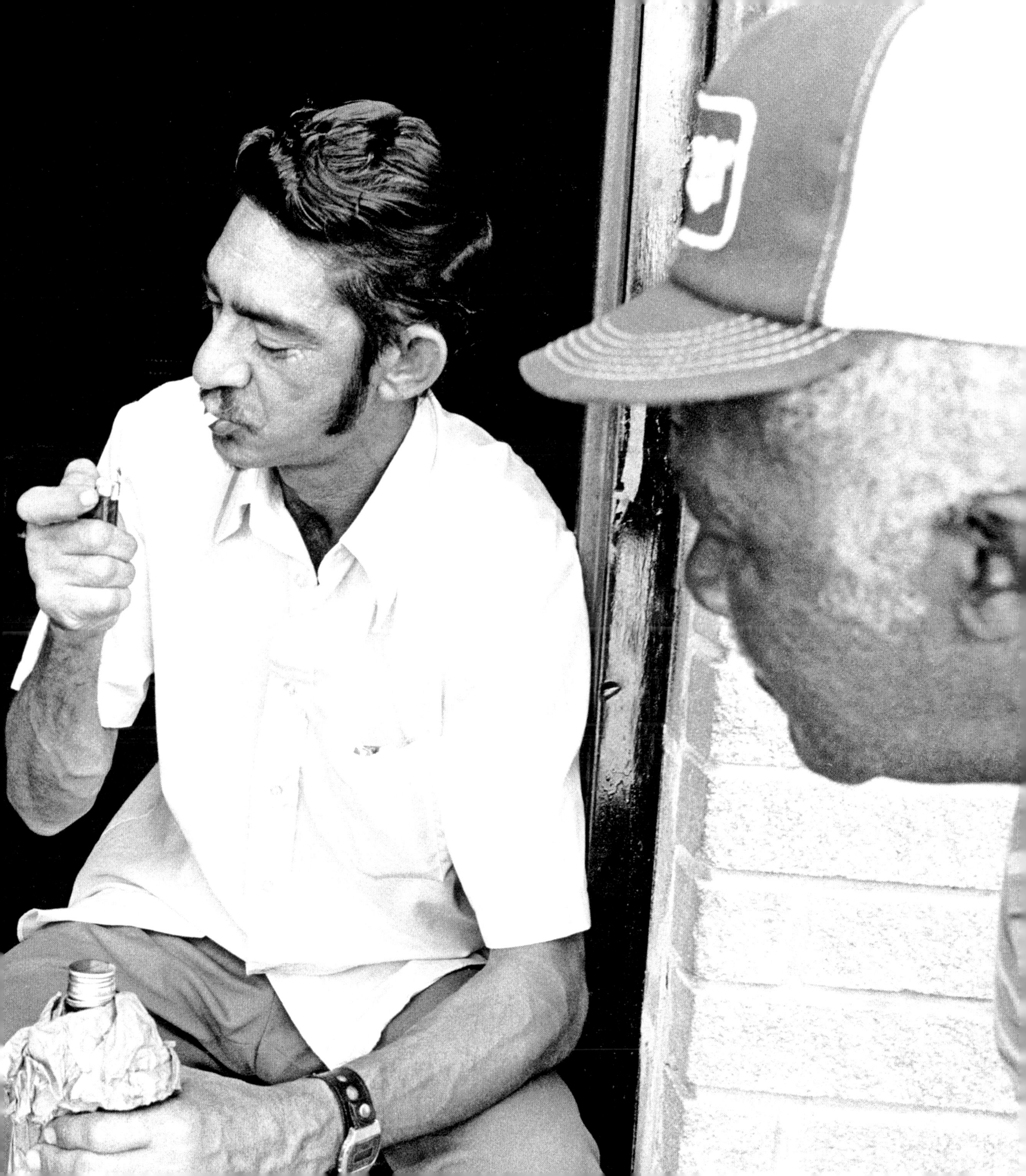

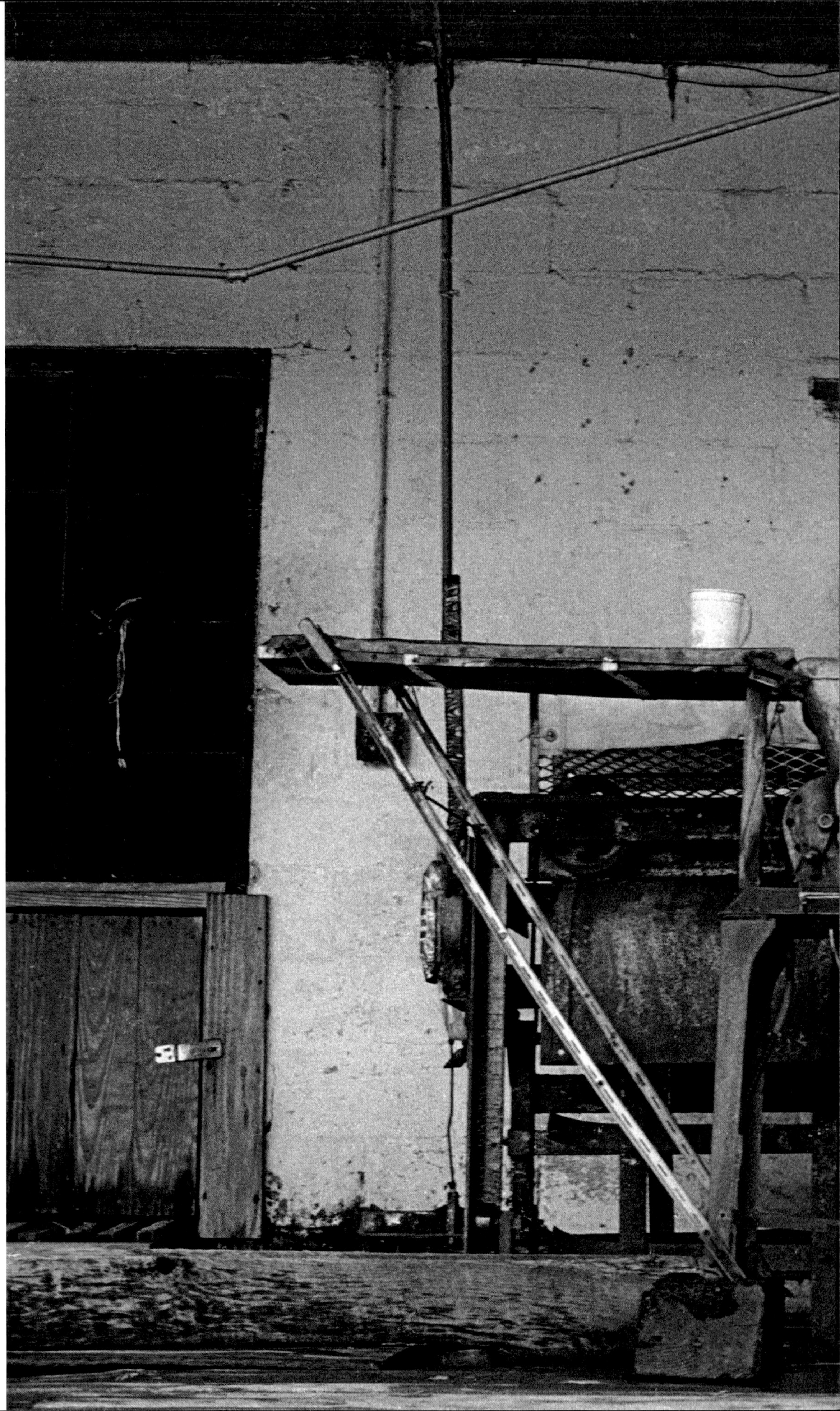

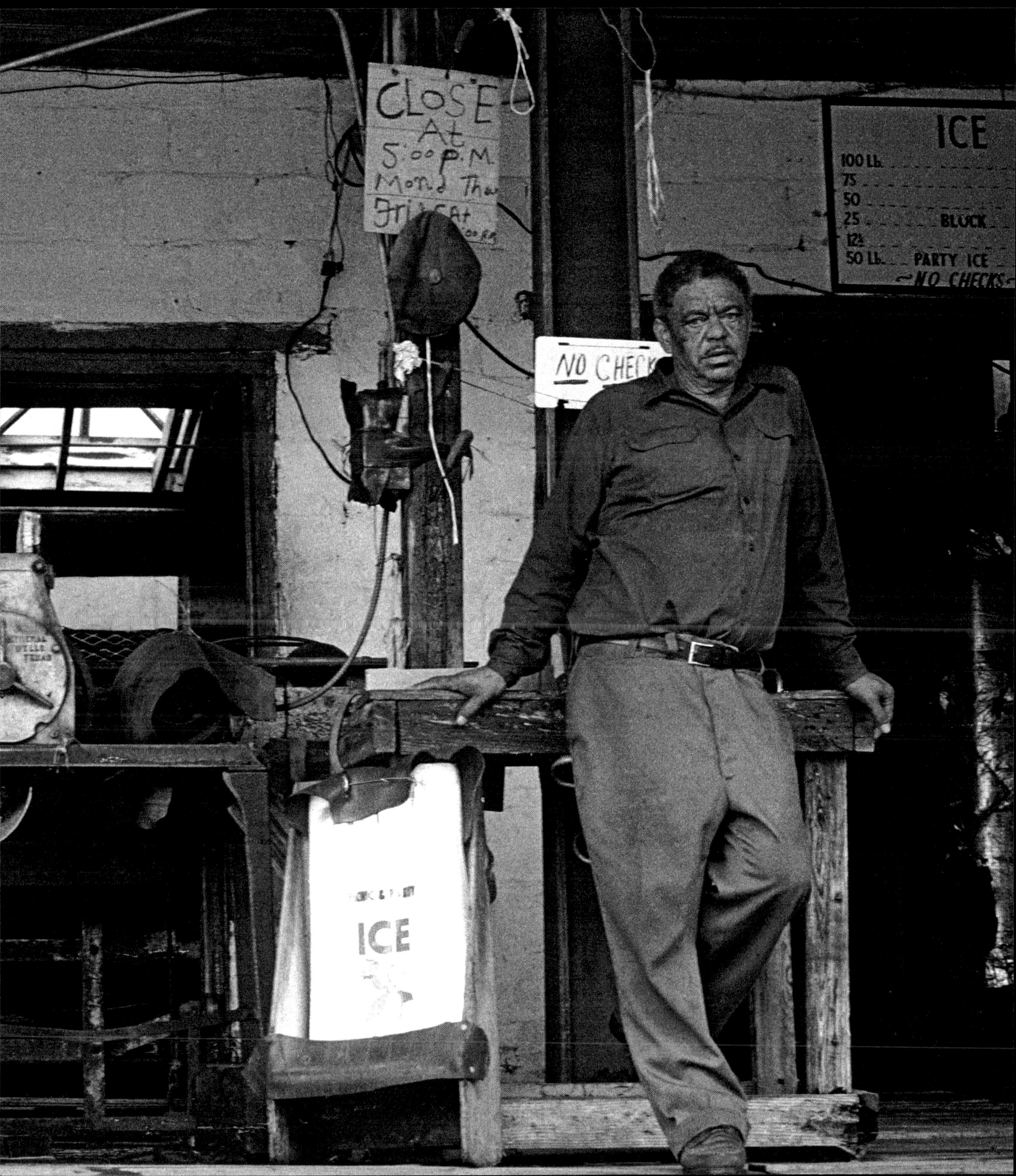
CLOSE
At
5:00 P.M.
ICE
100 Lb.
75
50
25
BLOCK
50 Lb.
PARTY ICE
NO CHECKS
ICE

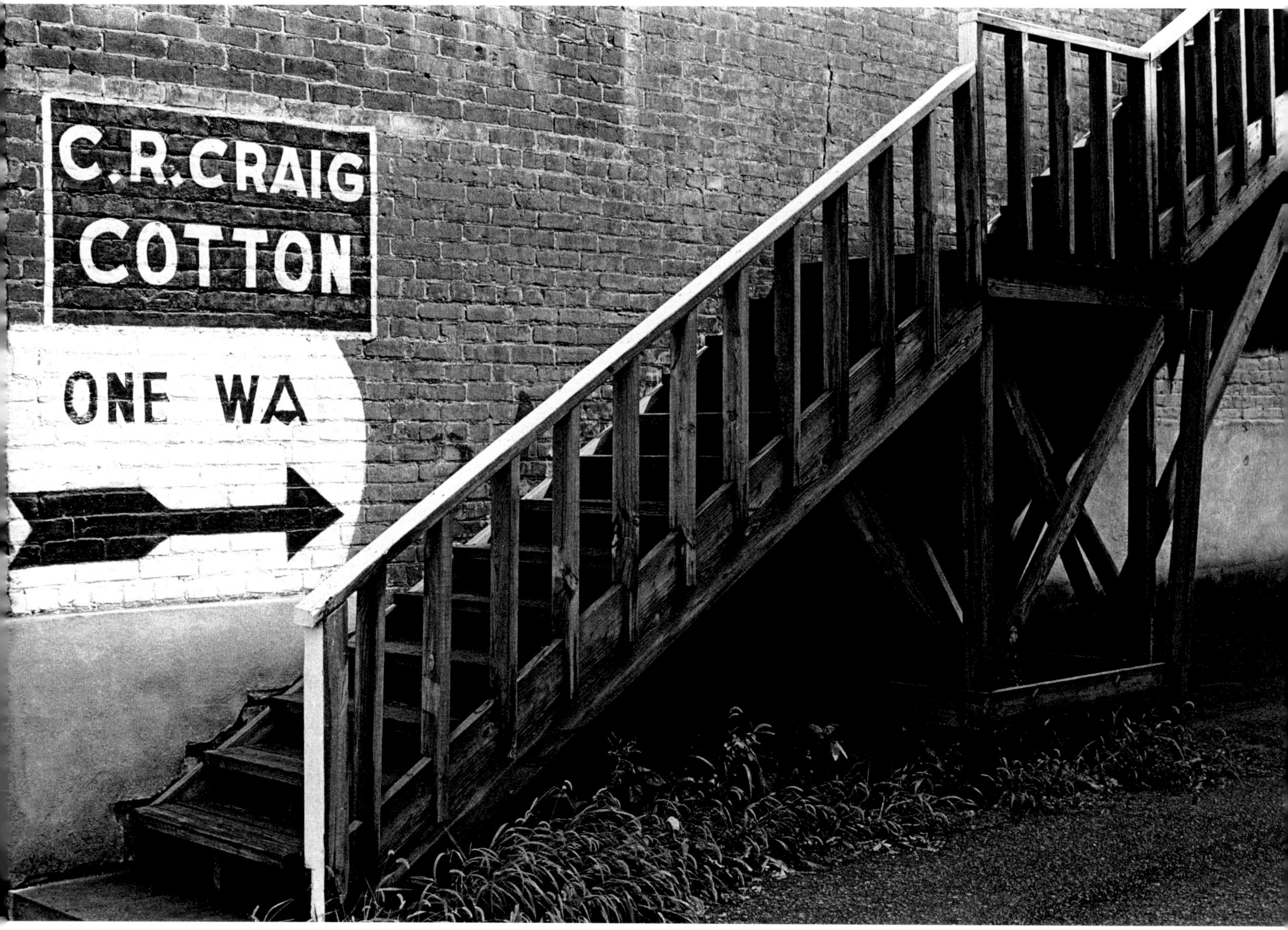
C. R. CRAIG
COTTON
ONE WA

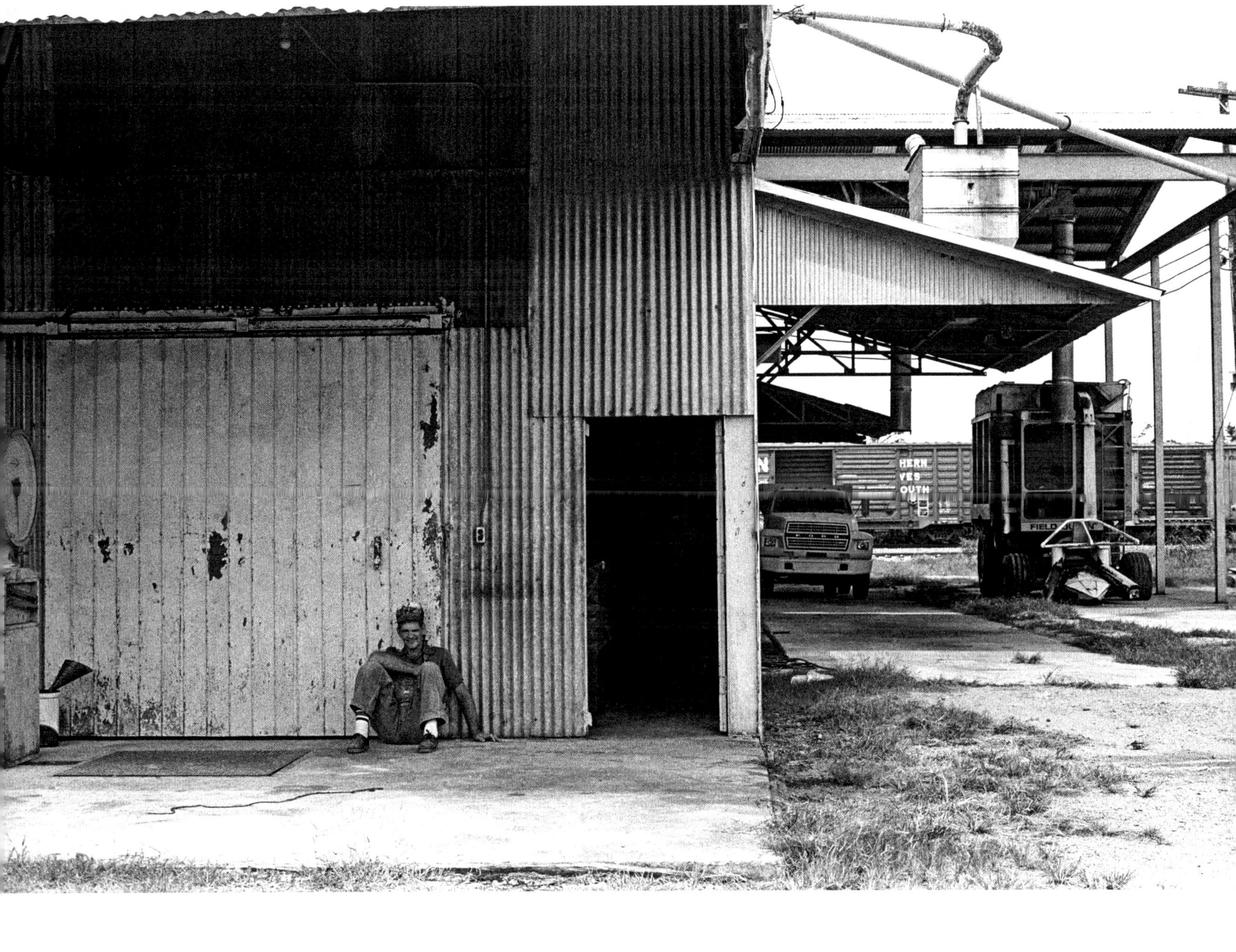

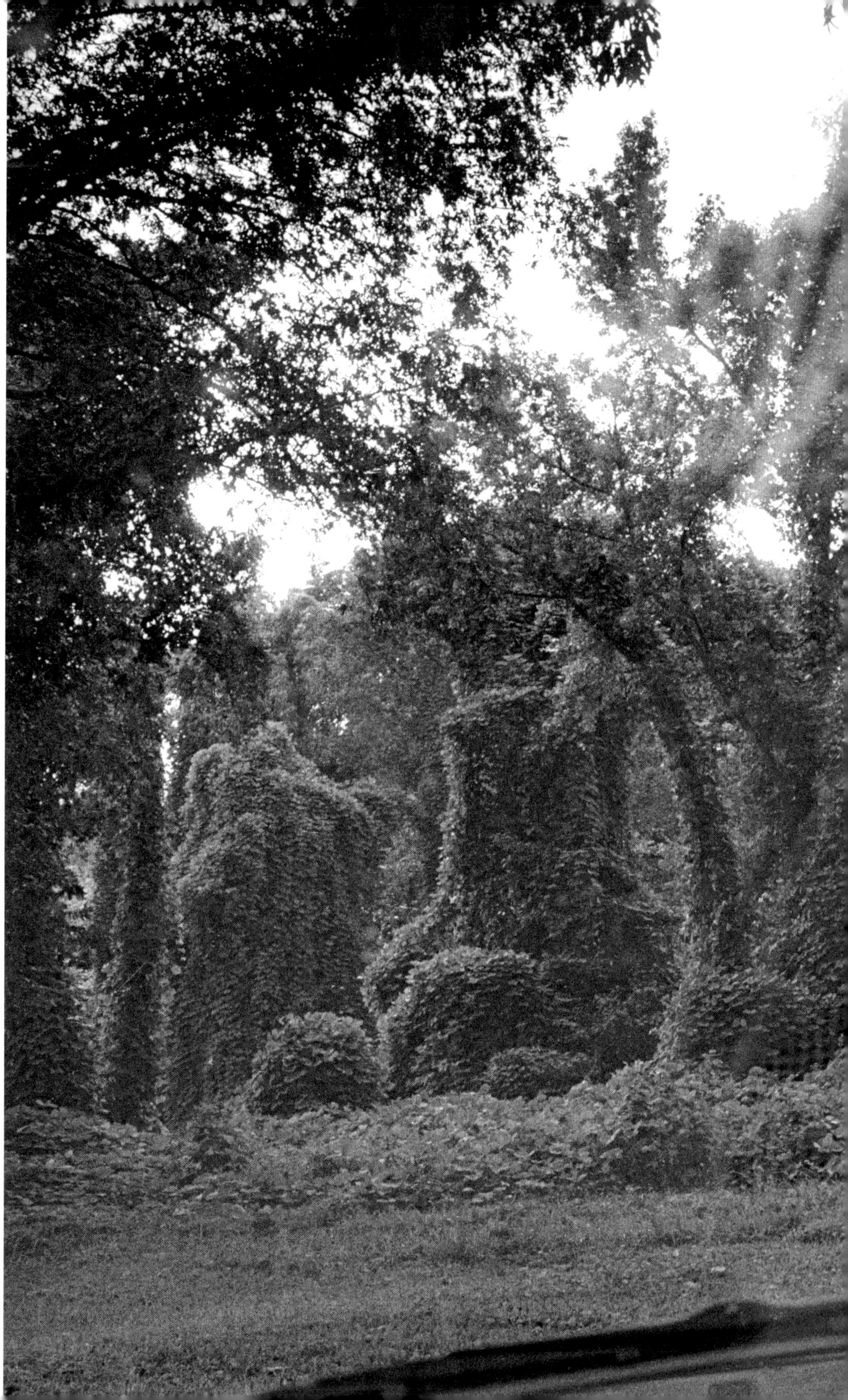

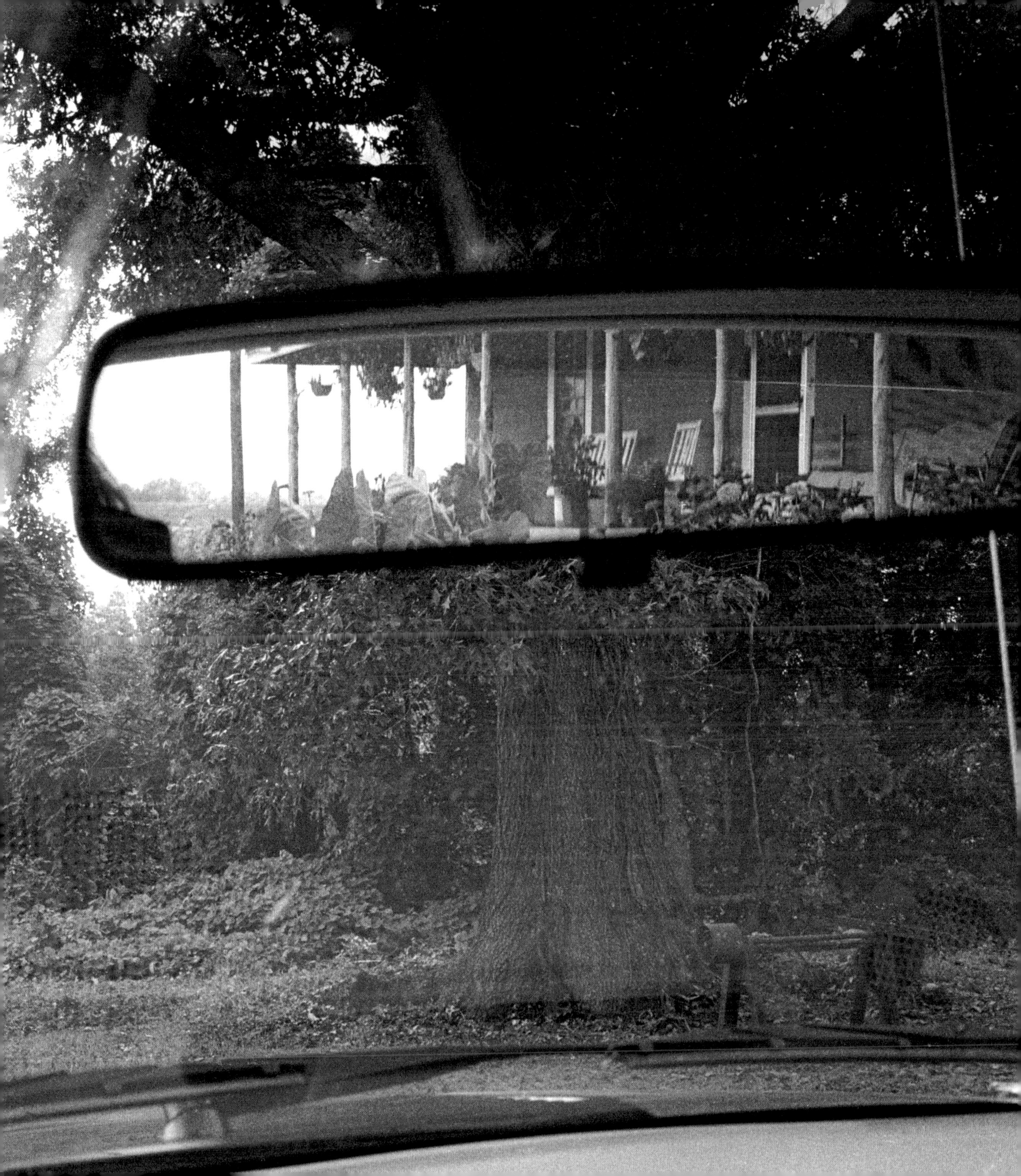

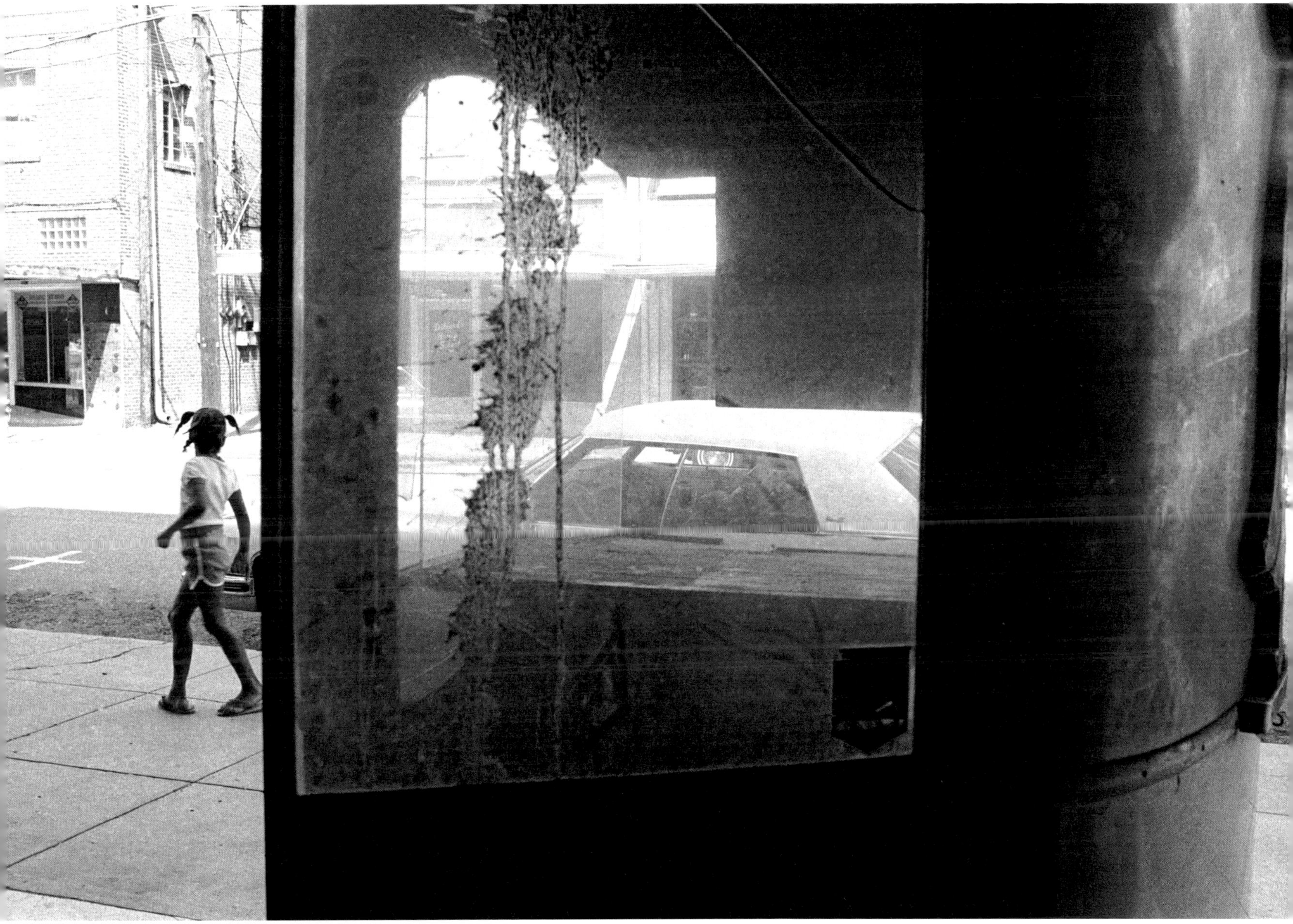

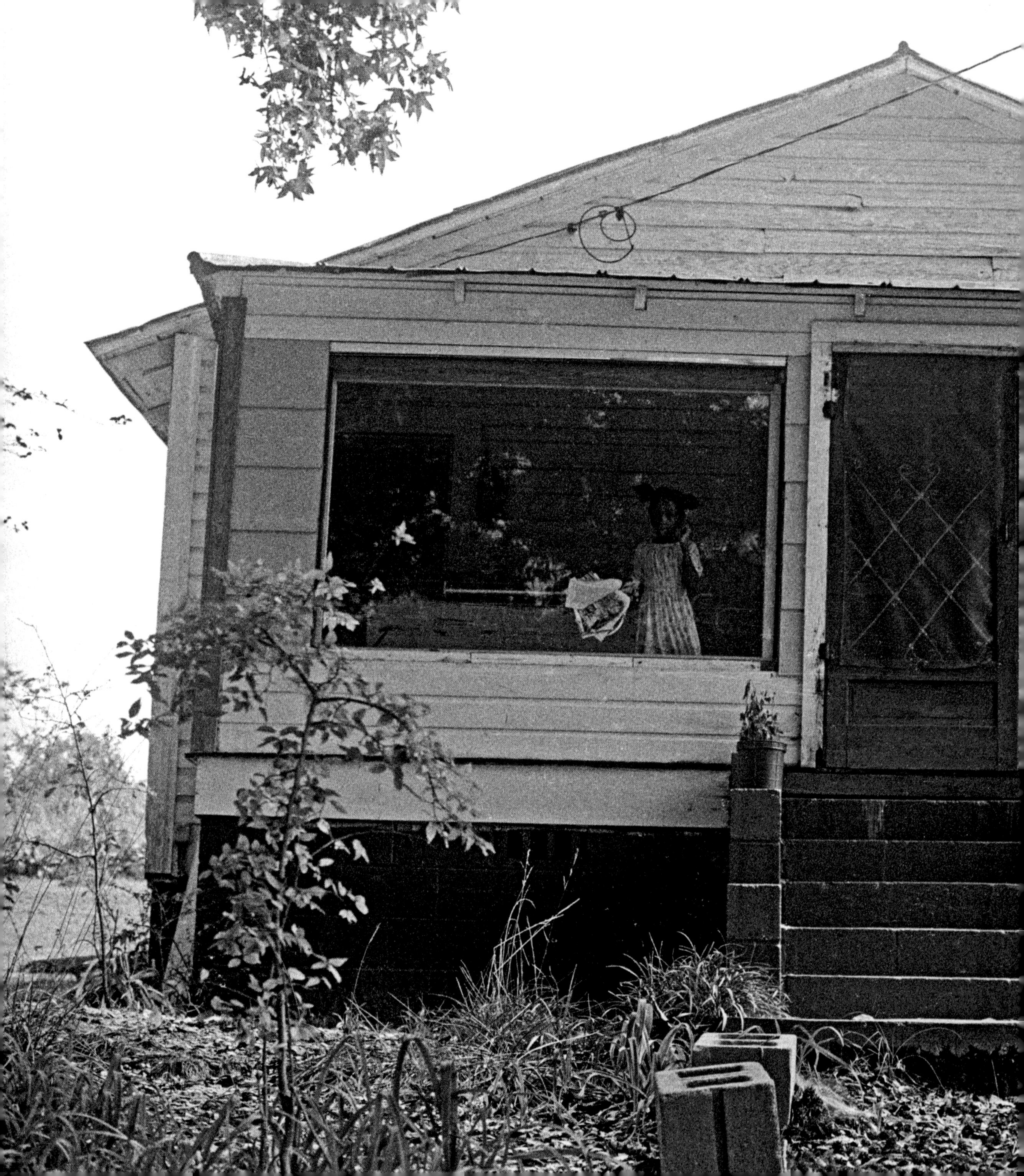

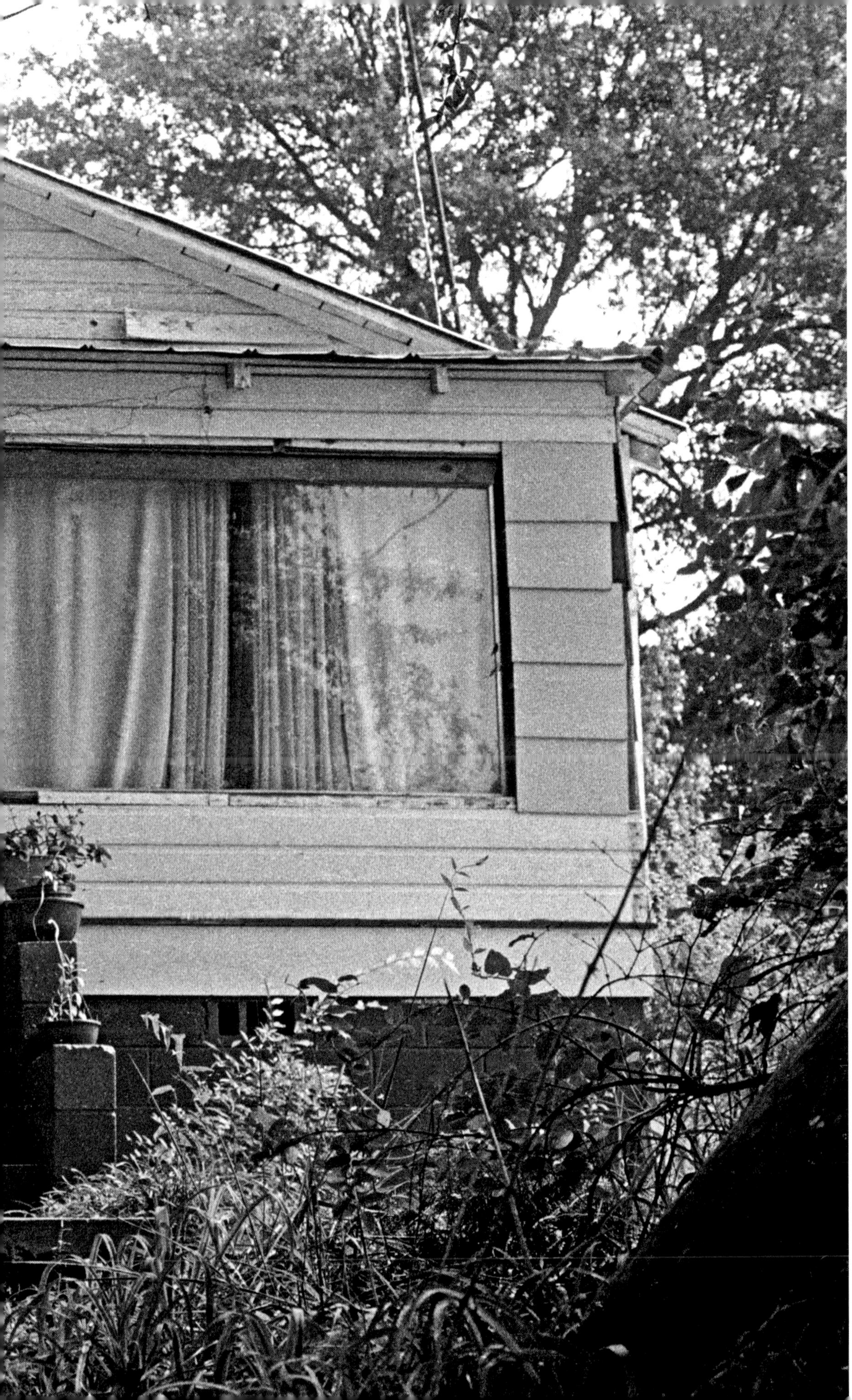

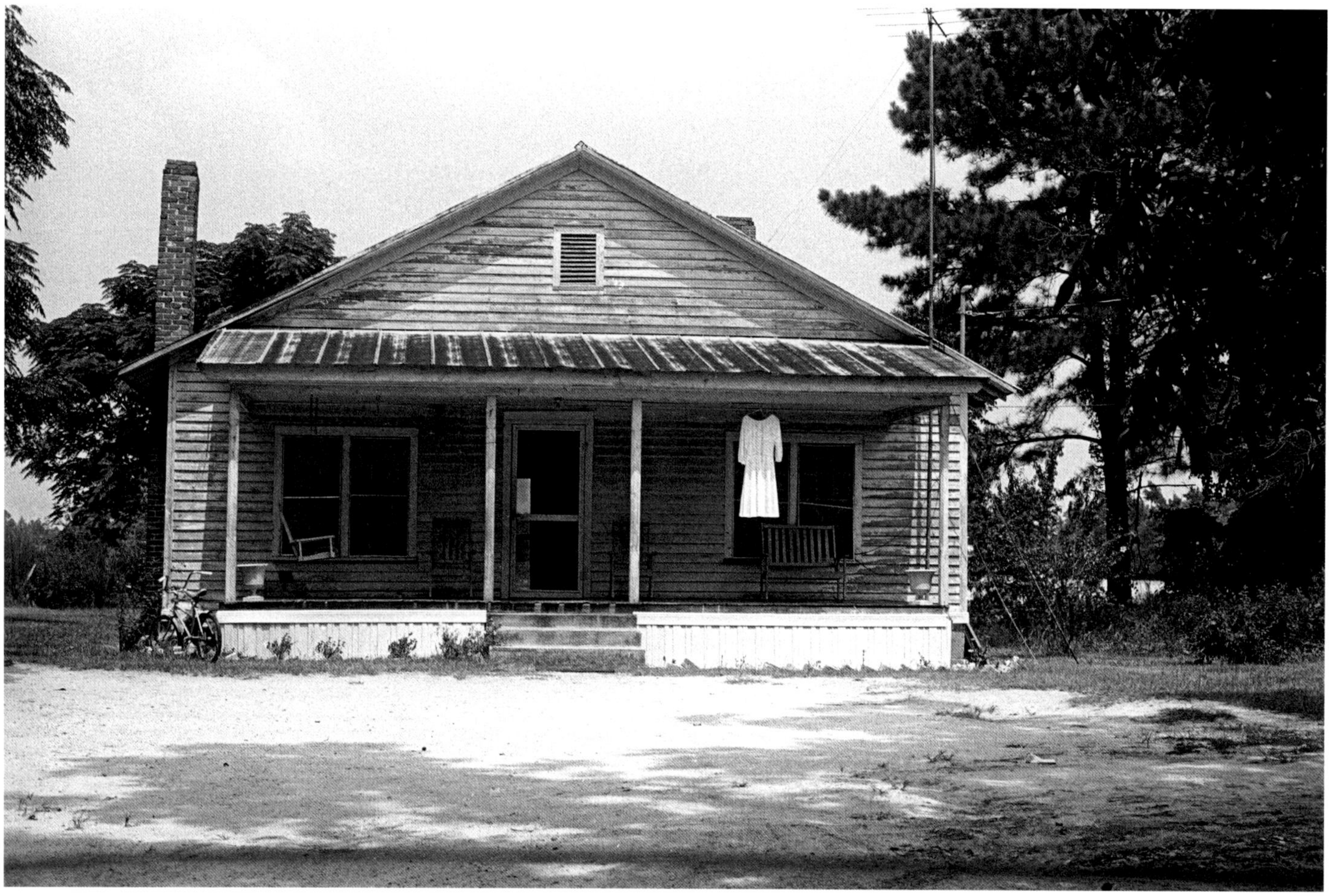

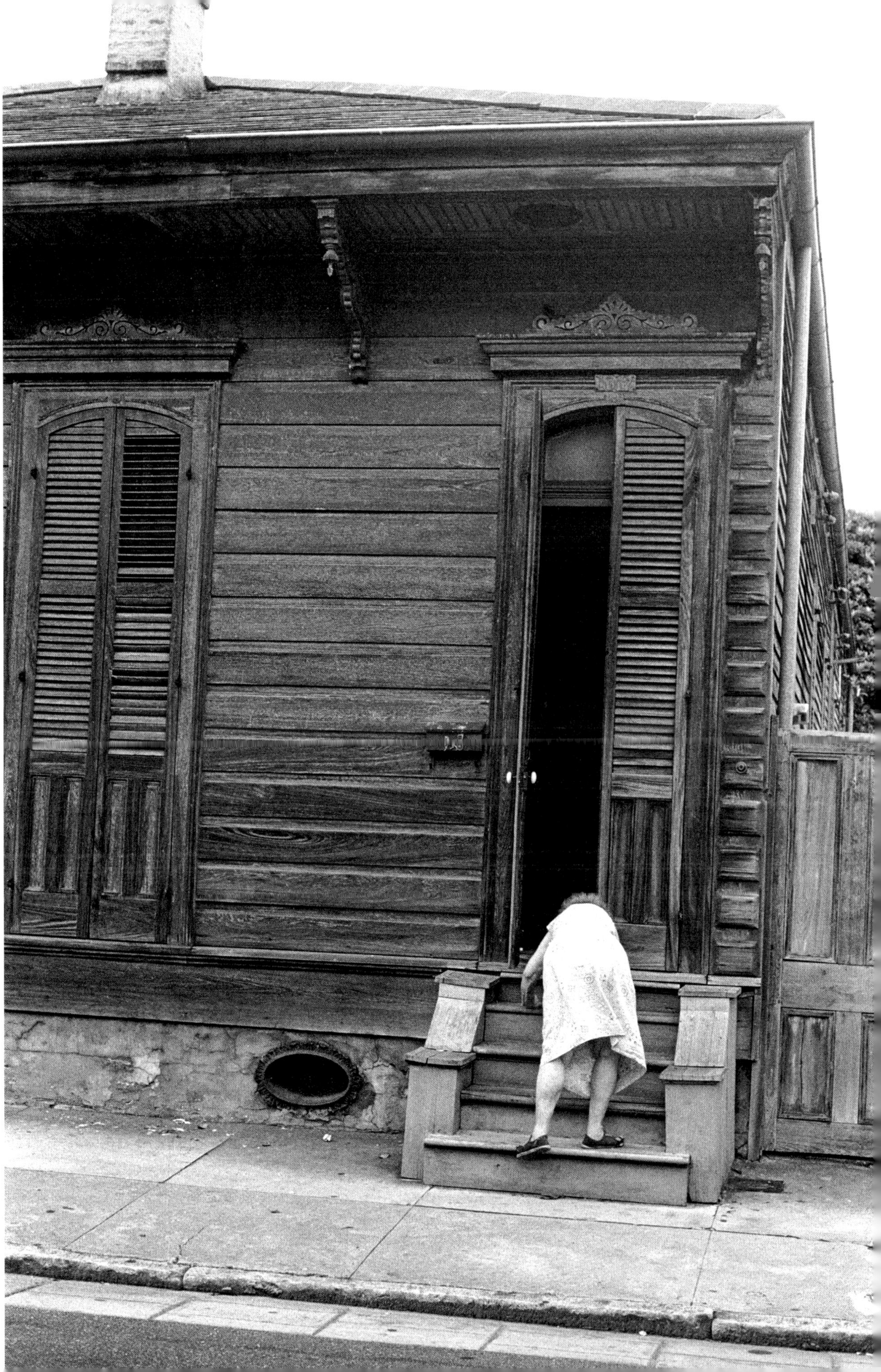

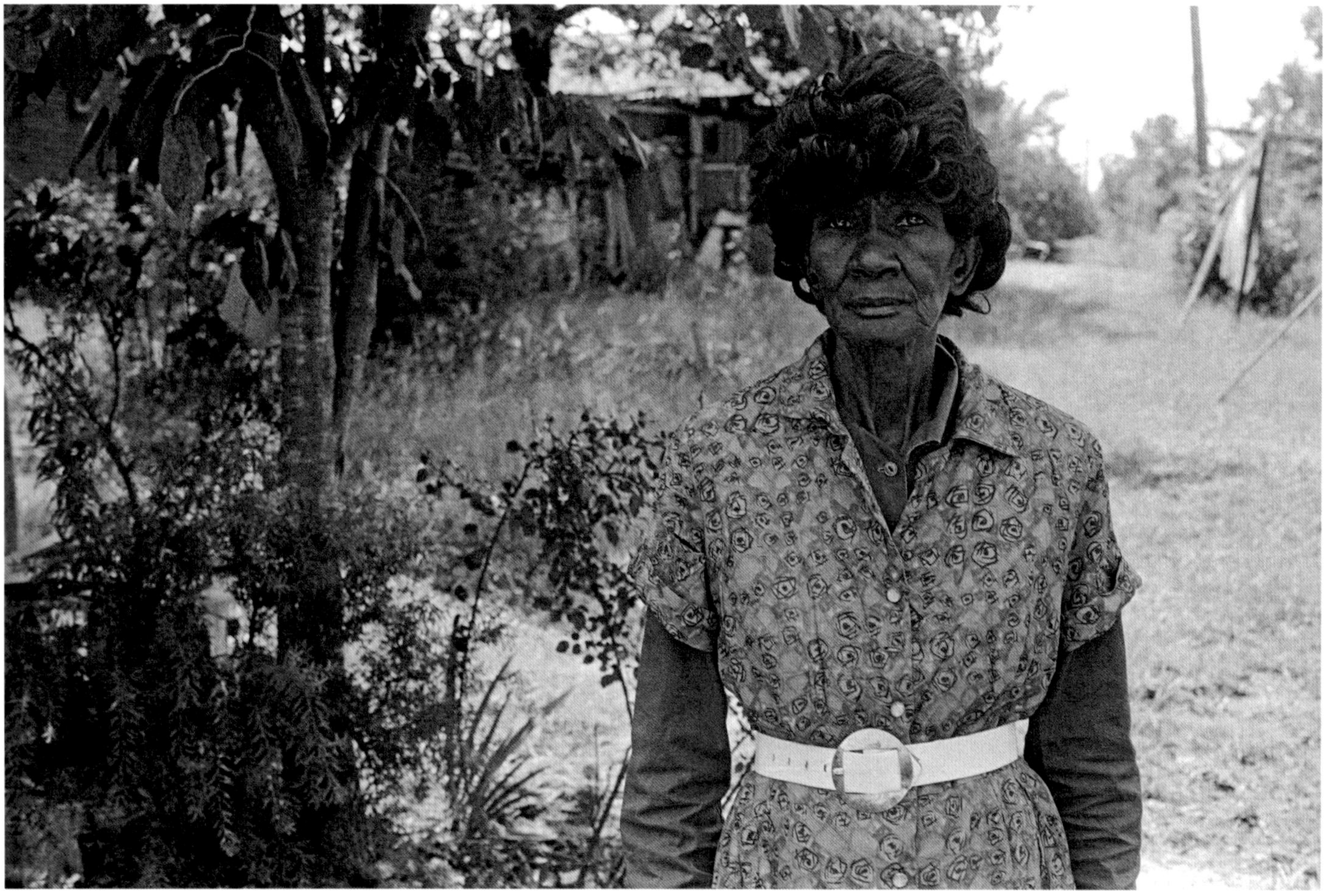

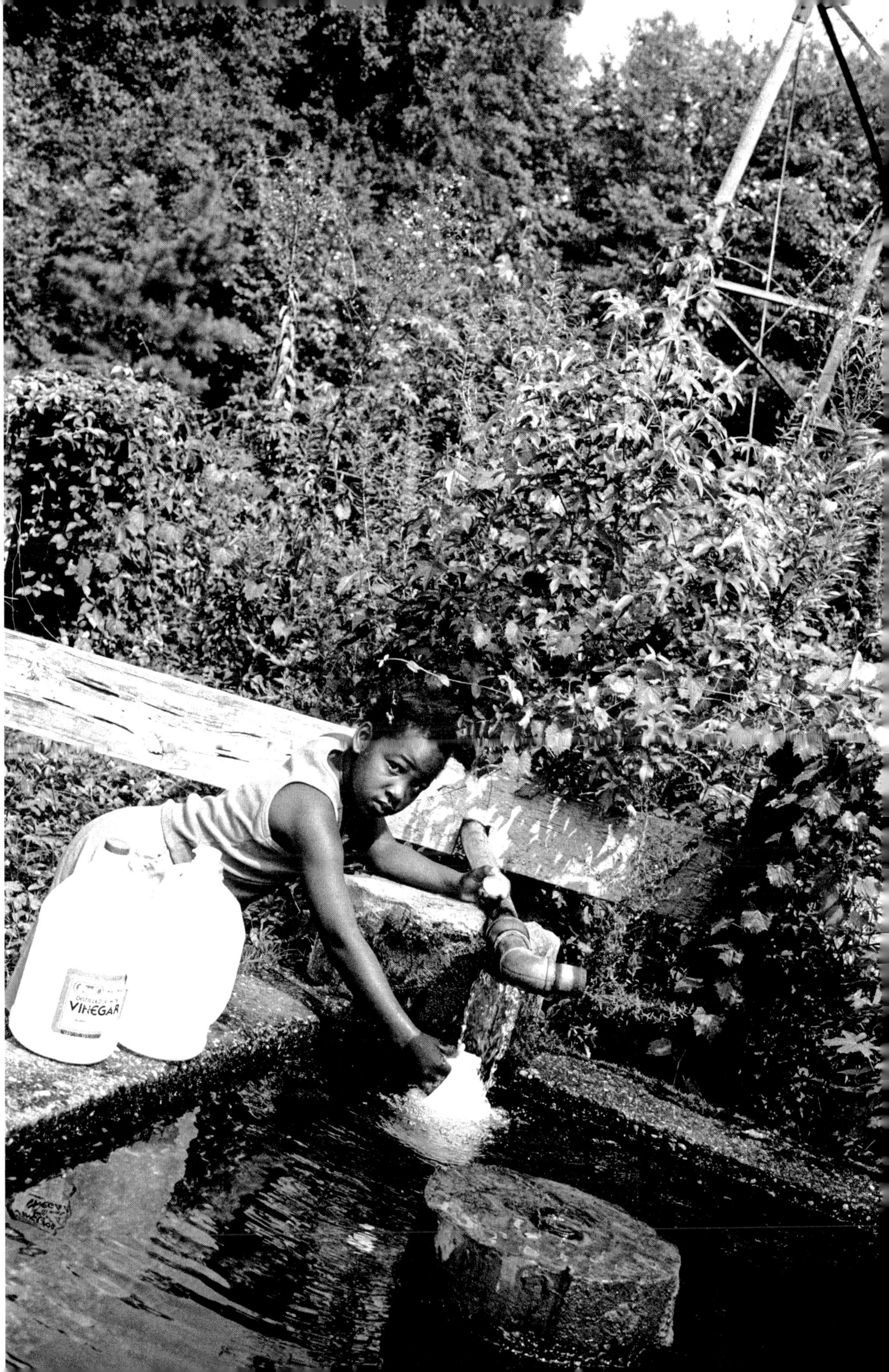
VINEGAR

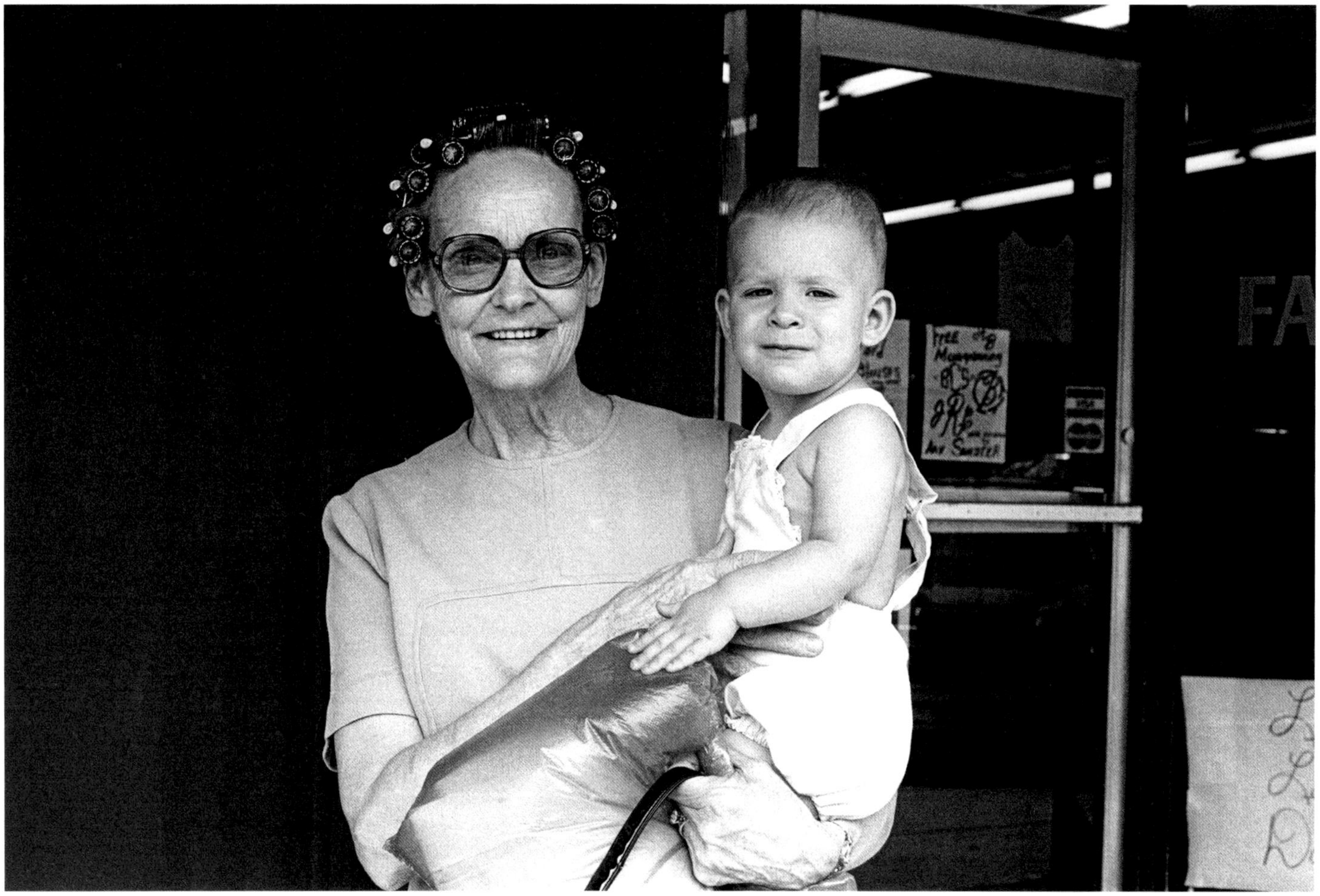

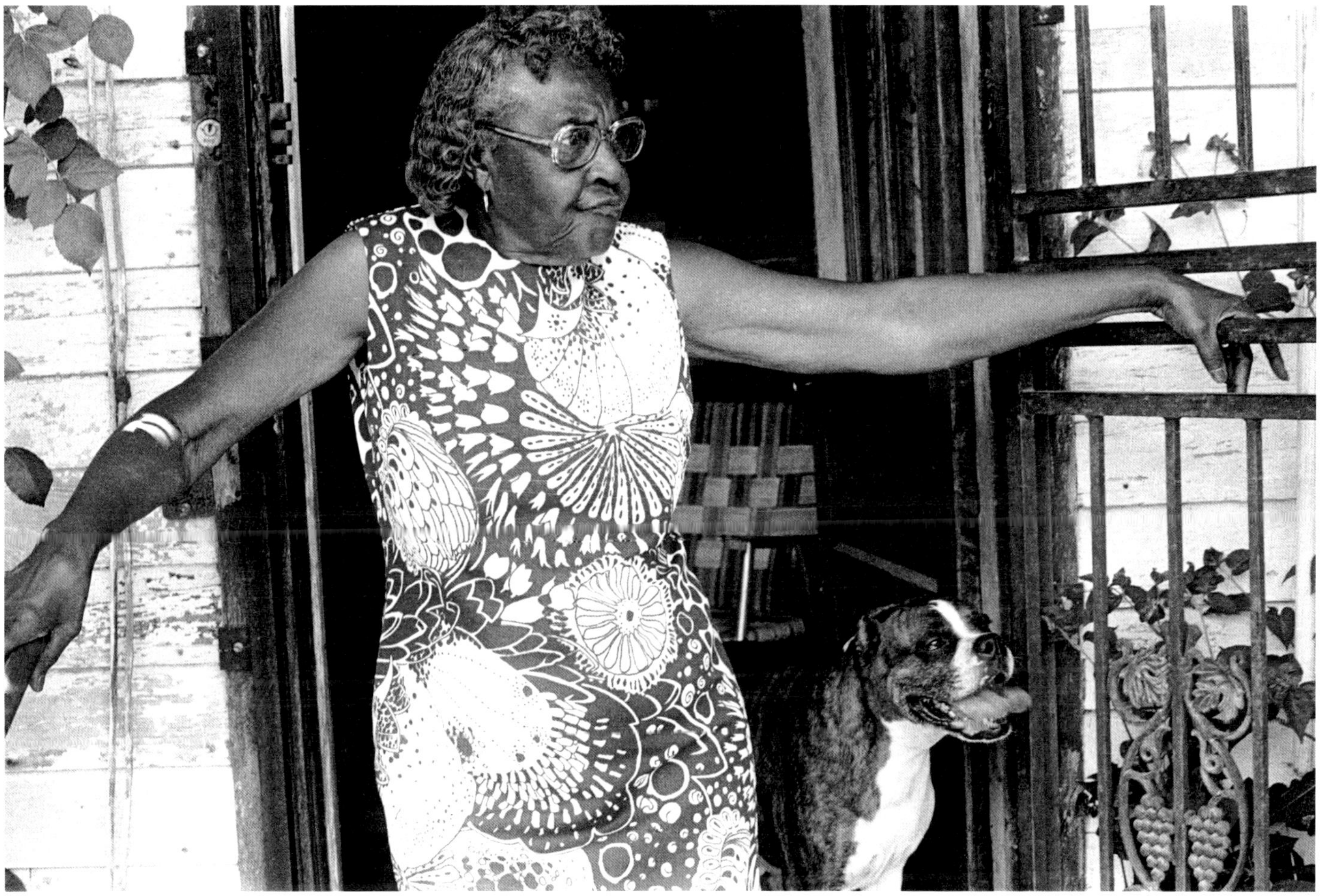

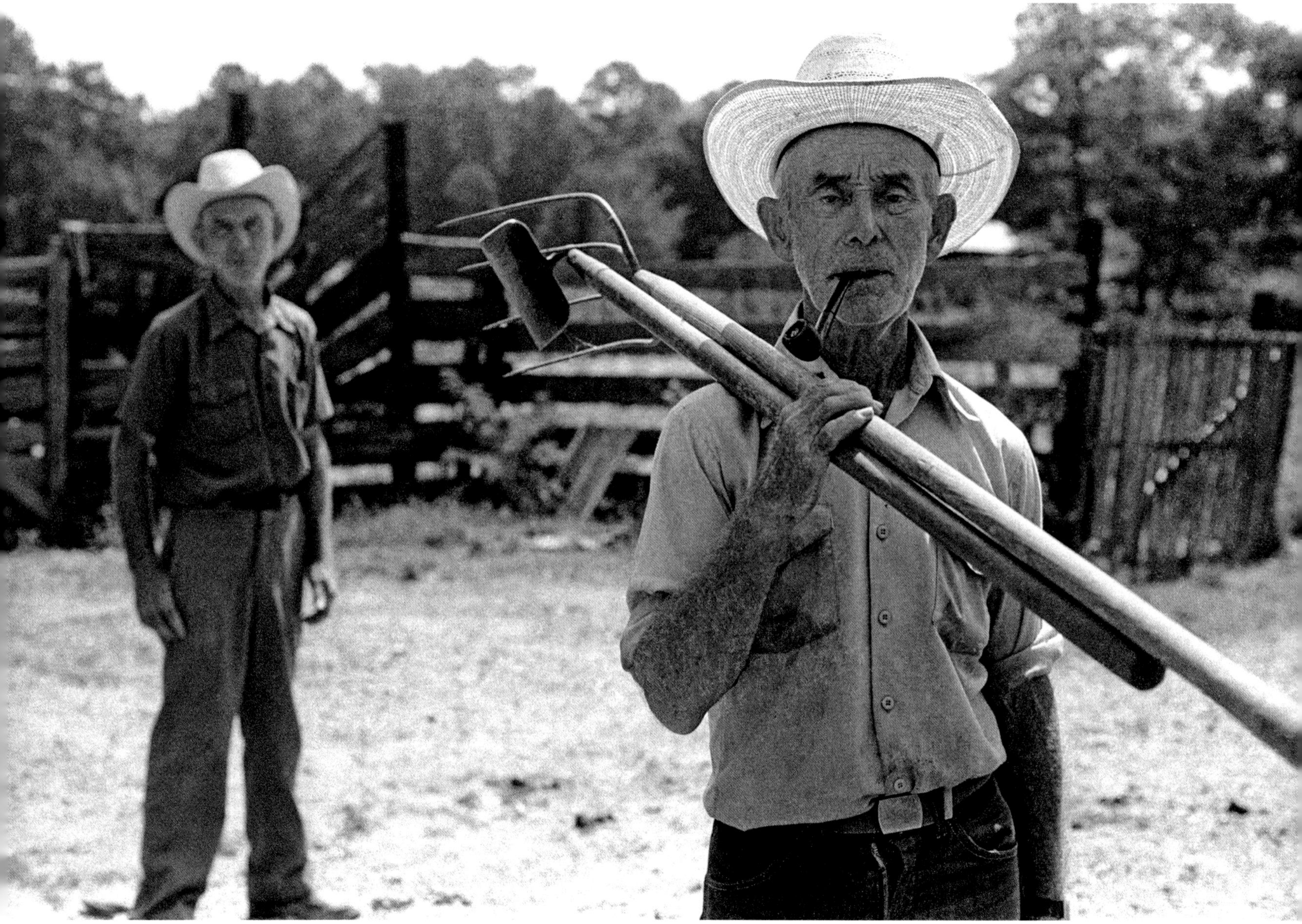

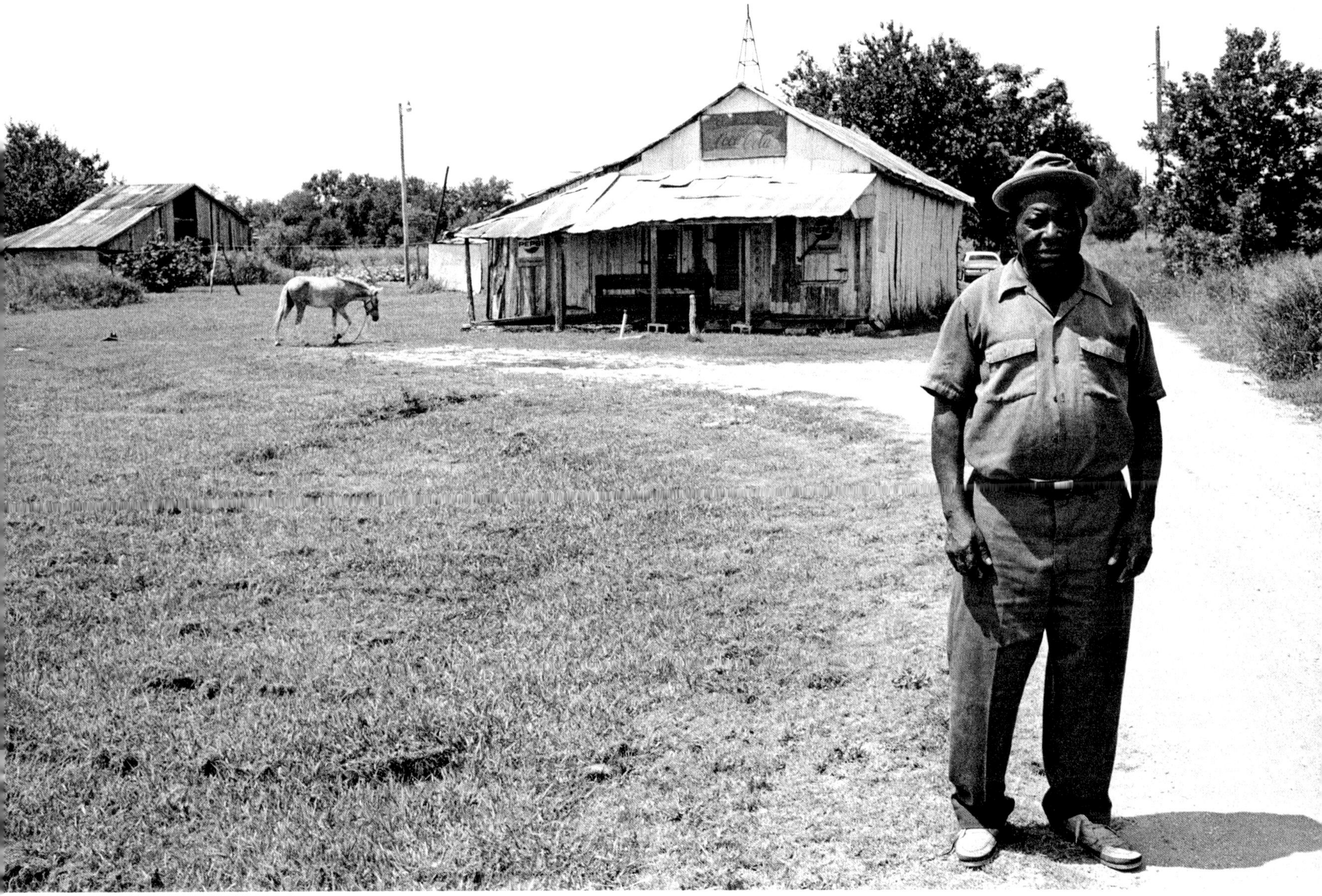

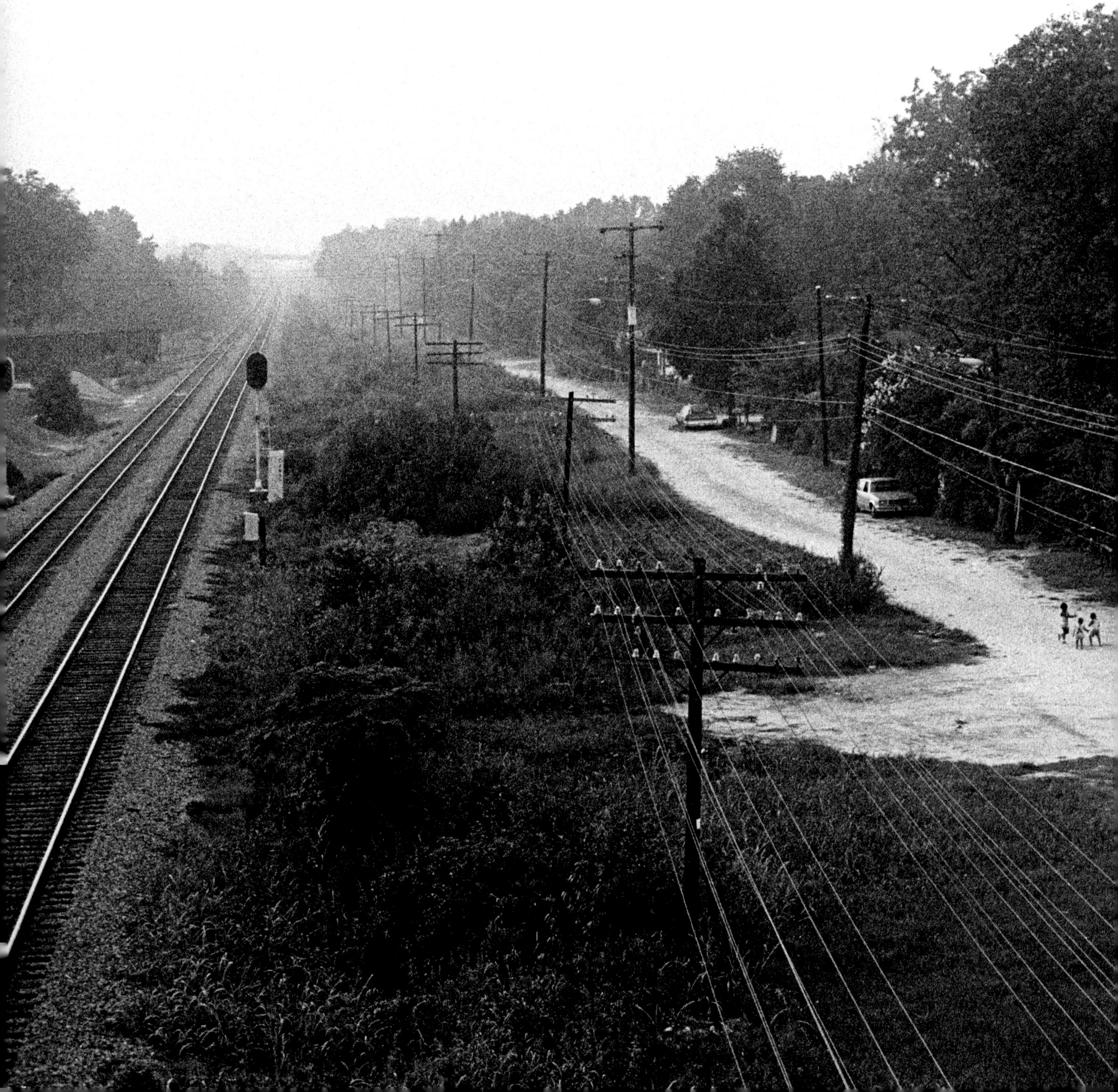

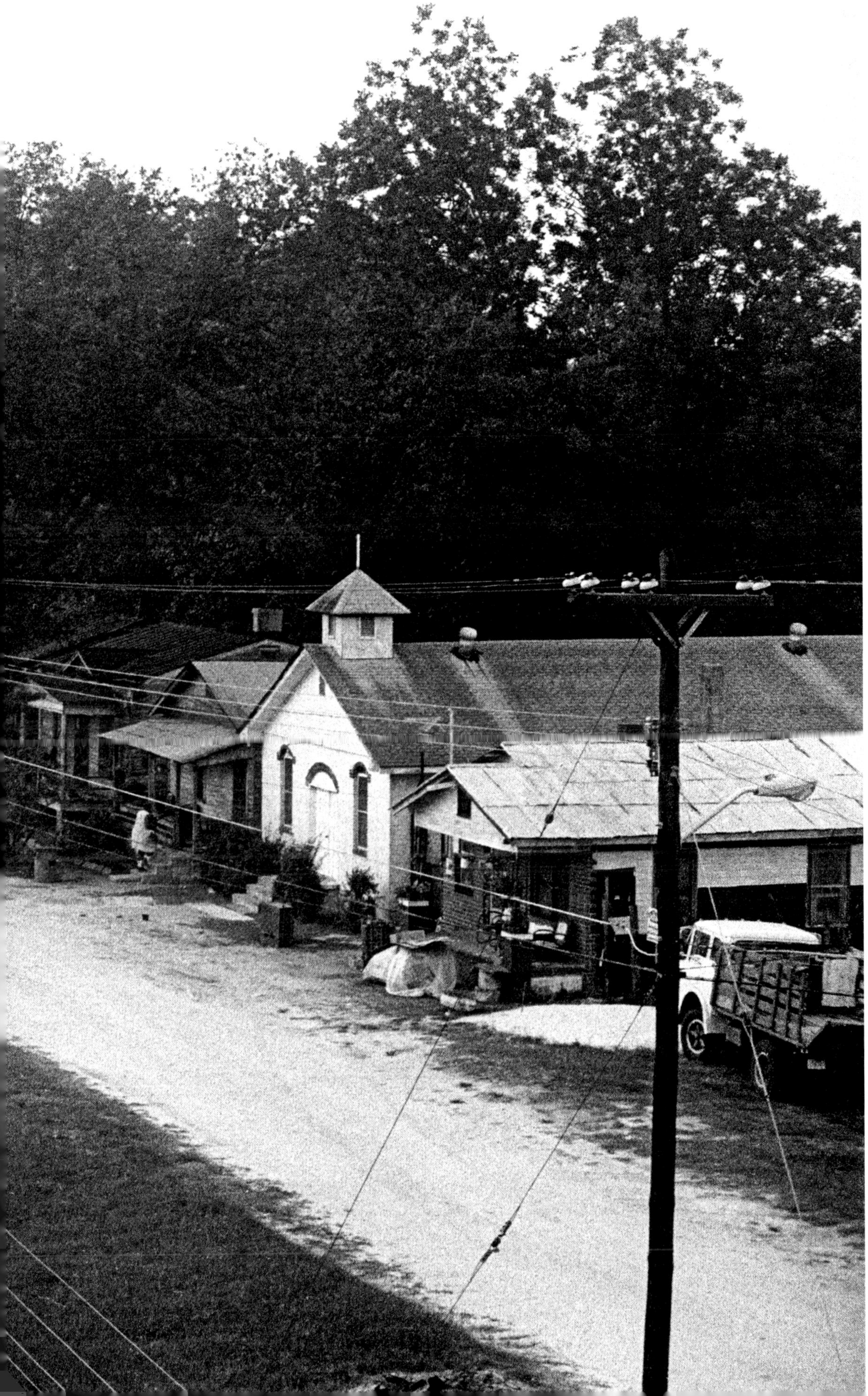

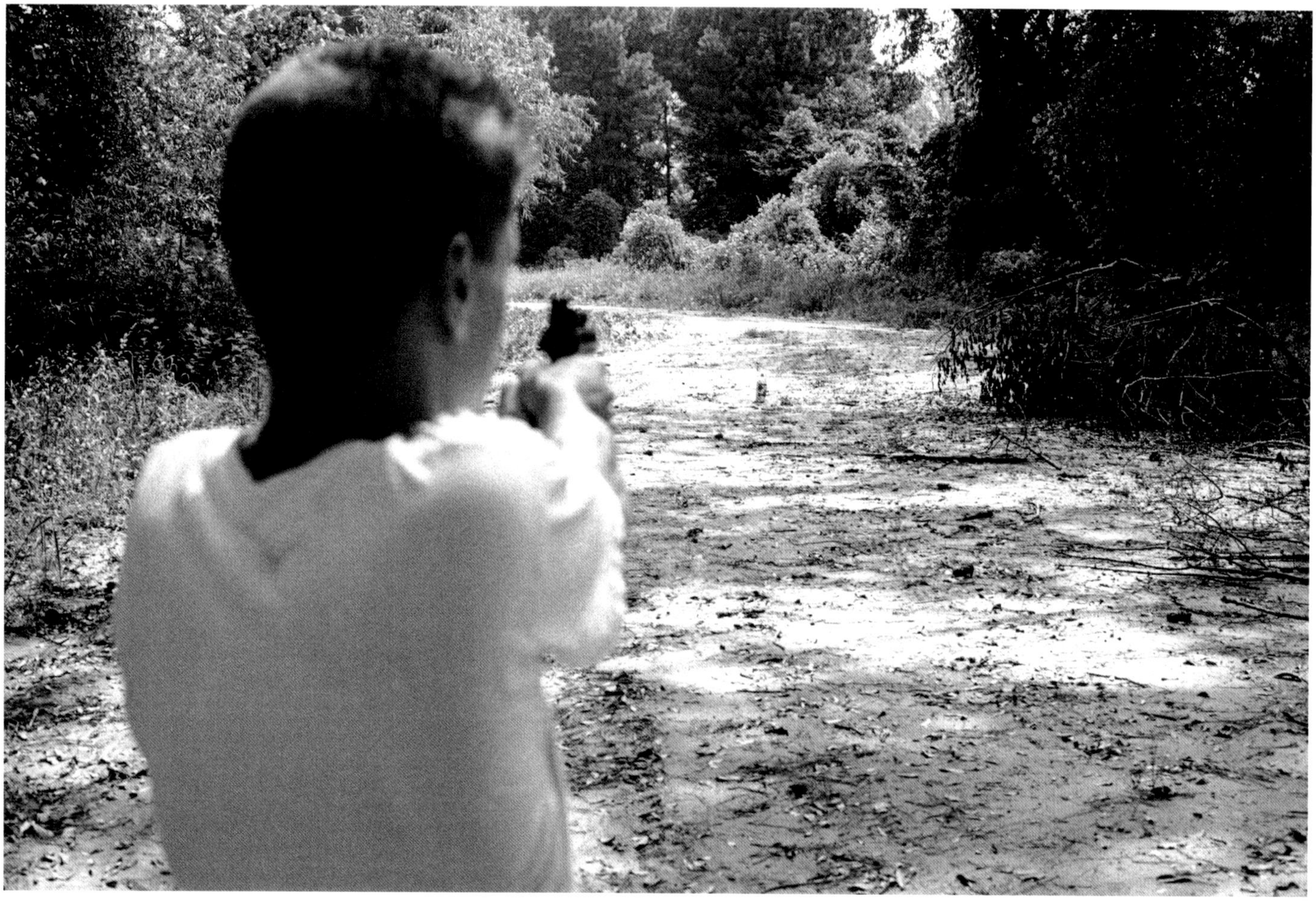

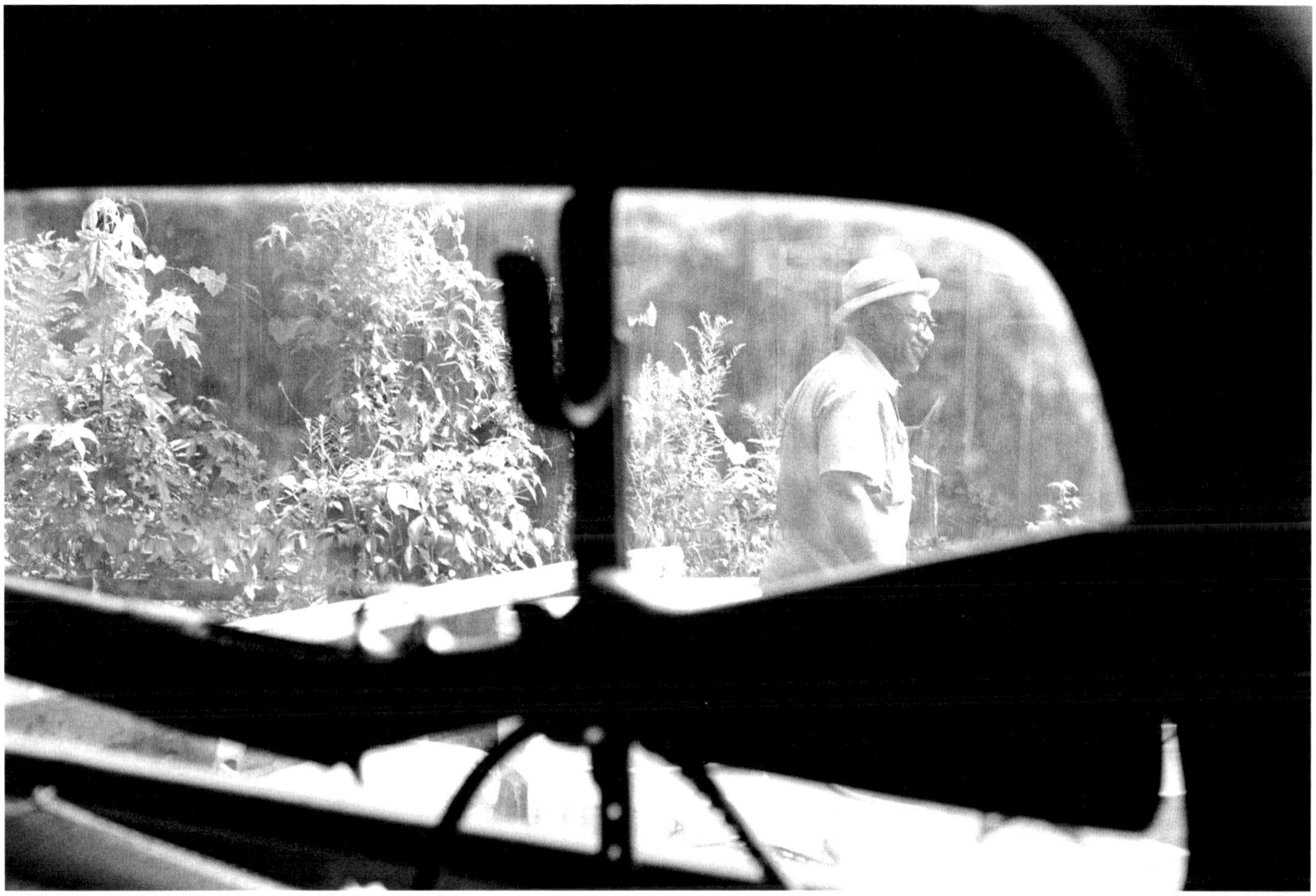

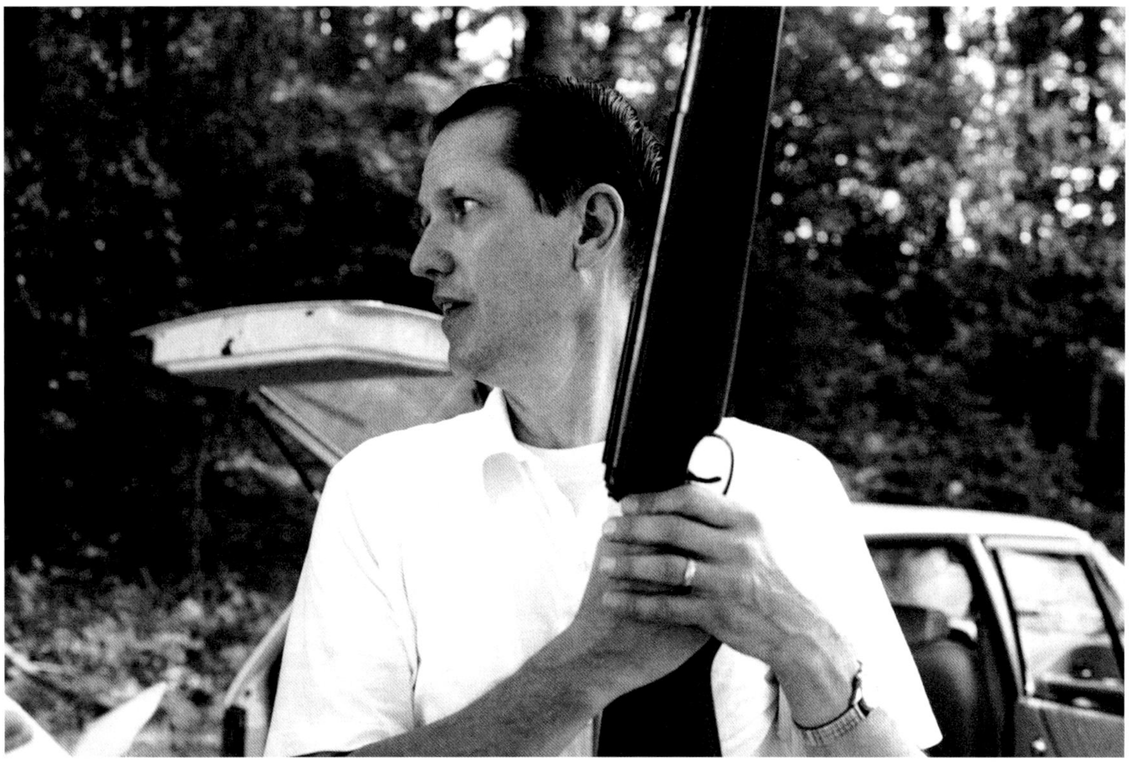

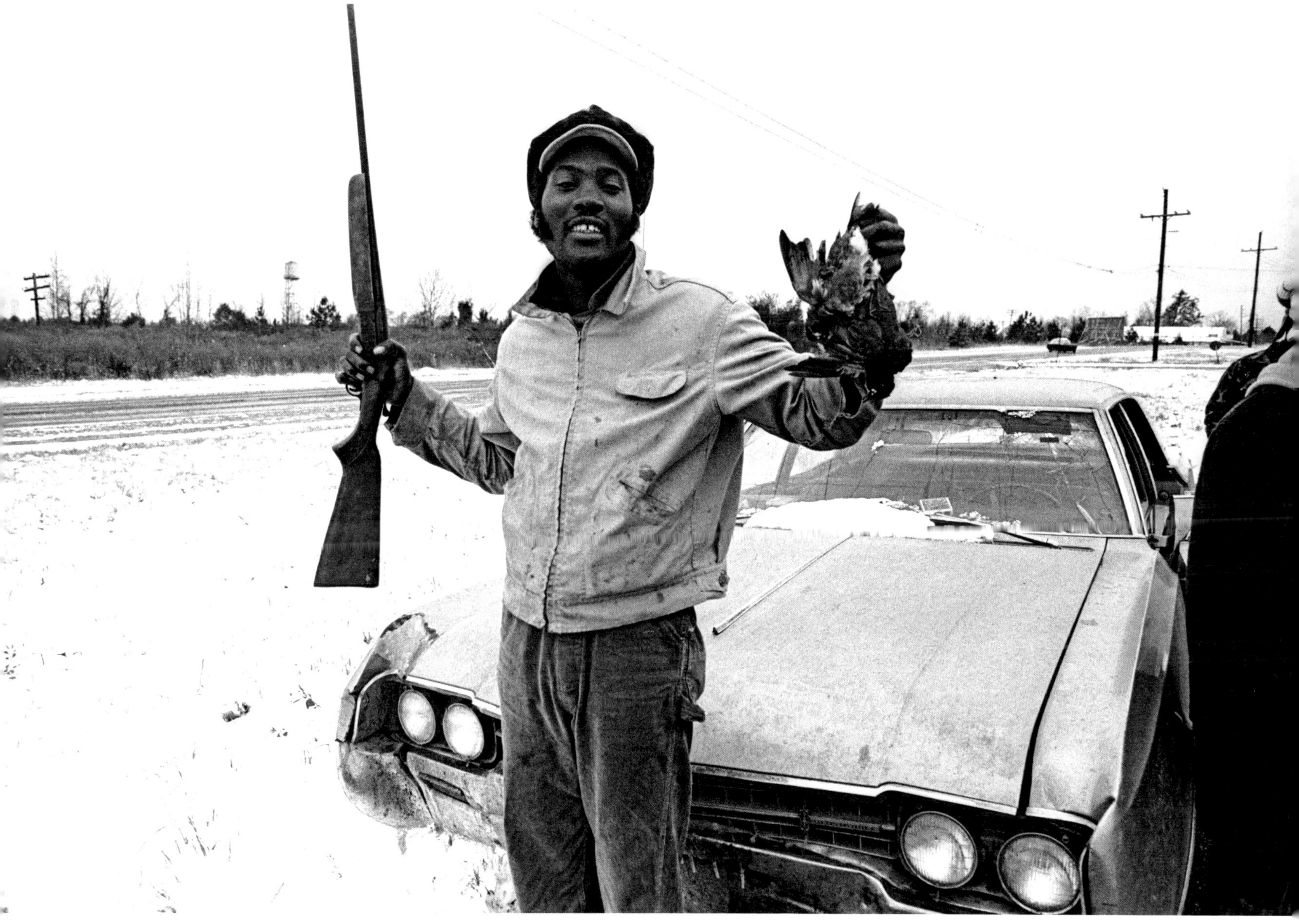

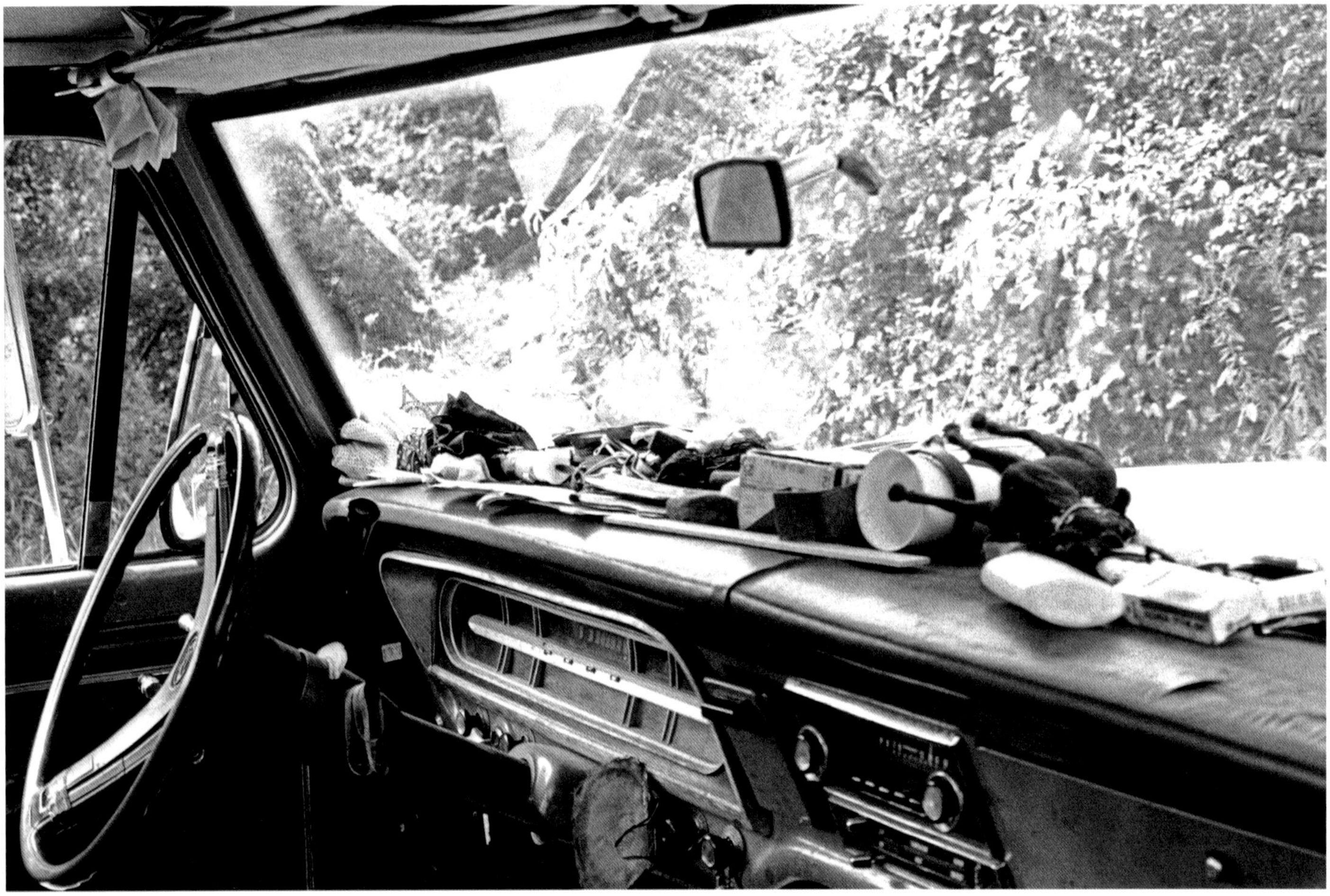

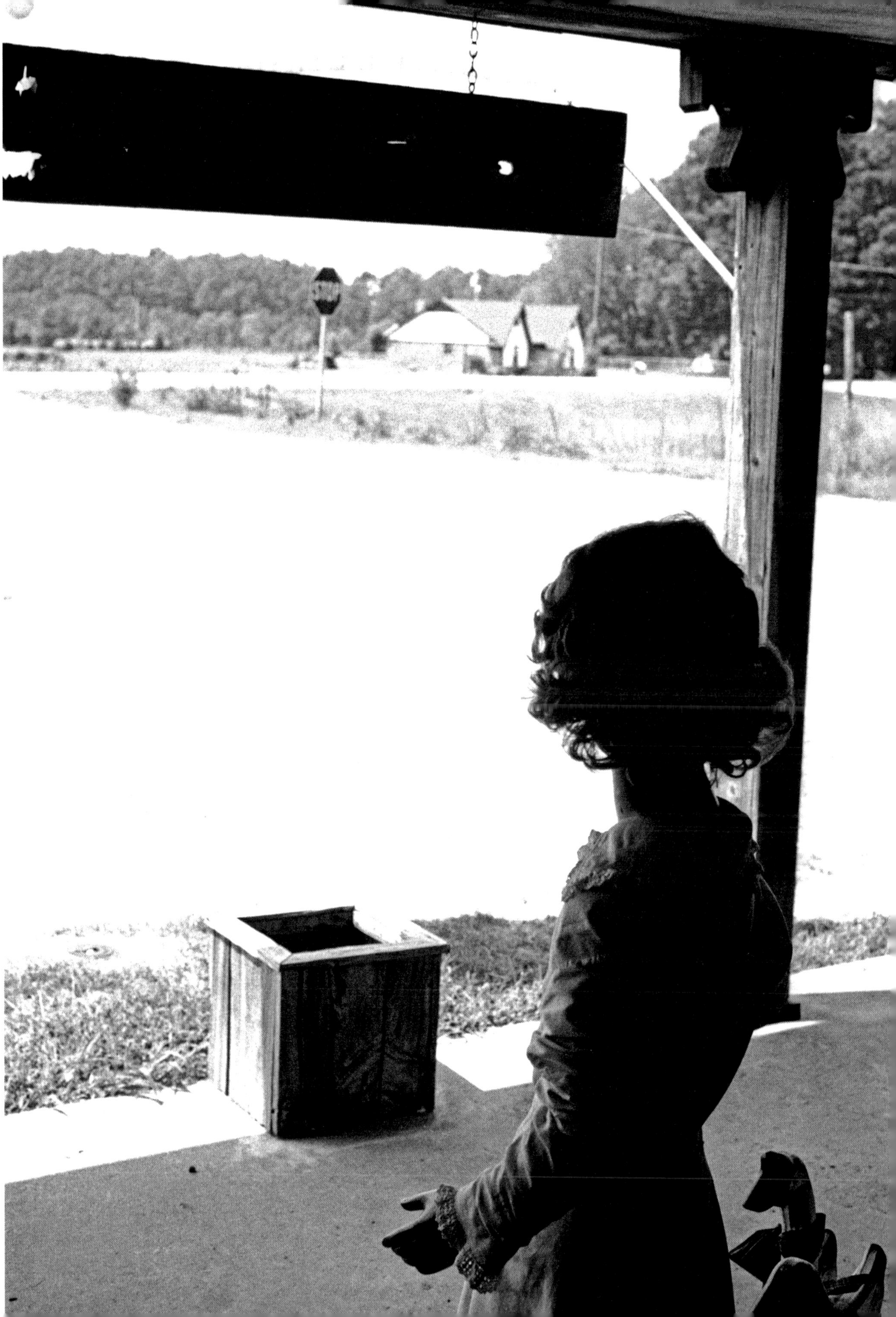

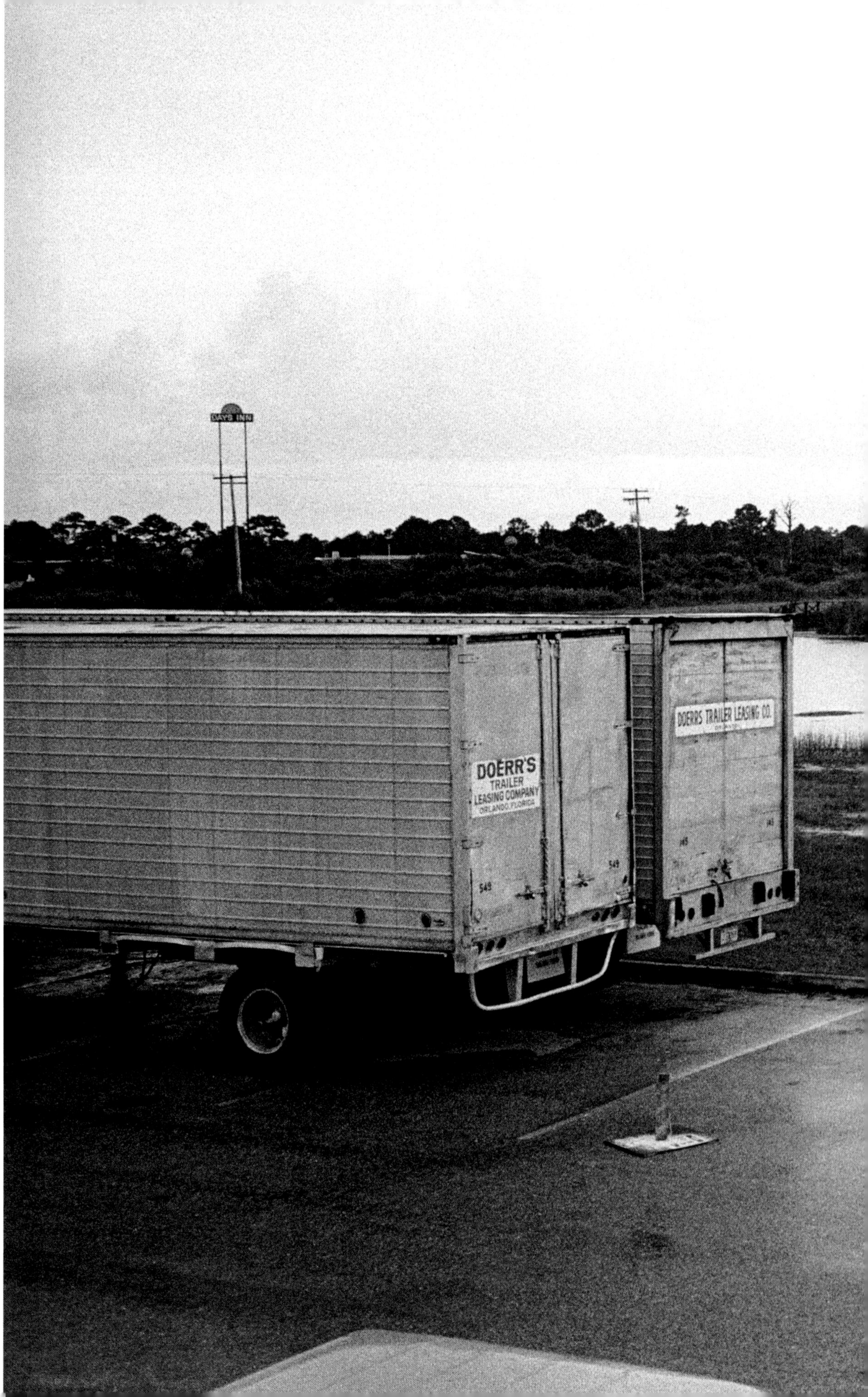
DAYS INN
DOERR'S
TRAILER
LEASING COMPANY
ORLANDO, FLORIDA
DOERRS TRAILER LEASING CO.

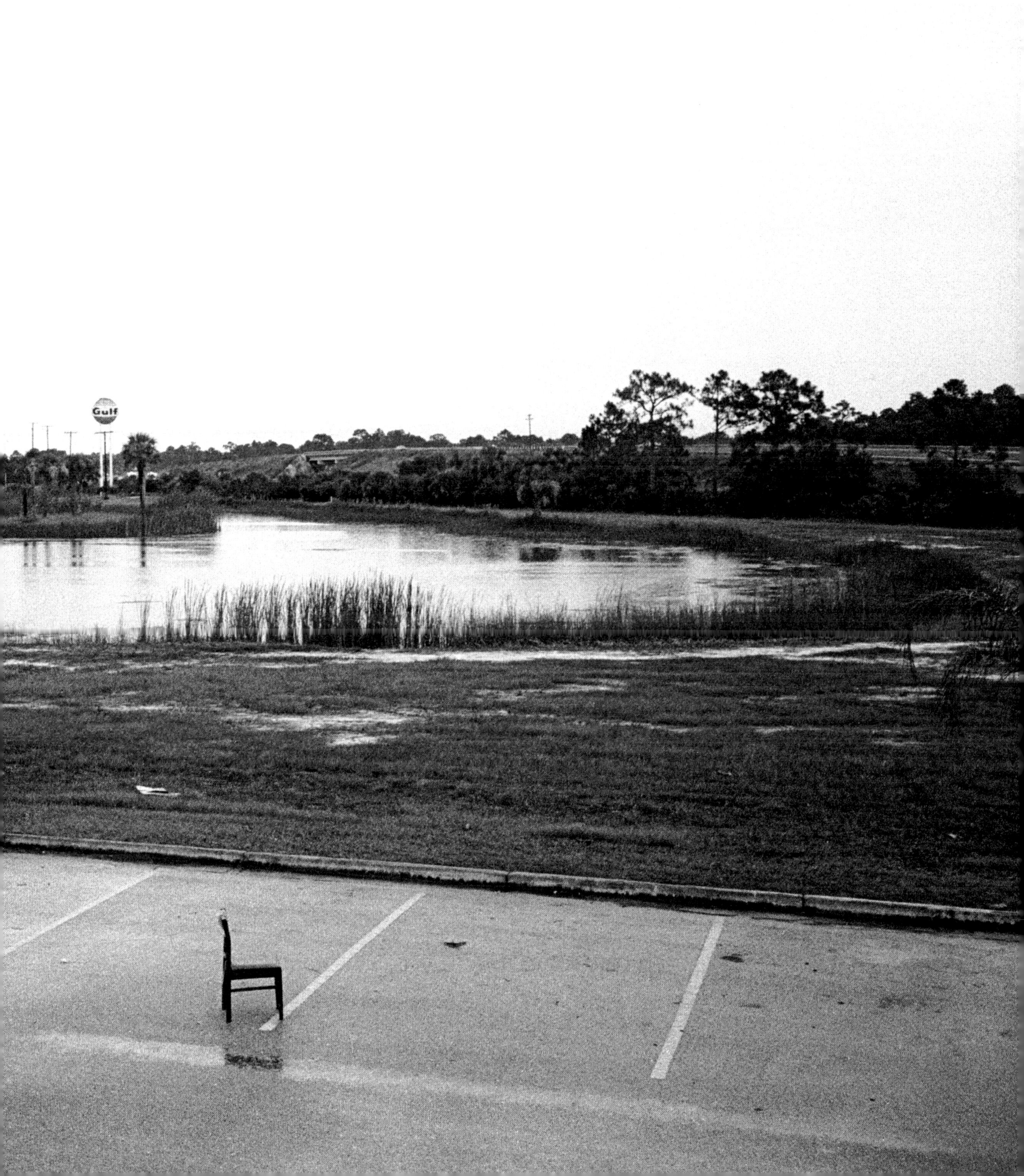
Gulf

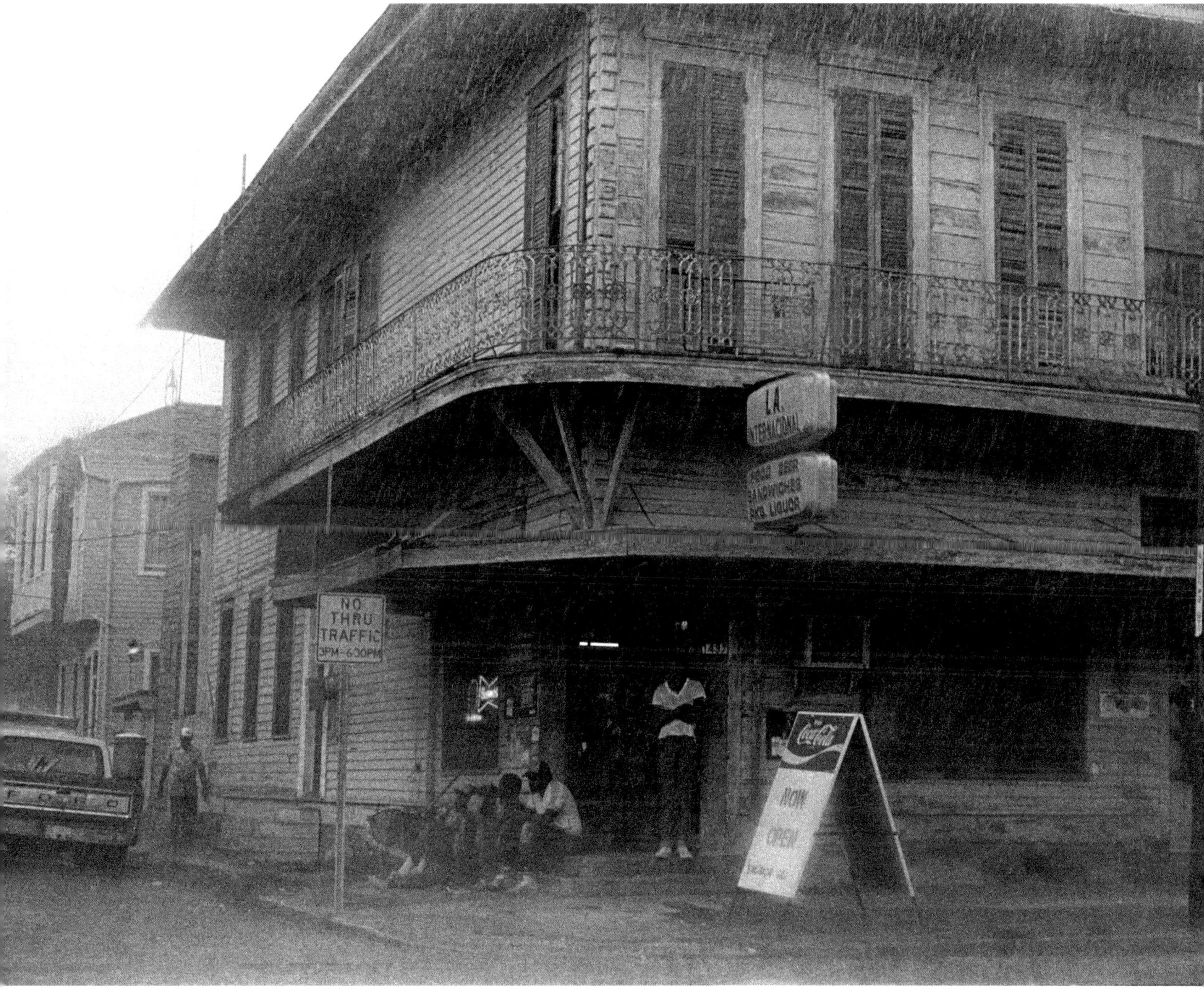
L.A.
INTERNACIONAL
SANDWICHES
PKG. LIQUOR
NO
THRU
TRAFFIC
Coca-Cola
NOW
OPEN

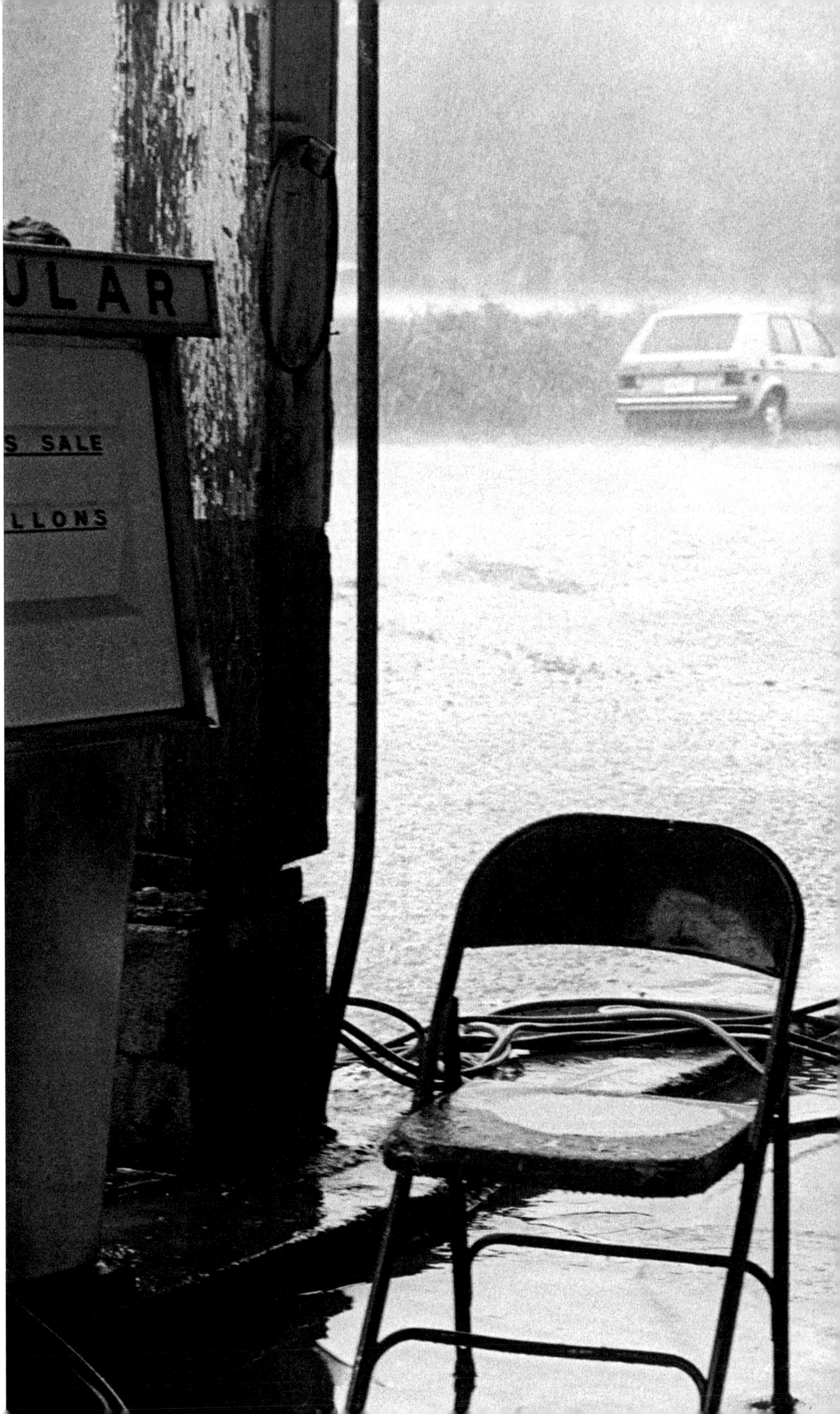
ULAR
S SALE
LLONS

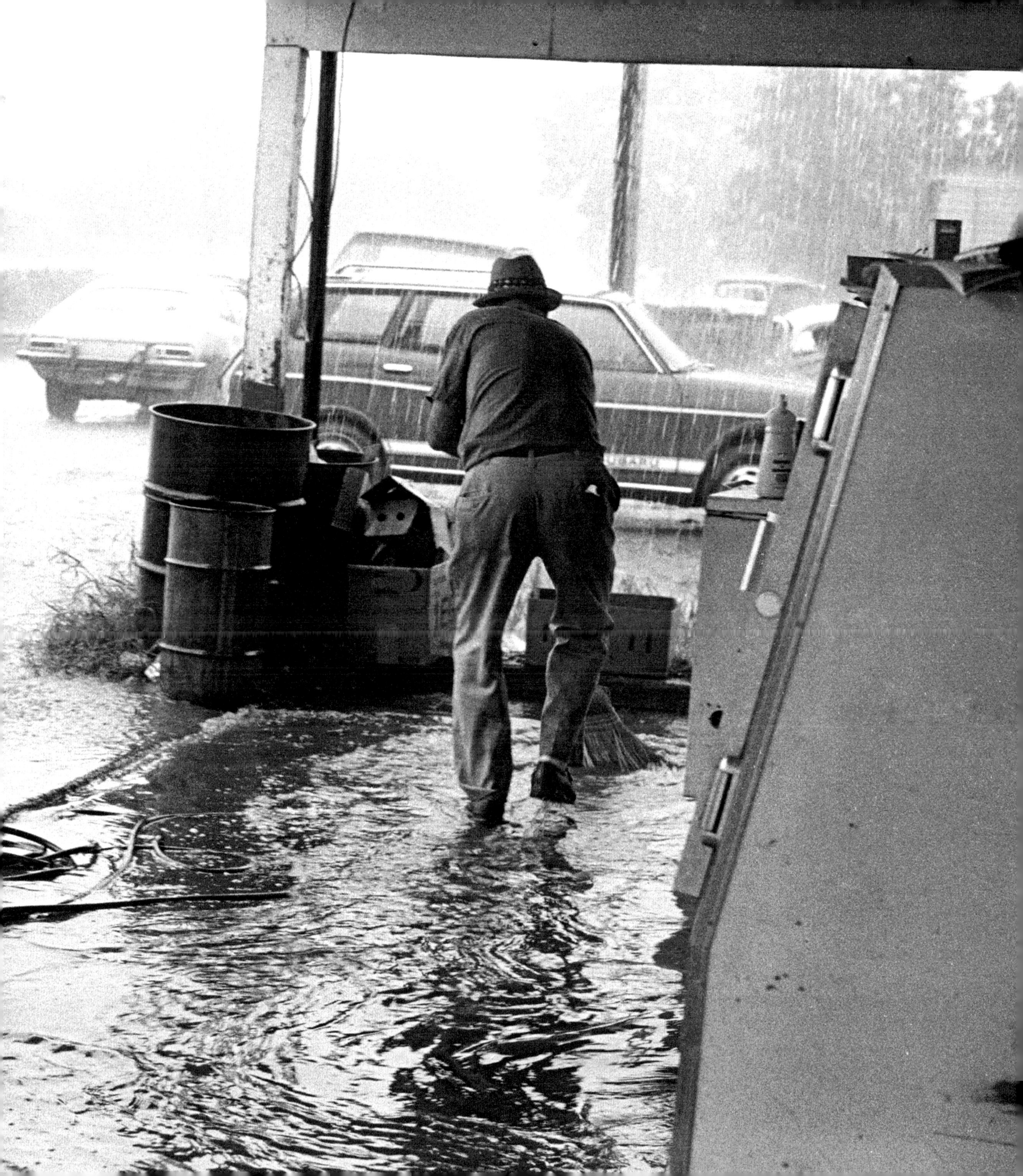

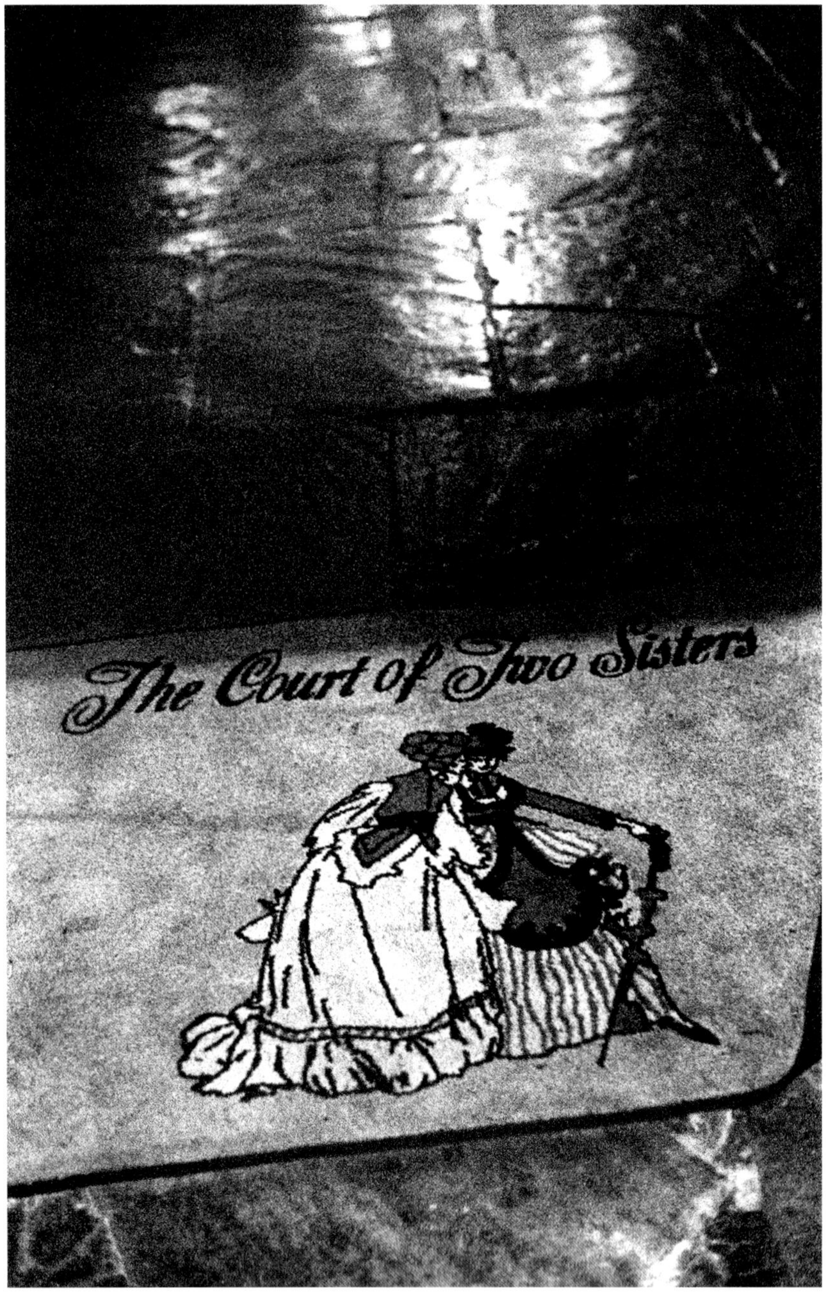
The Court of Two Sisters

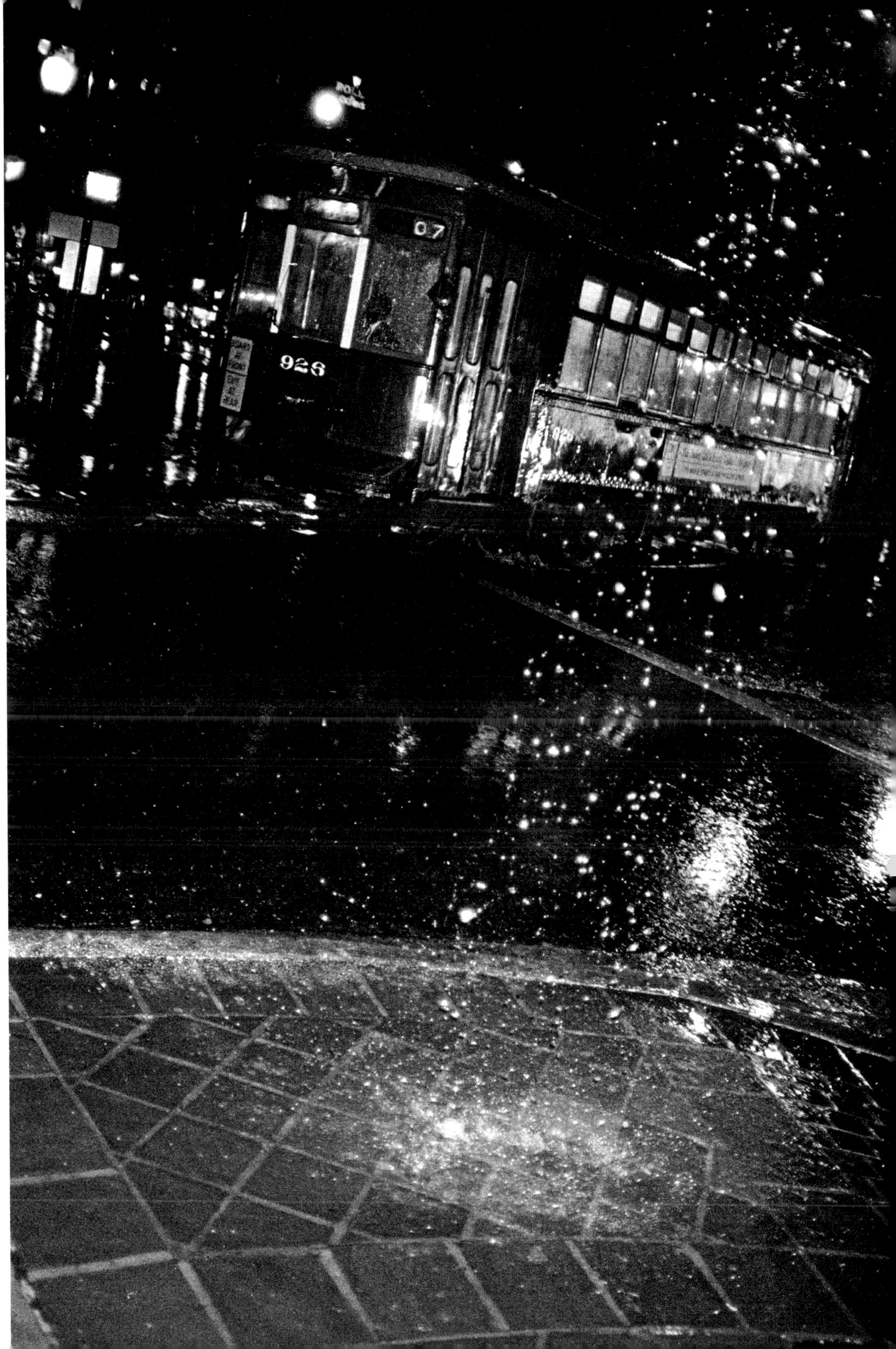
07
926

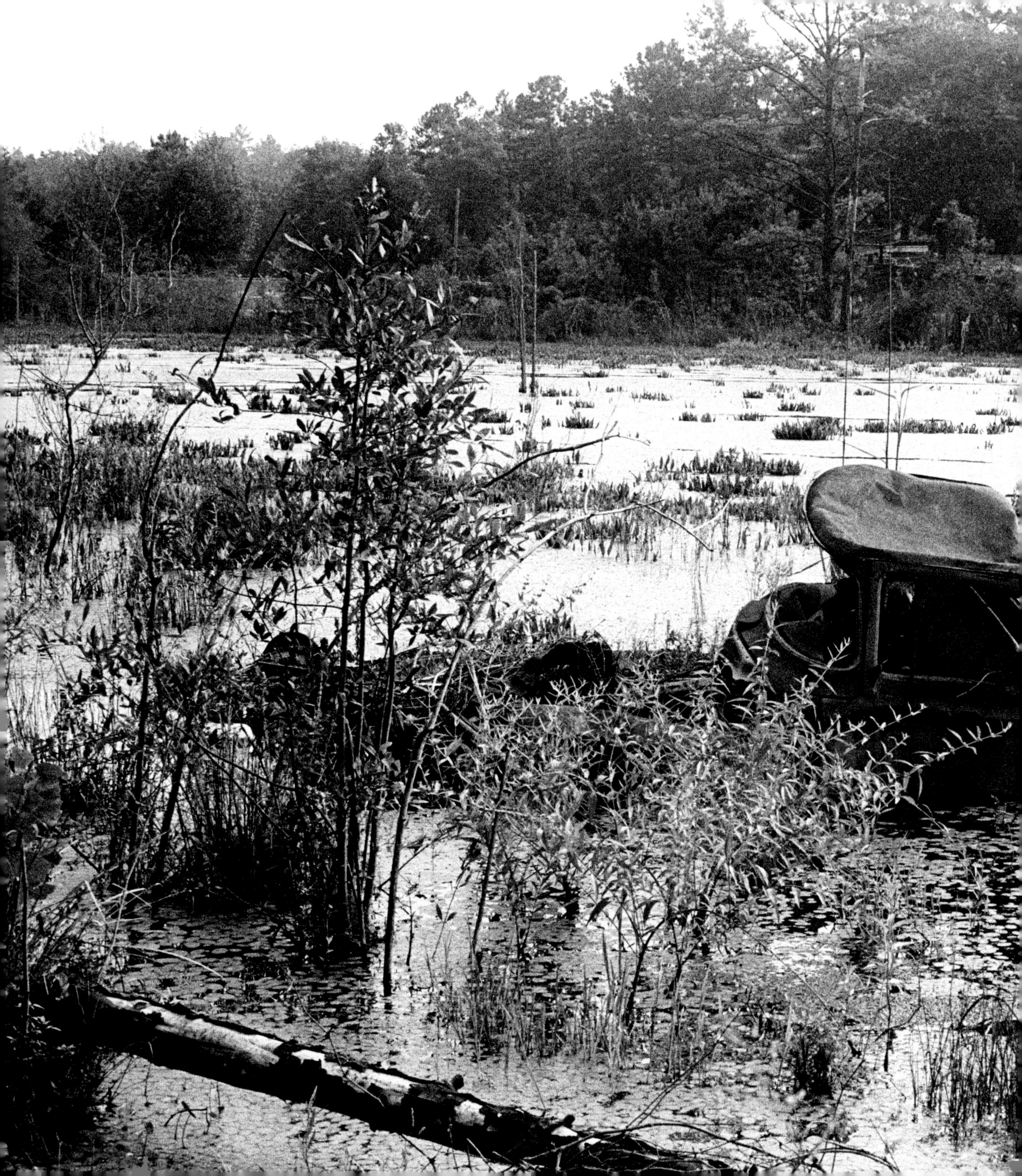

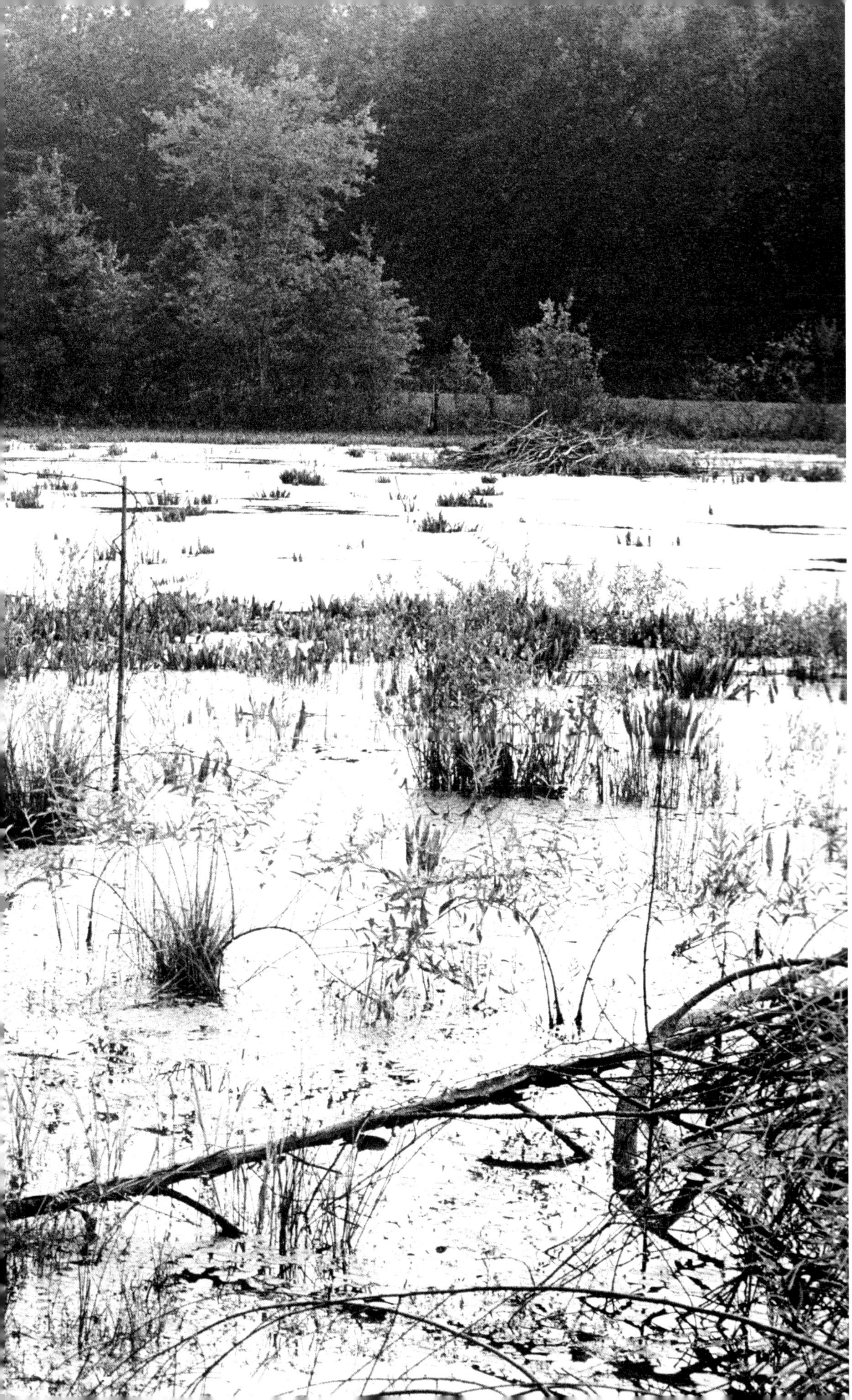

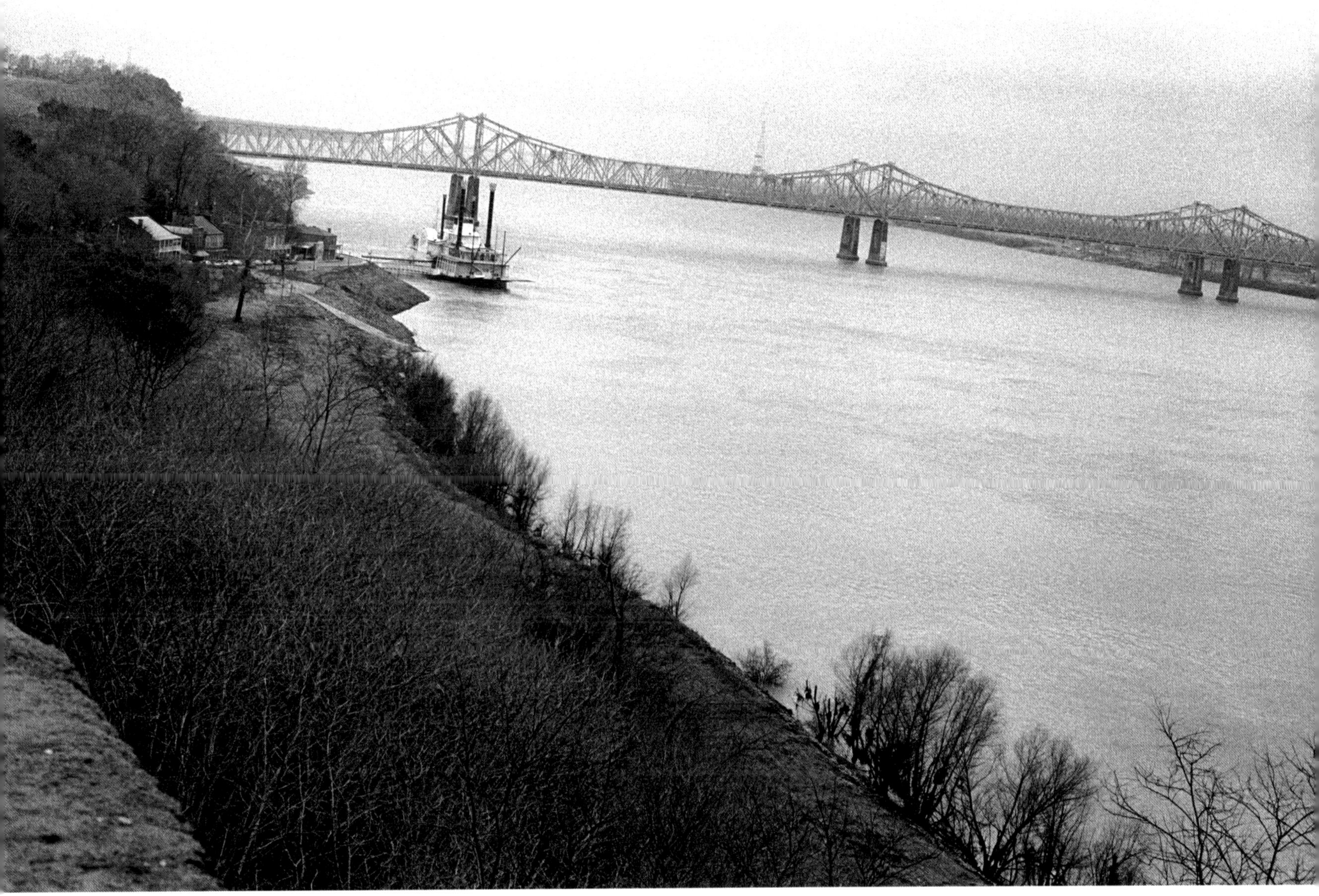

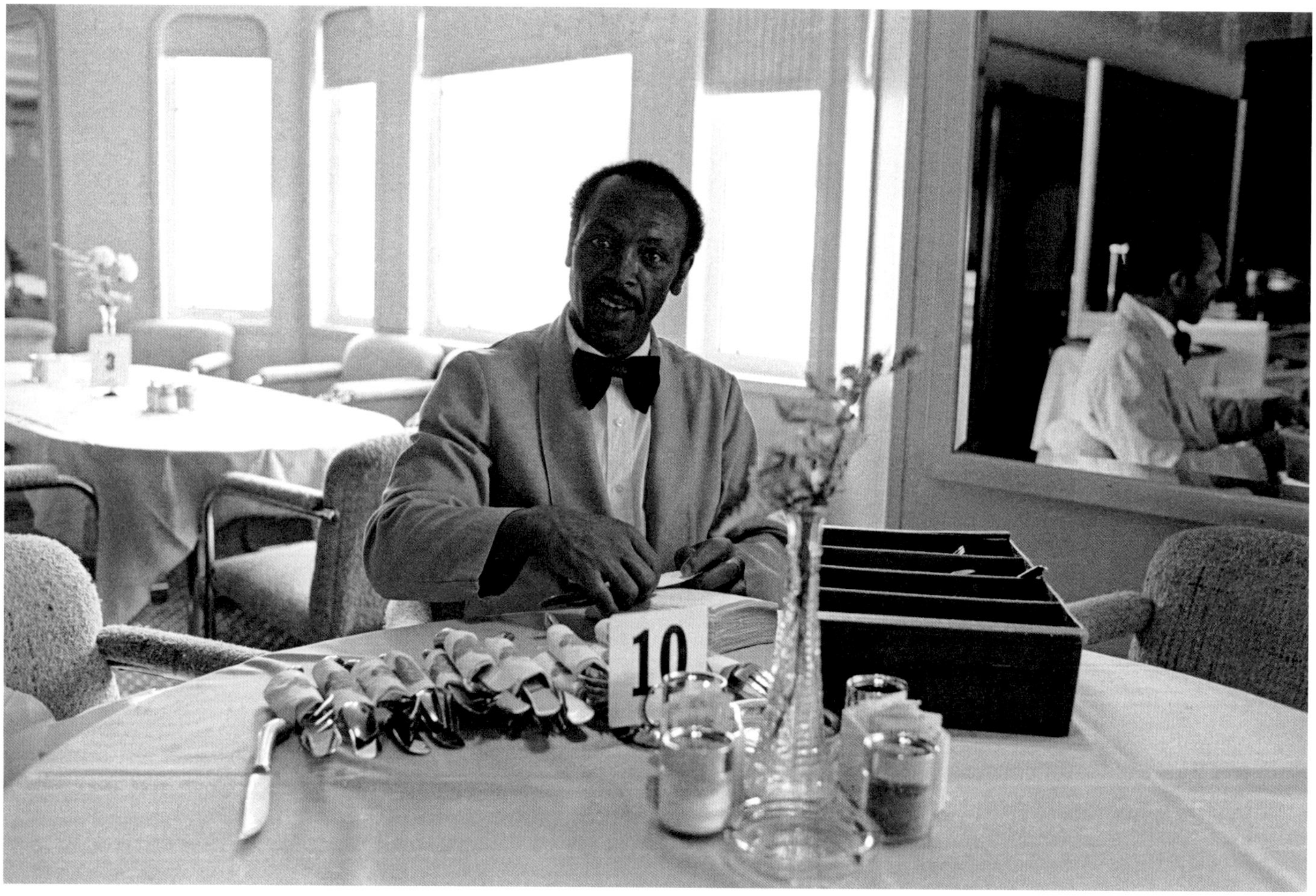

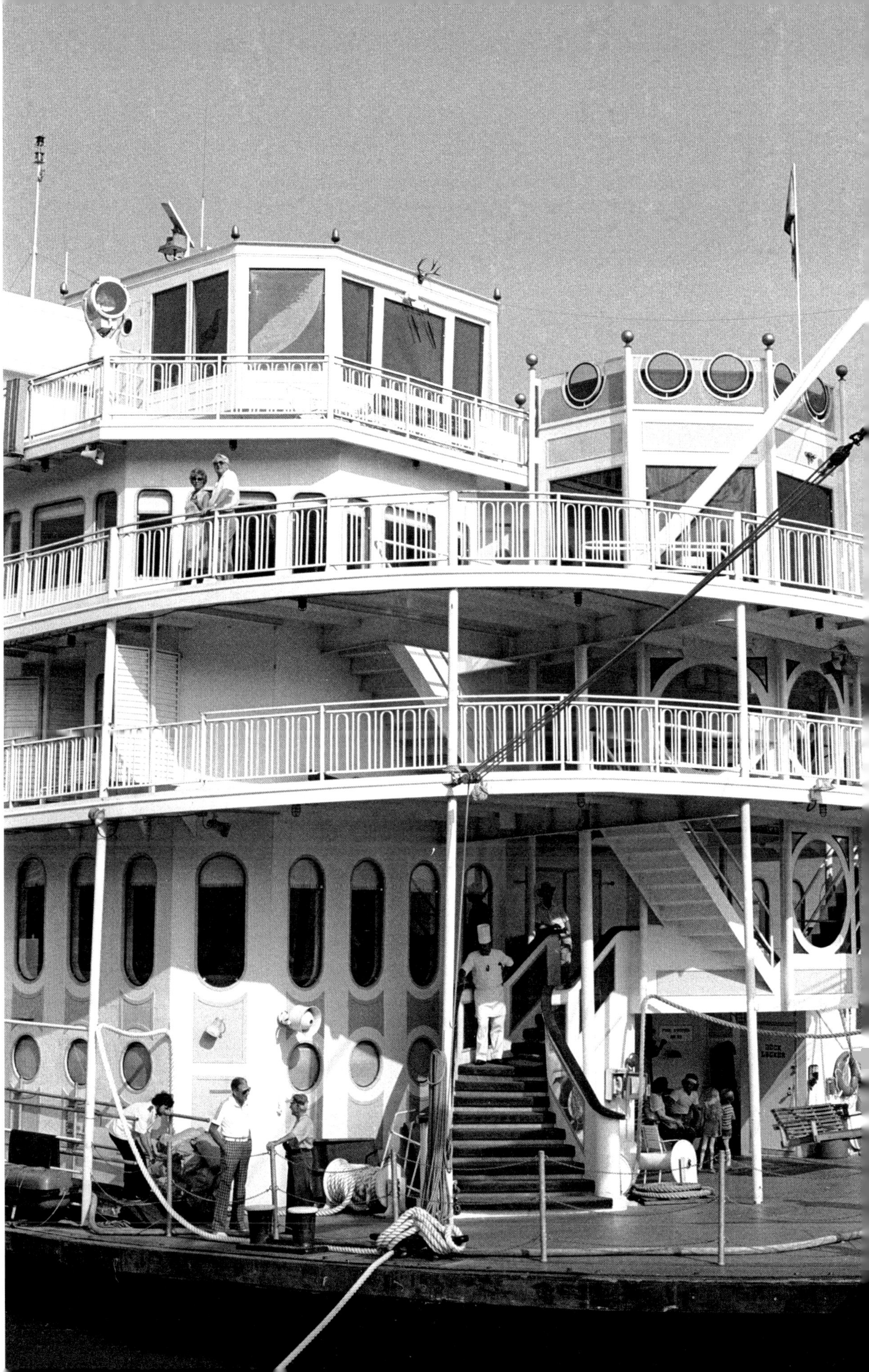

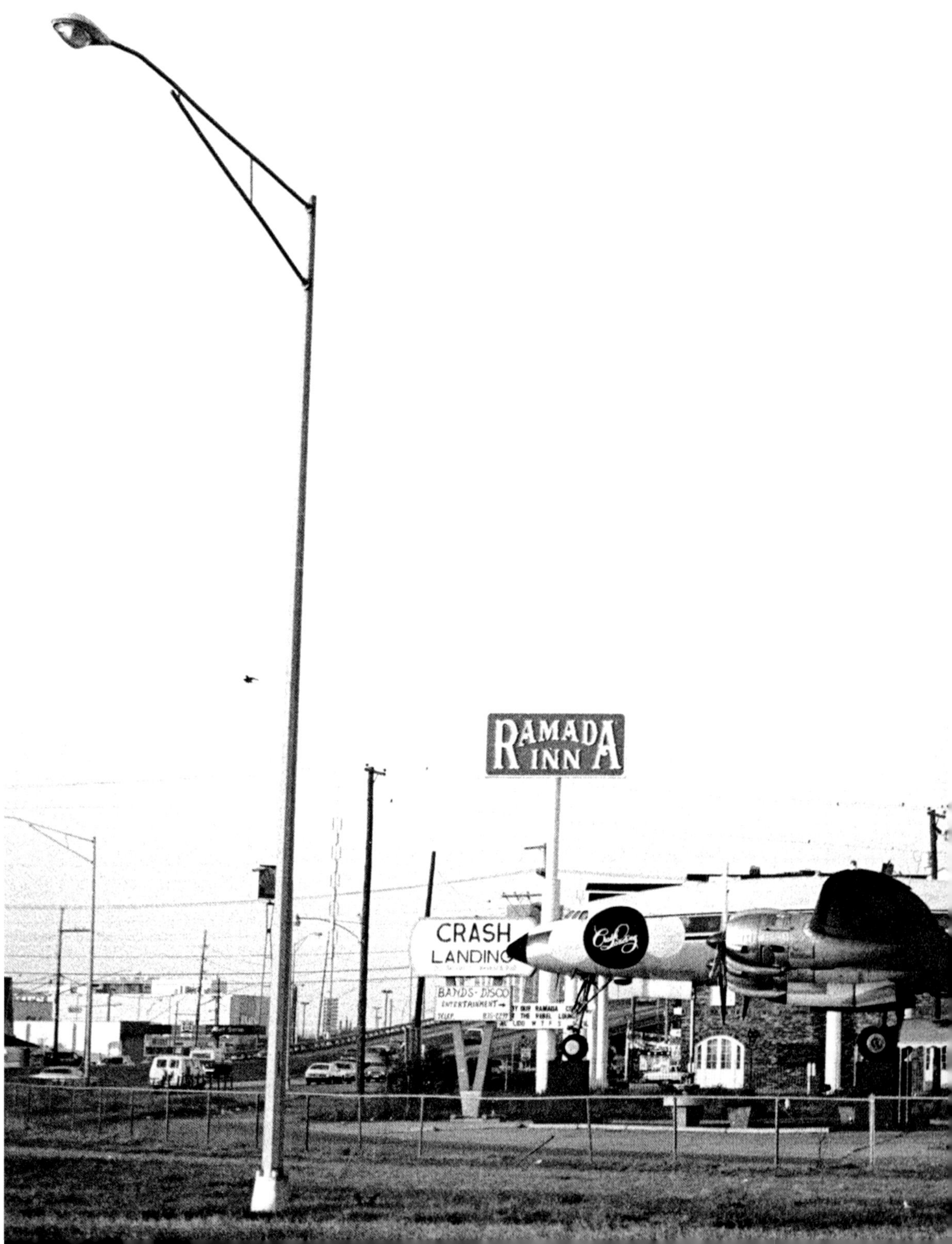
RAMADA INN
CRASH
BANDS-DISCO
ENTERTAINMENT

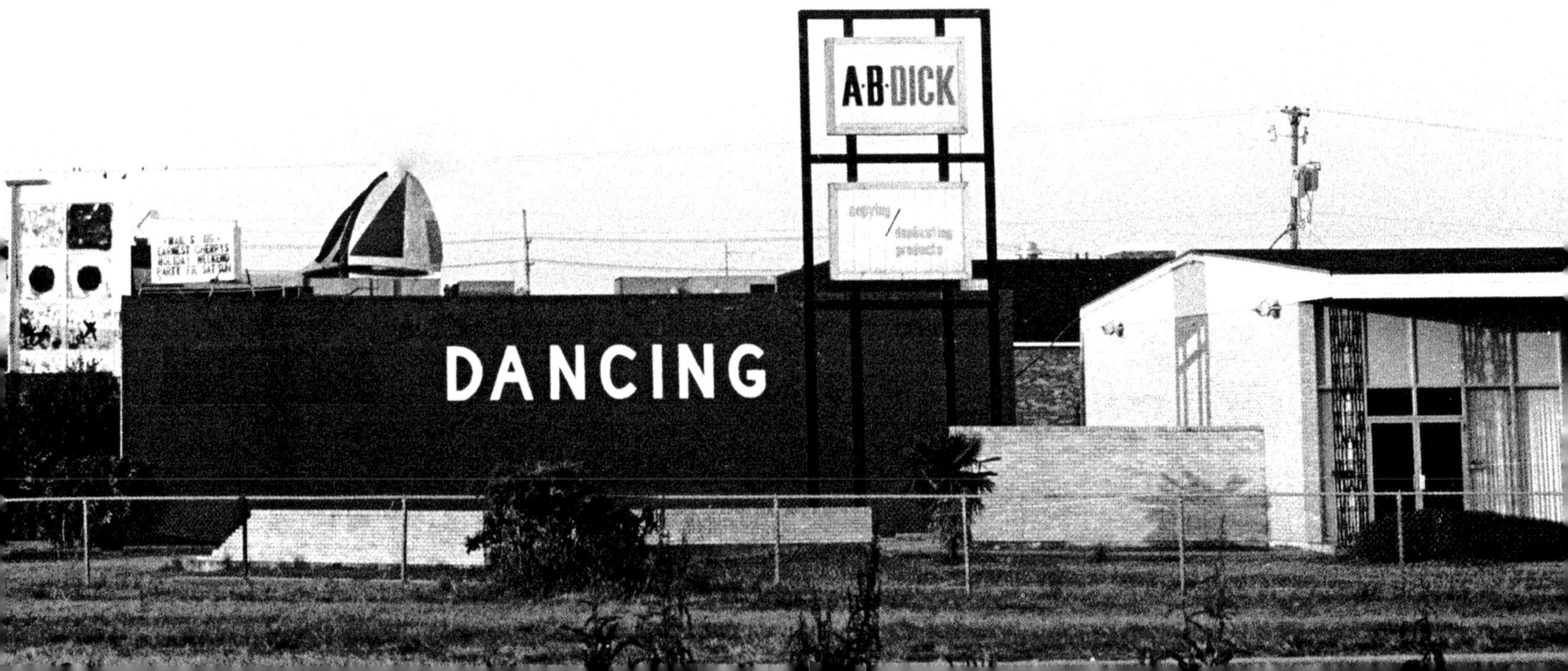
A·B·DICK
copying / duplicating products
DANCING

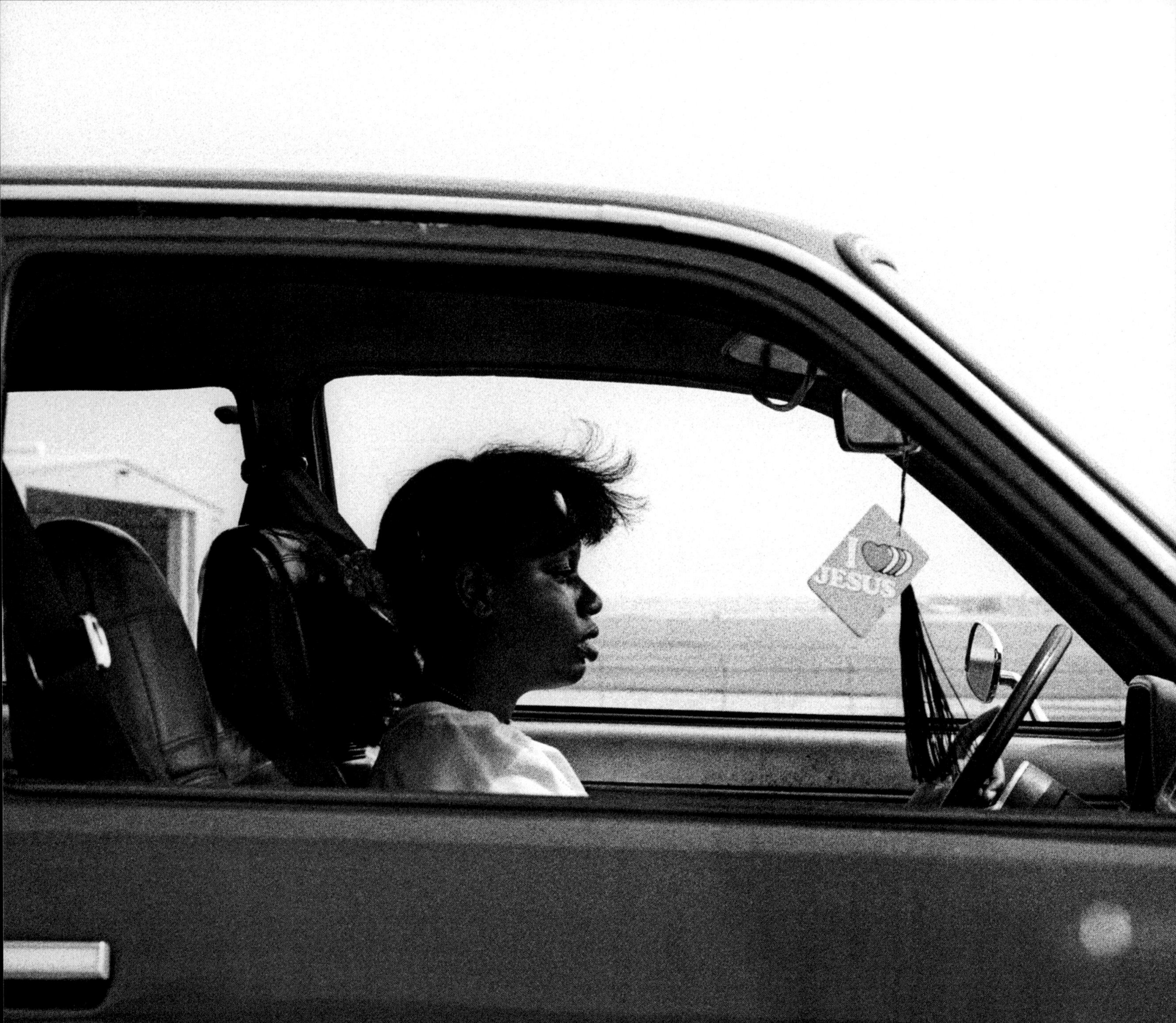
I
JESUS

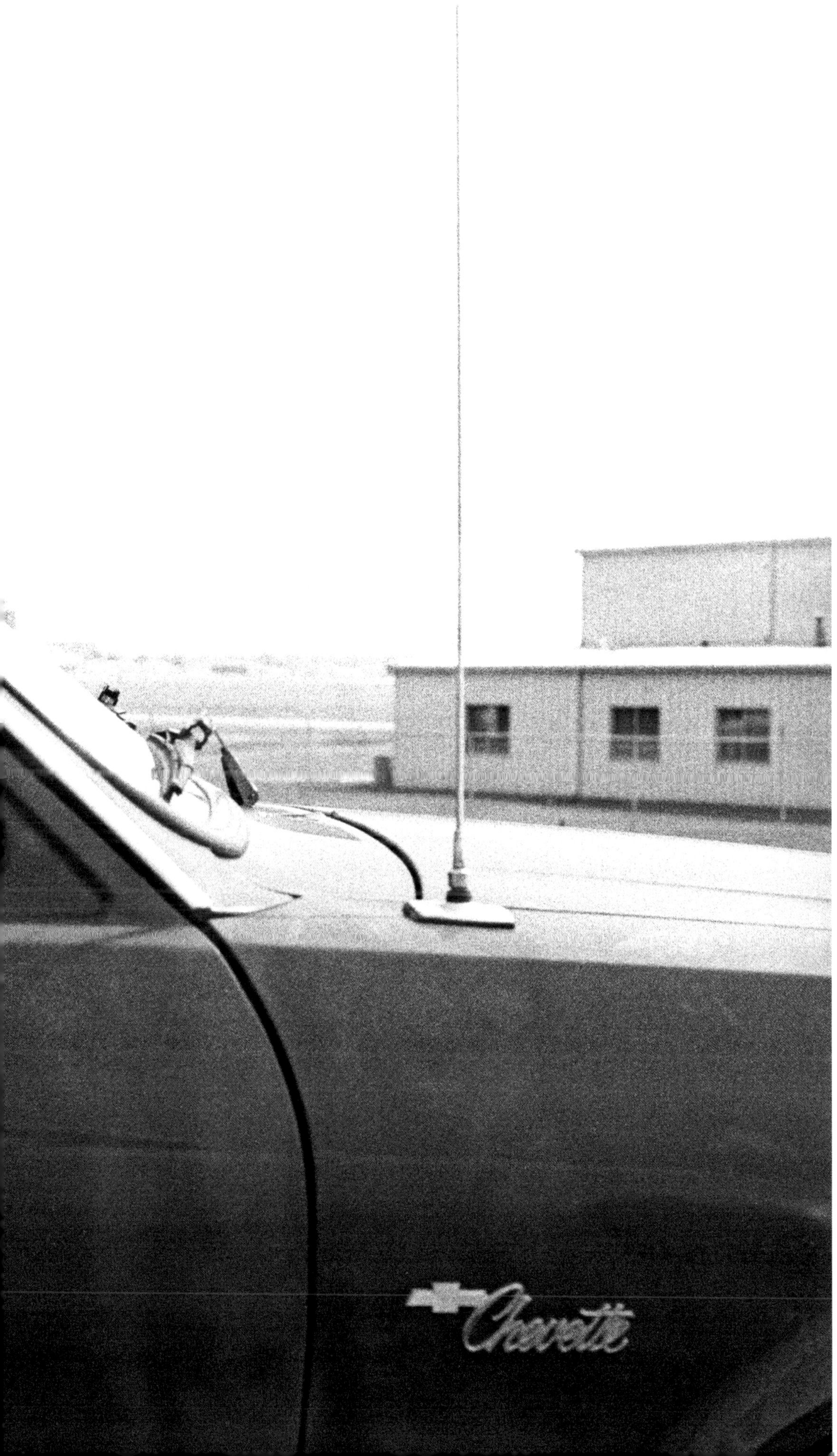
Chevette

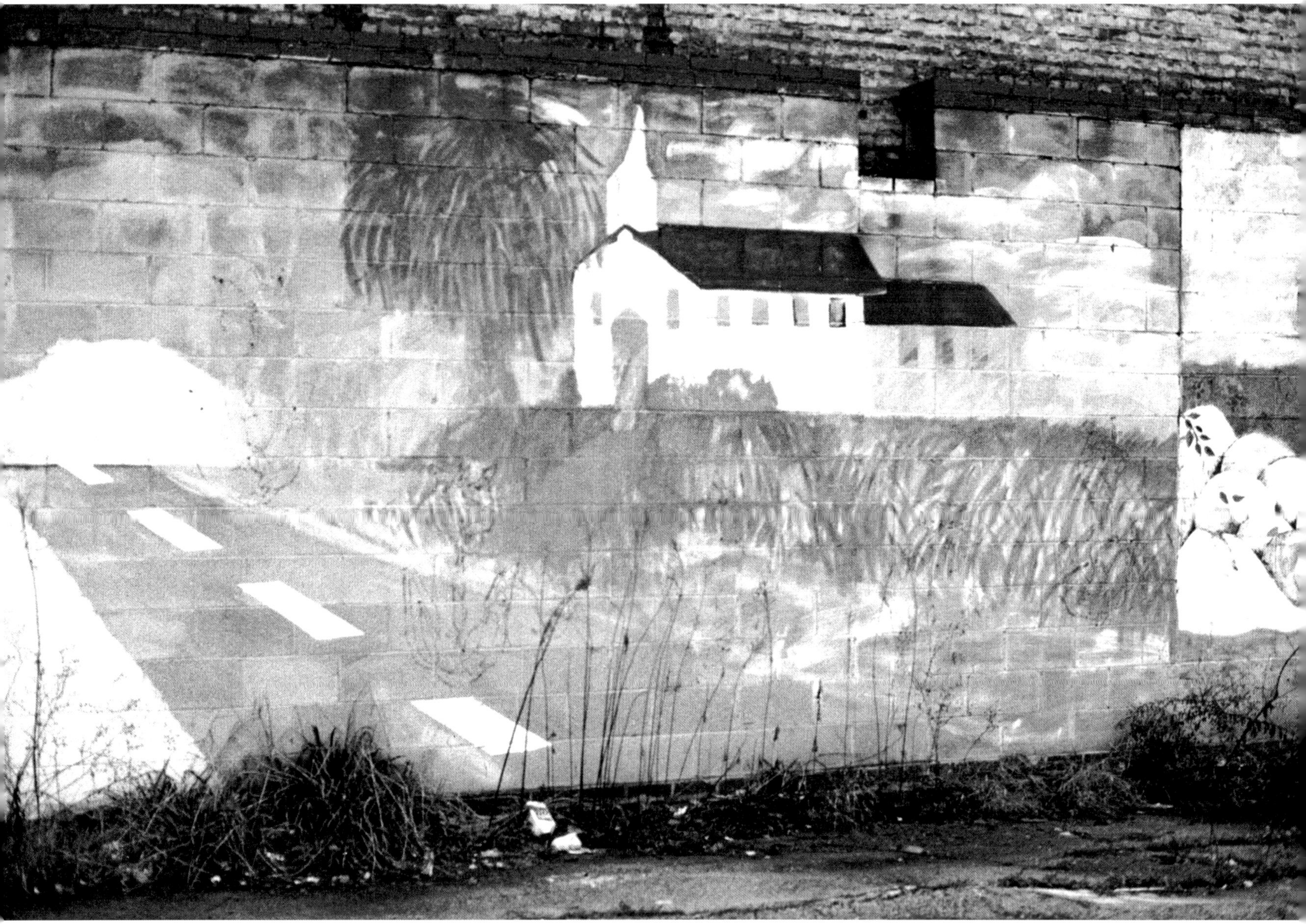

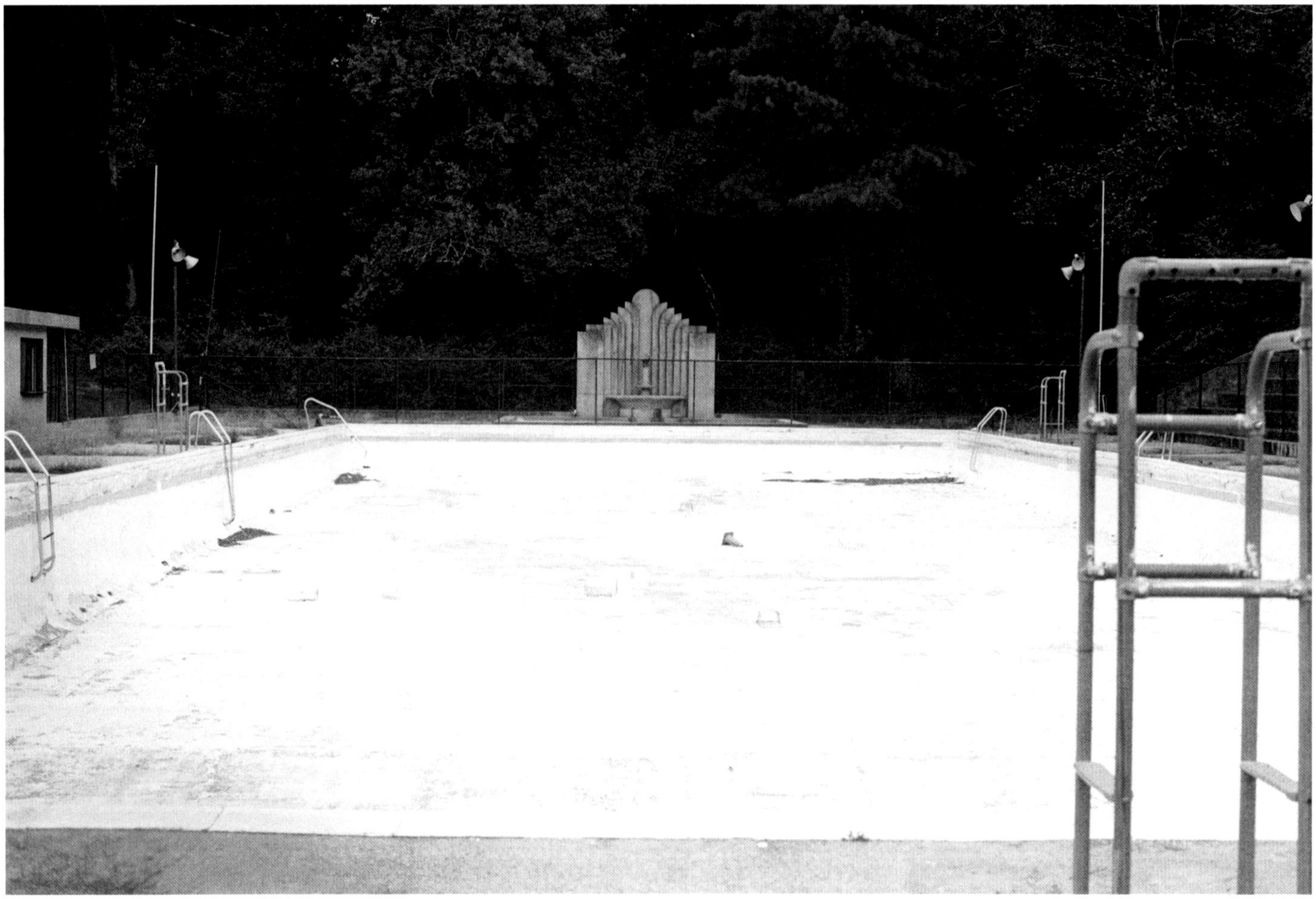

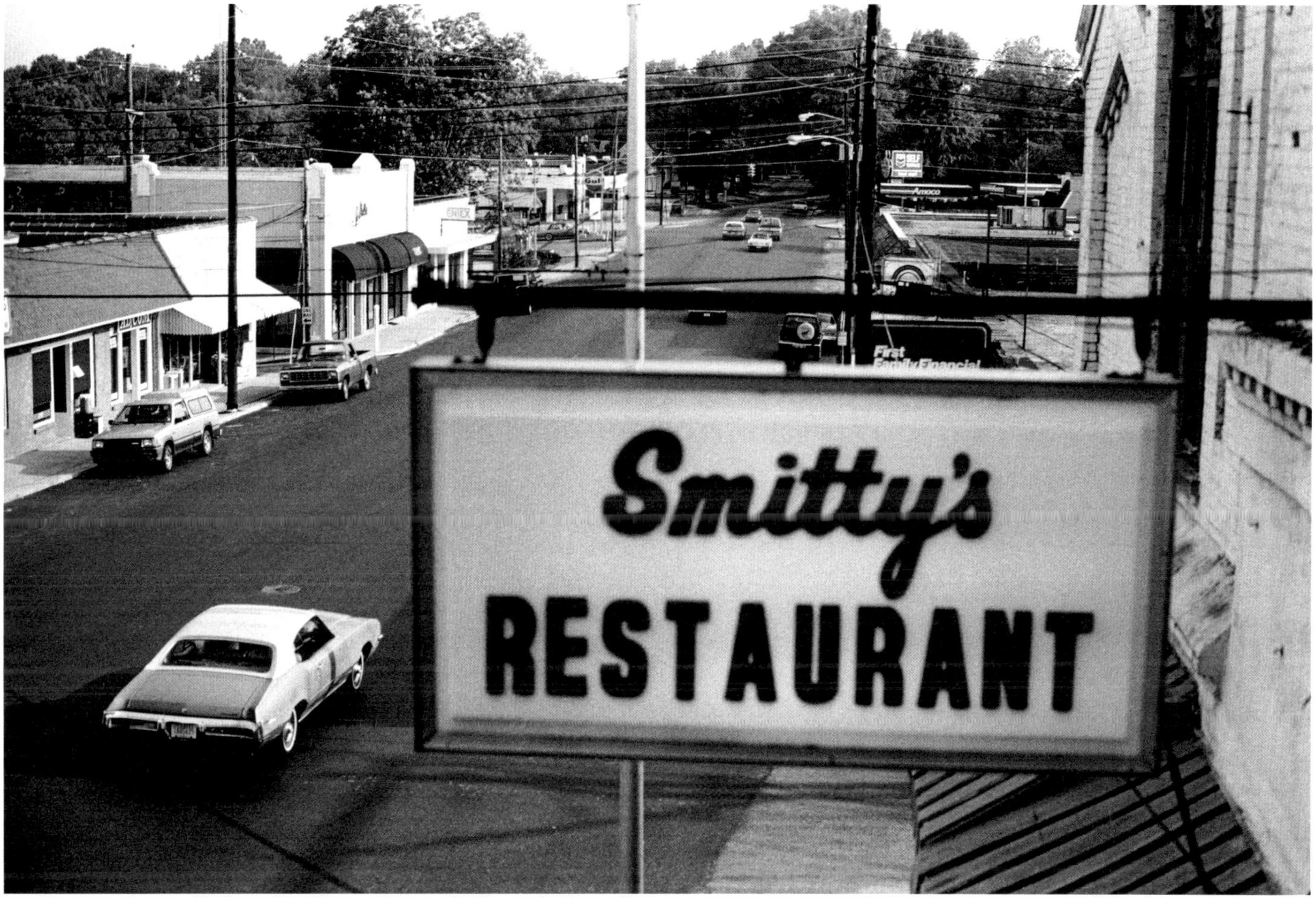
Smitty's
RESTAURANT

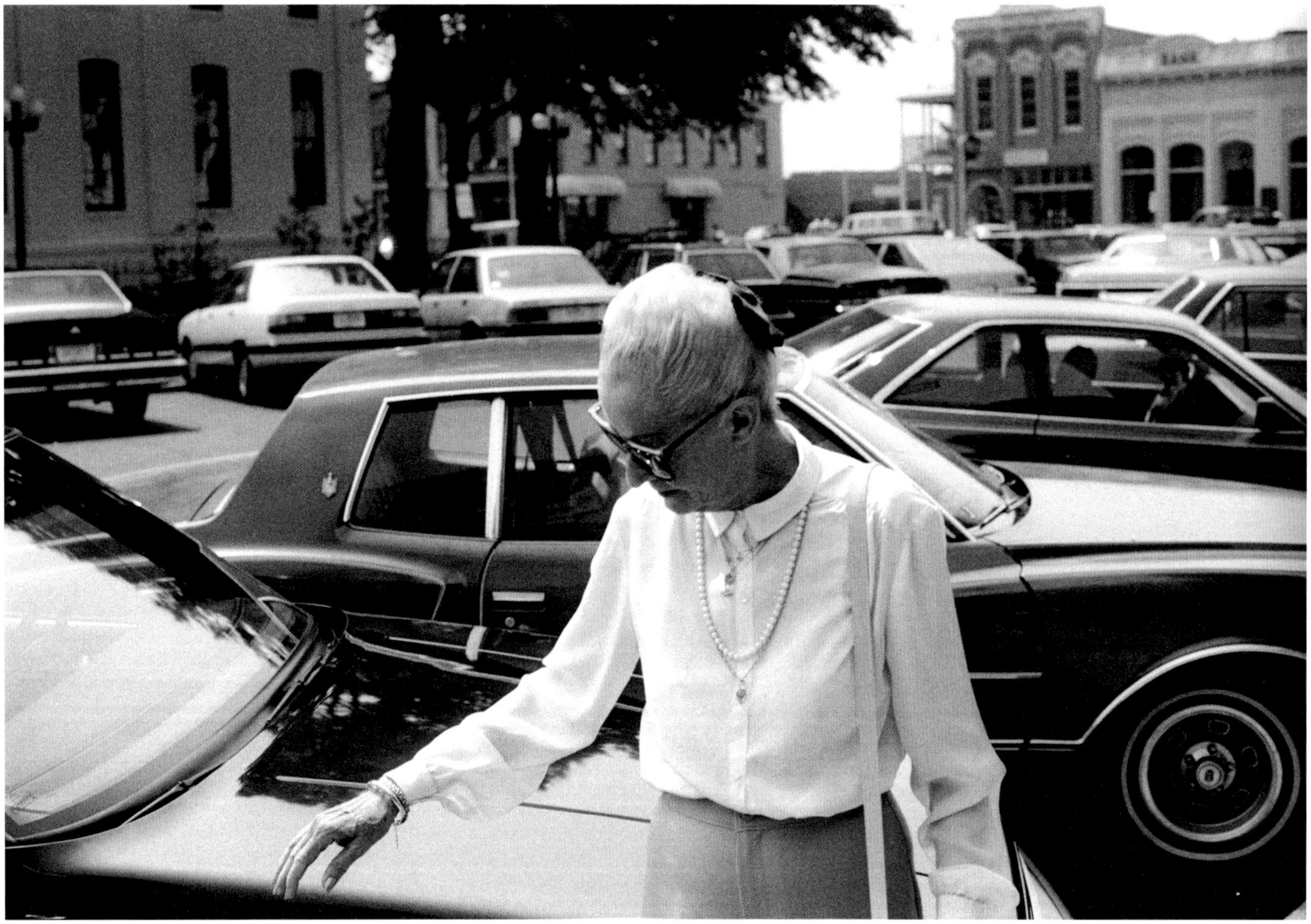

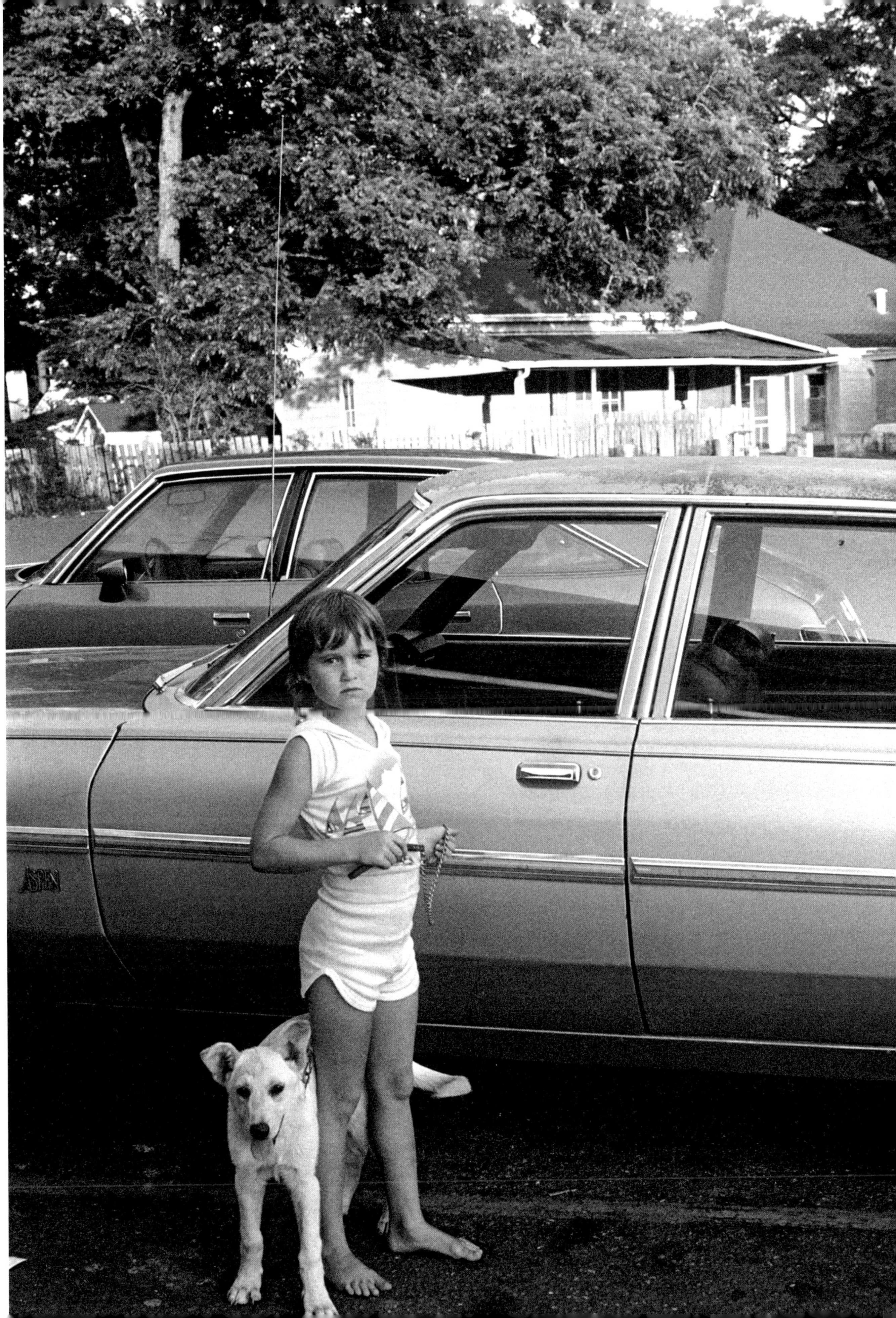

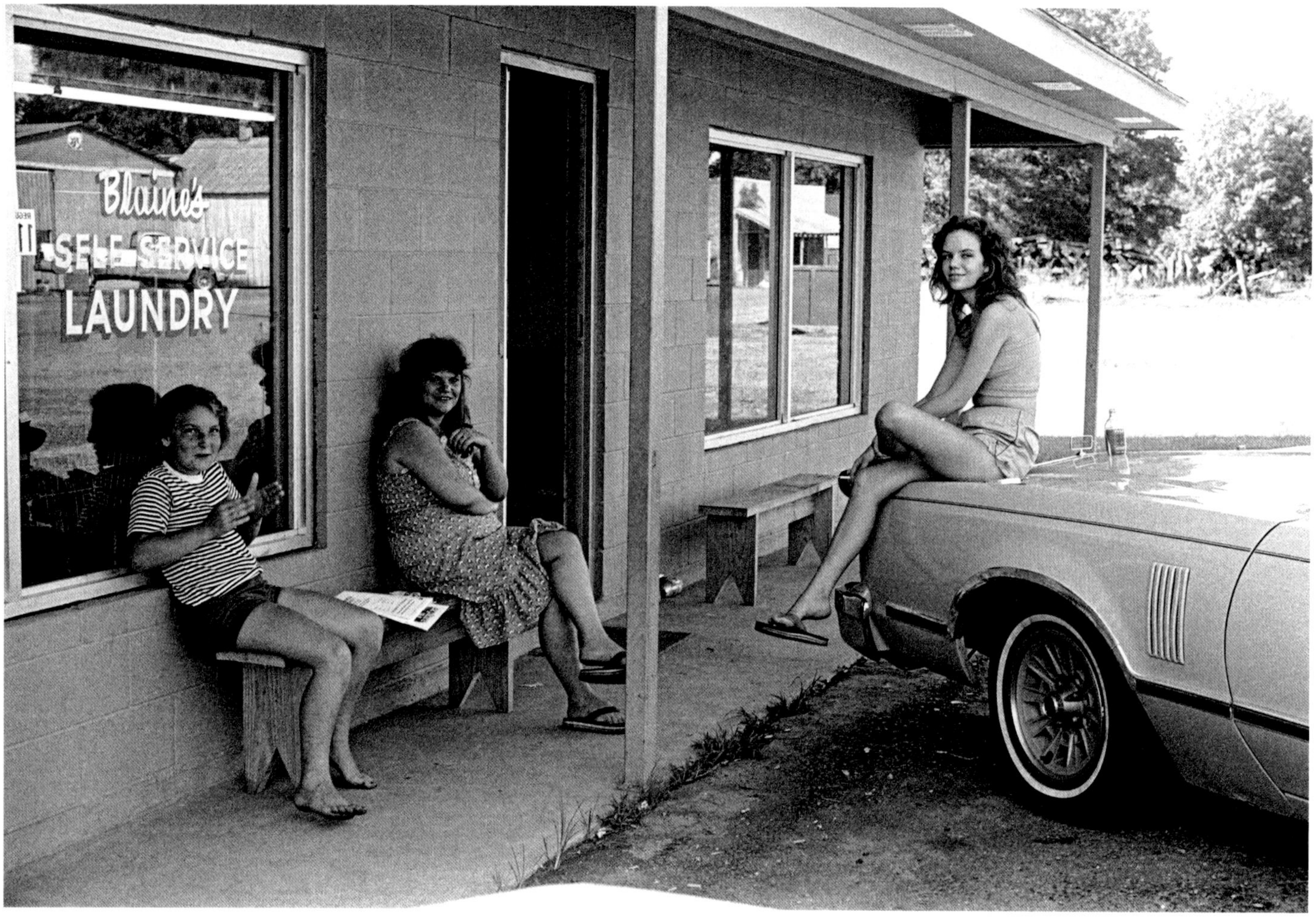
Blaine's
SELF SERVICE
LAUNDRY

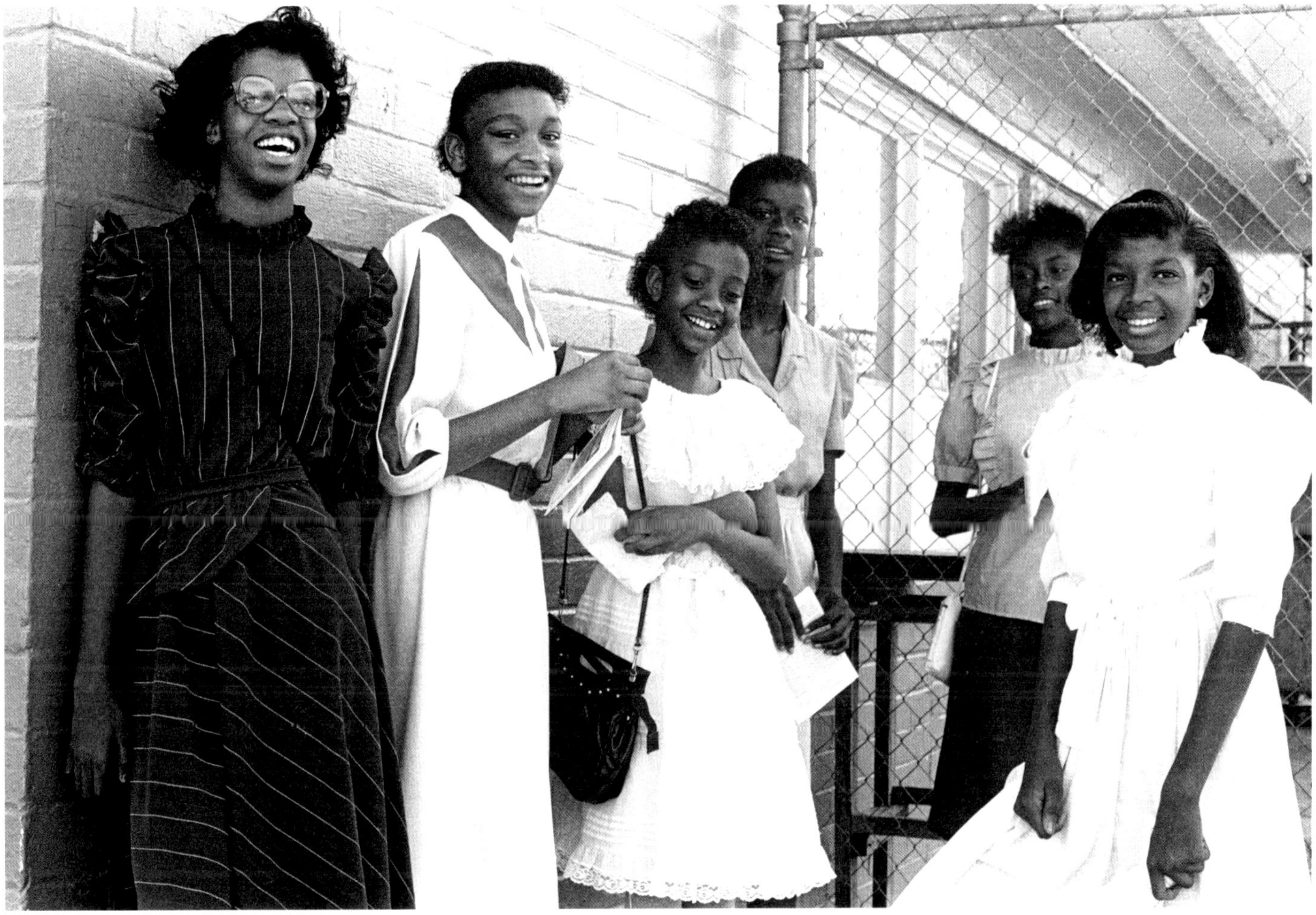

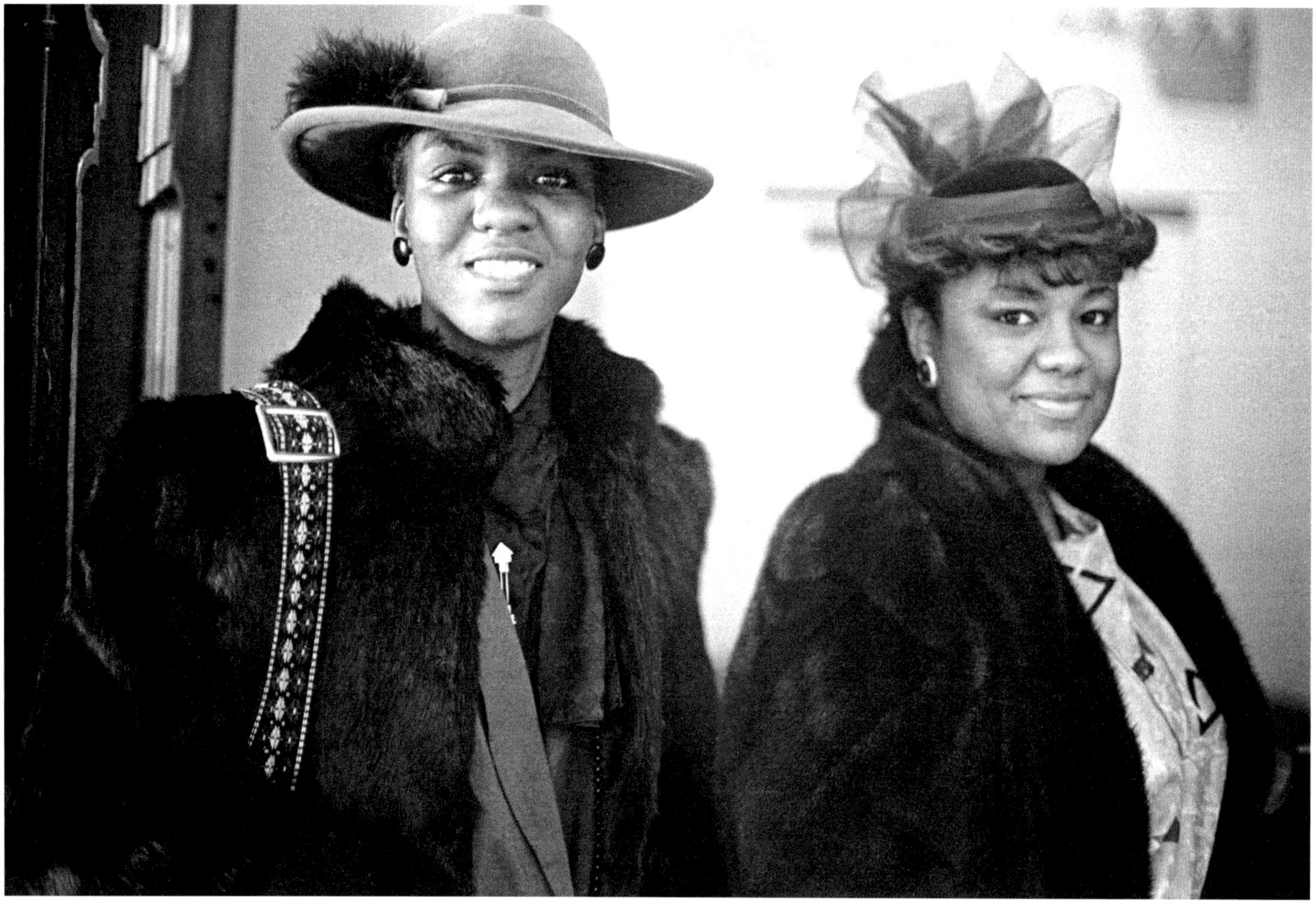

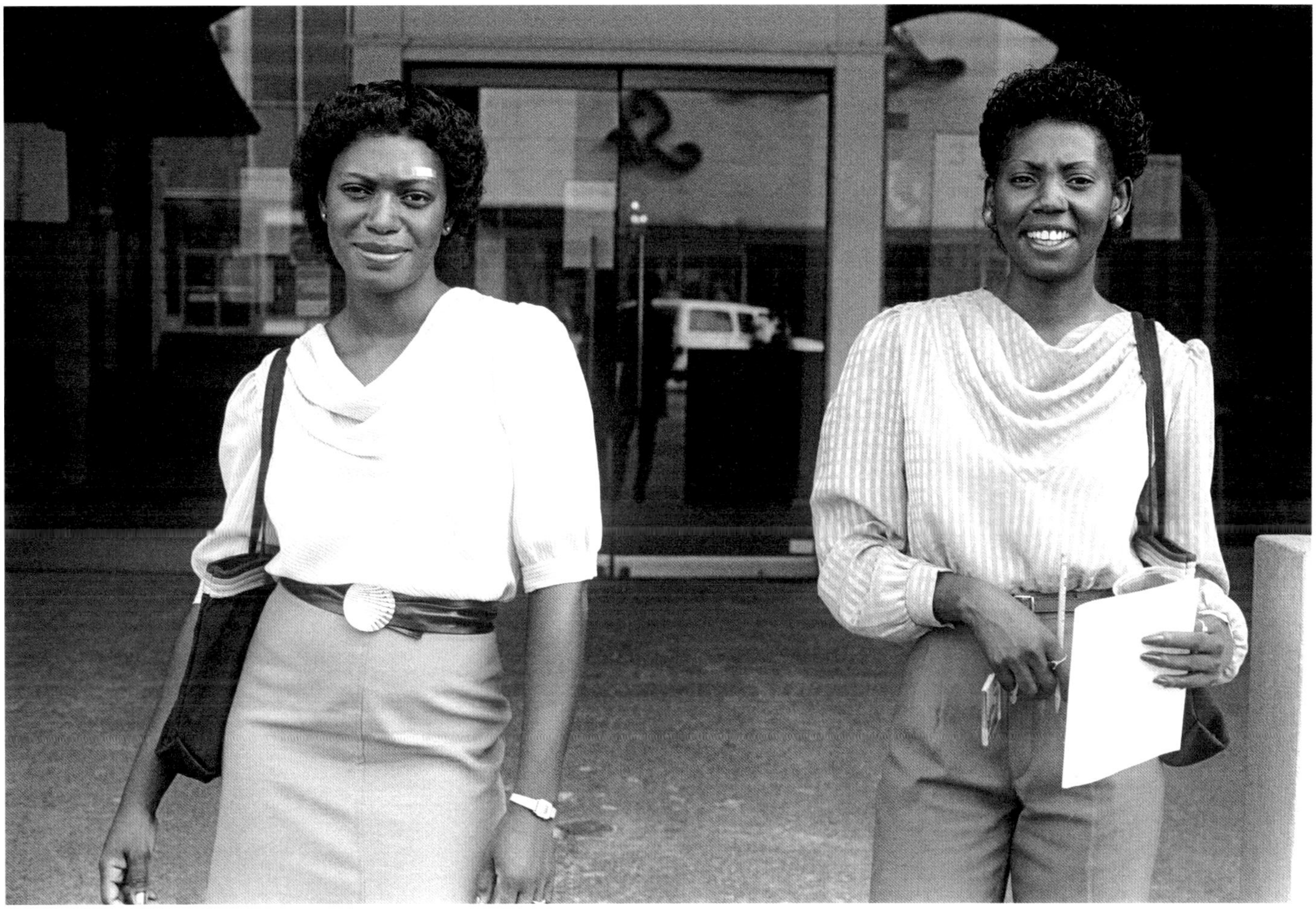

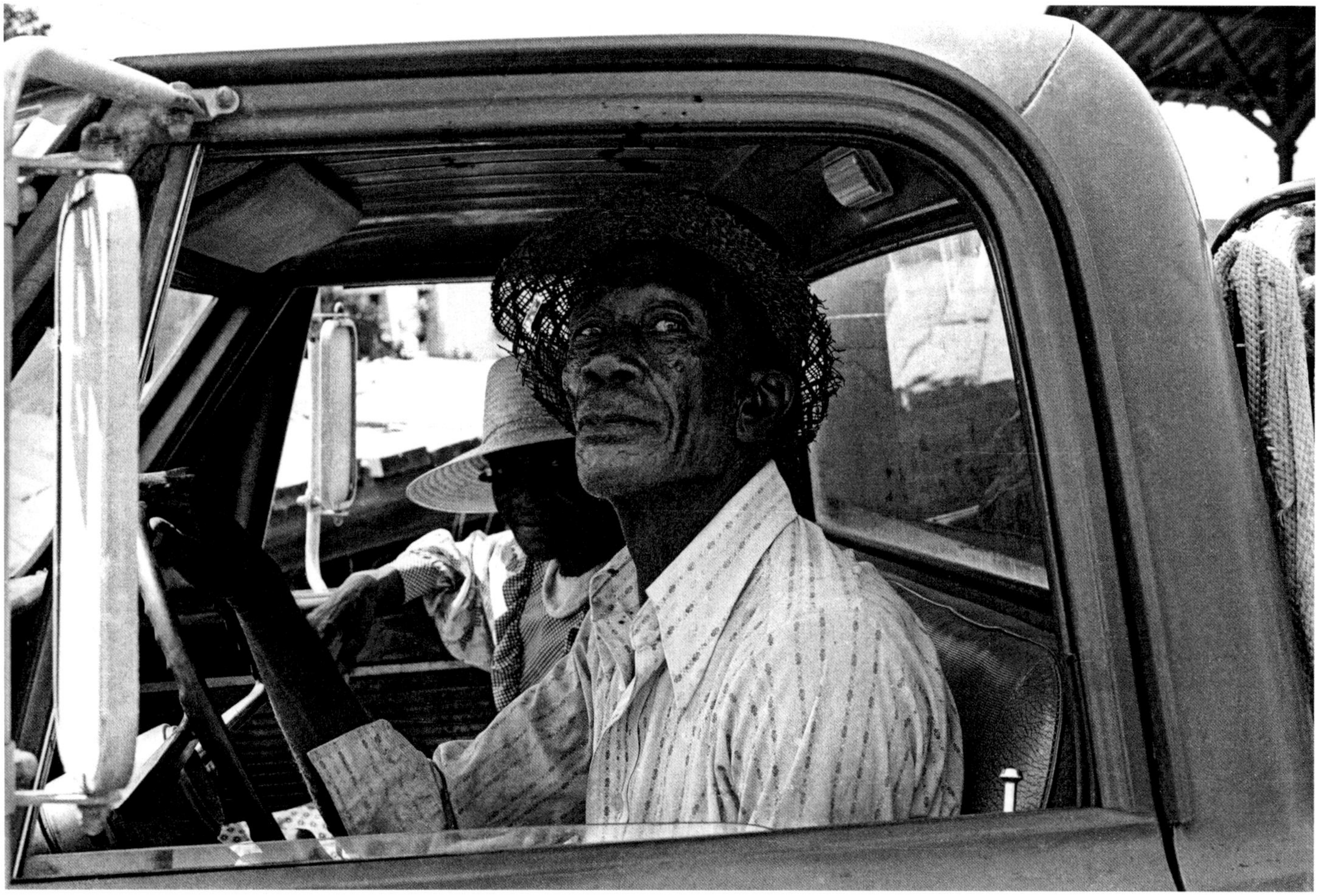

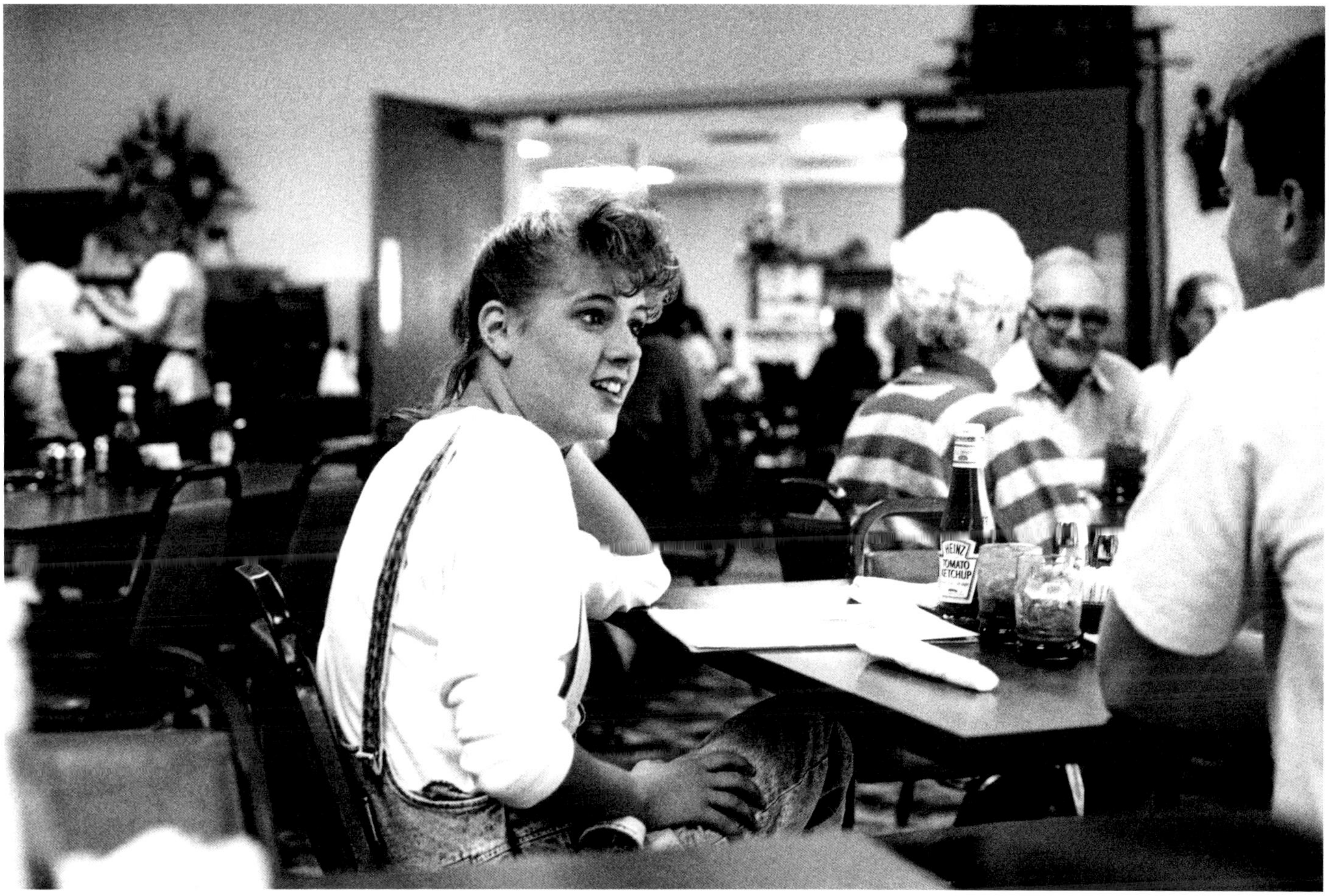
HEINZ
TOMATO

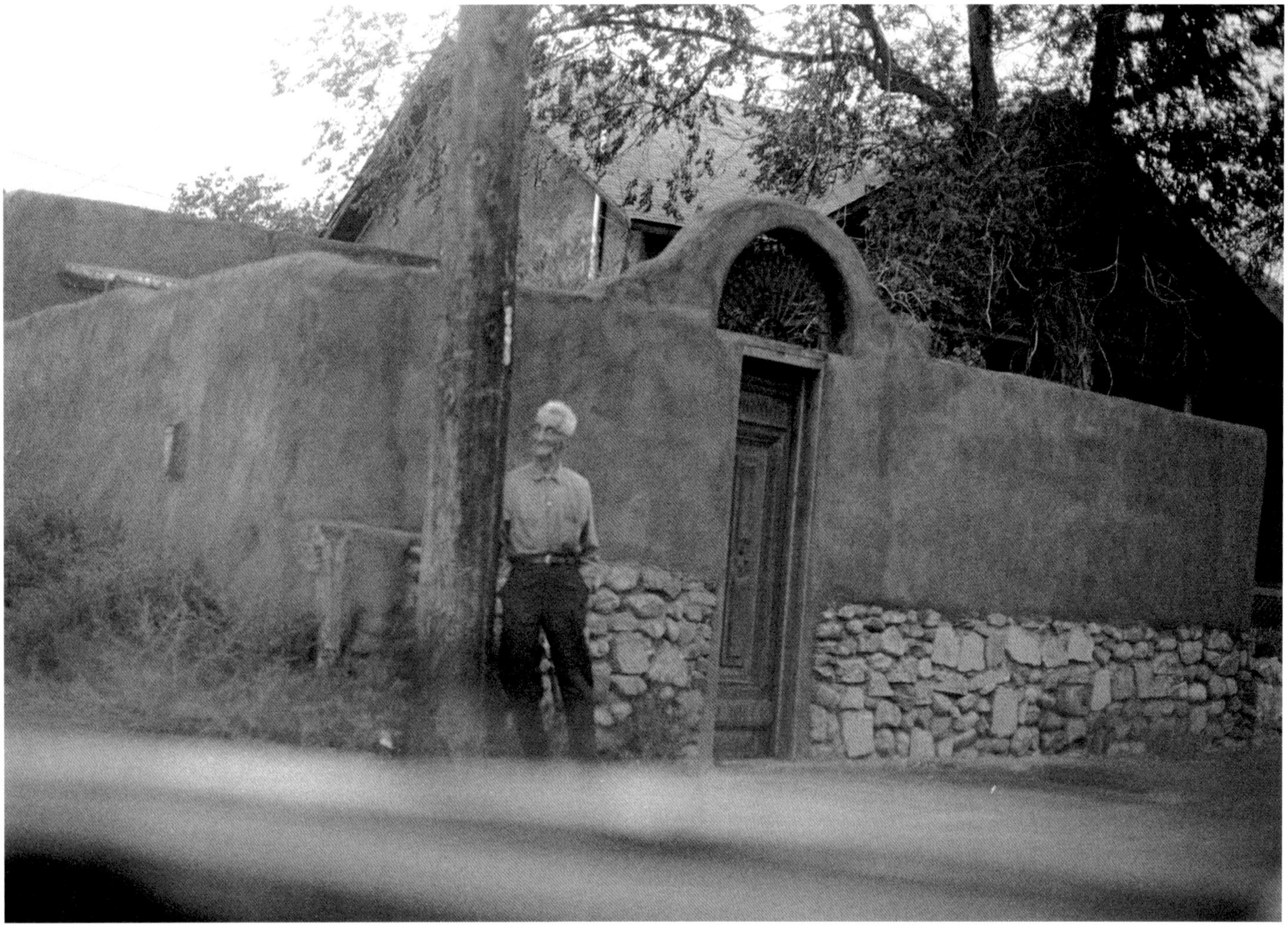

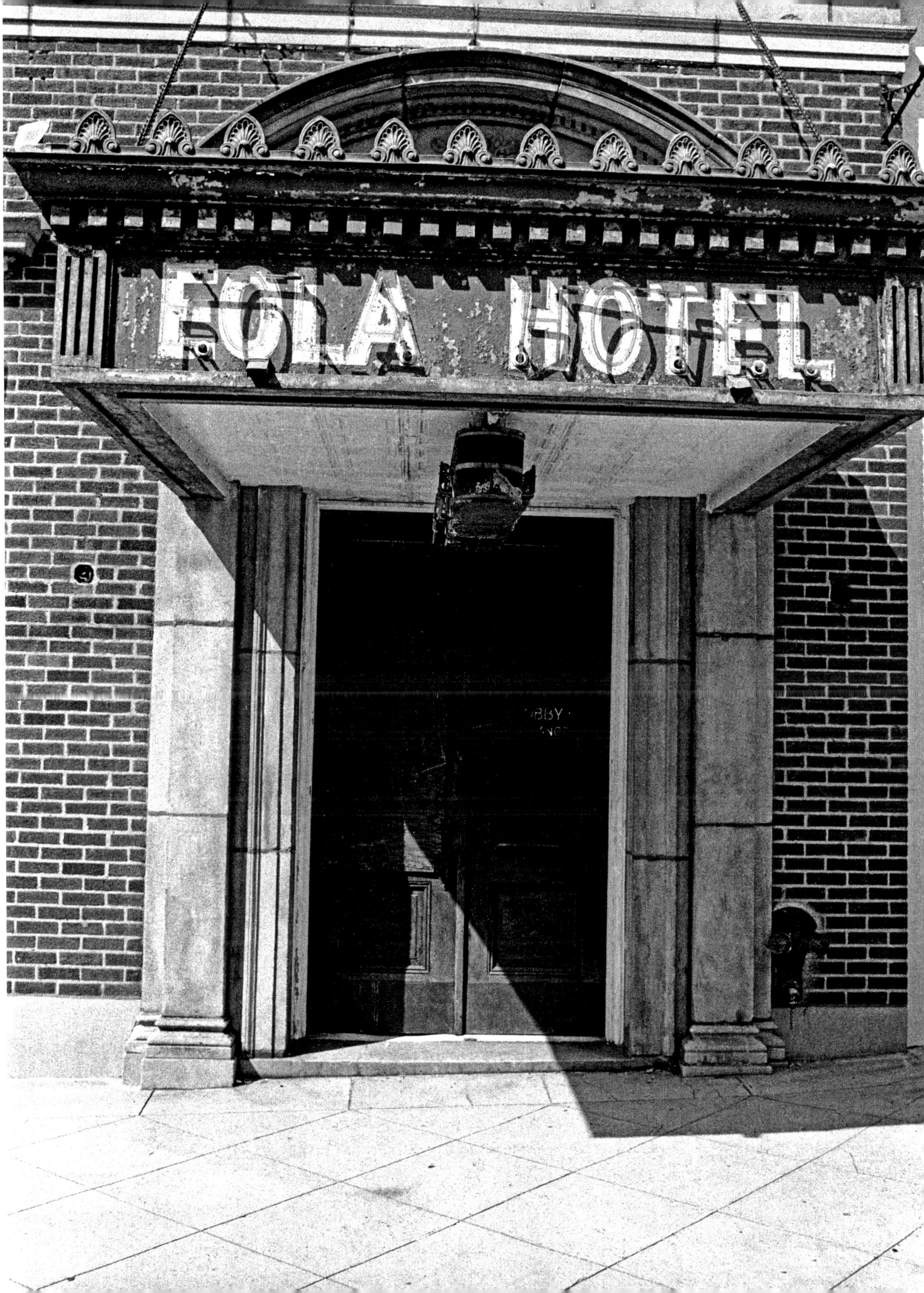
EOLA HOTEL

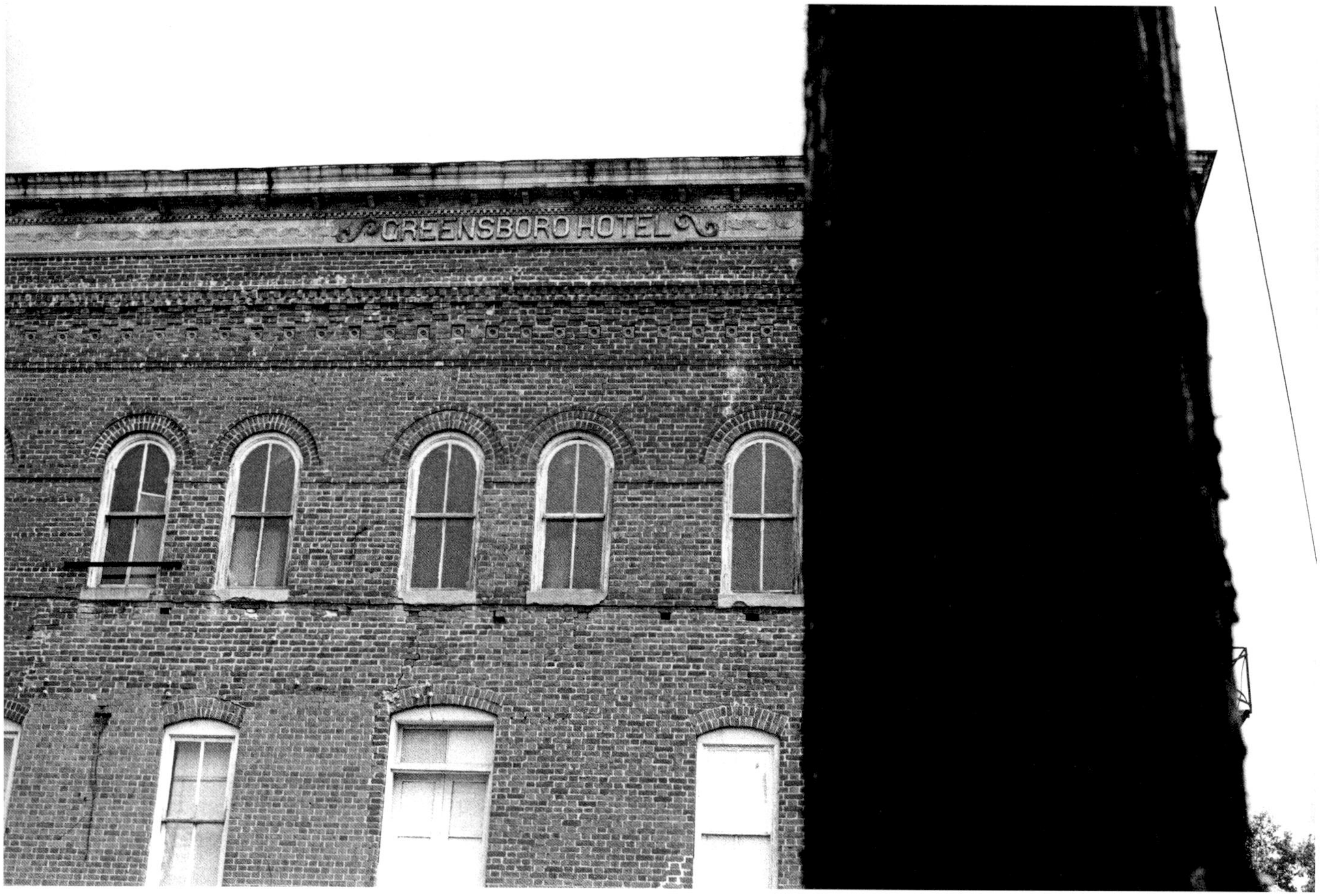
GREENSBORO HOTEL

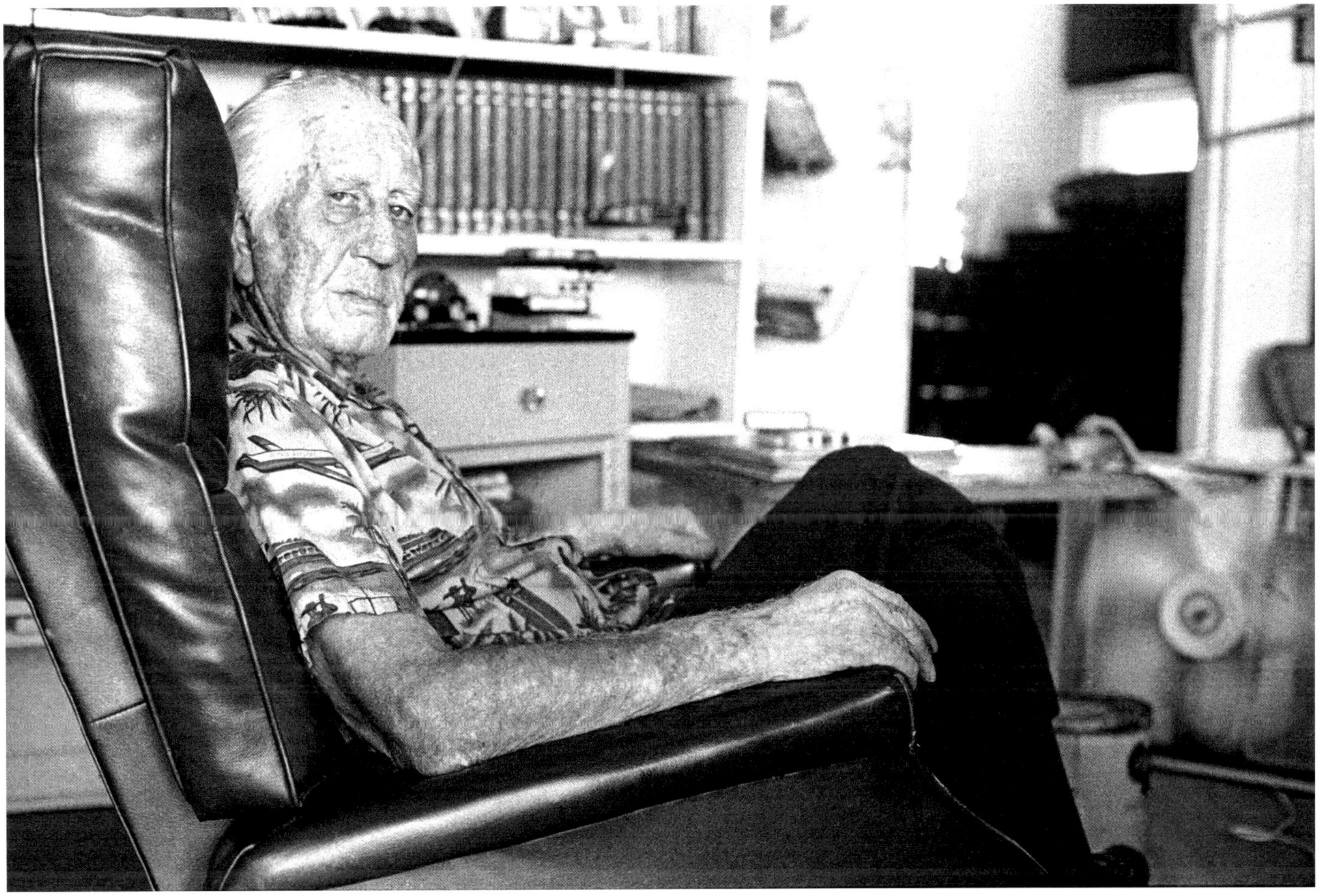

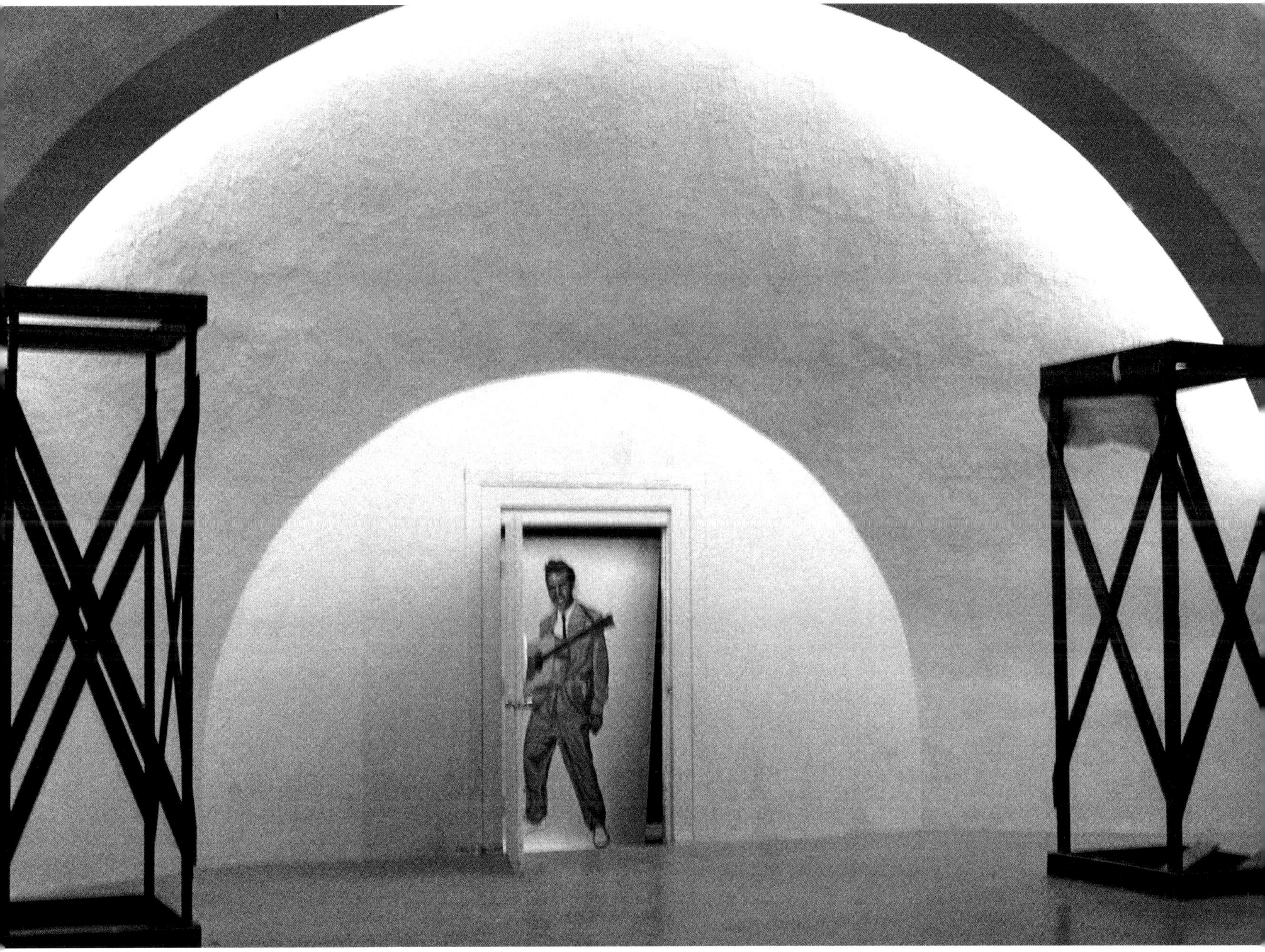

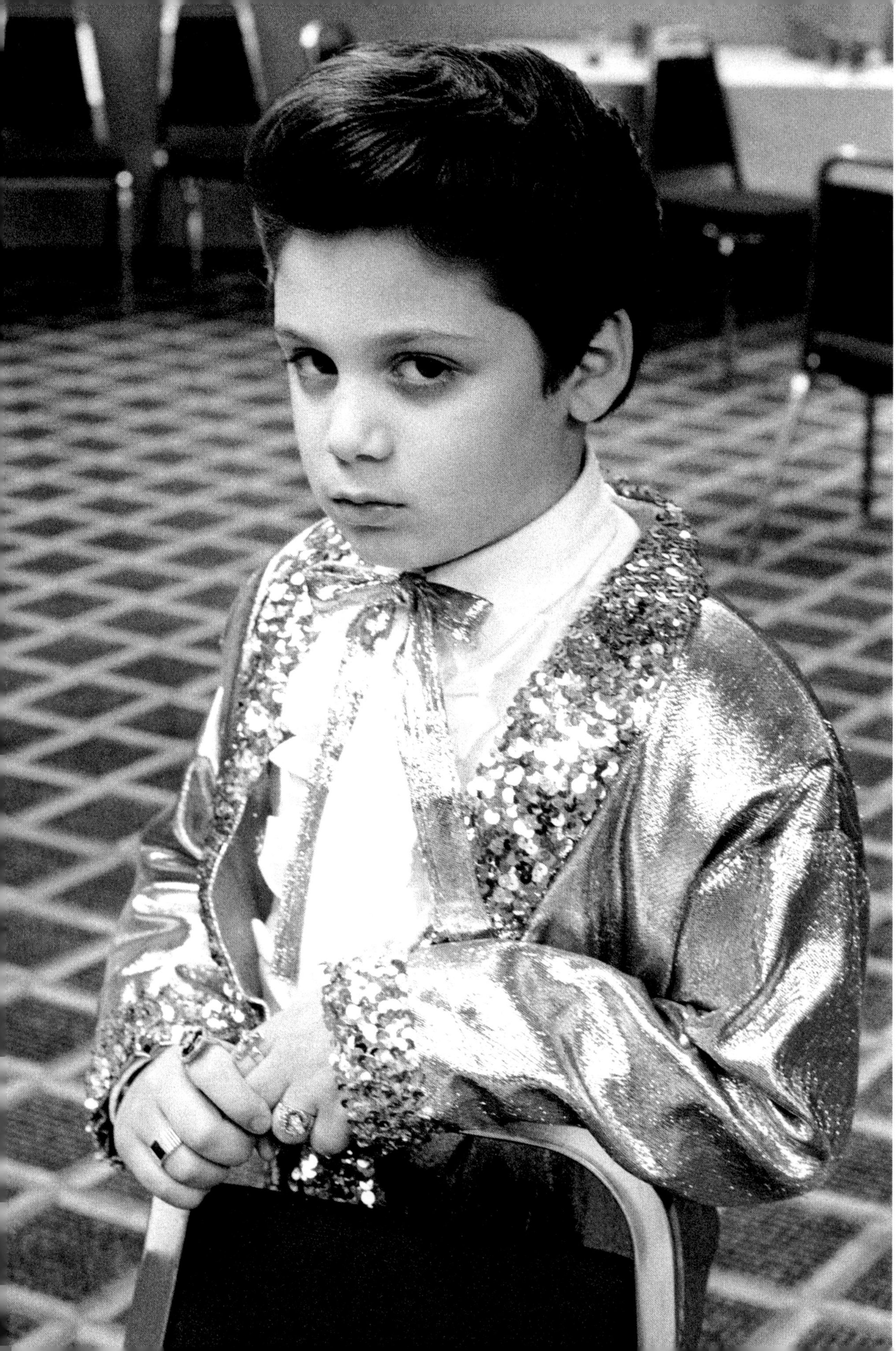

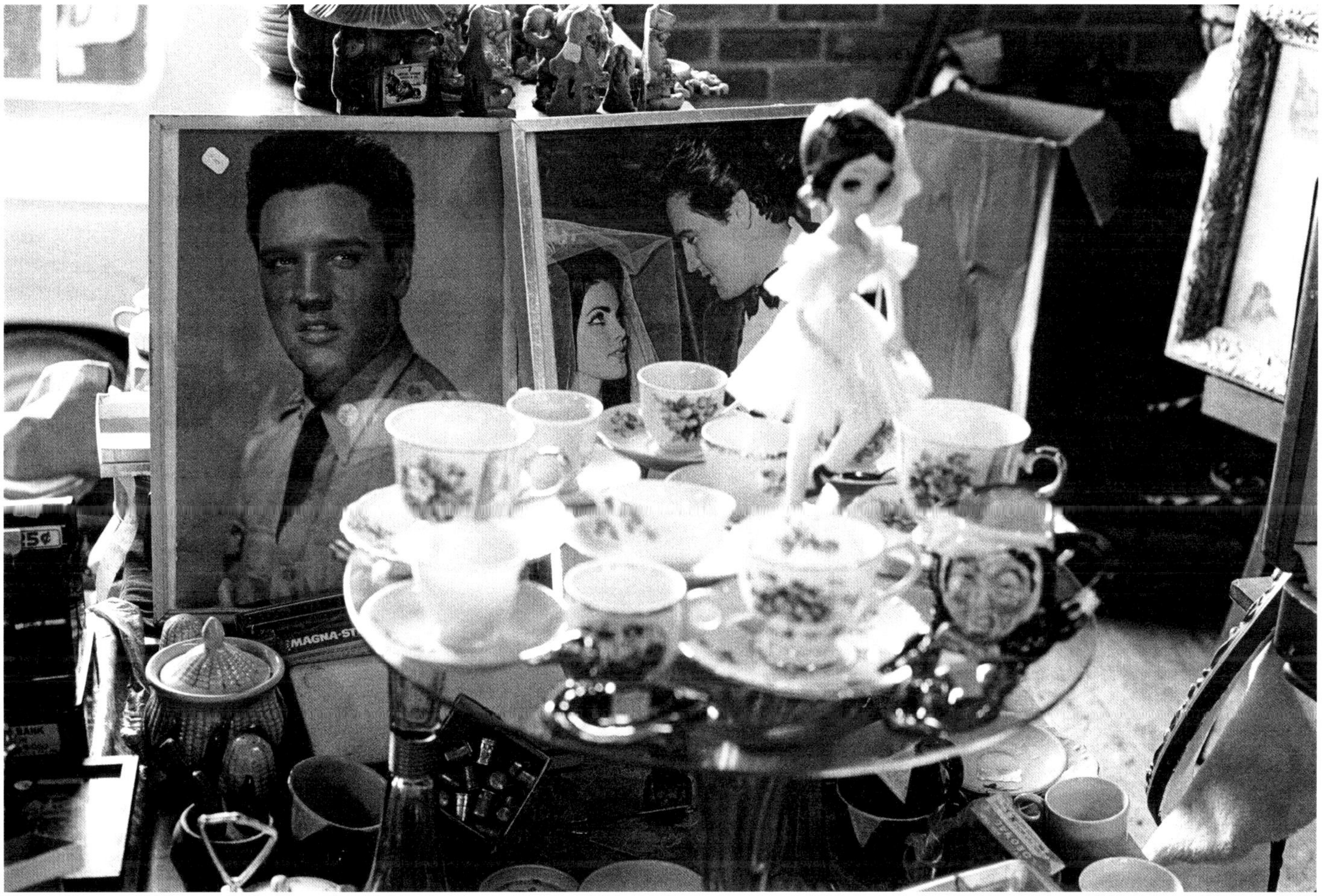

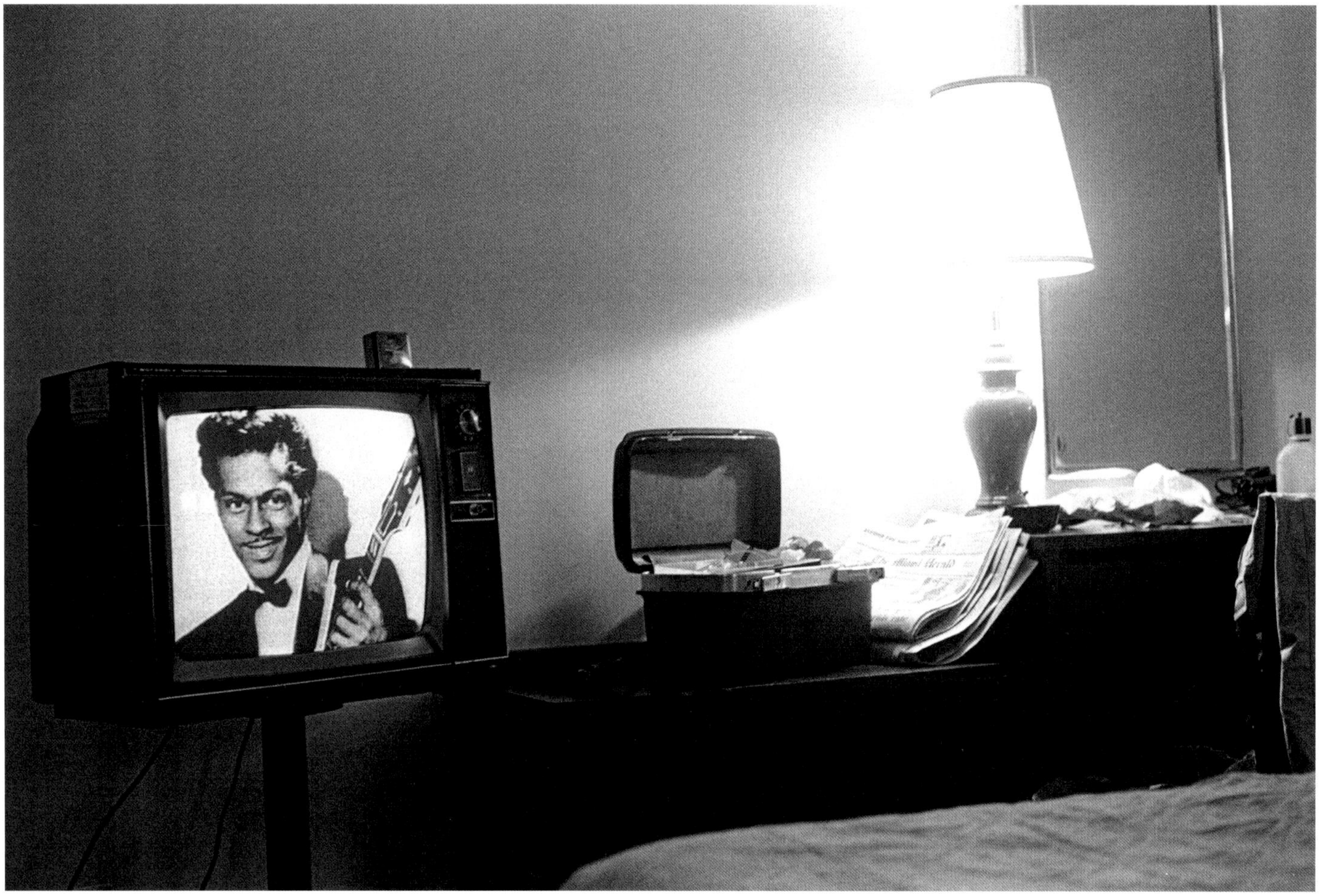

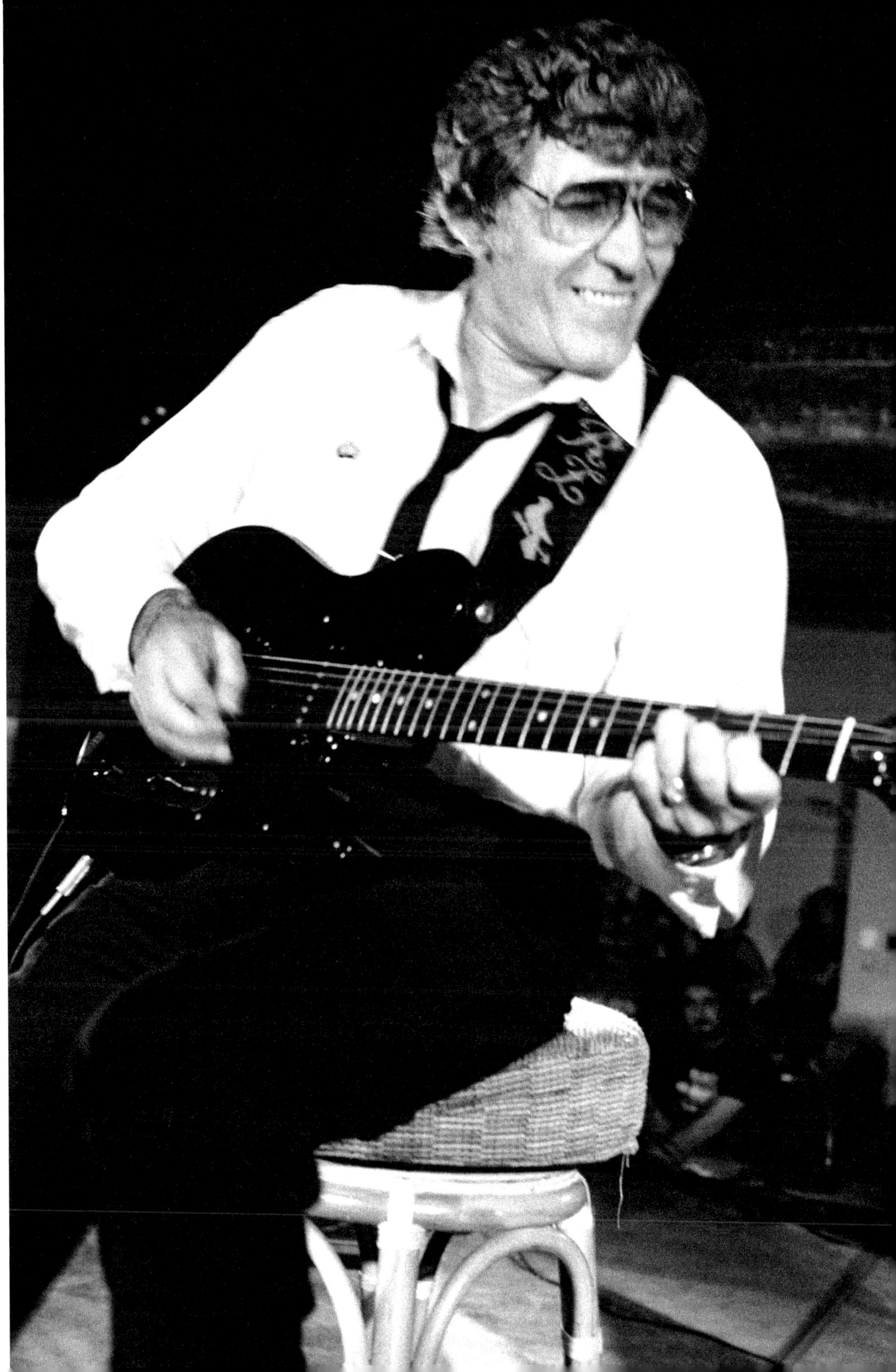

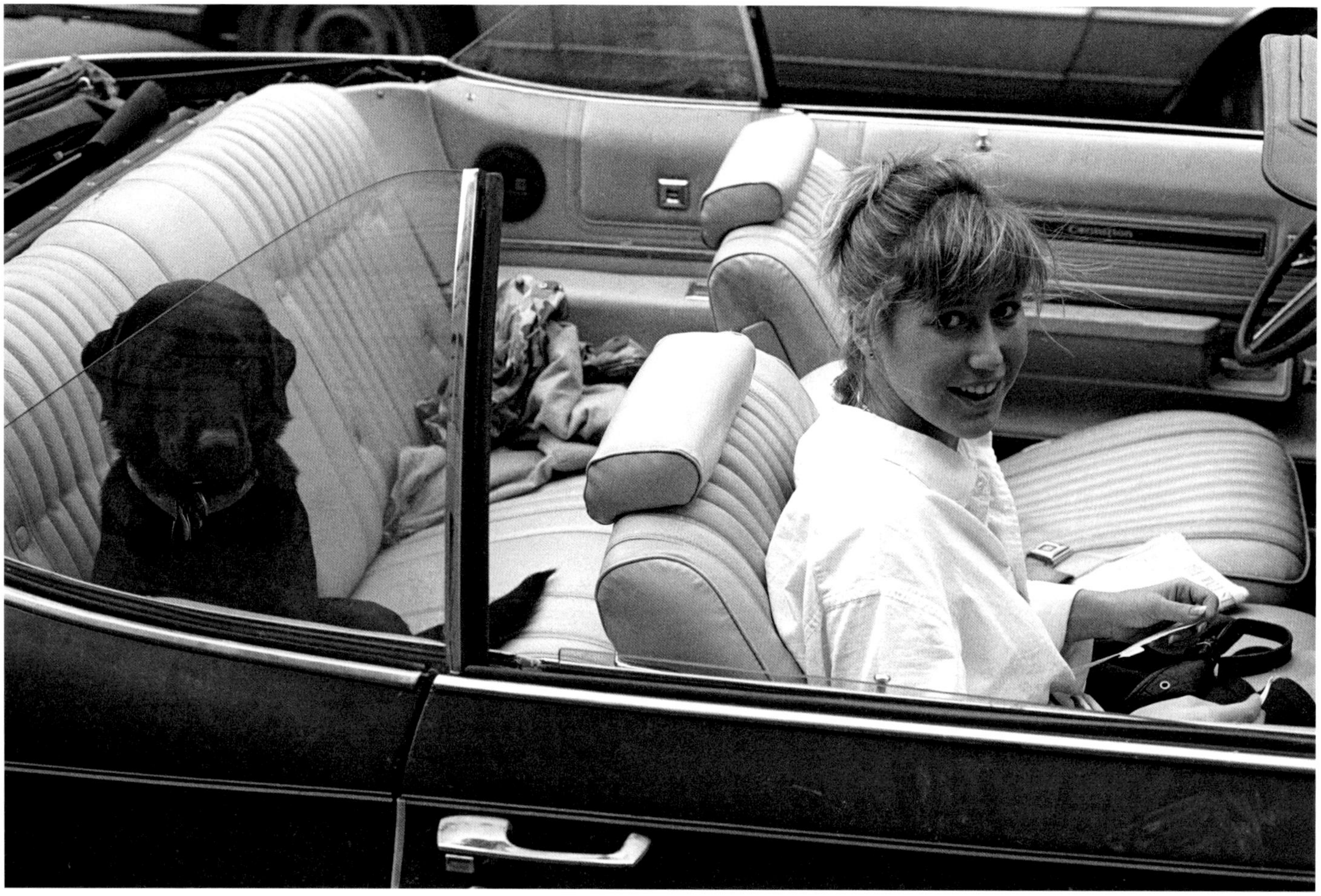

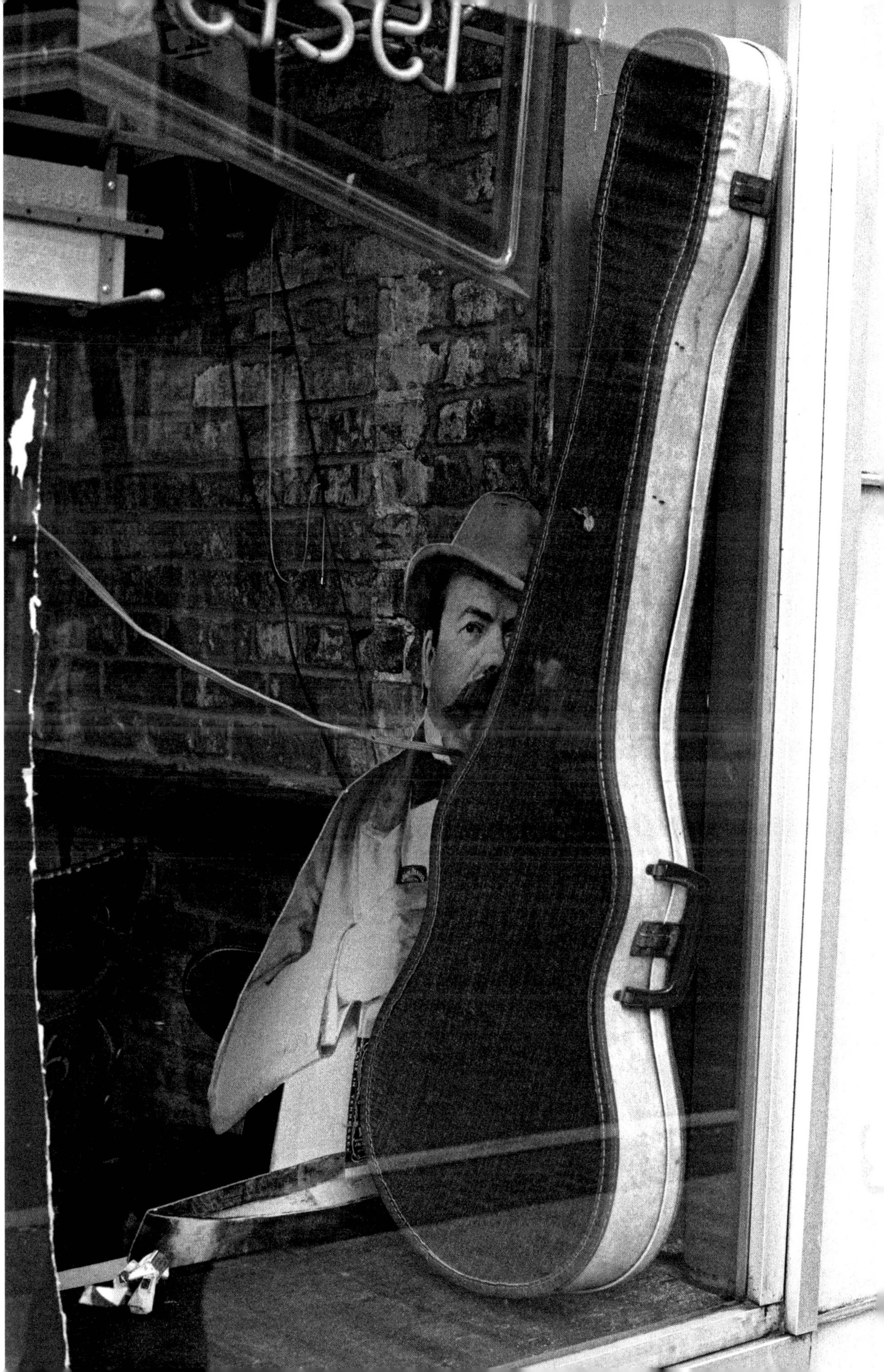

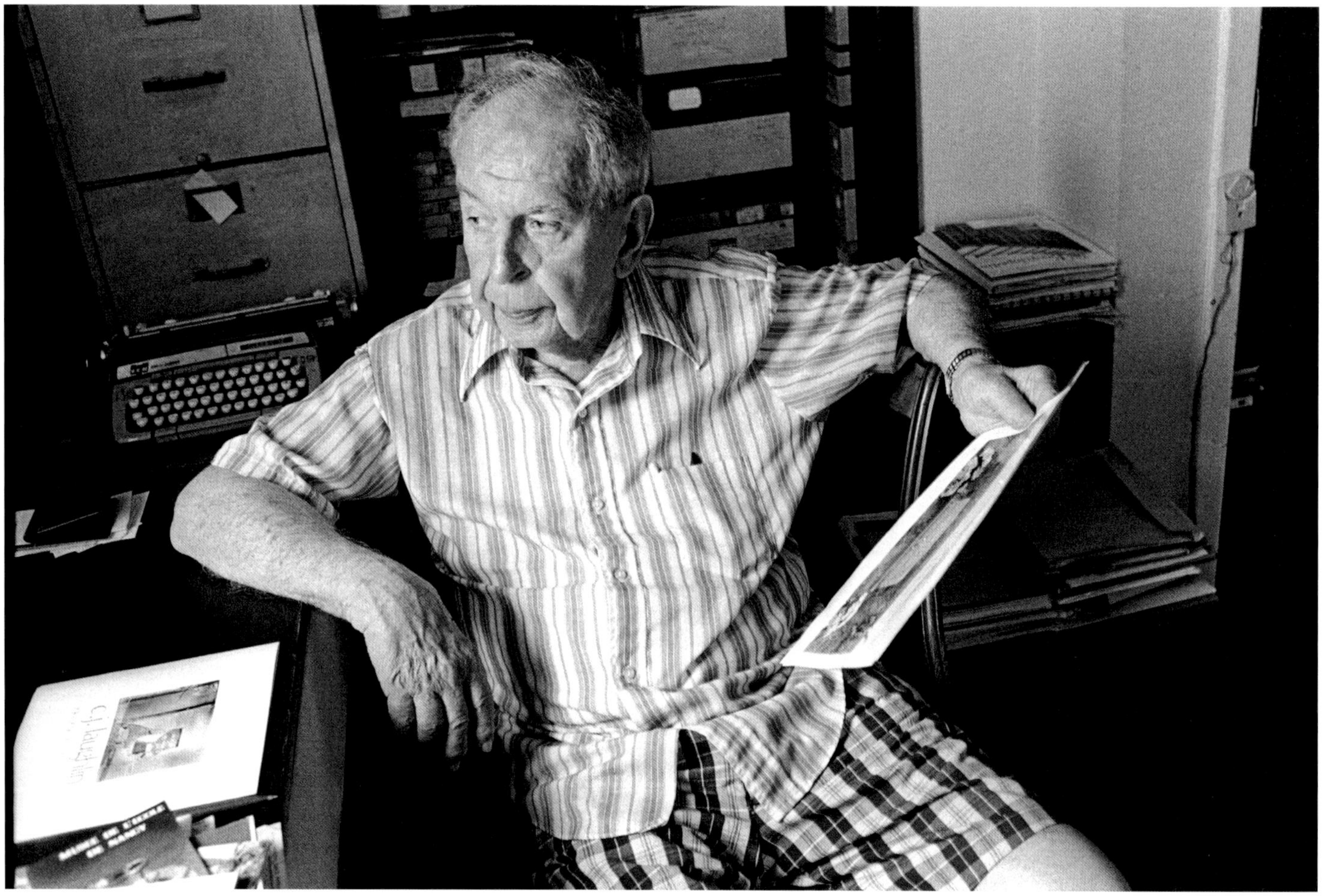

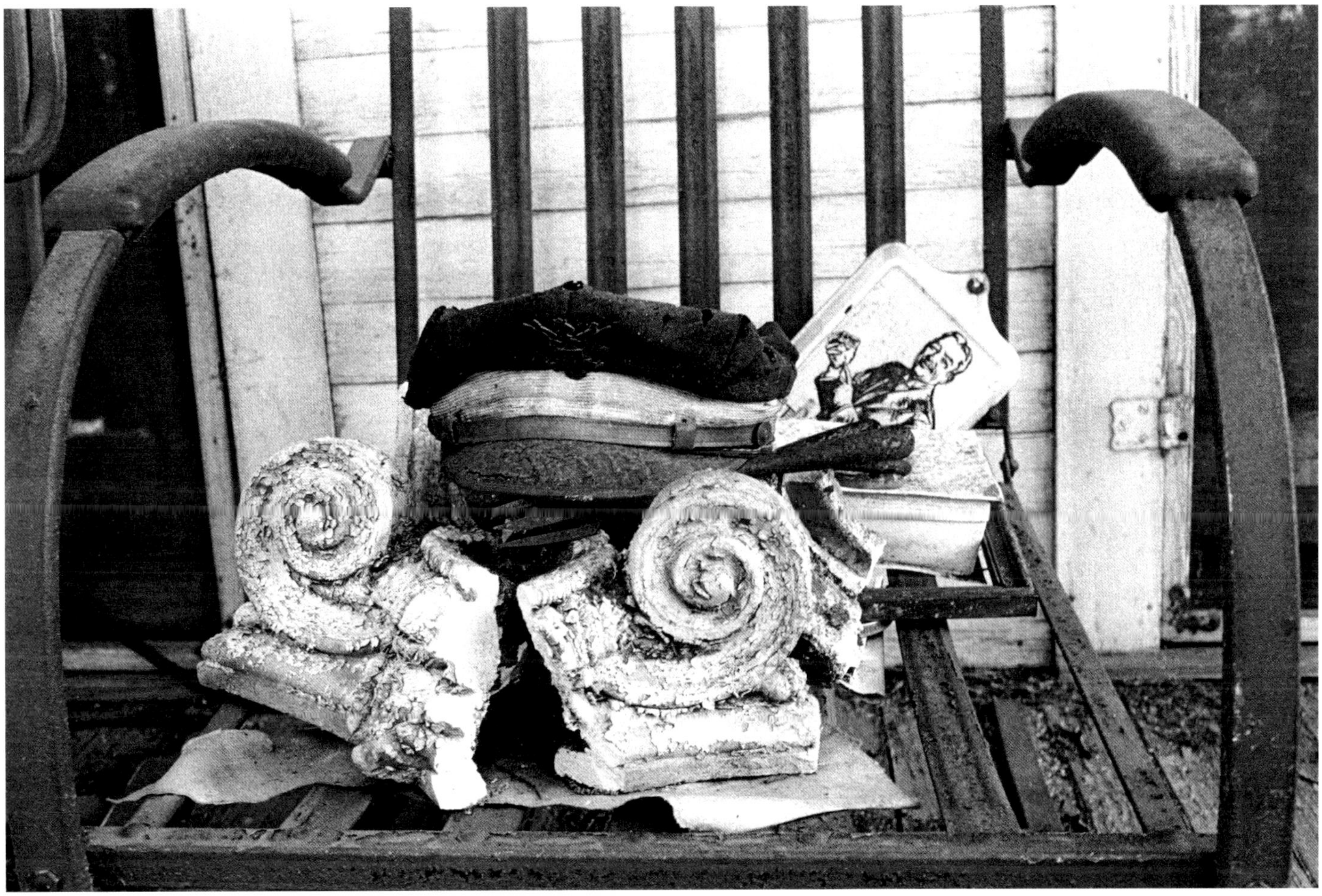

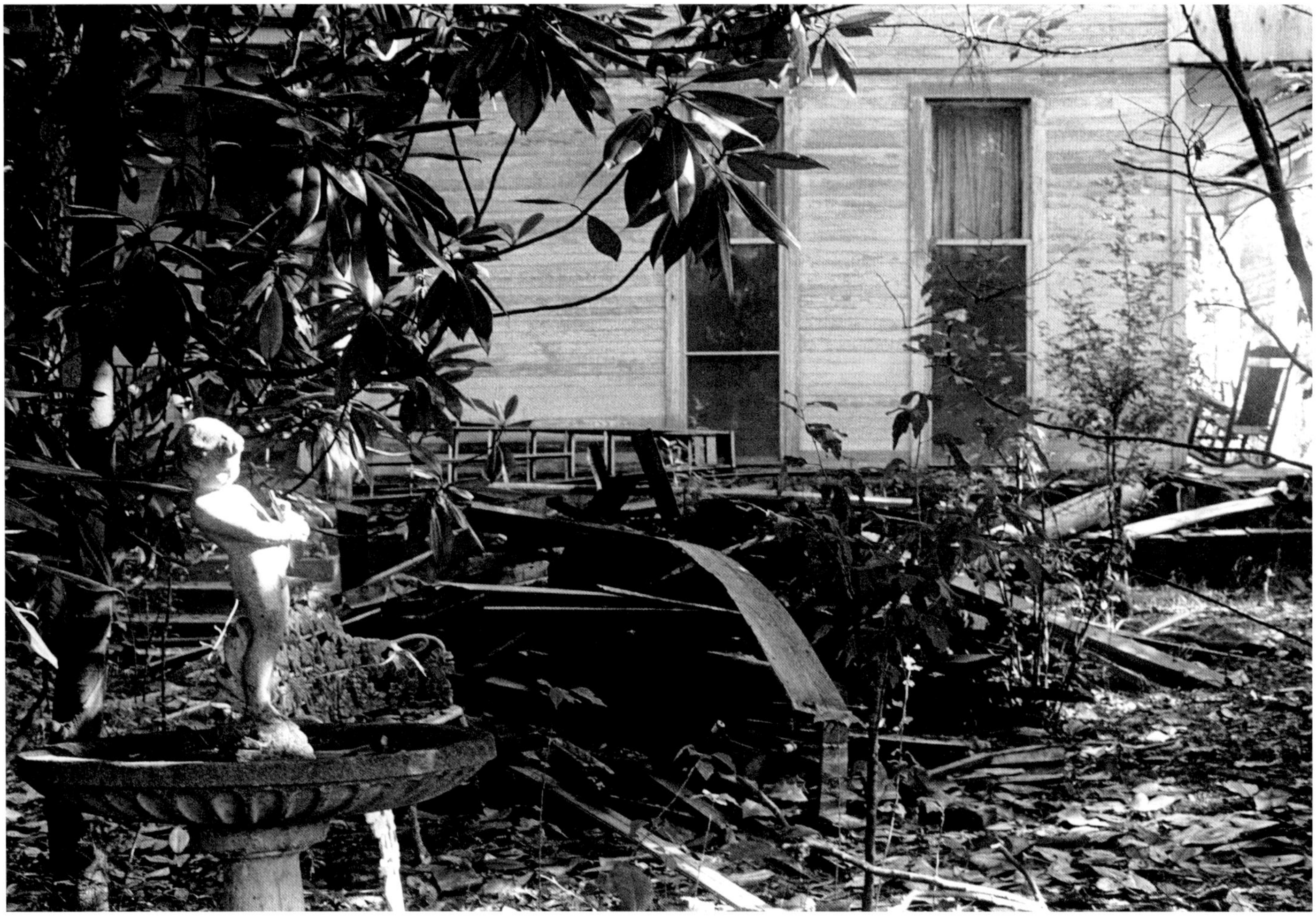

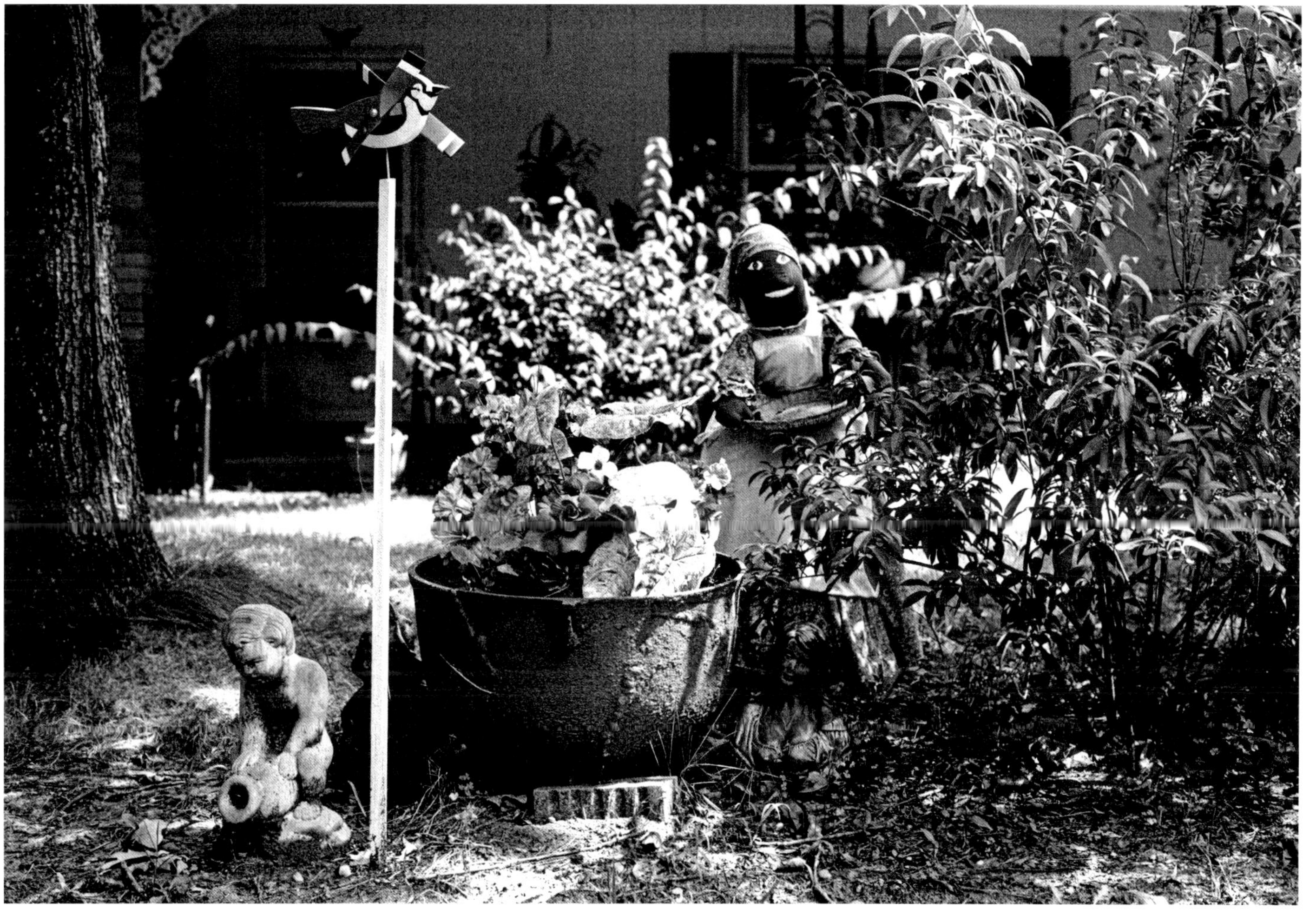

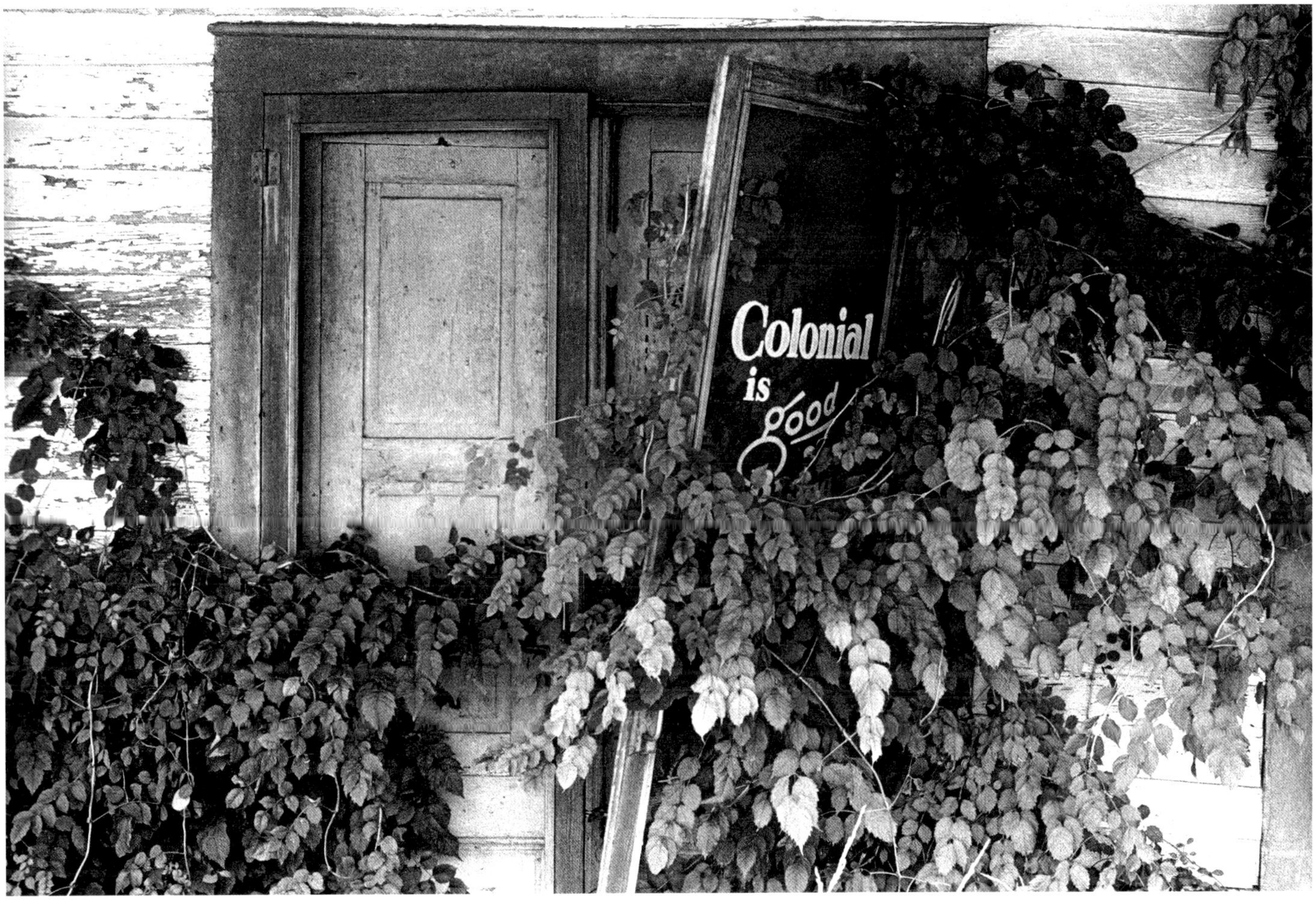
Colonial
is
good

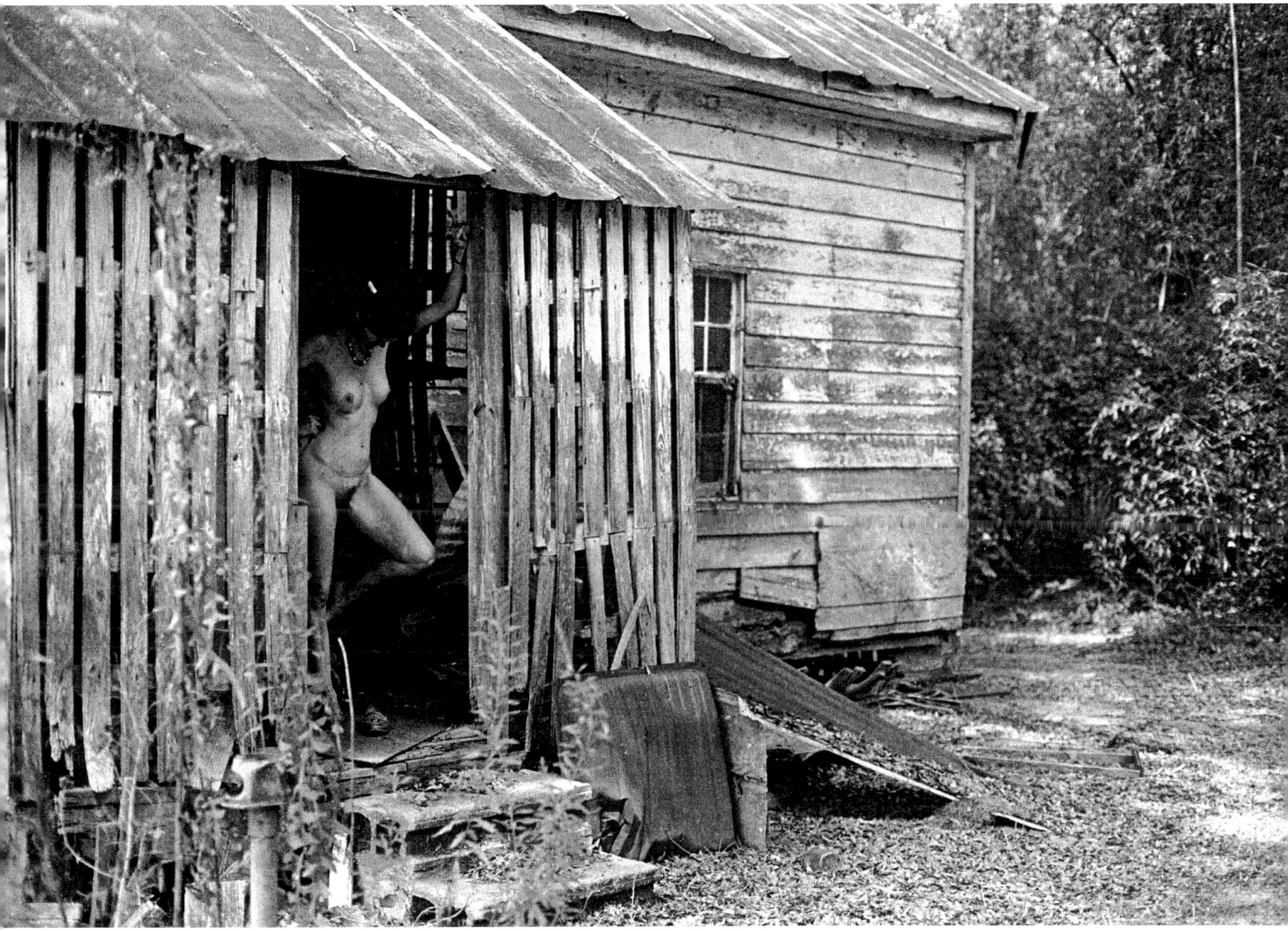

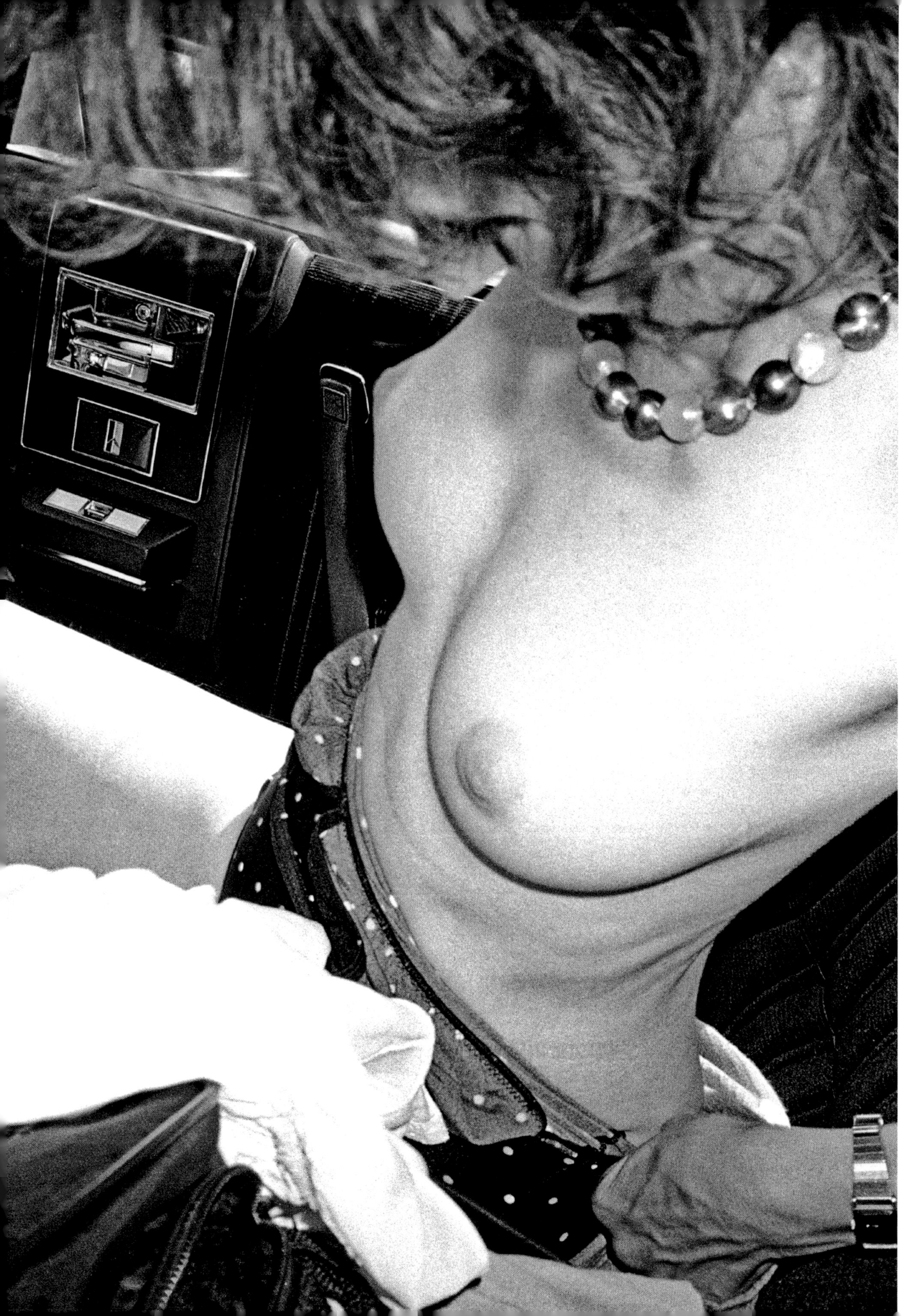

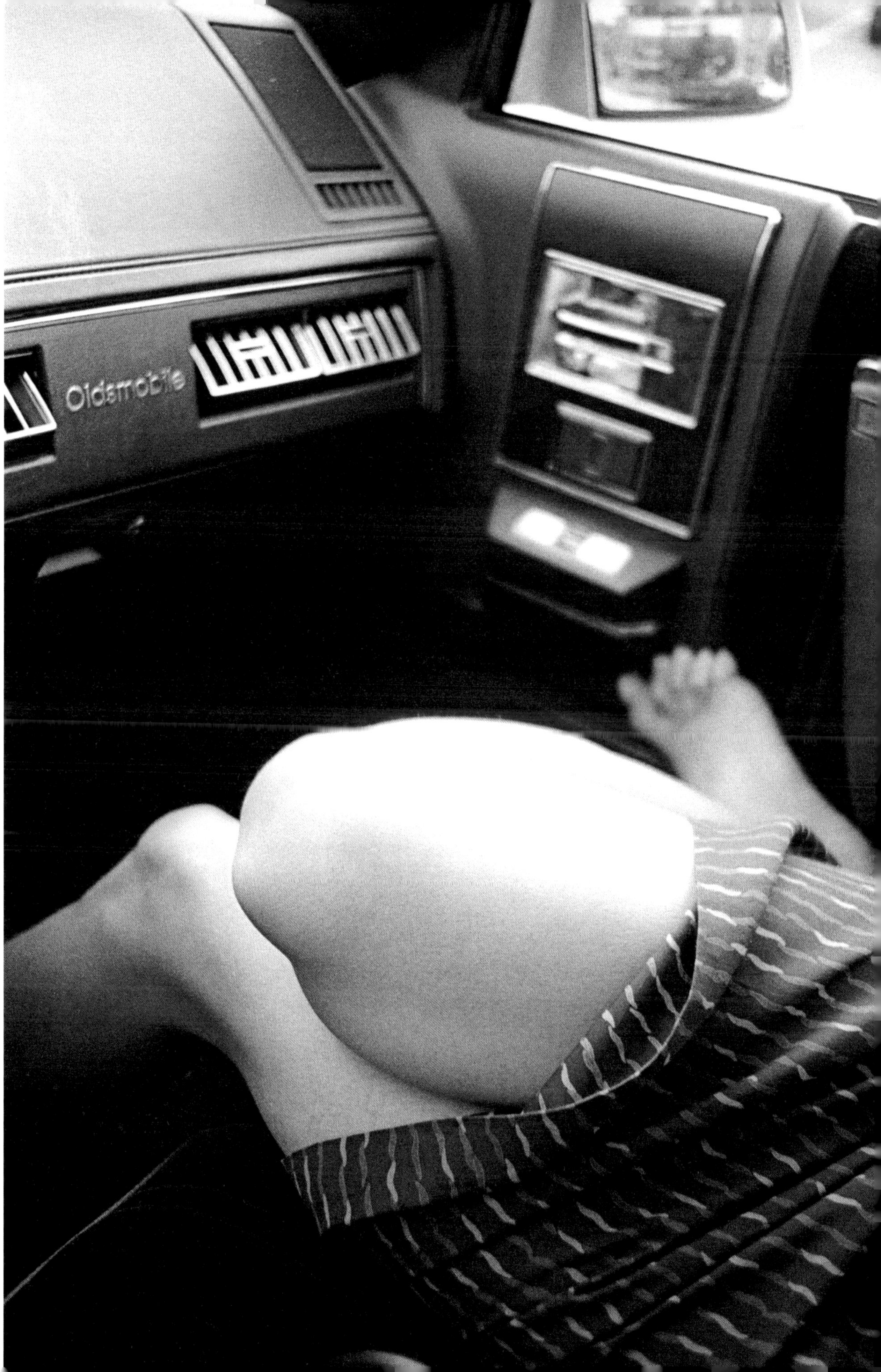
Oldsmobile

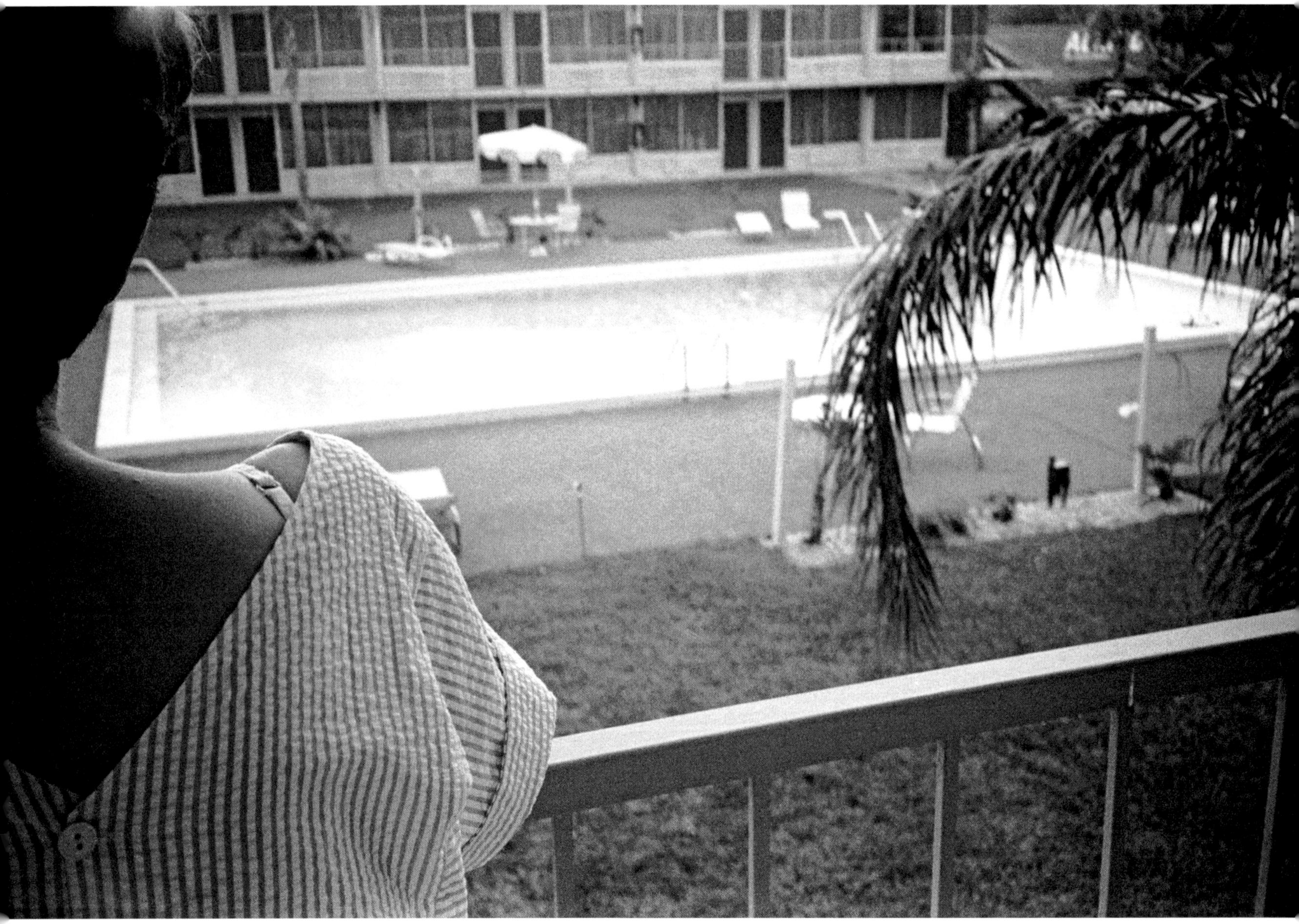

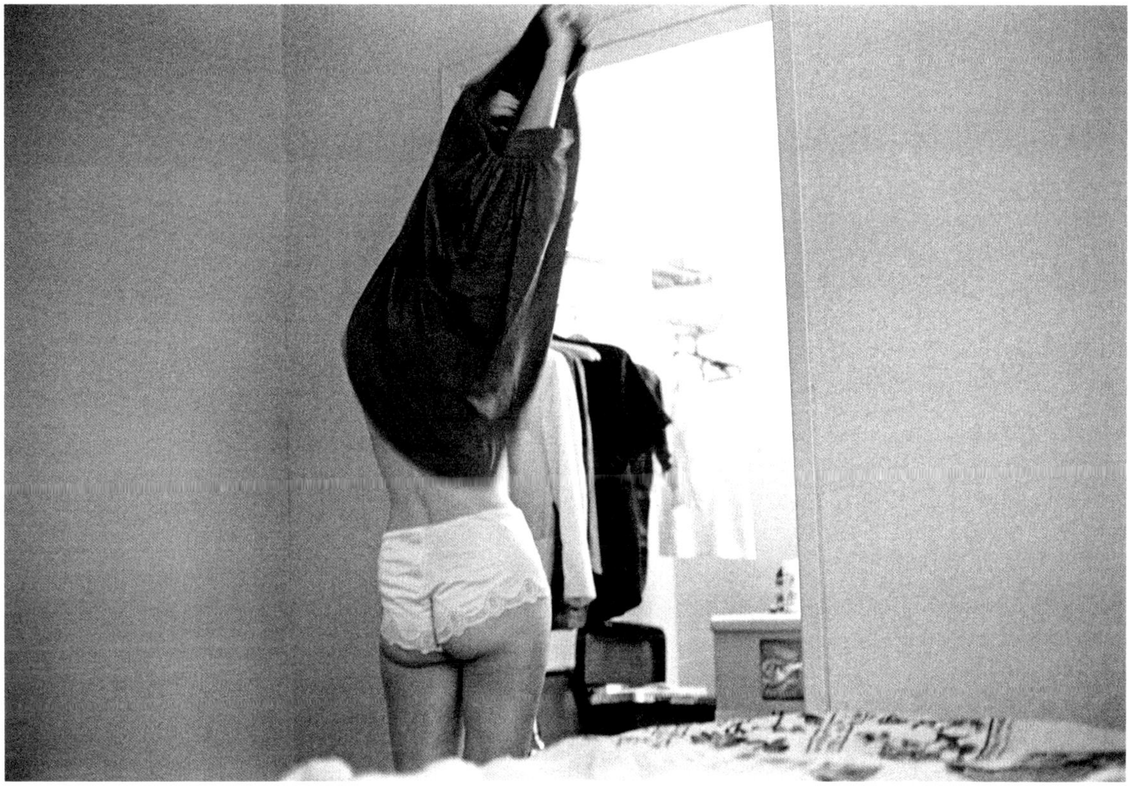

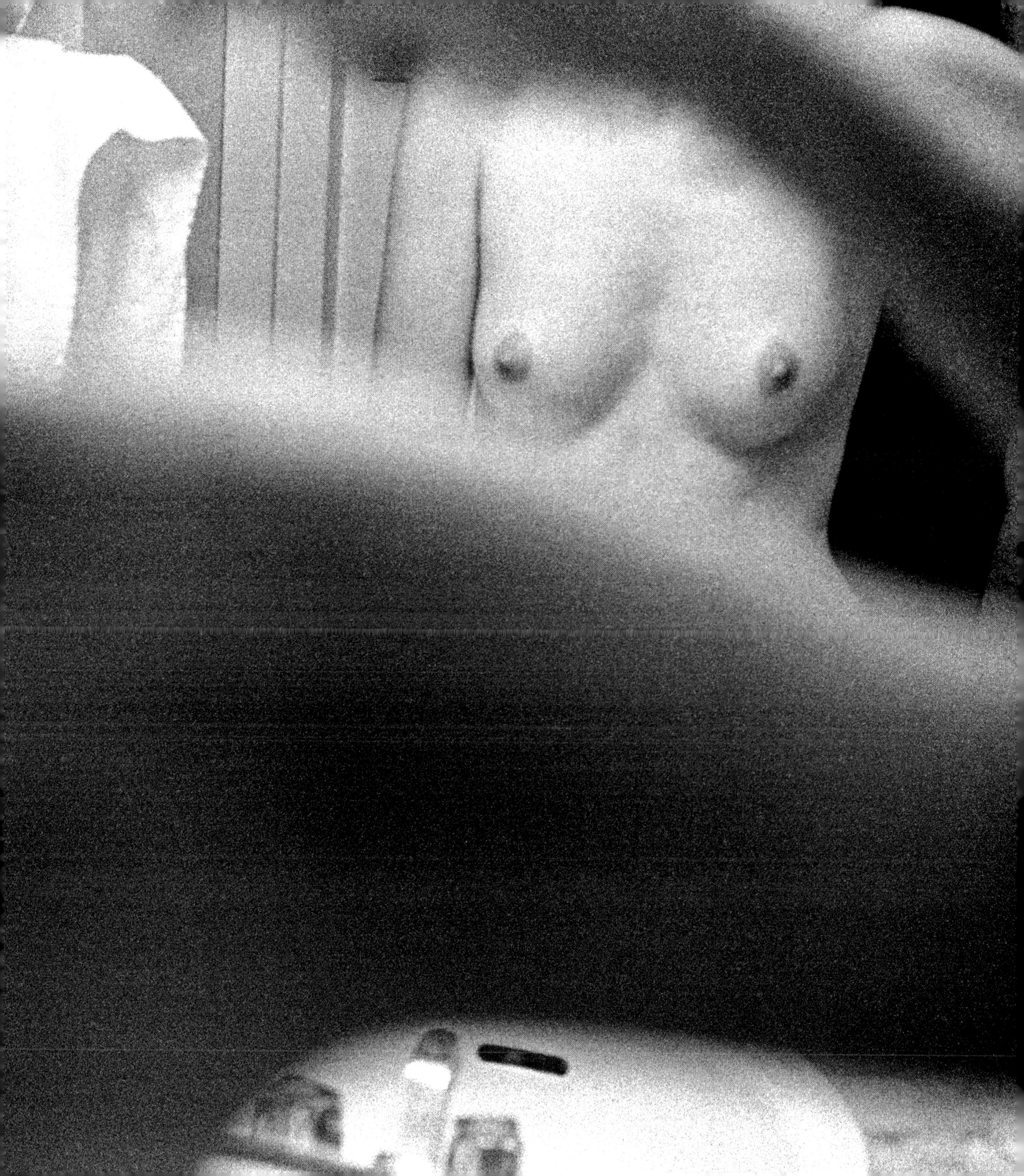

SOUTHERN
LEATHER CO.

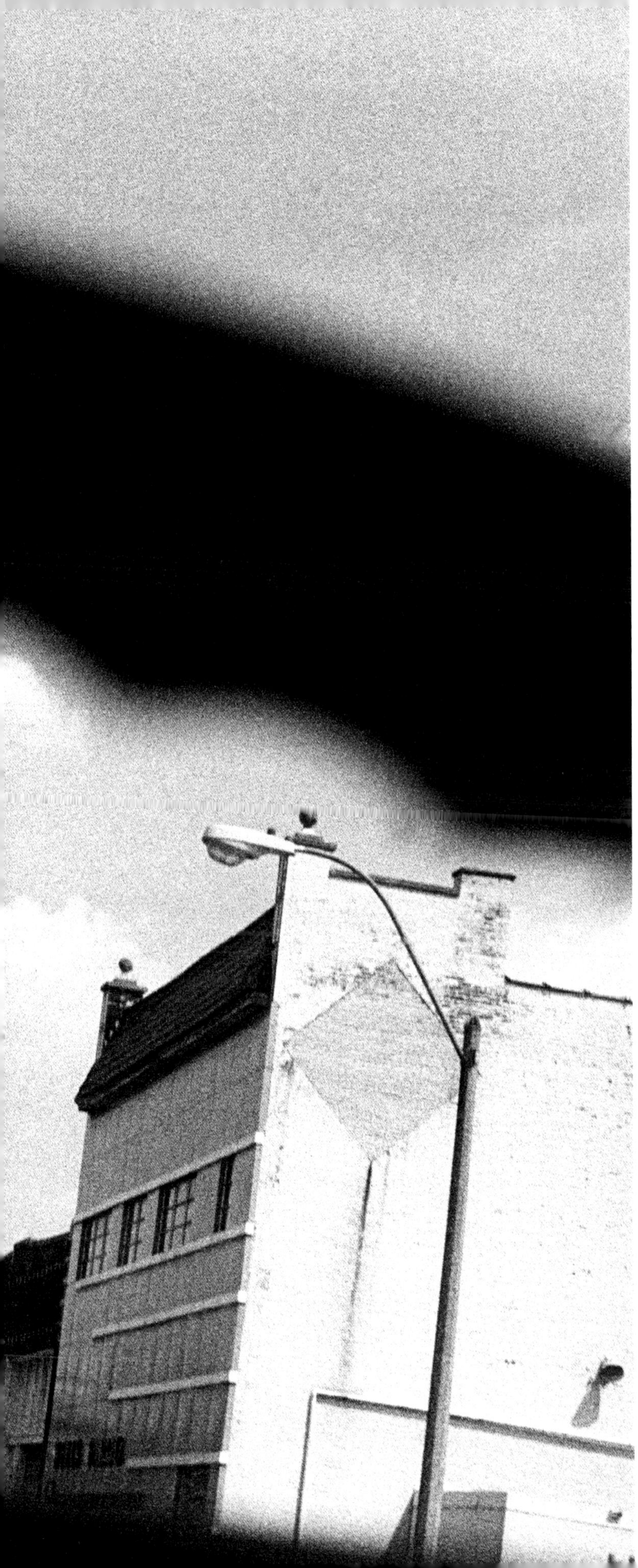

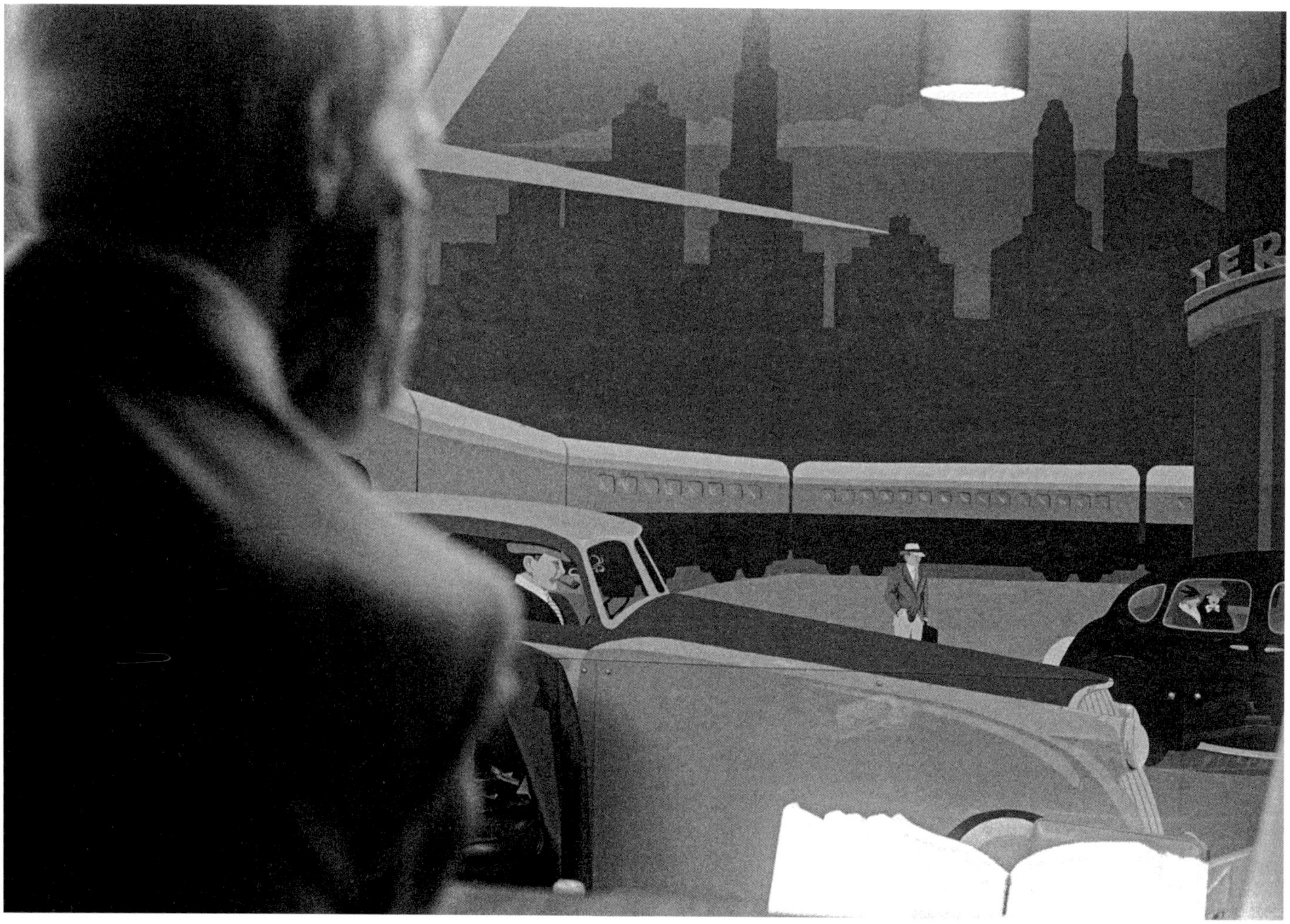

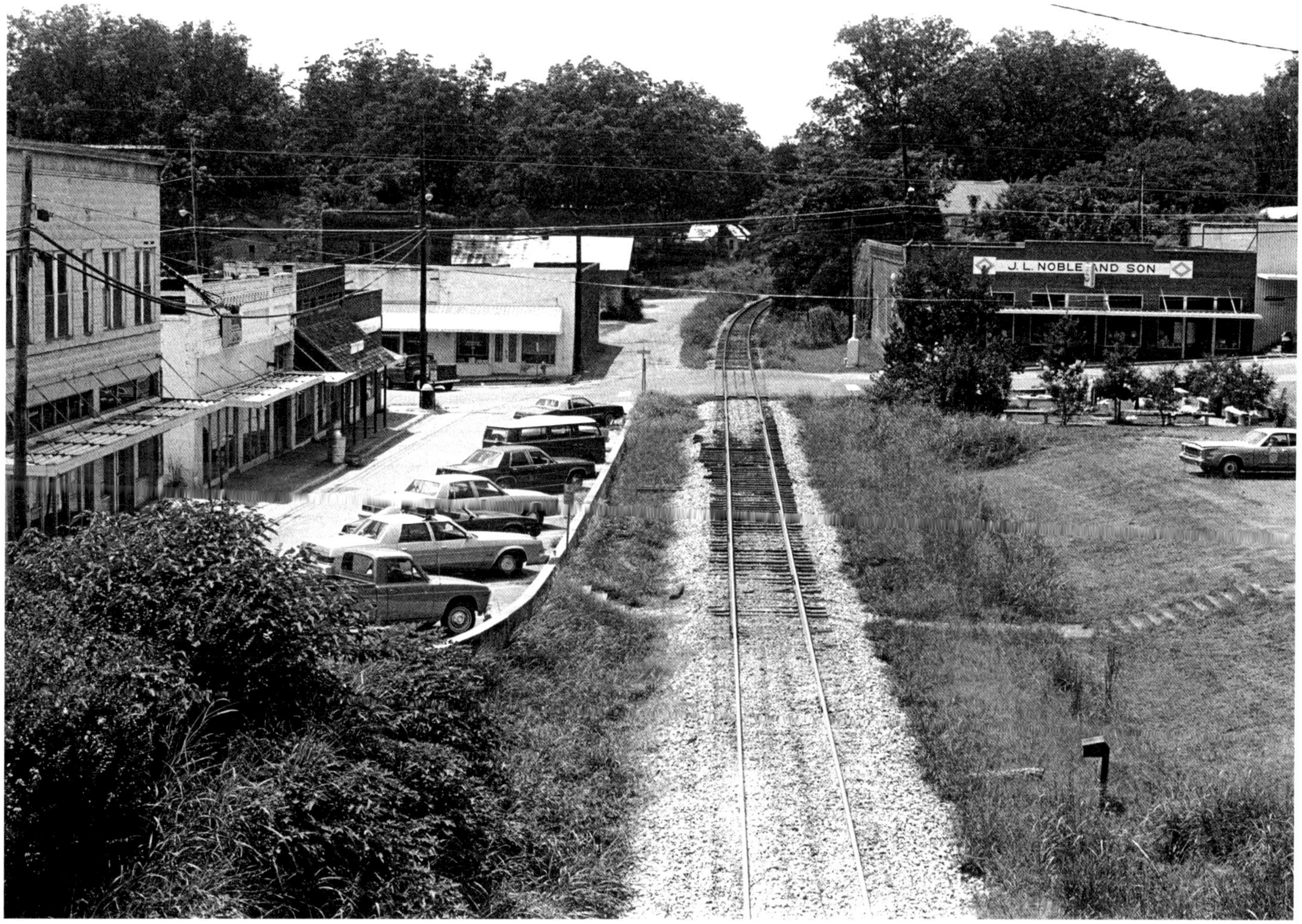
J. L. NOBLE AND SON

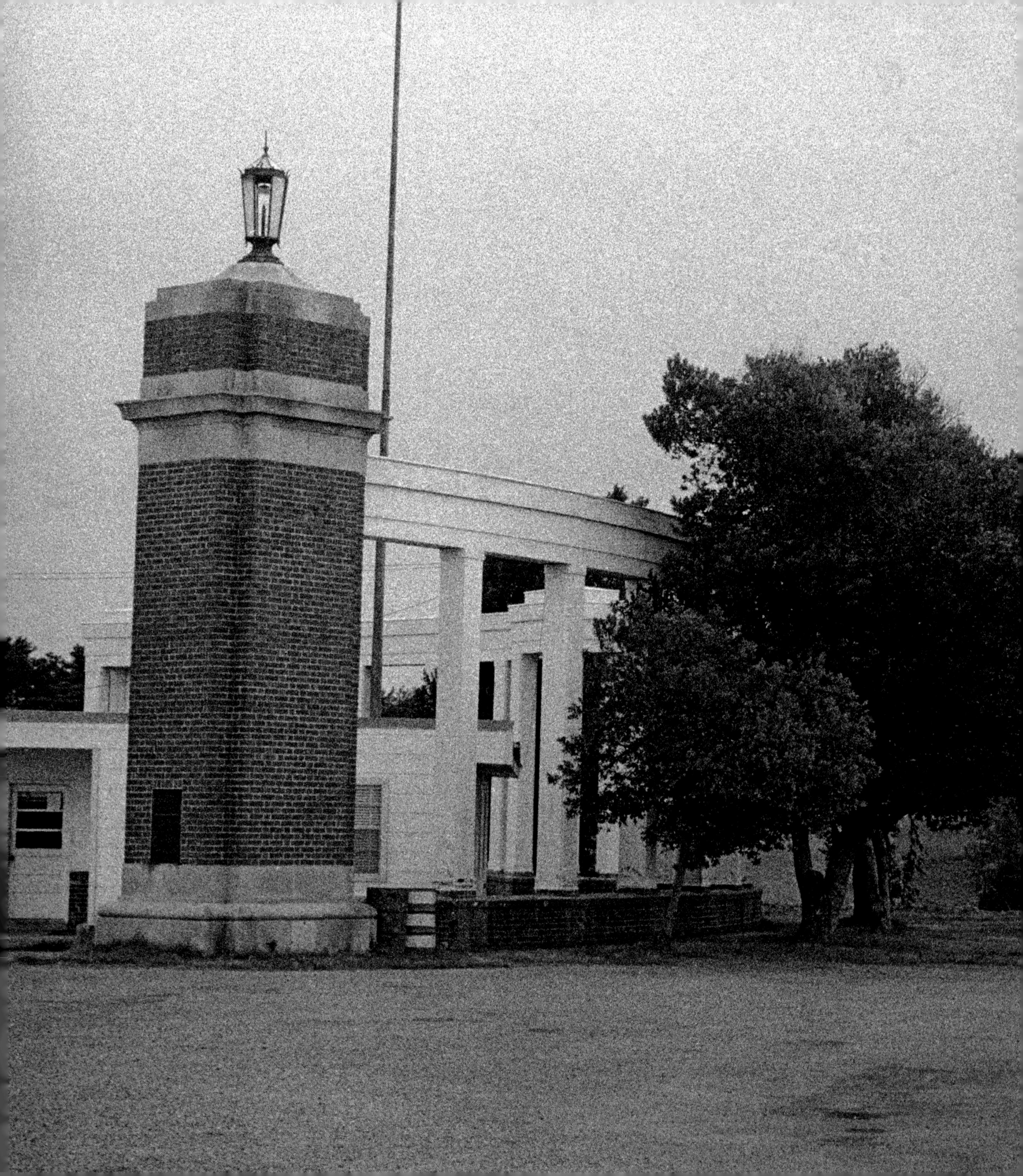

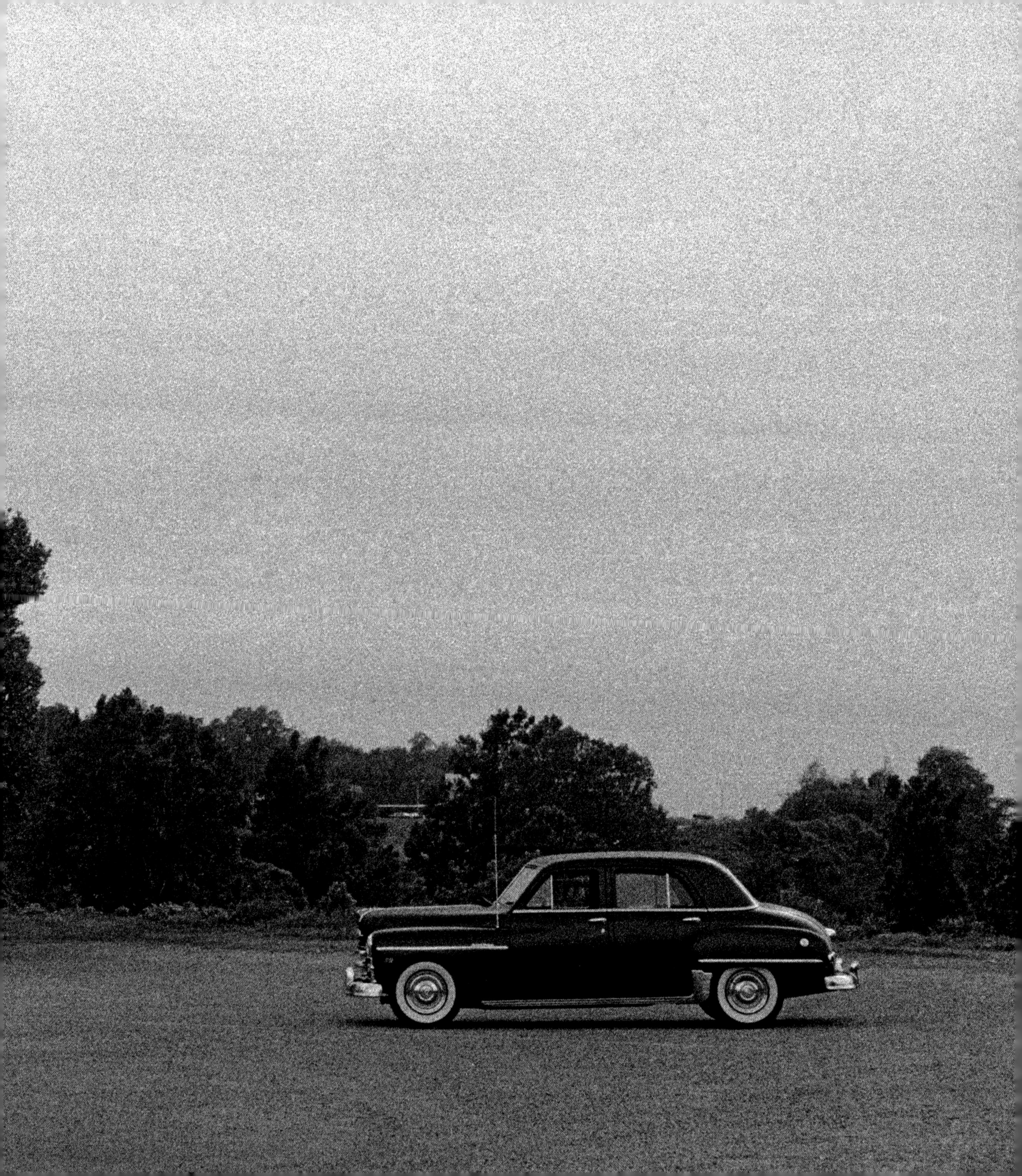

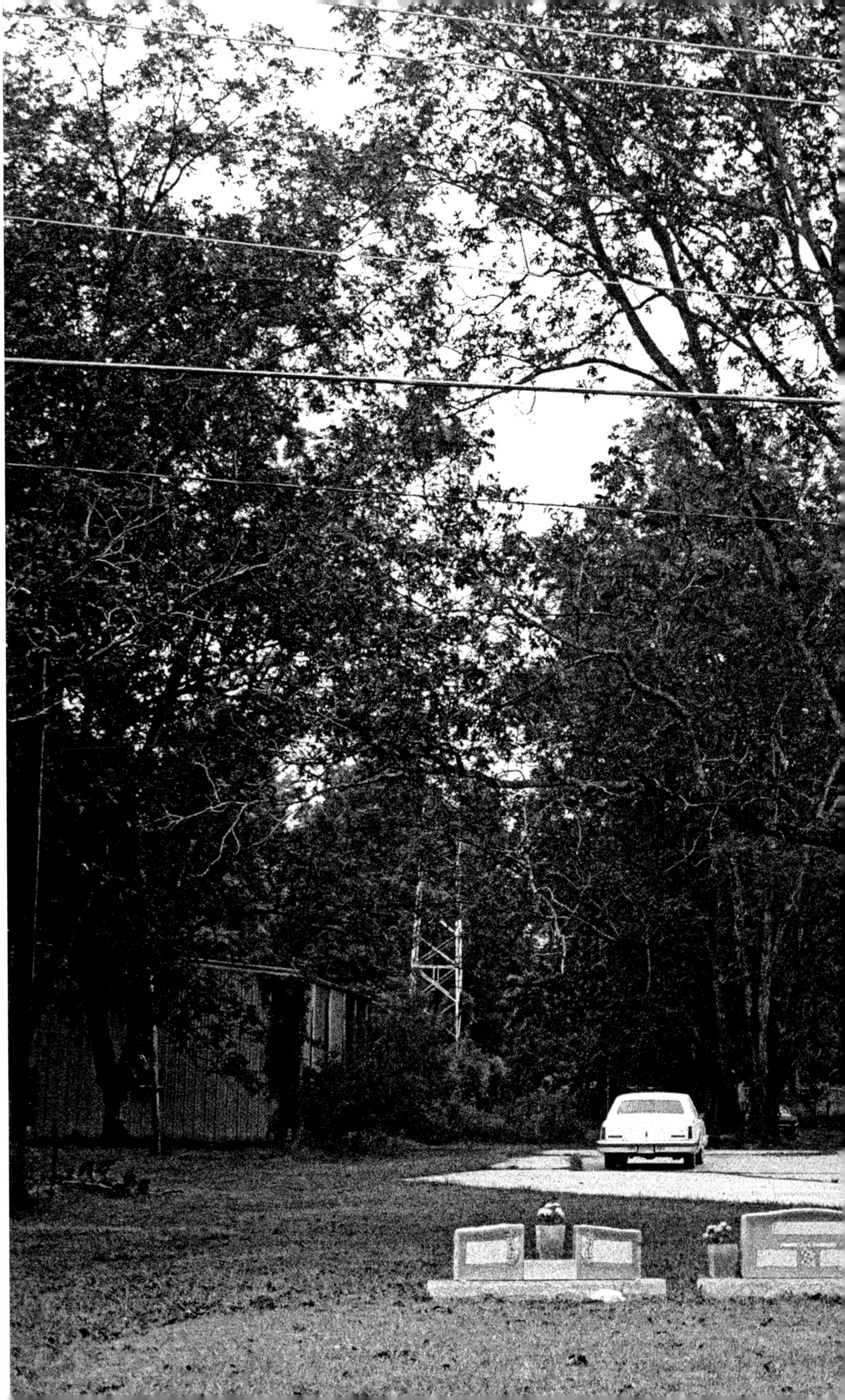

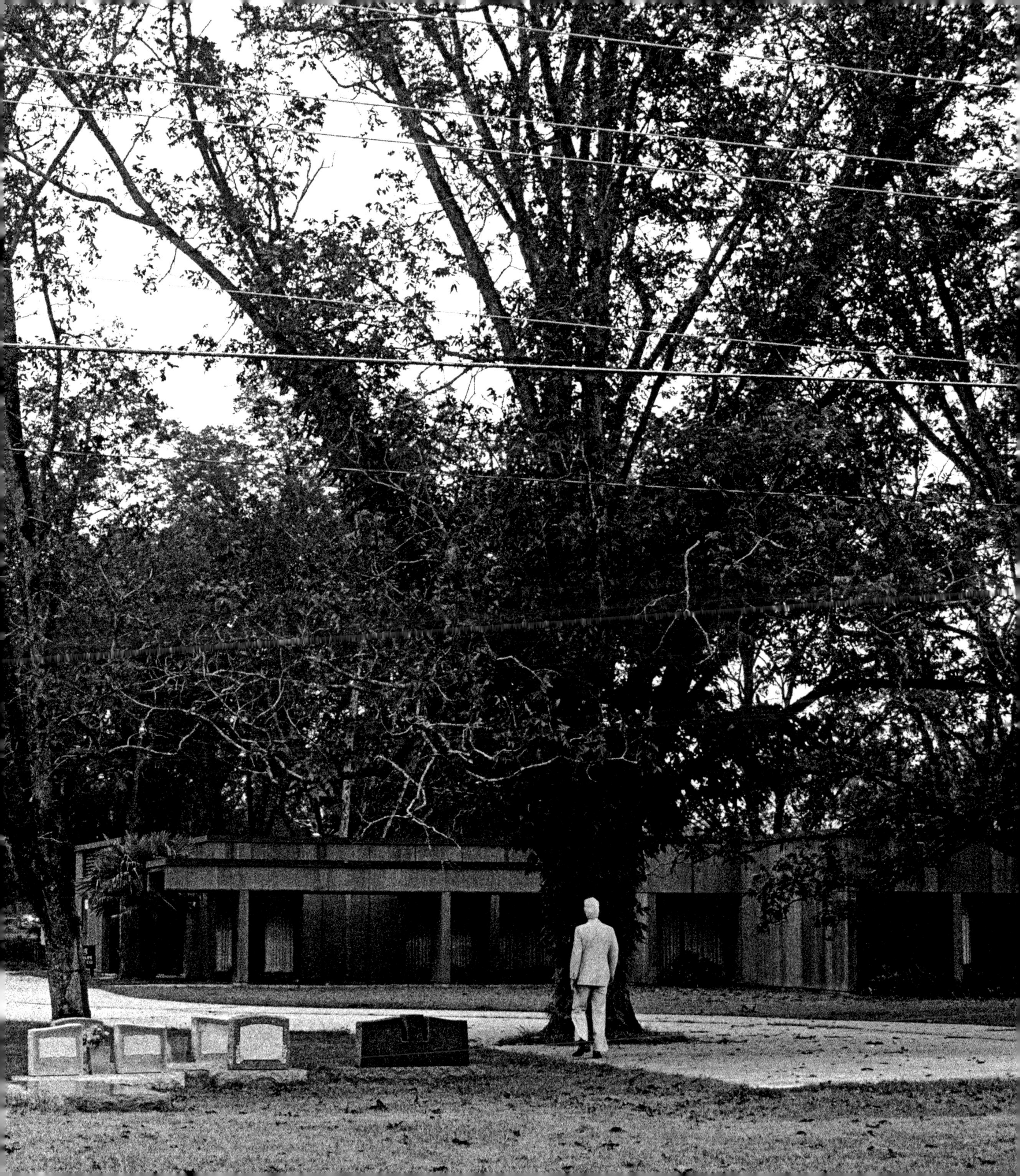

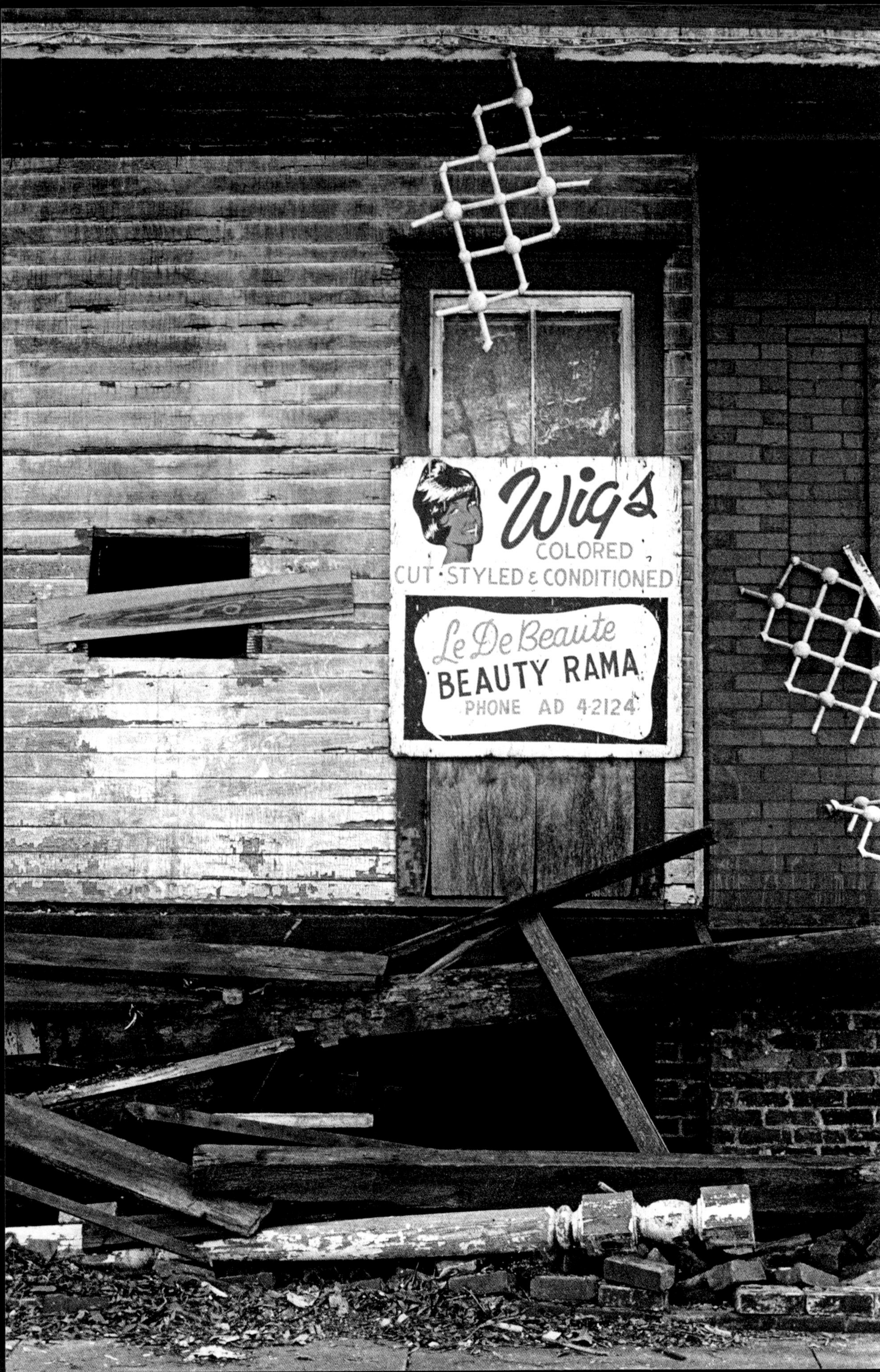
Wig's
COLORED
CUT·STYLED & CONDITIONED
Le De Beaute
BEAUTY RAMA
PHONE AD 4-2124

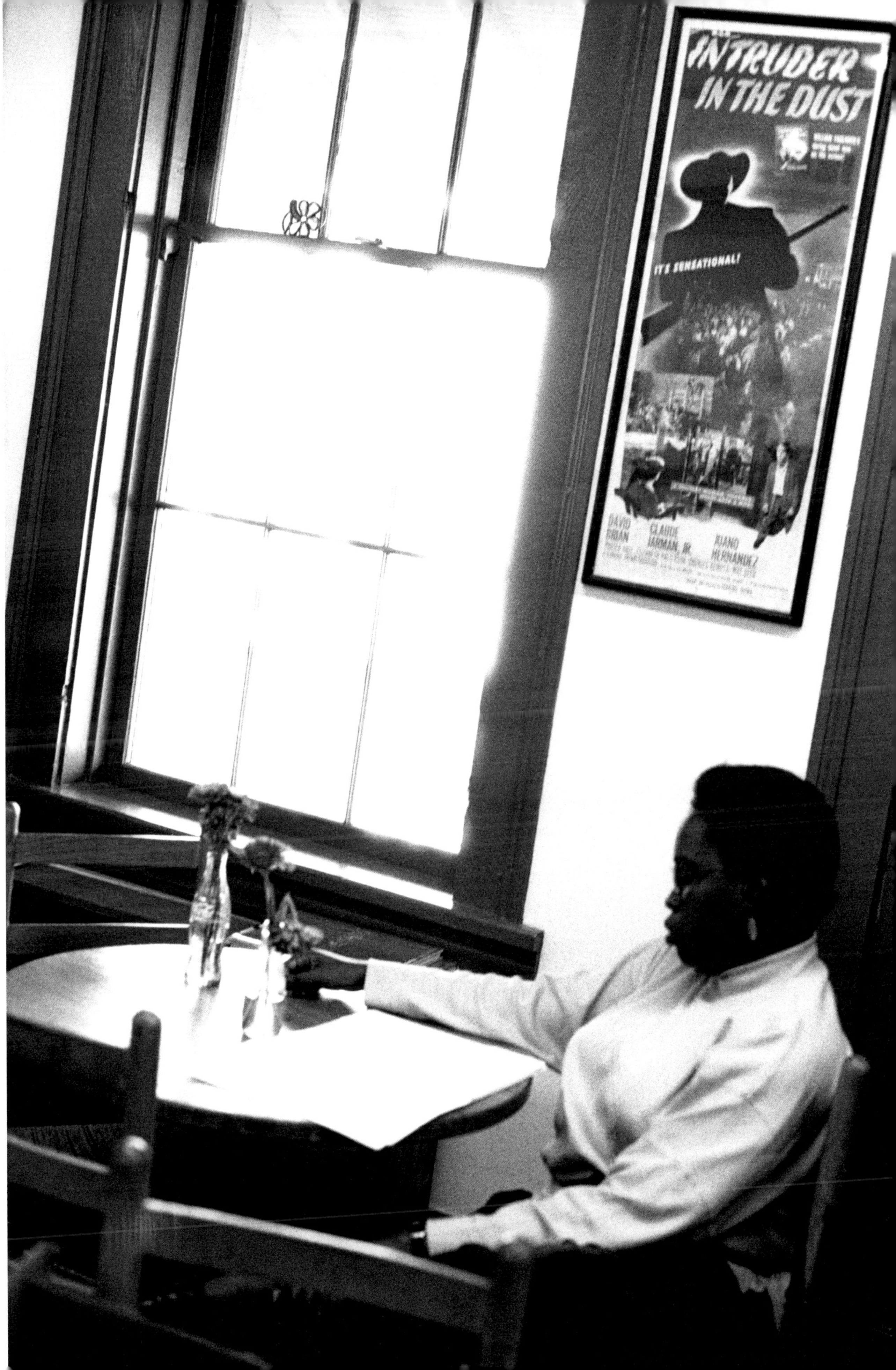
INTRUDER IN THE DUST
IT'S SENSATIONAL!
DAVID BRIAN
CLAUDE JARMAN, JR.
JUANO HERNANDEZ

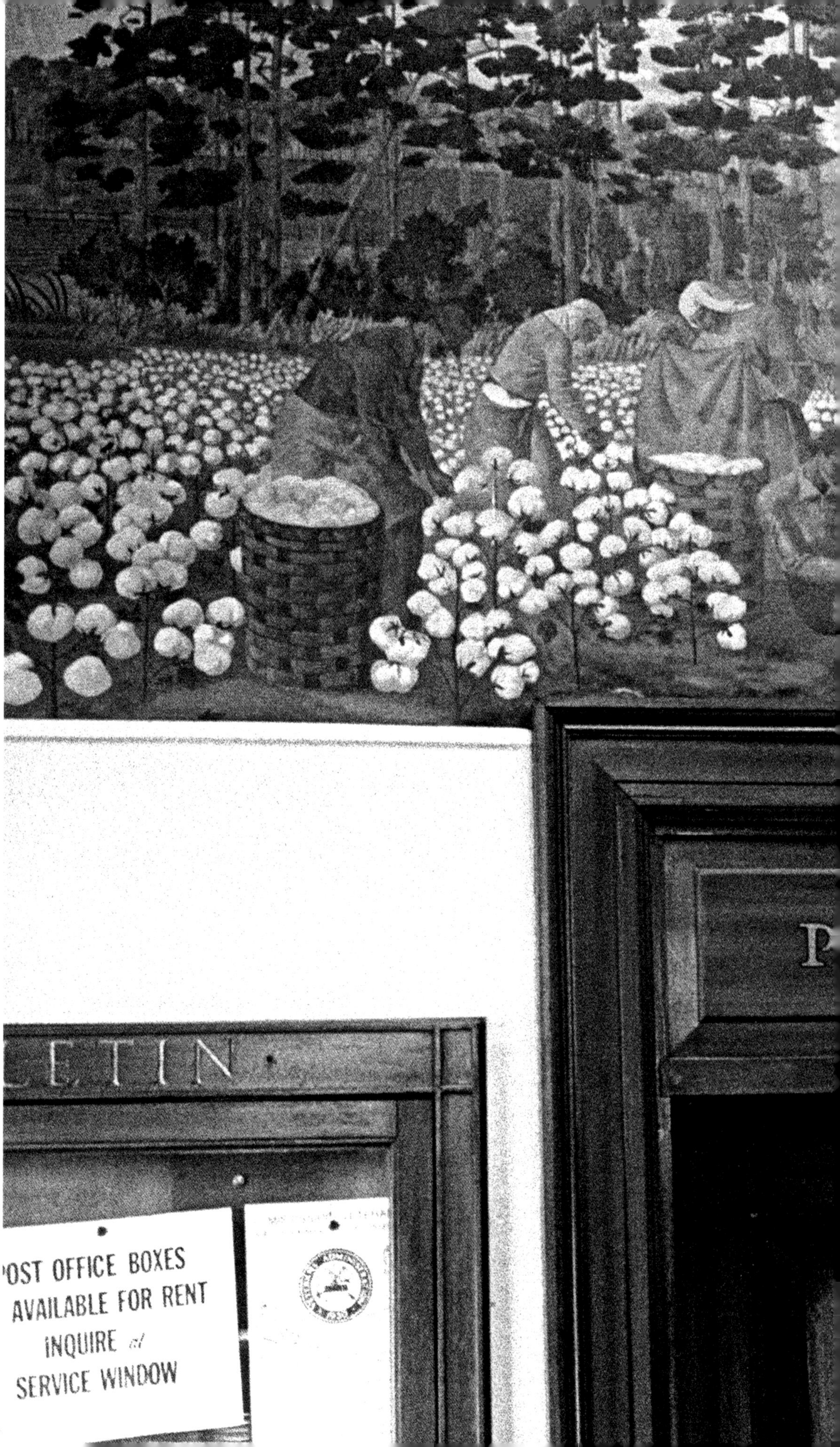
OST OFFICE BOXES
AVAILABLE FOR RENT
INQUIRE at
SERVICE WINDOW

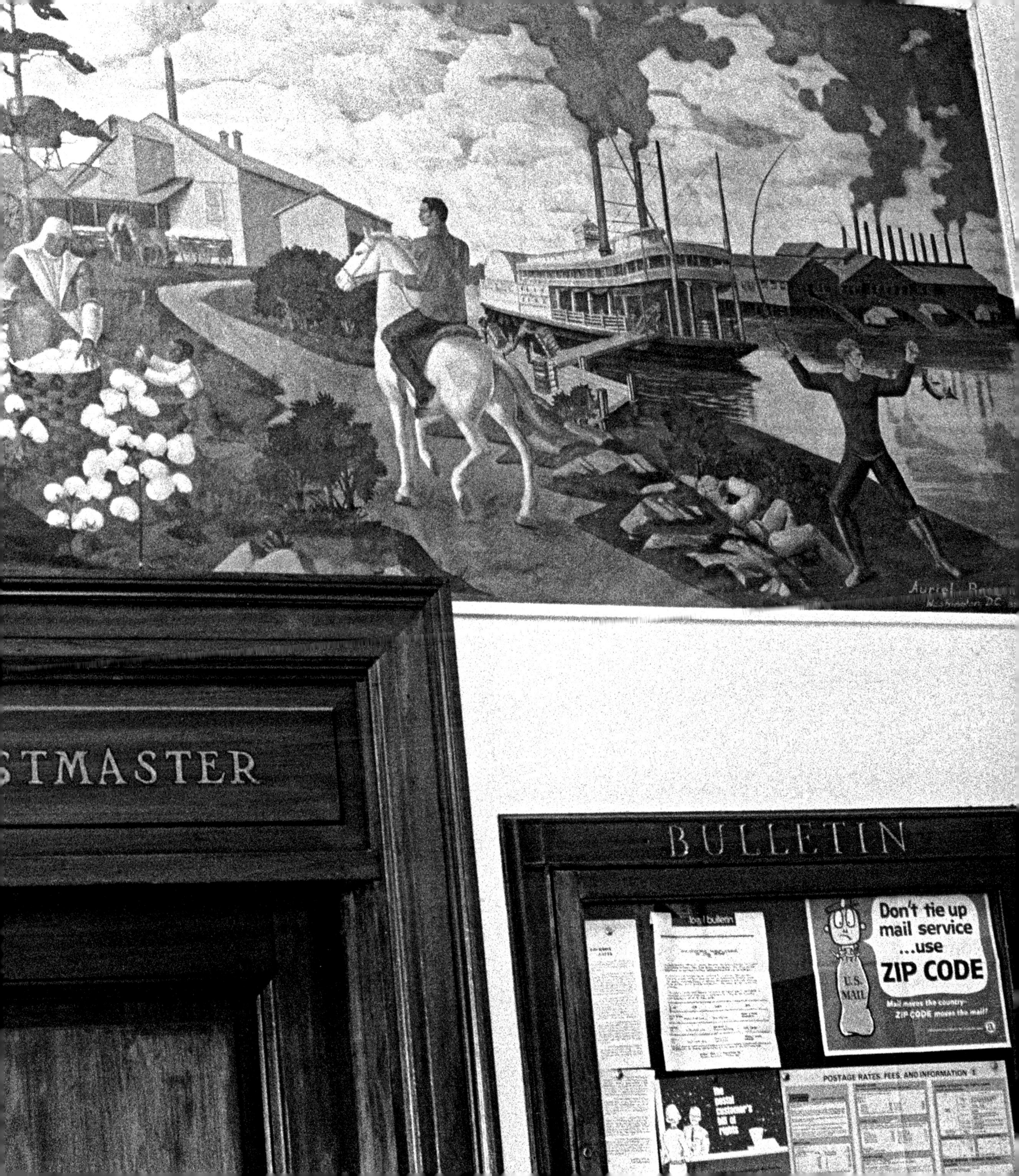
STMASTER
BULLETIN
Don't tie up
mail service
...use
ZIP CODE
U.S.
MAIL
Mail moves the country-
ZIP CODE moves the mail!
POSTAGE RATES, FEES, AND INFORMATION

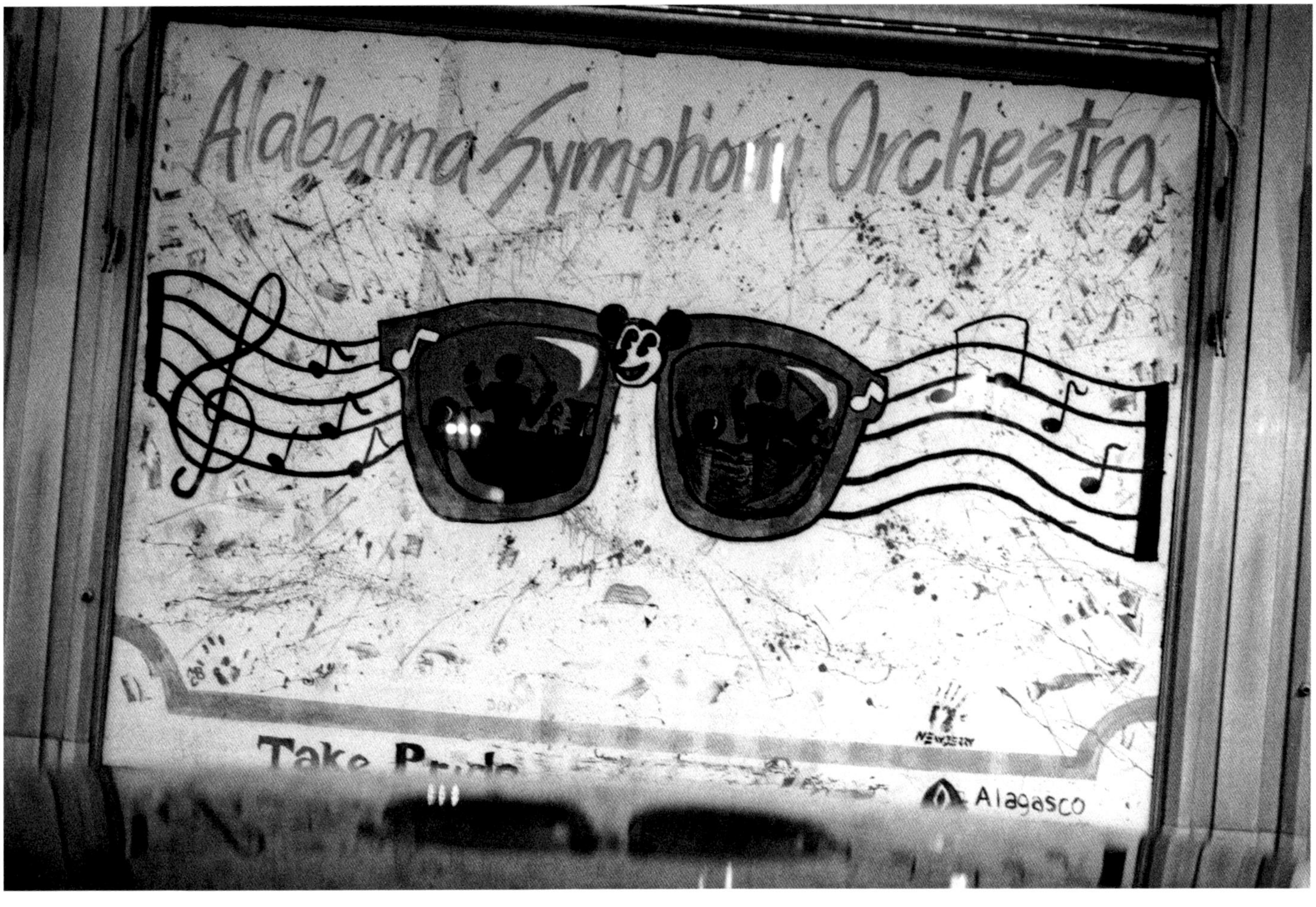
Alabama Symphony Orchestra
Alagasco

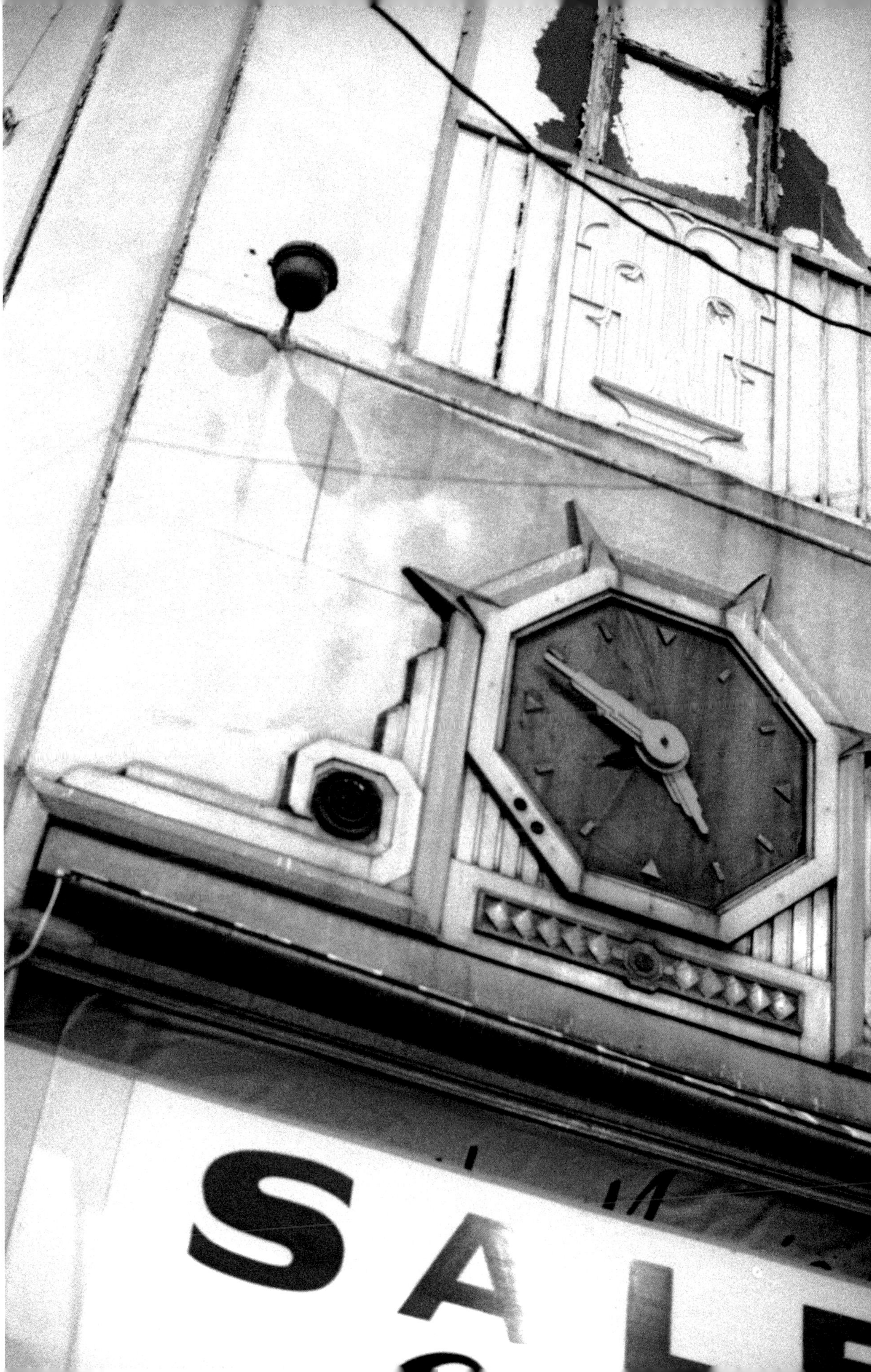
SAL

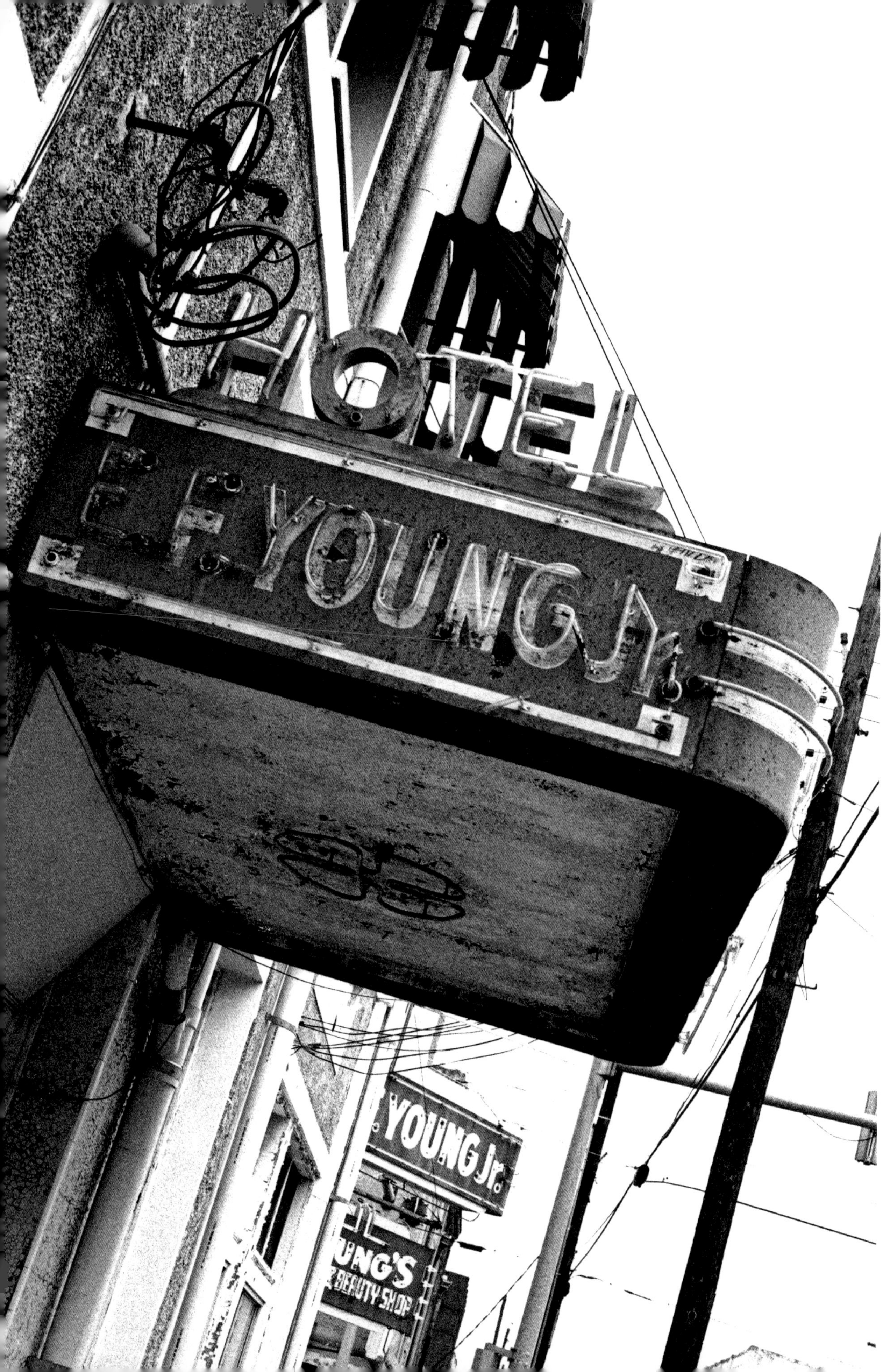
HOTEL
E.F. YOUNG Jr.
YOUNG Jr.
BEAUTY SHOP

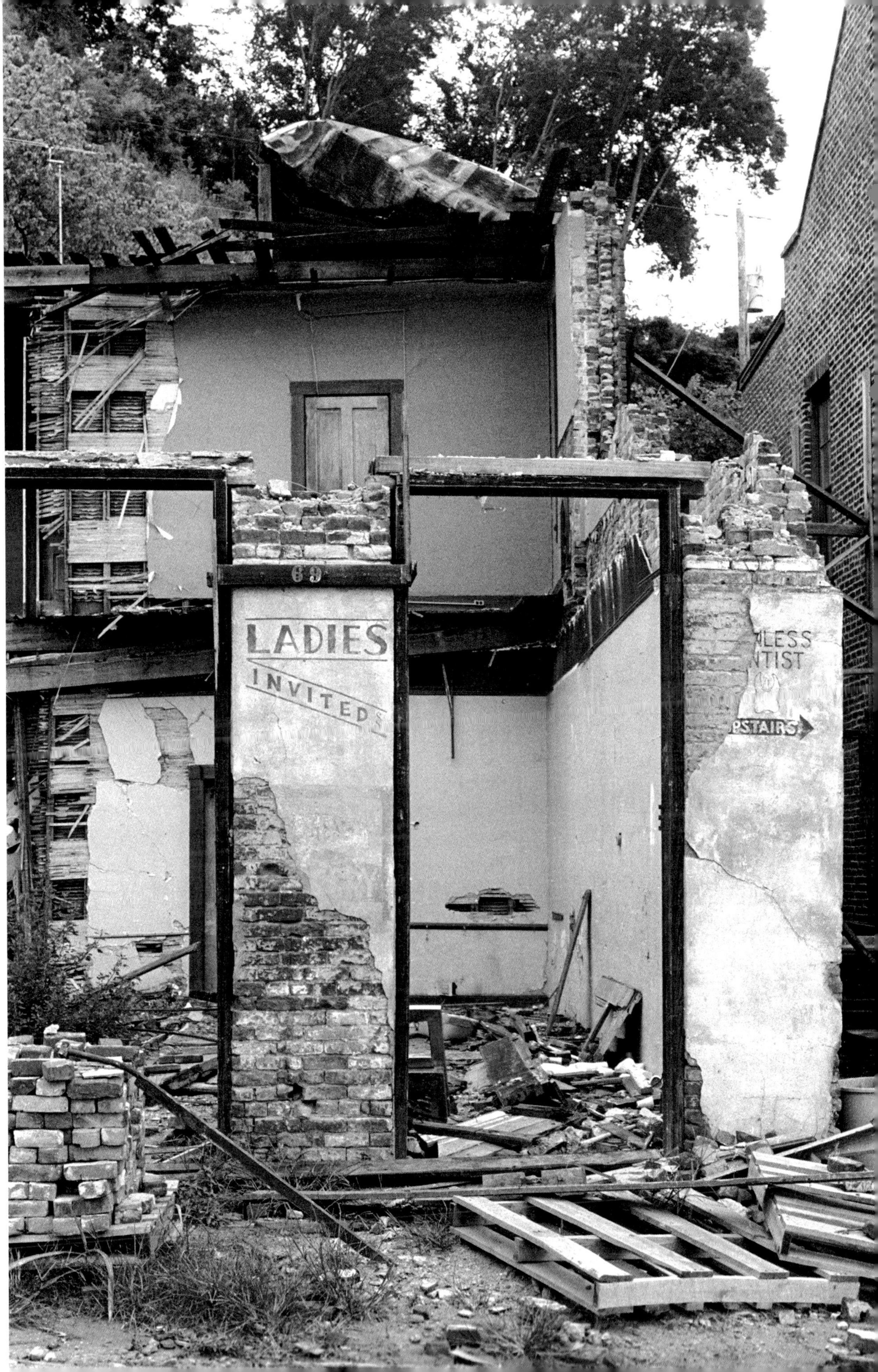
69
LADIES
INVITED

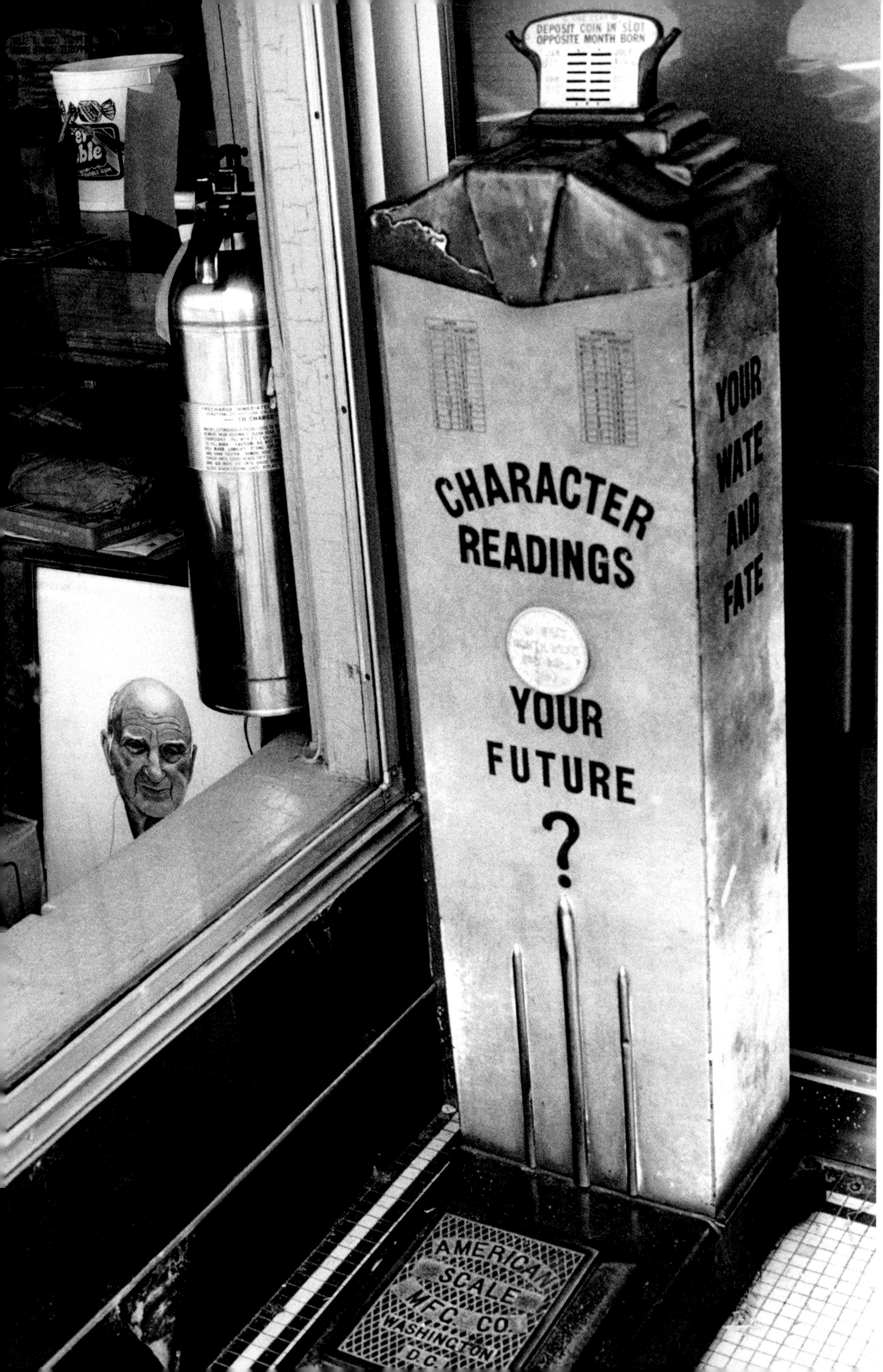
DEPOSIT COIN IN SLOT
OPPOSITE MONTH BORN
CHARACTER
READINGS
YOUR
FUTURE
?
YOUR
WATE
AND
FATE
AMERICAN
SCALE
MFG. CO.
WASHINGTON
D.C.

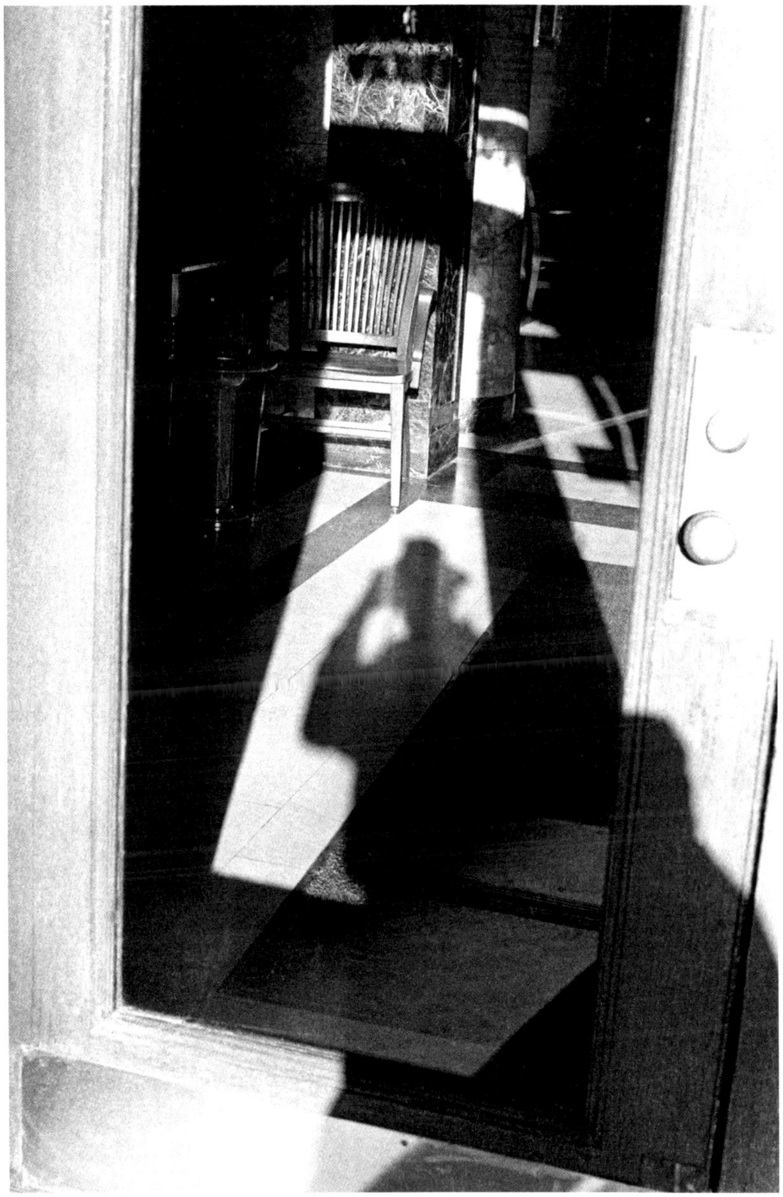

# CAPTIONS

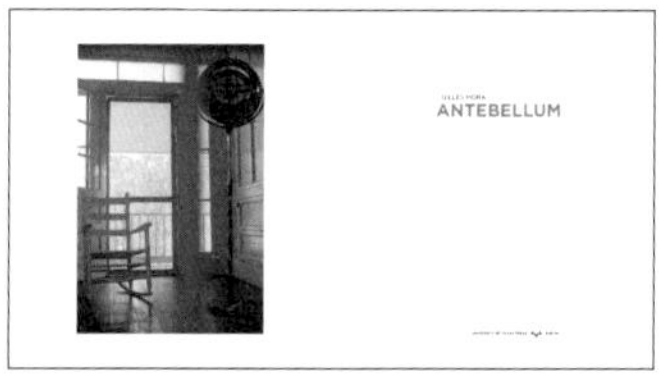


William Faulkner's bedroom, Rowan Oak,
Oxford, Mississippi, 1982

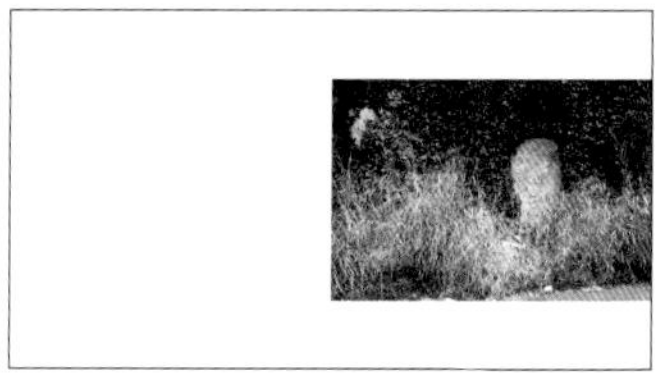

Columbus, Mississippi, 1990

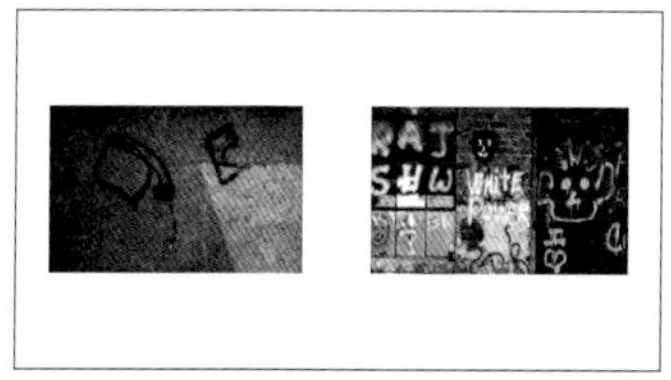

Meridian, Mississippi, 1989
Columbus, Mississippi, 1990

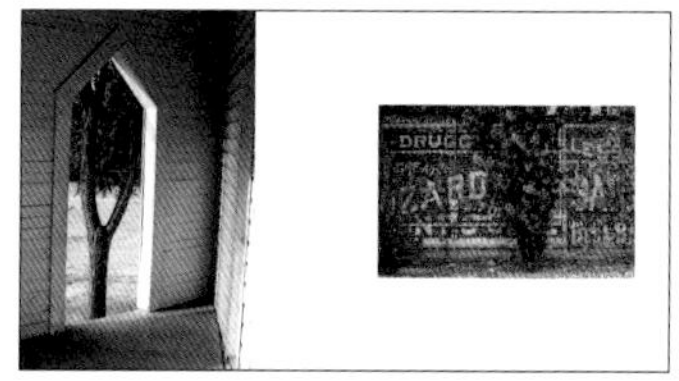

Alabama, 1990
Columbus, Mississippi, 1990

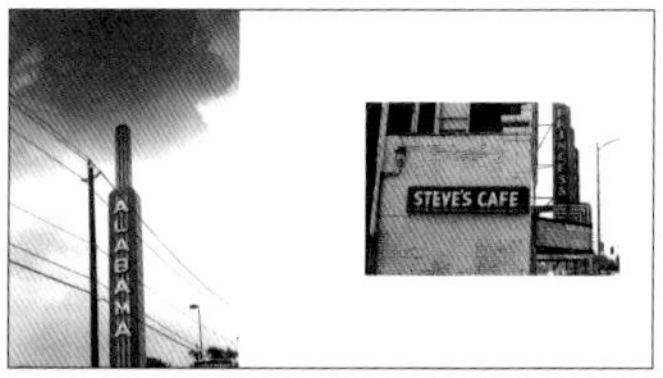


Birmingham, Alabama, 1991
Birmingham, Alabama, 1989

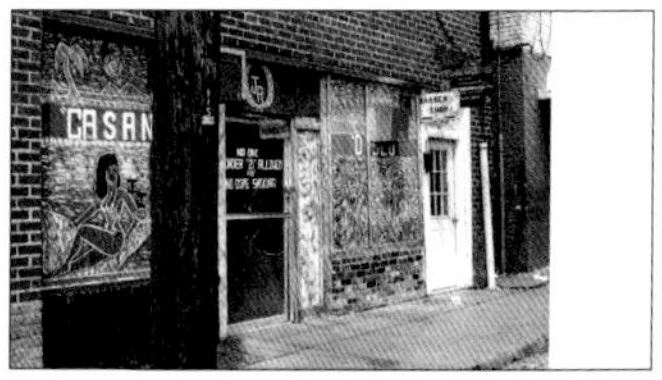

Meridian, Mississippi, 1989

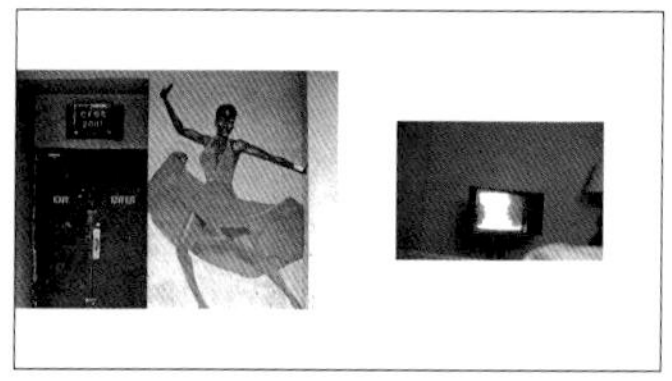

Jackson, Mississippi, 1984
Alabama, 1982

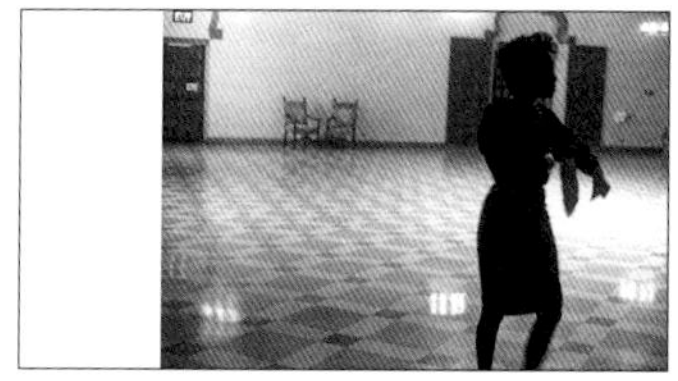

Atlanta, Georgia, 1986

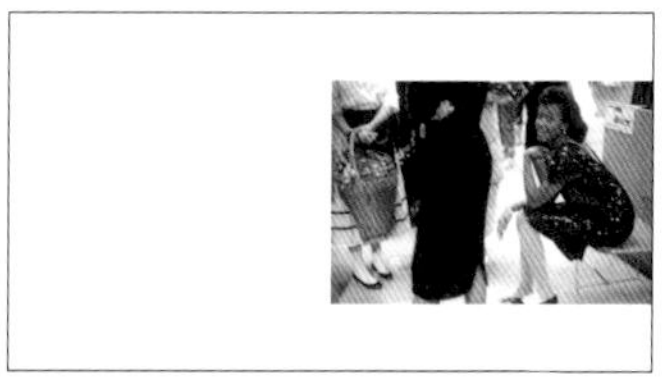

Atlanta, Georgia, 1987

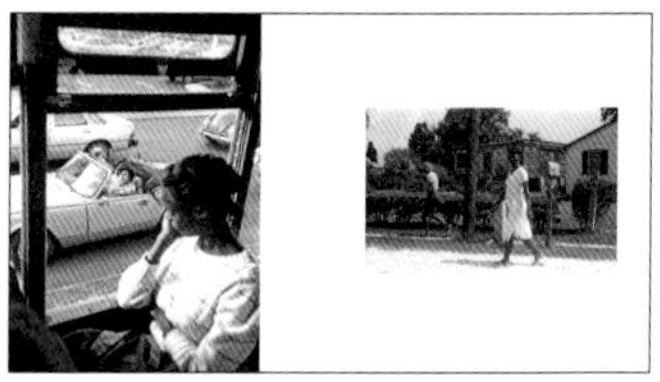

New Orleans, Louisiana, 1986
Louisiana, 1984

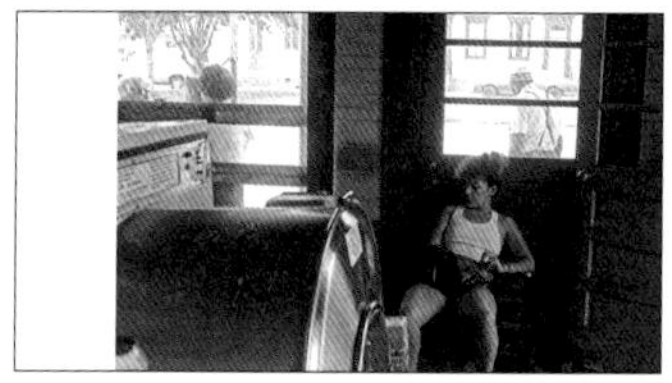

New Orleans, Louisiana, 1984

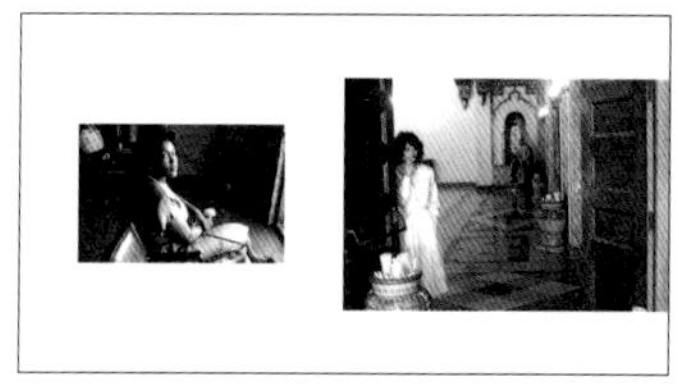

Memphis, Tennessee, 1986
Fox Theatre, Atlanta, Georgia, 1987

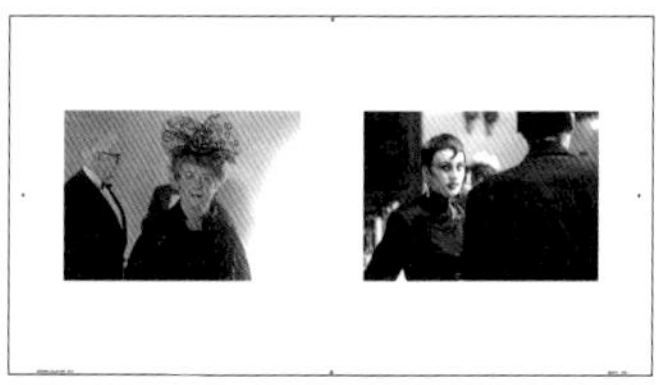

Georgia, 1986
Atlanta, Georgia, 1987

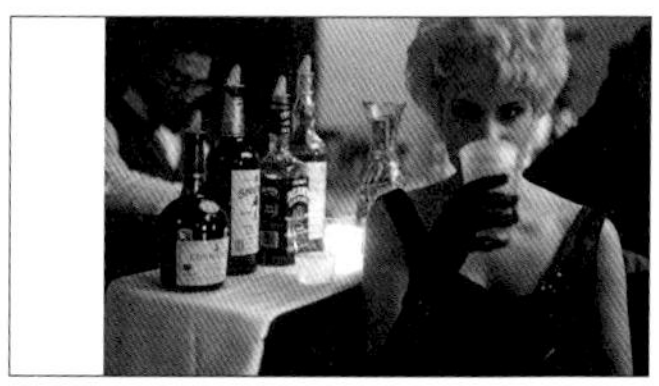

Georgia, 1986

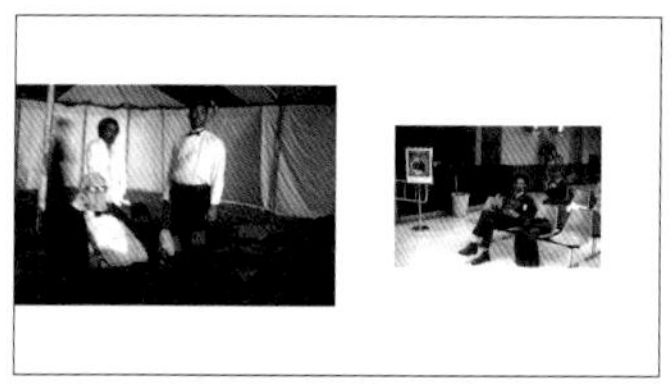

Georgia, 1986
Atlanta, Georgia, 1987

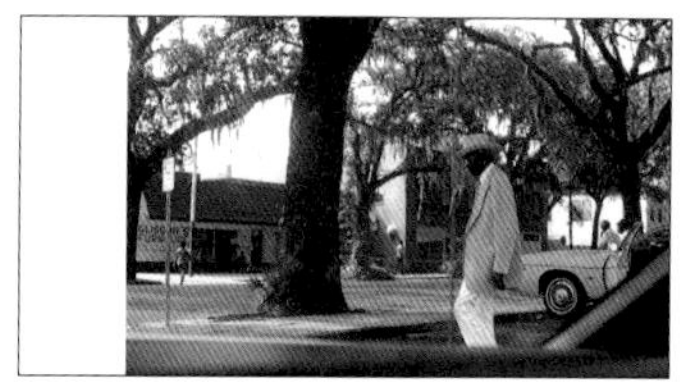

Savannah, Georgia, 1983

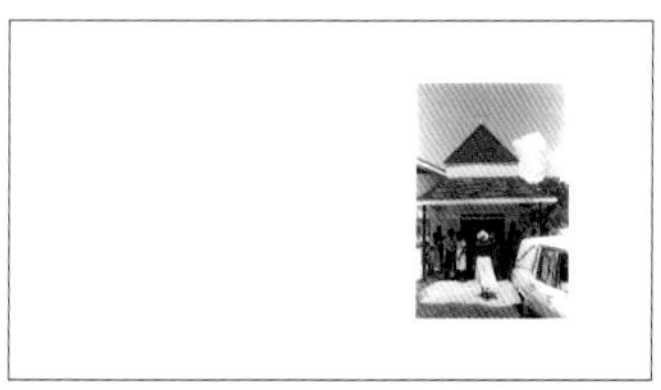

Louisiana, 1980

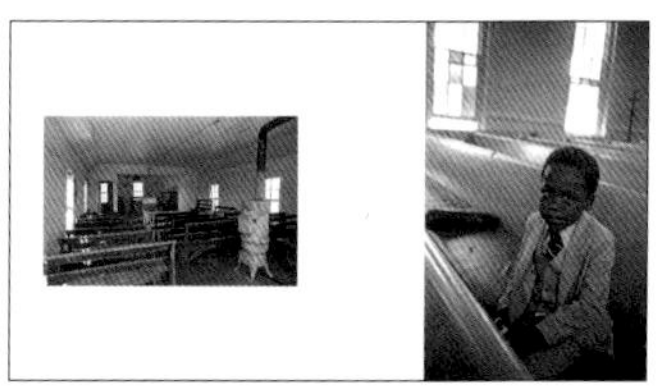

Black church, Jonesville, Louisiana, 1973
Natchez, Mississippi, 1979

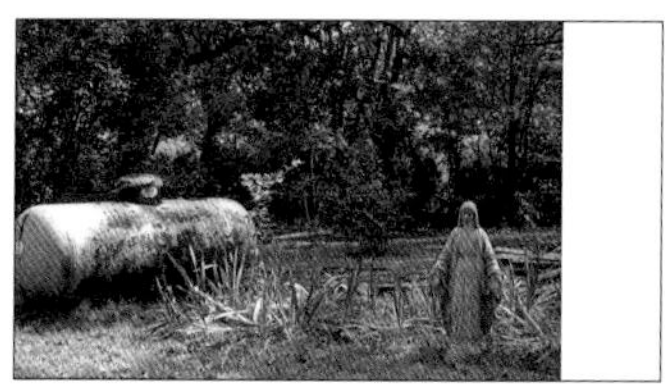

Arkansas, 1982

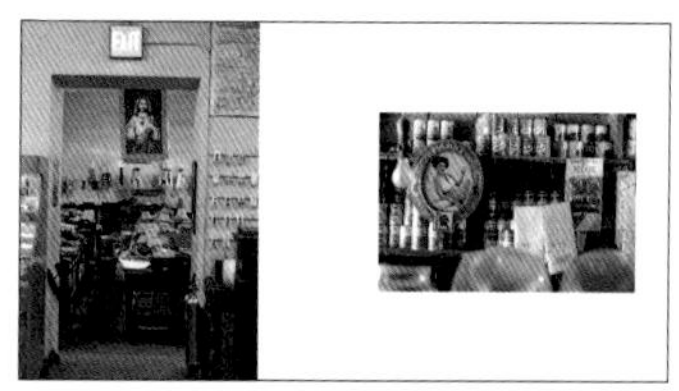

Alexandria, Louisiana, 1974
Ville Platte, Louisiana, 1979

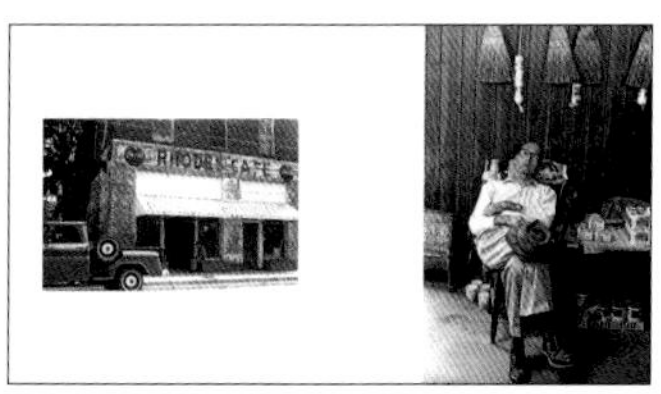

Alabama, 1982
Milledgeville, Georgia, 1983

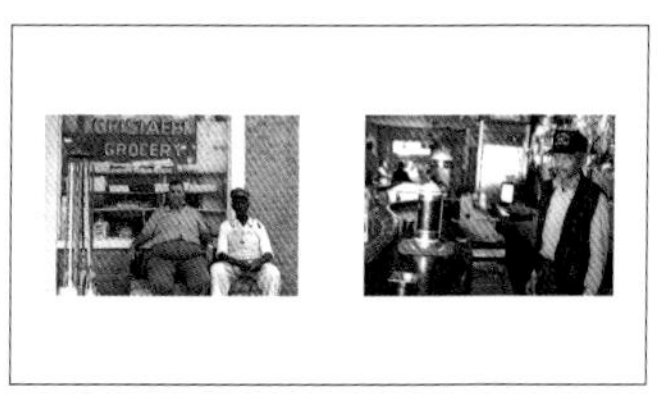

South Louisiana, 1979
Meridian, Mississippi, 1989

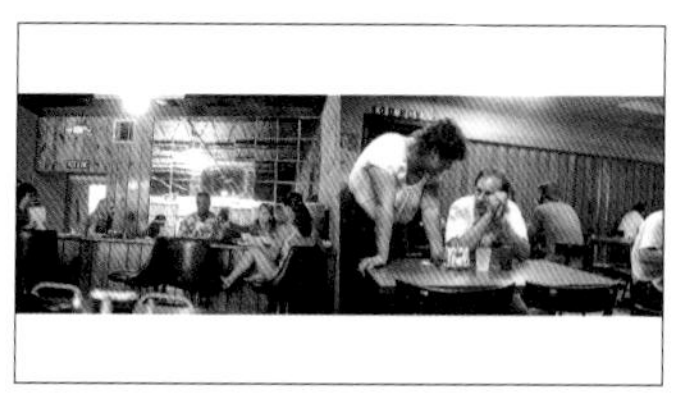

Ferriday, Louisiana, 1974
Monroe, Louisiana, 1973

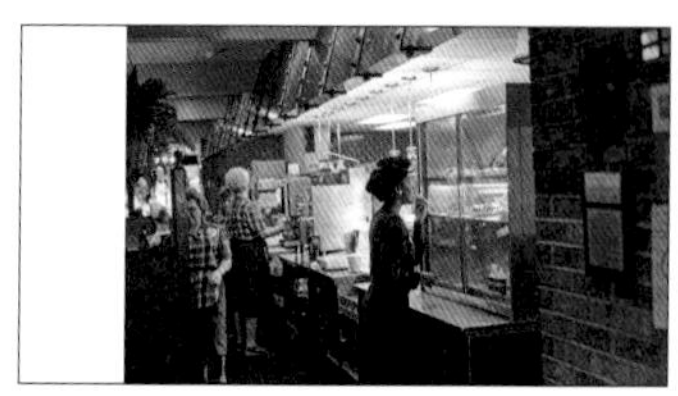

Birmingham, Alabama, 1988

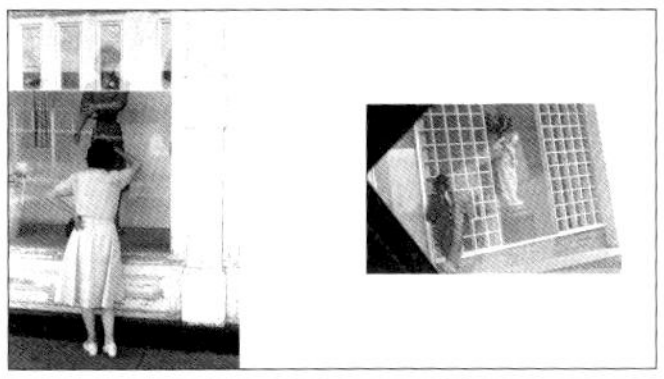
Selma, Alabama, 1982
Macon, Georgia, 1983

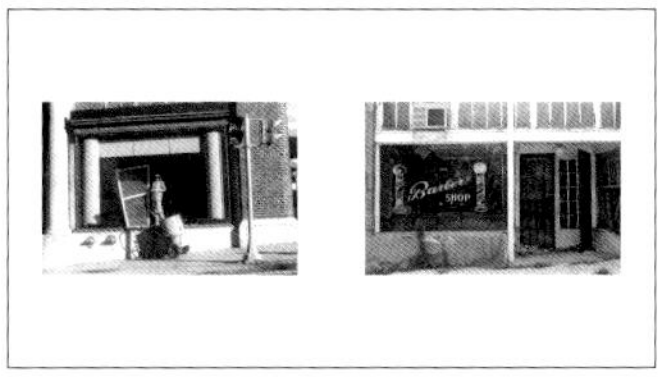
Atlanta, Georgia, 1986
Jackson, Mississippi, 1979

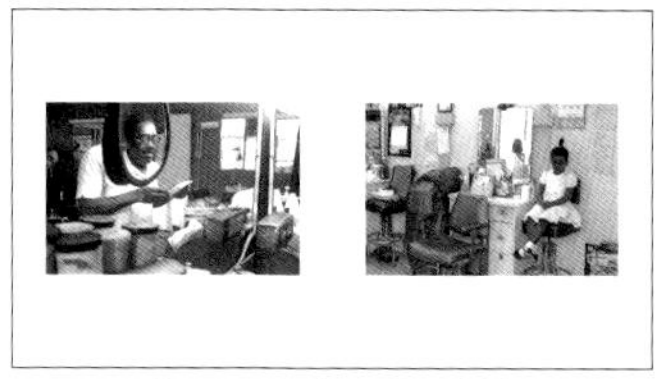
Savannah, Georgia, 1982
Memphis, Tennessee, 1996

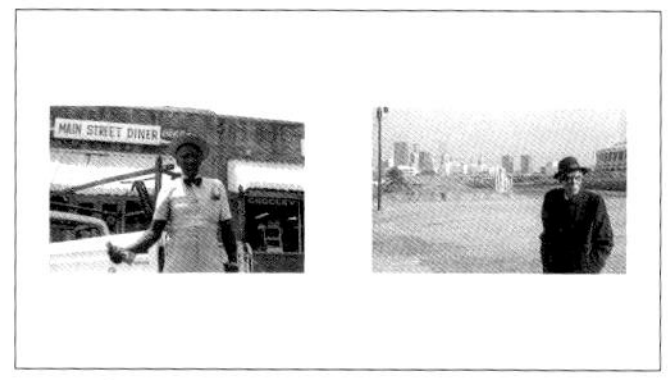
Charleston, South Carolina, 1987
Atlanta, Georgia, 1986

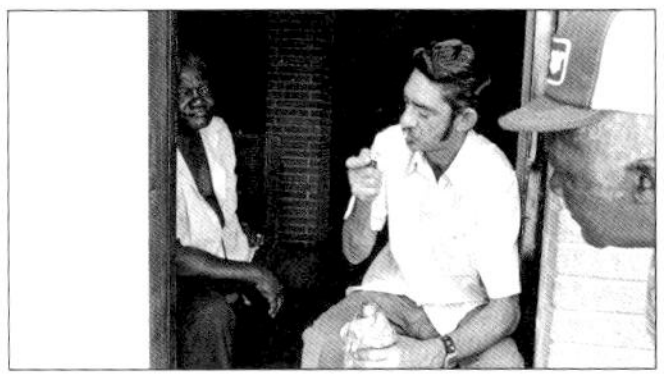
Opelousas, Louisiana, 1984

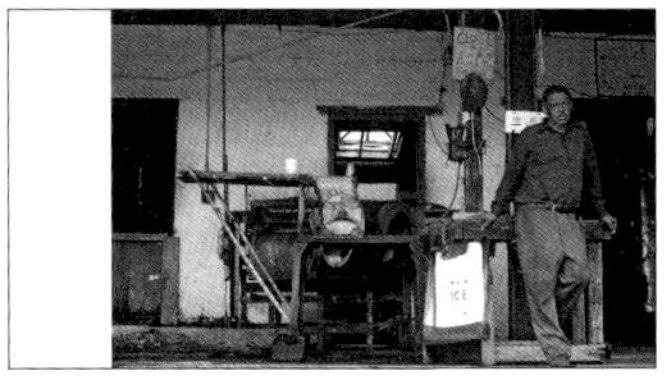
Oxford, Mississippi, 1982

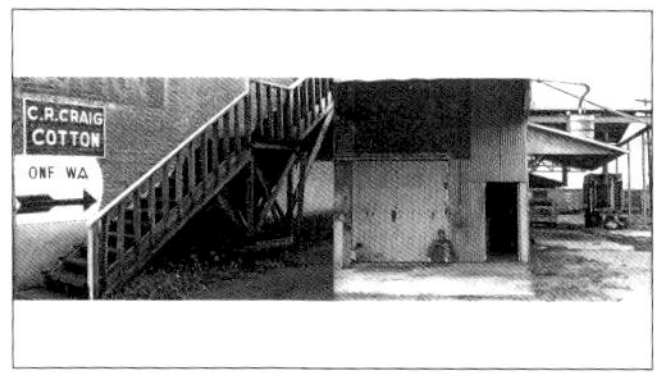
Mississippi, 1982
Tupelo, Mississippi, 1990

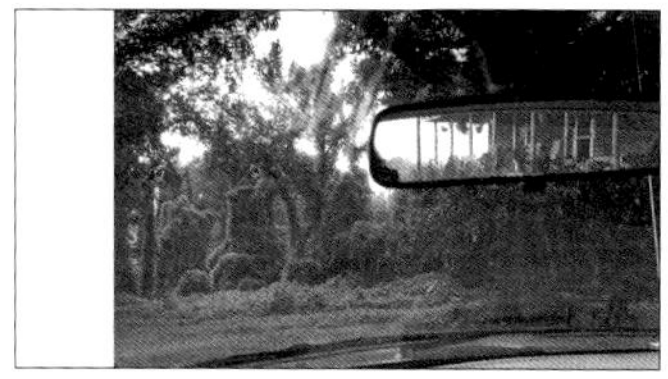
Alabama, 1982

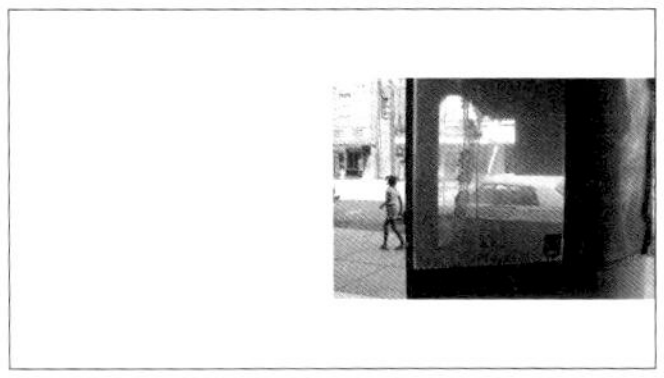
Natchez, Mississippi, 1979

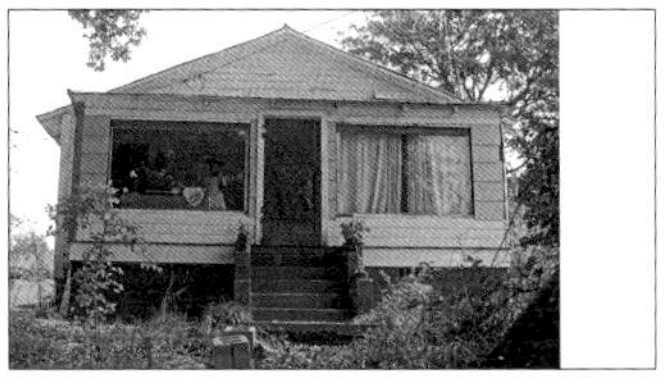
Alabama, 1982

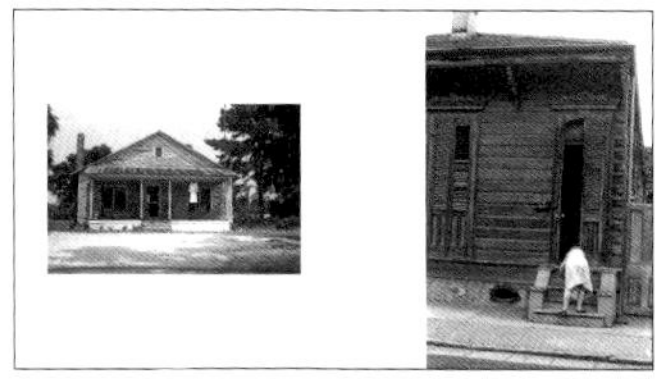
Arkansas, 1983
New Orleans, Louisiana, 2010

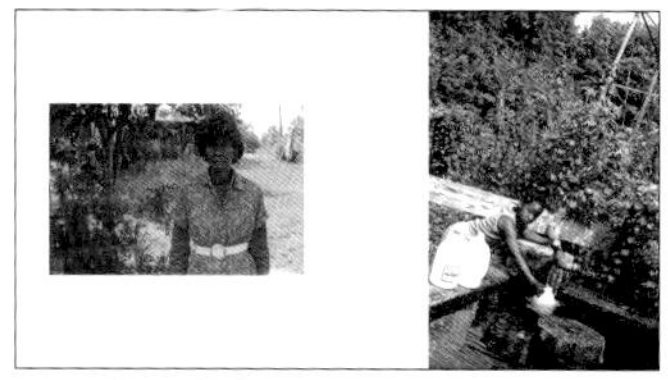
Near Oxford, Mississippi, 1982
Hale County, Alabama, 1990

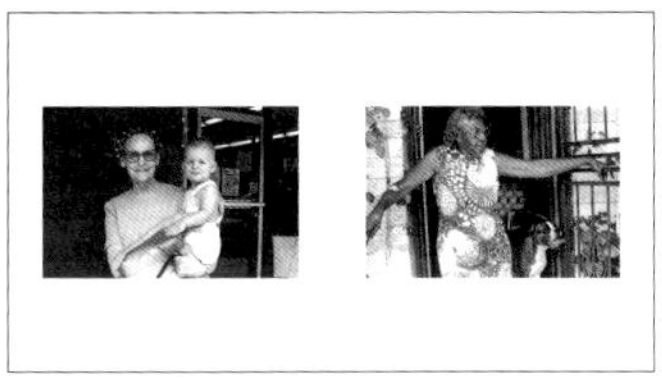
New Albany, Mississippi, 1982
South Louisiana, 1984

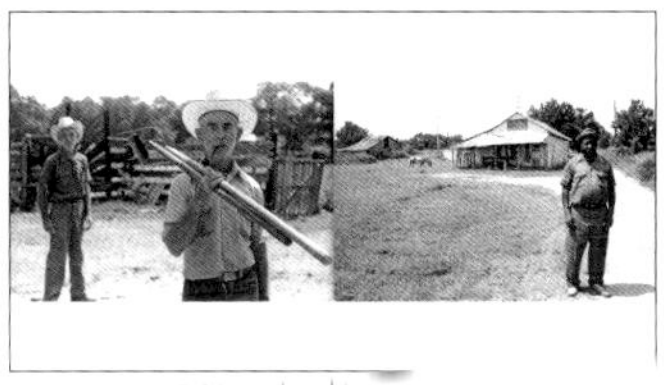
Hale County, Alabama, 1982

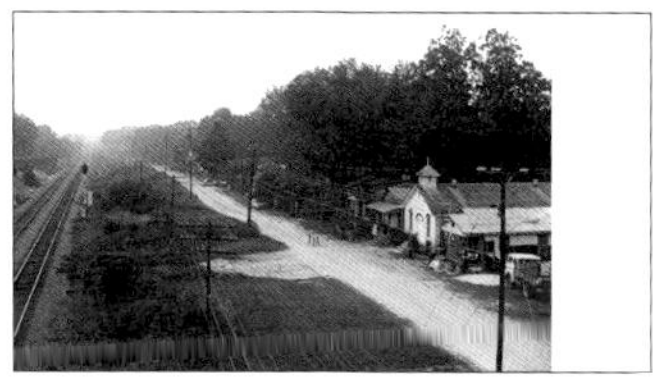
Savannah, Georgia, 1983

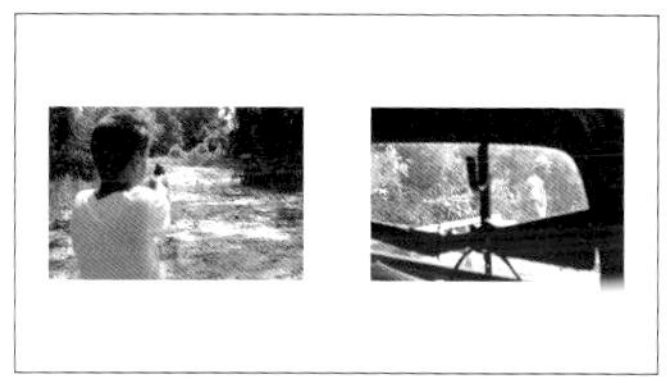
Selma, Alabama, 1990
Louisiana, 1974

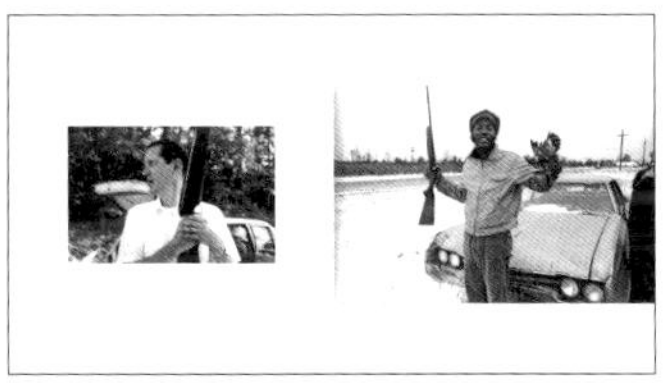
William Christenberry, Hale County, Alabama, 1990
Jena, Louisiana, 1973

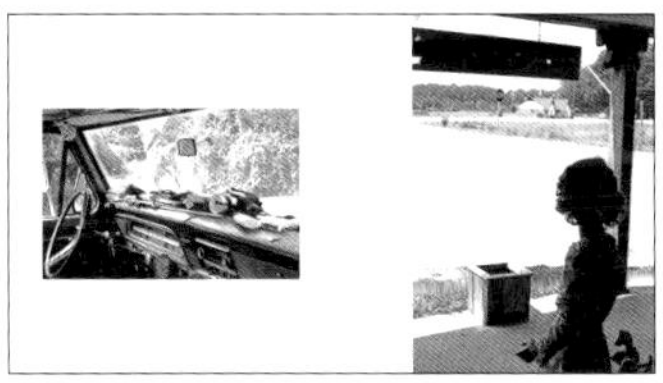
Tennessee, 1986

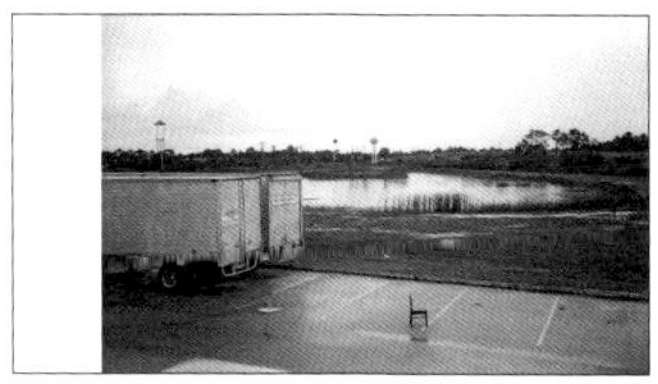
Florida, 1984

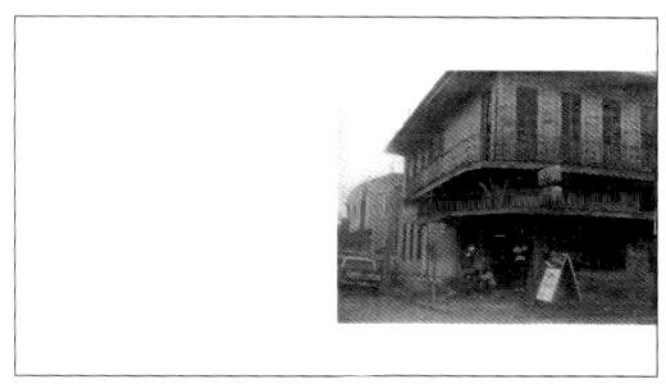
New Orleans, Louisiana, 1980

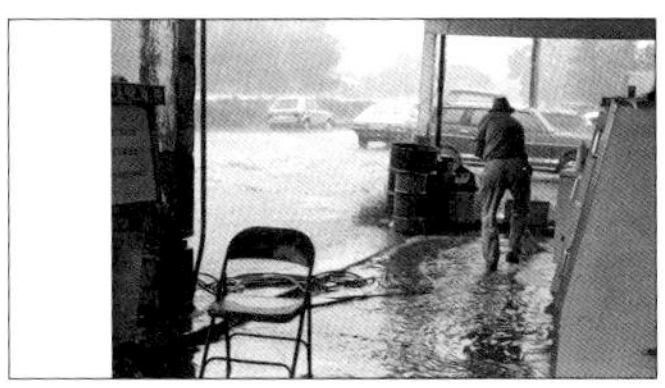
New Albany, Mississippi, 1982

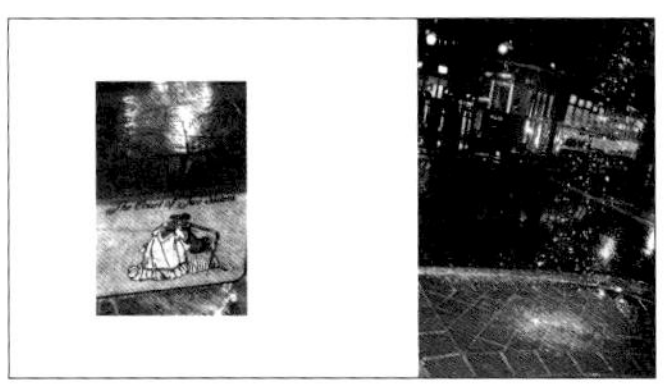
New Orleans, Louisiana, 2010
New Orleans, Canal Street, 1987

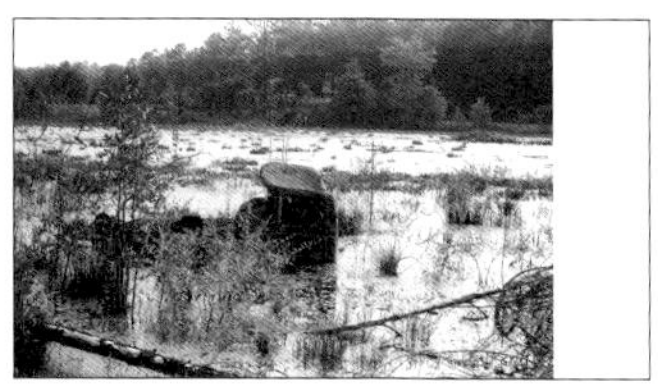
Louisiana, 1983

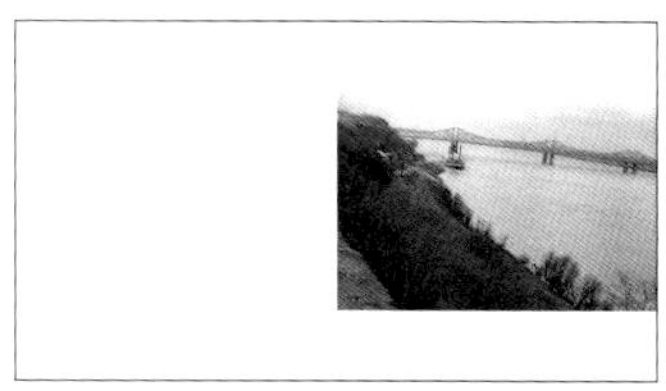
Natchez, Mississippi, 2010

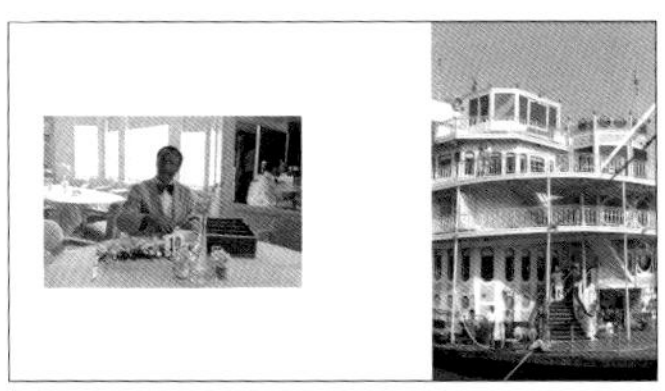
A waiter onboard *Delta Queen*, Mississippi, 1980
*Delta Queen*, Natchez, Mississippi, 1980

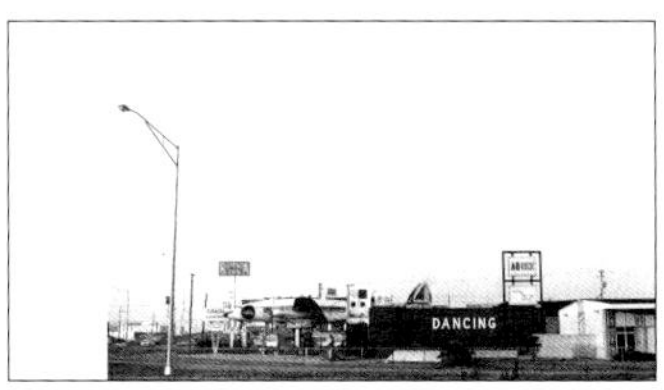
New Orleans, Louisiana, 1981

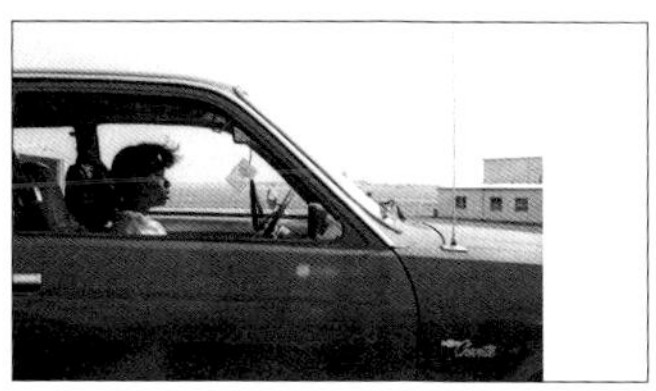
Alabama, 1990

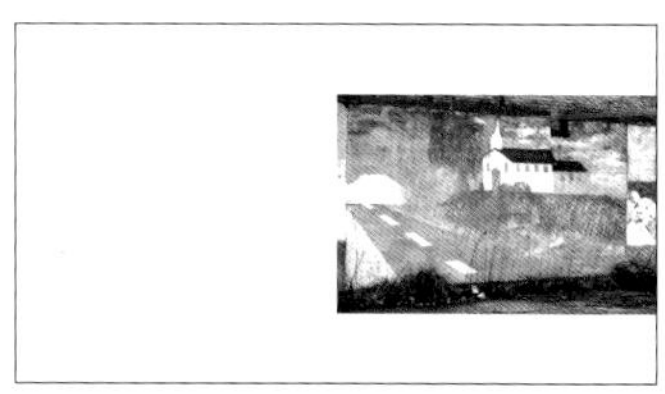
Tennessee, 1996

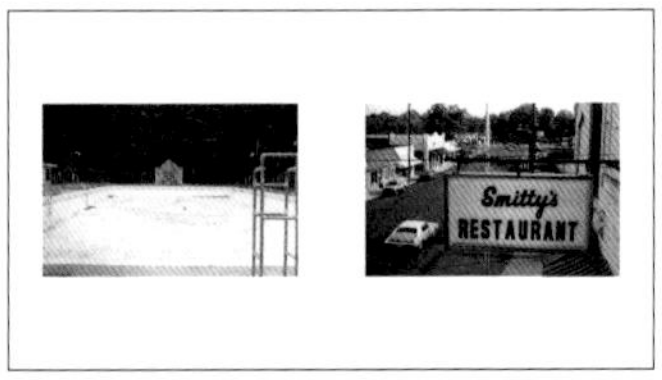
Tiptonville, Tennessee, 1990
Oxford, Mississippi, 1990

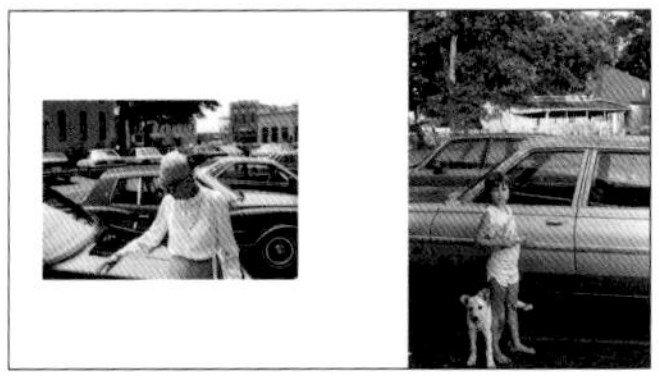
Oxford, Mississippi, 1990
Arkansas, 1990

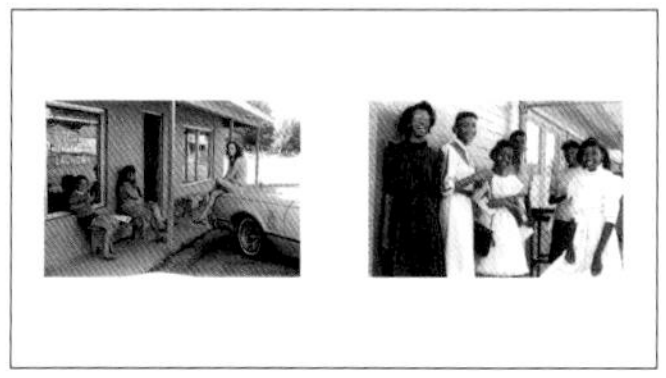
South Louisiana, 1979
Natchez, Mississippi, 1974

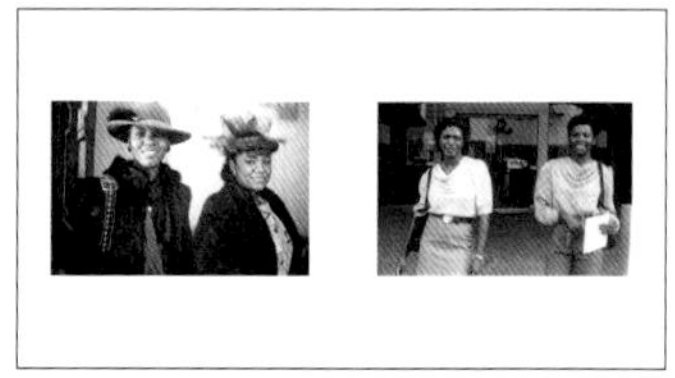
Georgia, 1987
Augusta, Georgia, 1983

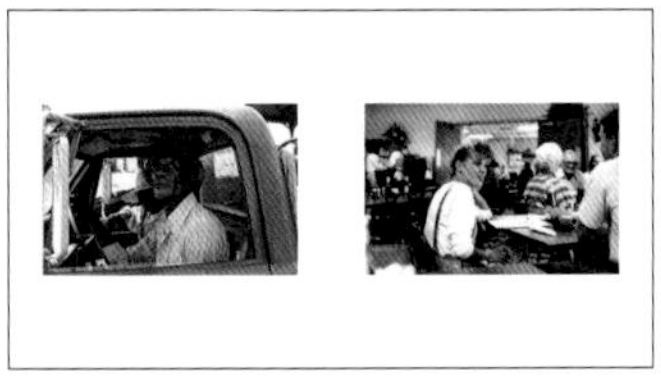
Louisiana, 1980
Alabama, 1989

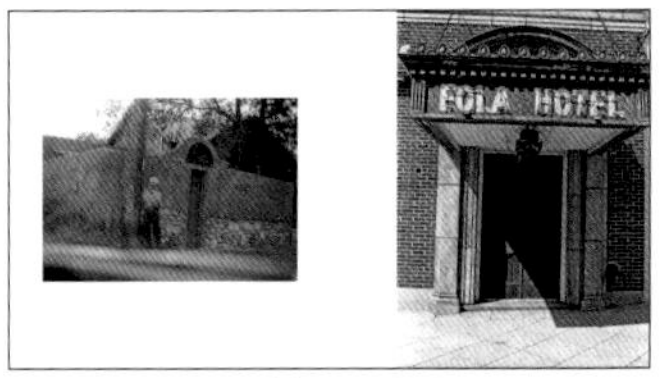
Louisiana, 1979
Natchez, Mississippi, 1973

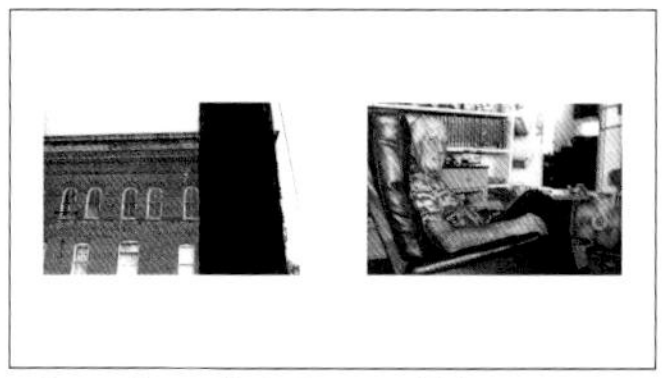
Greensboro, Hale County, Alabama, 1982
Vicksburg, Mississippi, 1979

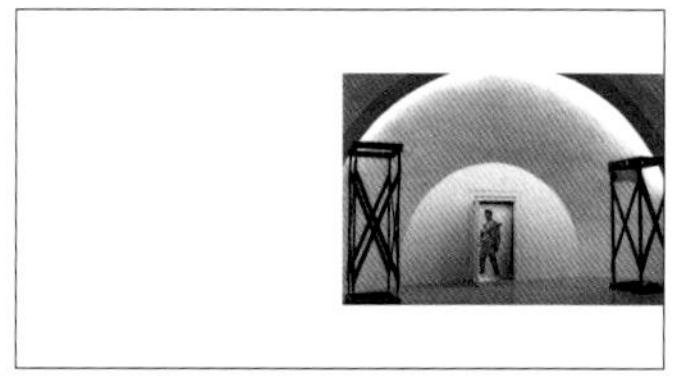
Overton Square, Memphis,
Tennessee, 1990

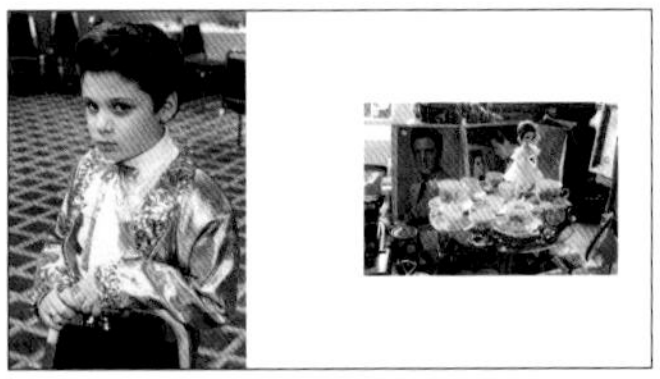
Memphis, Tennesse, 1990
Natchez, Mississippi, 1973

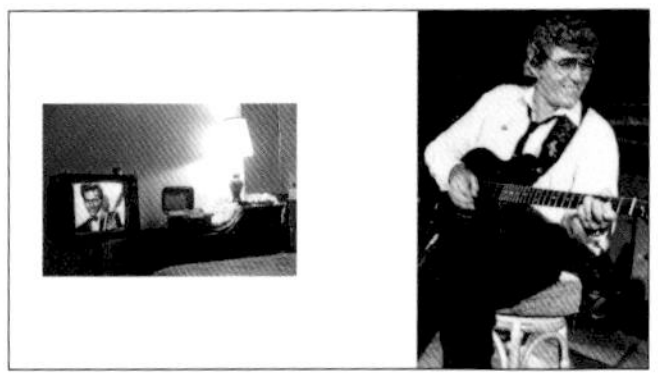
Nashville, Tennessee, 1989
Carl Perkins, Memphis, Tennessee, 1990

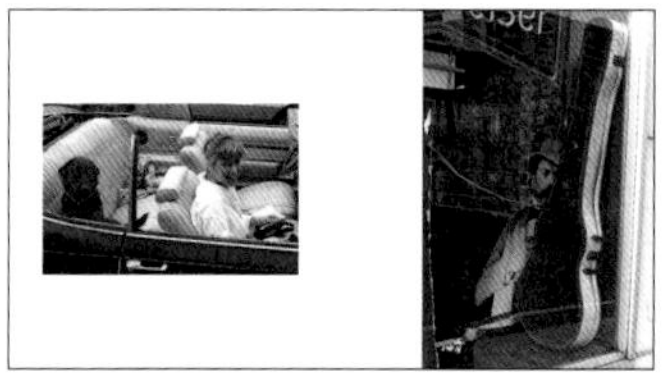
Nashville, Tennessee, 1989
Clarksdale, Mississippi, 1996

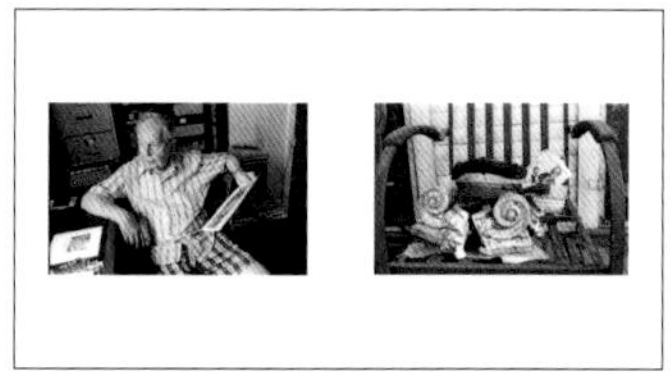
Clarence John Laughlin, New Orleans,
Louisiana, 1979
Kosciusko, Mississippi, 1984

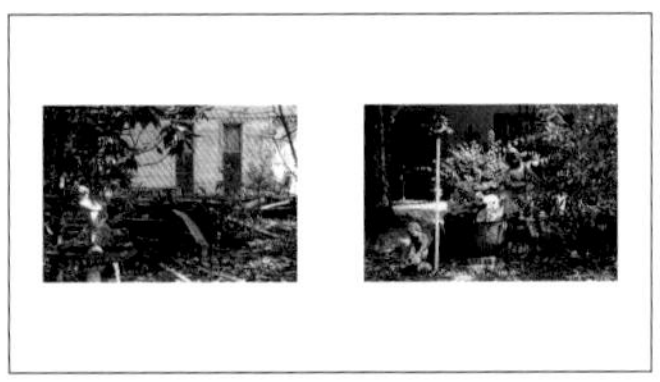
Louisiana, 1979
Mississippi, 1984

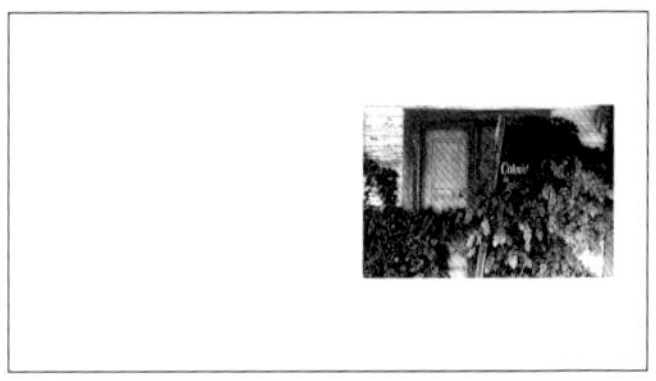
South Carolina, 1987

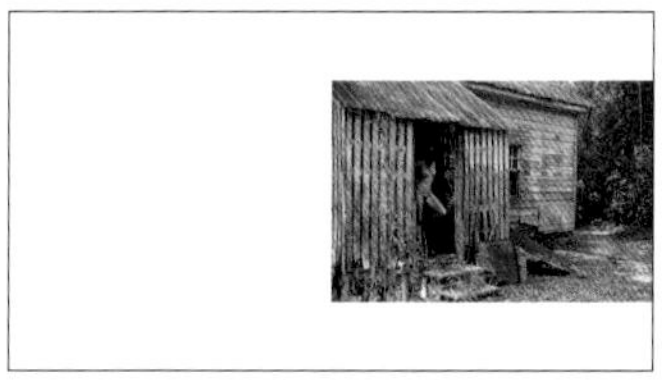
South Carolina, 1987

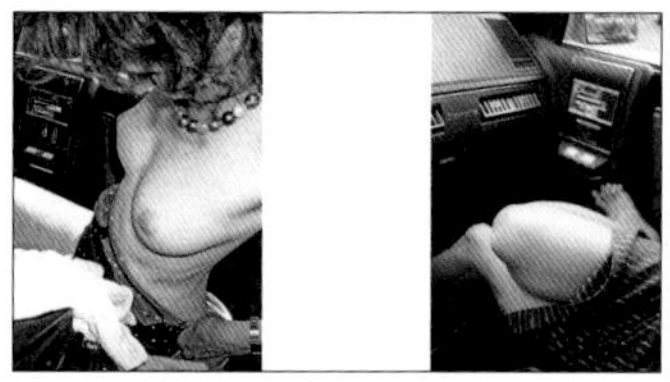
Savannah, Georgia, 1987
Georgia, 1987

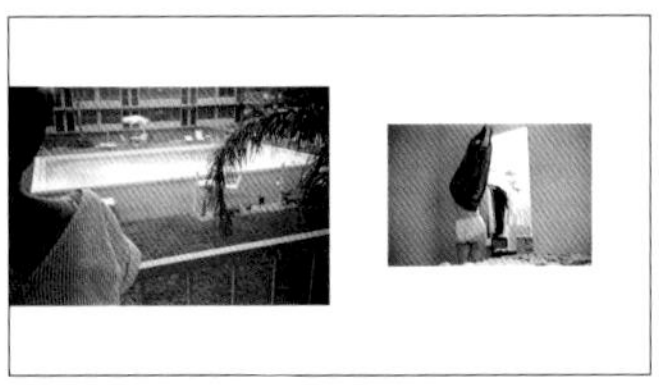
Florida, 1984
Oxford, Mississippi, 1984

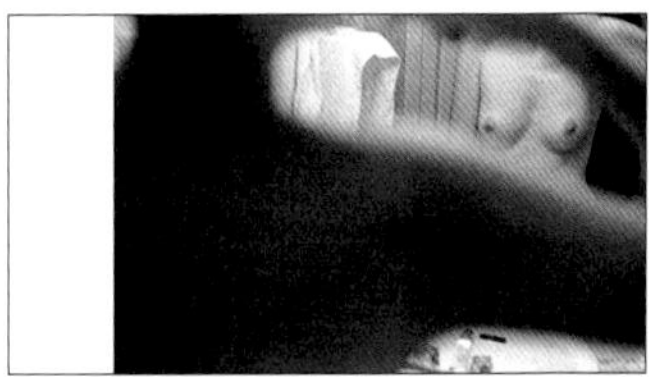
Mississippi, 1984

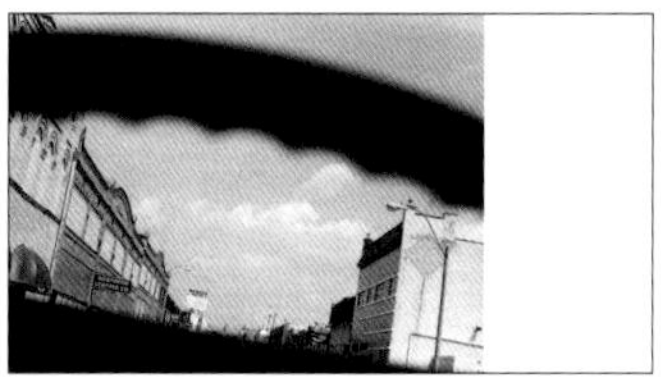
Memphis, Tennessee, 1984

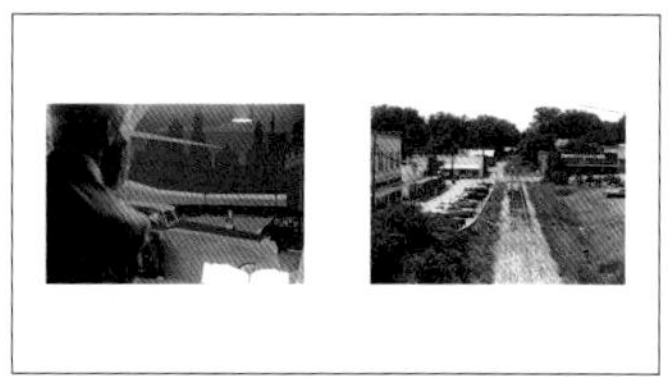
New Orleans, Louisiana, 1986
Edwards, Mississippi, 1982

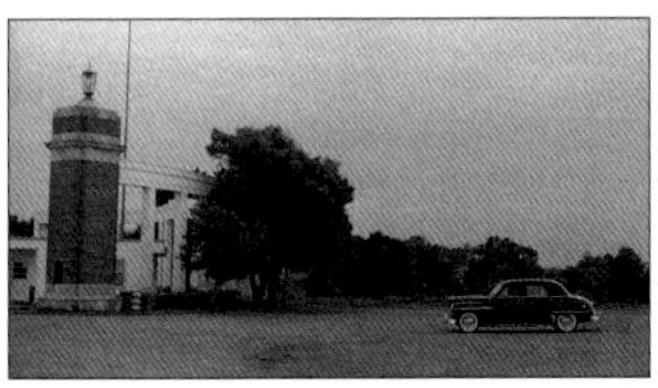
Natchez, Mississippi, 1979

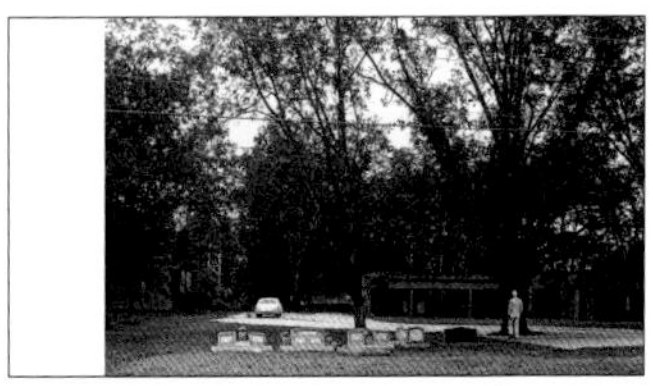
Ferriday, Louisiana, 1973

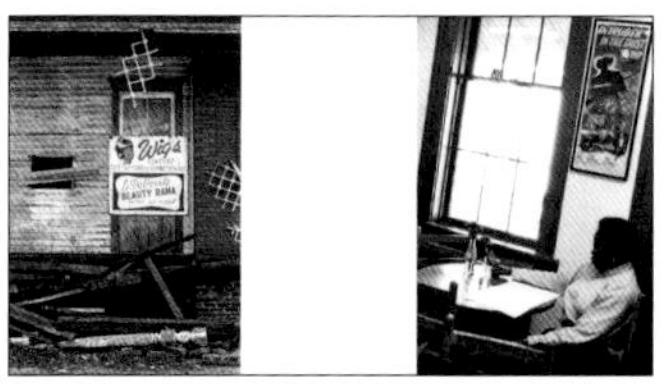
Alabama, 1990
Oxford, Mississippi, 1996

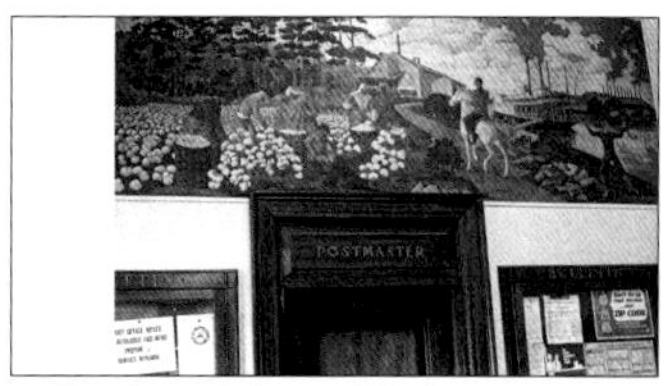
Ben Shahn's fresco, Mississippi, 1983

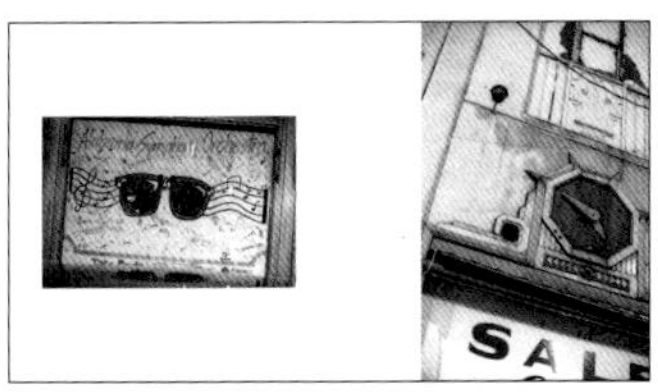
Birmingham, Alabama, 1979
Birmingham, Alabama, 1989

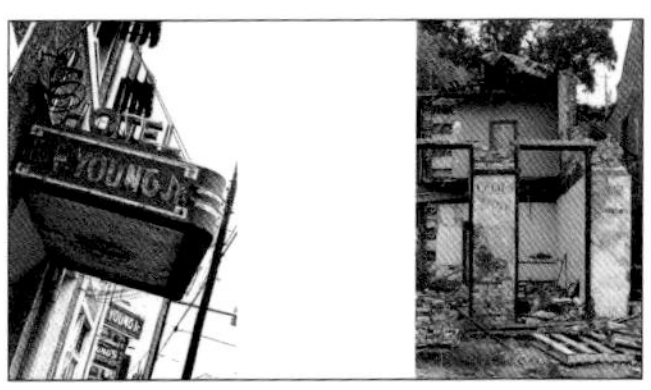
Jackson, Mississippi, 1979
Natchez Under-the-Hill, Mississippi, 1984

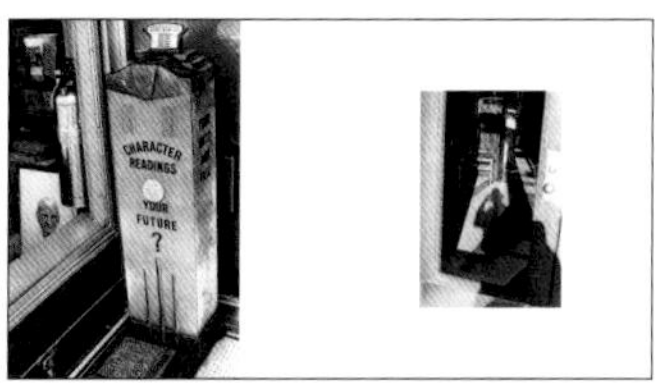
Memphis, Tennessee, 1989
Self-portrait, Birmingham, Alabama, March 1989

Published by arrangement with éditions lamaindonne, France

Translation by Anne Marcy-Benitez

Printed by Escourbiac in France
Fedrigoni Symbol Tatami White, 150 g
First edition, 2016



Library of Congress Cataloging-in-Publication Data
Names: Mora, Gilles, 1945– author.
Title: Antebellum / Gilles Mora.
Description: First edition. | Austin : University of Texas Press, 2016.
Includes bibliographical references and index.
Identifiers: LCCN 2016018941
ISBN 978-1-4773-1184-4 (cloth : alk. paper)
Subjects: LCSH: Southern States–Pictorial works.
Classification: LCC F210 .M83 2016 | DDC 975.0022/2–dc23
LC record available at https://lccn.loc.gov/2016018941

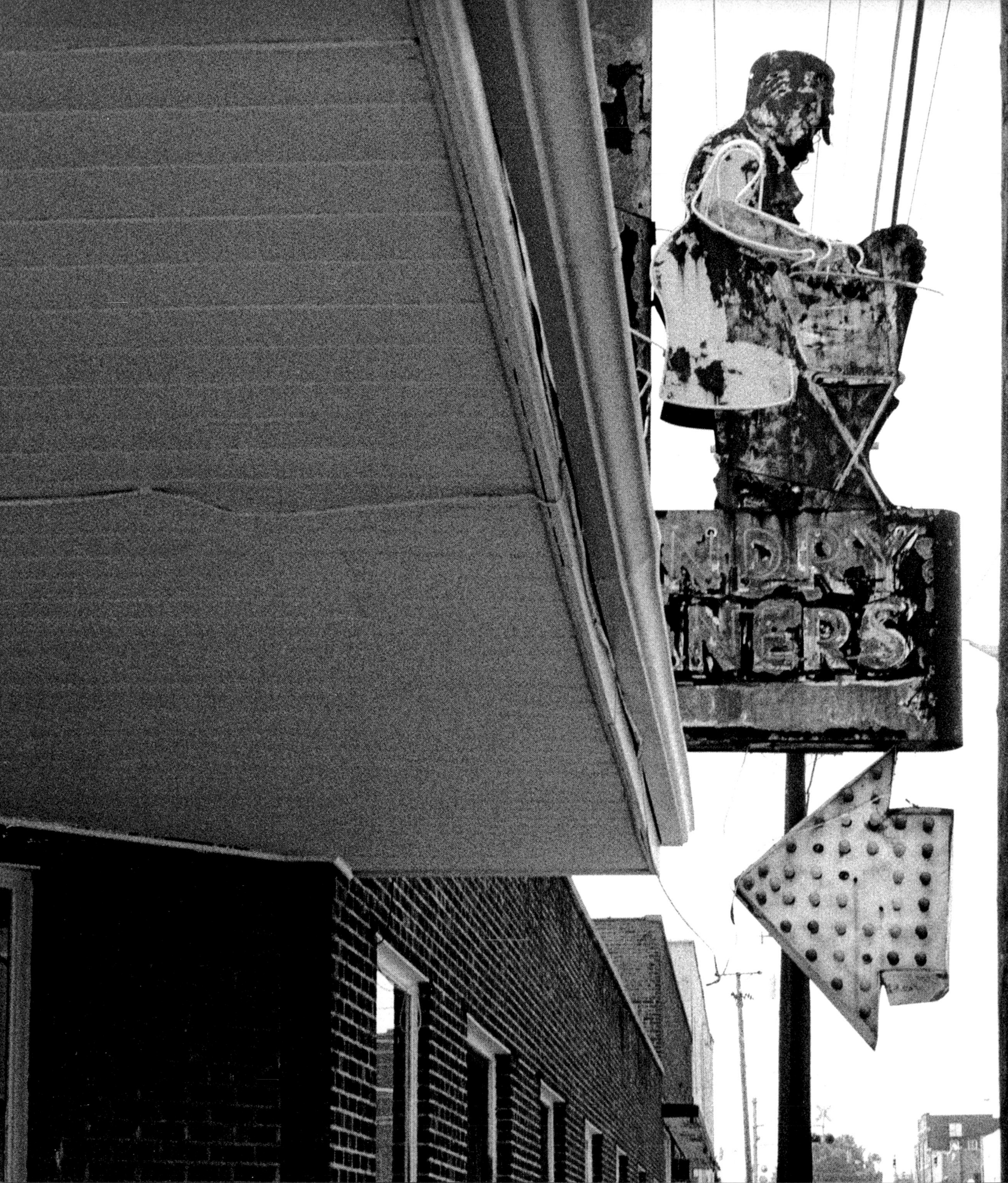